Lessons From Freedom Summer

Lessons From Freedom Summer

Ordinary People Building Extraordinary Movements

Kathy Emery, Linda Reid Gold & Sylvia Braselmann

COMMON COURAGE PRESS
MONROE, MAINE

COMMON COURAGE PRESS
P.O. Box 702 or
121 Red Barn Road
Monroe, ME 04951
207-525-0900
FAX (207) 525-3068
orders-info@commoncouragepress.com
www.commoncouragepress.com

Text design by Chris Hall/Ampersand

Cover design by Sylvia Braselmann
Cover photos copyright Matt Herron and Take Stock where indicated (MH)
(http://www.takestockphotos.com/imagepages/collections.php)
*Photos (from left to right and top to bottom): Frederick Douglass; Ida B. Wells;
Bob Moses (MH); Ella Baker (MH); Ed King and Aaron Henry (MH); Septima
Clark at Highlander; David Dennis (MH); Fannie Lou Hamer (MH); James
Forman (MH); Bayard Rustin (MH); Hollis Watkins (MH); Andrew Goodman;
Martin Luther King, Jr. (MH); Michael Schwerner*

ISBN 13 paper: 9781567513882
ISBN 13 hardcover: 9781567513899

Library of Congress Cataloging-in-Publication Data is available on request from
the publisher.

Printed in Canada

First Printing

Acknowledgements

The idea for this book emerged out of a discussion between Linda and Ellen Reeves, editor at The New Press, over ten years ago. The original concept was to publish the 1964 Mississippi Freedom School Curriculum in its entirety, put it in its historical context, and provide teaching materials that would "bring it up-to-date." Kathy came on board to edit the documents and write the teaching materials. Linda began the long process of researching and writing the historical context. It is her Herculean effort that resulted in most of the text you will read in this book. Sylvia adopted the project and helped Kathy lead it through the long process of rewriting and re-conceptualizing the manuscript, and the search for a publisher. Along the way and in response to comments from editors, we decided to put all the Freedom School Curriculum materials we could track down on a website (www.educationanddemocracy.org) in order to make them freely available to all.

Our thanks to all those who agreed to talk to Linda in the early research phase, especially Hollis Watkins and Edwin King, and to the support from the staff of different archives and collections. We would like to thank Ellen Reeves from The New Press and Danny Miller from Heinemann for valuable suggestions, as well as several reviewers along the way for their input.

We are most grateful for the early and consistent support and encouragement from Howard Zinn, which really kept us going. Howard Zinn's support of the book led us to ask him to write the foreword for this publication, which he graciously agreed to do. Howard also led us to our editor Greg Bates at Common Courage Press. We are deeply grateful for Greg's enthusiasm and insightful editing.

Friends and family have all played an important part in keeping the project alive during the last ten years and we are extremely grateful for their encouragement, advice and comfort.

Finally, we would like to acknowledge and thank the following donors, whose financial support made this publication possible:

St. Francis Foundation, St. Francis Lutheran Church, San Francisco

Carolyn Goodman and the Andrew Goodman Foundation

Anonymous donor through the Tides Foundation

Bruce Jervis and Jim Kowalski

Sherri and Joseph Sawyer, Jr.

Kelly Emery

Dorothy Emery

Keith McWalter

Kathy Emery, Linda Reid Gold, and Sylvia Braselmann
2008

Contents

Foreword

SURELY ONE OF THE GREAT social movements in the history of the United States is that extraordinary burst of energy and courage that took place in the 1950s and 1960s in the South—the struggle for equal rights for African Americans. Its roots went far back, to the anti-slavery movement in the decades before the Civil War, and to that brief period after the war when black people voted, held office, demanded that promises of land and freedom made in the heat of the war be fulfilled.

Those promises—embodied in the Fourteenth and Fifteenth Amendments to the Constitution—were not kept, and there followed almost a hundred years of segregation, humiliation, brutality, poverty, lynching, all enforced by the states with the tacit consent of the national government. In reaction to that terrible period, African Americans, their indignation long pent-up, rebelled all over the South, and changed not only that section of the country, but the consciousness of the nation itself.

The highlights of that story have been told many times—the Montgomery bus boycott, the sit-ins, the Freedom Rides, the street demonstrations in Birmingham, Alabama, the march from Selma to Montgomery—all of that agitation forcing the passage of the Civil Rights Act of 1964 and the Voting Rights Act of 1965. The heroes of that struggle have become known: Martin Luther King, Jr., Rosa Parks, Fannie Lou Hamer, and Stokely Carmichael.

However, the history of our country, as told in our textbooks, and in the culture at large, is mostly still confined to those highlights, still focused on certain important individuals. There are a thousand stories that are part of the larger one and remain untold. There are countless individuals, anonymous, unheralded, whose commitment, whose bravery, have not been recognized.

This book is one of many attempts to recognize the untold history of that time, to tell, in this case, one important story—of the Mississippi Freedom Summer of 1964, and the Freedom Schools that emerged during that summer. And also to bring to the forefront some of those unnamed individuals who played a crucial part in the struggles of that summer.

In doing that, this book is challenging not only the orthodox history of those years, but the very idea of a history told from the point of view of the authorities—a history confined to the "important" people, and therefore ignoring the struggles of ordinary people. This orthodox approach perpetuates the idea that history is made from the top, and leaves to the mass of the people the most feeble of roles—that of voting every four years for a member of the Establishment chosen by the elite of the two major parties.

In recounting the history of the Mississippi Freedom Summer of 1964, and the extraordinary experience of the Freedom Schools, this book does more than suggest a different view of history. It presents a unique approach to education, one that is not the outcome of abstract theorizing, but that has been forged out of a rare educational experiment, carried out, unbelievably and yet necessarily, in the midst of an ongoing social struggle.

The Freedom Schools were a challenge not only to the social structure of Mississippi, but to American education as a whole. They began with the provocative suggestion that an entire school system can be created in a community outside the official order, and critical of its suppositions.

That experience, and this book, ask questions that get at the heart of what education should be about. Can we, somehow, bring teachers and students together, not through the artificial sieve of certification and examination, but on the basis of their common commitment to an exciting social goal? Can we solve the old educational problem of how to teach children crucial values, while avoiding a blanket imposition of the teacher's ideas?

(The key to that, suggested in the pages that follow, is in asking questions rather than always providing answers.)

Can we forthrightly accept, as an educational goal, that we want better human beings in the rising generation than we had in the last, and that this requires a bold declaration that the educational process cherishes equality, justice, compassion, and a global community? Is it possible to create a hunger for those goals through the fiercest argument about whether or not they are indeed worthwhile? And can the schools have a running, no-ideas-barred exchange of views about alternative ways to those goals?

Is there, in the war-torn, troubled atmosphere of our time, a national equivalent to the excitement of that great social movement of the Sixties? Can a new movement in our time be strong enough in its pull to create a motivation for learning that even the enticements of monetary success cannot match? Would it be possible to declare, boldly, that the aim of the schools is to find solutions for poverty, for injustice, for race and national hatred, for violence and war? Can we turn all educational efforts into a national striving for those solutions?

There is certainly no point expecting the government to initiate such an inquiry. Social movements like the one in the South came into being precisely because government ignored its charge, made in the Declaration of Independence, to assure for everyone an equal right to life, liberty, and the pursuit of happiness. The people themselves will have to begin, perhaps to set up other pilot ventures, imperfect, but suggestive like that of the Mississippi Freedom Summer. Education can, and should, be dangerous to the existing social structure.

Howard Zinn, 2008

Introduction

IN THE SUMMER OF 1964, nearly one thousand volunteers, mostly northern white college students, went to Mississippi to join local blacks in a struggle to gain civil rights for all Mississippians and to end segregation in the South. The Mississippi Summer Project, later known as "Freedom Summer," aimed at and succeeded in ending the isolation of Mississippi from the rest of the nation, and was the point of no return for legal segregation in the United States. Such a pivotal event in the Southern Freedom Movement, not surprisingly, necessitated the joining of the rank and file members of the four major Civil Rights organizations of the time. This effort was directed by an umbrella organization, the Council of Federated Organizations. COFO coordinated the efforts of four Civil Rights groups:

NAACP, the National Association for the Advancement of Colored People, founded in 1911;

CORE, the Congress on Racial Equality, founded in 1942;

SCLC, the Southern Christian Leadership Conference, founded in 1957; and

SNCC, the Student Non-Violent Coordinating Committee (pronounced "snick"), founded in 1960.

The long-term aim of Freedom Summer was to transform the power structure of Mississippi. The short-term aim of the Freedom School was to challenge the legitimacy of the all-white Mississippi Democratic Party at the Democratic National Convention in Atlantic City in August of 1964. To do this, organizers decided to create a parallel state party that was truly representative of the people of Mississippi—both blacks and whites.

To support the voter registration drives, community centers and Freedom Schools were opened across the state. Forty-one Freedom Schools opened in the churches, on the back porches, and under the trees of Mississippi. The students were native Mississippians, their teachers were volunteers, for the most part still students themselves. The task of this small group of students and teachers was daunting. They set out to replace the fear of nearly two hundred years of violent control with hope and organized action. Both students and teachers faced the possibility, and in some cases, the reality, of brutal retaliation from local whites. They had little money and few supplies. Yet the Freedom Schools set out to alter forever the state of Mississippi, the stronghold of the Southern way of life.

This book tells the story of Freedom Summer primarily through the stories of some of the people connected to the wider struggle for civil rights and the Mississippi Summer Project. We have chosen to do this for the same reason that the authors of the original Freedom School Curriculum chose their content—to empower our readers to be active agents of social change. In the Freedom Schools, students were taught a strong sense of their value as creators of history. "We are living," they were told, "in the middle of the revolution and in the middle of a new history."[1] Many of those who participated in the Mississippi Summer Project, and the movement of which it was a part, felt that each of their actions, however small, was a significant part of history. In the sit-in, the bus boycott, the walk to the courthouse, individuals found small actions, grounded in the routines of ordinary life that symbolized resistance, summoned courage, and inspired hope. This lived belief in the value of the individual challenges conventional history, which acknowledges only the wealthy and powerful. In *A People's History of the United States,* Howard Zinn writes that most histories "teach us that the supreme act of citizenship is to choose among saviors, by going into a voting booth every four years to choose between two white and well-off Anglo-Saxon males of inoffensive personality and orthodox opinion. . . . We have learned to look to stars, leaders, experts in every field, thus surrendering our own strength, demeaning our own ability, obliterating our own selves."[2]

By organizing our text around profiles of "ordinary" people, we hope to accomplish two things: to validate the political actions of individuals and to establish the historical network from which those actions emerged. Often, we are taught to view events as isolated, disregarding the models and inspirations for them; such teaching does not apply to social movements. Activist David Dennis described the Civil Rights Movement as a vast network extending over time and space, something only partially visible to history. The stories told in this book are part of this network, a series of interconnected events that spans decades and centuries, and includes actions both celebrated and uncelebrated. We believe that our book can contribute to our reader's understanding of how he or she fits into that network, thereby understanding that one can, through action, become part of an ongoing movement for human dignity and social justice for all.

Freedom Summer was built on the centuries old struggle for equality, on the successes and failures of the past, and on the philosophies and tactics developed during this struggle. Learning this can empower people to carry on the struggle today. We begin in Chapter 1 with the anti-slavery movement and the nonviolent tradition. The fight for civil rights in the Sixties was an extension of the abolitionist movement in the 1830s. The theory of nonviolence as articulated and practiced by both Henry David Thoreau and Gandhi was used as a guide to action by all those who ended up in Mississippi in 1964. Freedom Summer was supported and developed by the Council of Federated Organizations. In chapters 2 to 5, we tell the history of each of the four major organizations of COFO from their origins to how each one became involved in the struggle in Mississippi by 1964. Chapters 6 to 10 deal with Freedom Summer itself, the preparations leading up to it, and the activities and events of the summer. In Chapter 11, we provide some sense of the aftermath of Freedom Summer and suggest what some of the "lessons" might be.

While reading this book, bear in mind that the words Negro, black, colored, and African American are used at different times in this book, reflecting the period in which the texts were written.

About Using This Book

MUCH HAS BEEN MADE of the failure of public high schools today to graduate many of their students. We suspect, based on our own experiences and research, that a profound change would occur in high school graduation rates if students were allowed to ask questions freely and those questions were taken seriously by teachers and other students. An equally profound change would occur in our society if citizens had the skills, disposition and knowledge to question and analyse what they are confronted with by the media, friends and fellow workers. In other words, there would be fewer bored and alienated students in school and more active citizens in society if the principles of the Mississippi Freedom School Curriculum were the foundation of current pedagogy, curricula and "water cooler" conversations. What passes for history in today's conventional public schools and what passes for news in today's media is increasingly superficial and is too often a laundry list of dates, people and events or entertaining gossip—information without context and increasingly unrelated to the serious issues facing youth and adults today.

There are several ways in which this book can be used to counter such disempowering effects of current institutions. In studying Freedom Summer and the 1964 Freedom School Curriculum, one can learn how to make questions the basis for learning. Questioning leads to the development of ideas, and ideas lead to action. Furthermore, in studying the 1964 Freedom School Curriculum in its historical context, one can analyze how social movements happen and, thereby, identify the role that individual action and authentic education can play in the process of organizing communities effectively around issues of social justice. Many people want to do something to improve the lives of their community. Yet, they don't. They are paralyzed because they can't believe any action on their part will make a difference, or they don't know what to do. Studying the details of what ordinary, everyday people did in Mississippi in preparation for and during Freedom Summer can inspire people to take action today.

This book was conceived during our research to assemble the materials that constituted the Mississippi Freedom School Curriculum. The FSC presents a stark contrast to current public and private school curricula. Our book puts the Freedom School Curriculum in its historical context. Throughout this text, there are references to parts of the original curriculum on the web to help the reader connect the history of Freedom Summer with the 1964 Freedom School Curriculum. Understanding the role that the Freedom Schools played in achieving the Summer's political goals can provoke questions about how current educational institutions function to maintain the status quo. The goal of the 1964 Freedom School Curriculum was "to encourage the asking of questions, and hope that society can be improved." Current high-stakes testing education reform has reduced the goal of education to raising test scores. One might better understand the significance of this if one considers why the Freedom School principles and methods were so different from those of the public schools both then and now. The Freedom School Curriculum emphasized the following:

- the school is an agent of social change;

- people must know their own history;

- the curriculum should be linked to the student's experience;

- questions should be open-ended; and

- developing problem-solving skills is crucial.

Each of the seven units of the Citizenship Curriculum was written as a series of questions and answers. For example, Unit V uses the answers to previous questions to set up another question.

As we saw. . .Negroes and whites are afraid. Negroes have reason to be afraid. Whites are afraid because of guilt. When Negroes are afraid, they continue to go along with the system. The same is true of whites. And so we say that: there is great fear in the South and it is from this fear that the "power structure" derives its power, from fear that the system keeps going. What do fear and lies do to people?[1]

By providing examples of how a Socratic dialogue could be developed, the authors of the Freedom School Curriculum encouraged teachers to use a Socratic teaching method. This progressive pedagogy allowed teachers to begin a discussion at the place where the students were and then take them, step by step, to where the teachers wanted the students to be. This place also was defined in terms of questions. Throughout the Citizenship Curriculum, teachers and students were reminded to ask and answer the Basic and Secondary Set of questions.

Basic Set of Questions:

1. Why are we (students and teachers) in Freedom Schools?

2. What is the Freedom Movement?

3. What alternatives does the Freedom Movement offer us?

Secondary Set of Questions:

1. What does the majority culture have that we want?

2. What does the majority culture have that we don't want?

3. What do we have that we want to keep?

This progressive pedagogy, and the questions themselves, can be modified to apply to most circumstances today.* We have written questions and activities for our text as suggestions of how to do so. The questions at the beginning of chapters and sections are intended to encourage the reader to adopt a critical stance toward the reading. We encourage you to go wherever your questions take you. Contrary to what many have experienced in their schooling, thinking is not confined to certain moments nor is think-

---

* The set of "Secondary Questions" are particularly relevant when thinking about how public schools, as a mechanism of socialization, are based on an assimilationist model with white middle-class culture being considered the norm to which all are expected to conform.

ing a linear process. We encourage you to keep this in mind when reading and discussing any part of this book. In the Appendix there are "further research questions," "debate resolutions" and "activities." Some of these will encourage the reader to act upon (in role play or real form) what he or she learned in studying the movement. Others are suggestions about how, beyond knowing the history and developing academic skills, connections can be made between the story of Freedom Summer and the reader's experience. The questions and activities vary greatly in scope and depth. We do not expect any one person or group to explore all or even most of them. We hope that the questions serve as models inspiring other questions and not limitations to think only about what those questions ask. One need not limit one's questions to those that "should" or "should not" be asked. Furthermore, the best questions are those to which no one, as yet, has a satisfactory answer and arise from the reader's own experiences. Often we learn much more in the process of answering questions than from the answer itself. Most importantly, answering questions that one truly wants answered leads to thinking and thought. Thought leads to action.

The story, as told in this text, does not end in 1964. Len Holt, lawyer, SNCC activist, and participant of Freedom Summer called his account "The Summer That Didn't End." As the Civil Rights workers stood on the shoulders of abolitionists and suffragists, they have in turn become inspiration and foundation for the ongoing struggle for equal rights today. The last chapter explains some developments that came out of Freedom Summer, and points towards the life changing effects on many who were touched by the Summer. Readers might wish to investigate the earlier or later careers of activists and artists who went to Mississippi in 1964. We also encourage readers to ask themselves about the untold story, the many contributions that are not included in this or other texts. There are places in the text where names are "dropped" without further reference to them. These persons can be the basis of further research. We hope that the readers of this book, with their own writing and research, continue and expand the story presented here.

In the same way, readers are asked to consider their own places in this social and historical network. We hope that all who encounter the story of Freedom Summer will regard their own experiences as part of an unfolding story; the book is organized to encourage their participation in the creating and the writing of history. The use of the profiles is intended to validate both the contributions of the well-publicized leaders and those of local activists whose risks and sacrifices were often equal if not greater. The profiles also offer a model for us to imitate. Readers may choose to profile local activists whose work continues in content or philosophy the work of those profiled here, or add one's own story, or the stories of one's parents, grandparents, friends, or teachers. As Staughton Lynd, Director of the Freedom Schools, wrote to students in a movement newspaper in 1964,

> You Are History. . . . We would like to include in this newspaper the history that YOU are making. . . . We ask you to send us an account of some experience you had, recently or long ago. We are particularly interested in hearing about what you are doing now to build the freedom movement.[2]

Dr. Lynd's invitation, prompted by the spirit of the Freedom Schools, is still open. You are history, and you are historians. In contributing to the telling of this story, we hope you are inspired to act in a way that makes your neighborhood, your city, your state, your country and the world a more just and humane place in which to live.

ONE

Abolitionists and the Nonviolent Tradition

THE MOMENT AFRICANS were sold into slavery, they struggled against it. The first slaves arrived in the Thirteen Colonies in 1619. When the institution of slavery became especially "peculiar"* by the 1830s, black advocates for the abolition of slavery were joined by white abolitionists in a powerful movement. This alliance, however, was full of tensions. The conflicts within the abolitionist movement foreshadowed similar obstacles faced by succeeding black/white alliances, including the architects of the Mississippi Summer Project in 1964. Experiencing and coping with racial tension was not the only legacy that abolitionists bequeathed to subsequent activists. Anti-slavery activity was one of many social protest movements during a time of religious revival. Abolitionism was a "crusade"; it had a moral dimension. Much of the power, courage and persuasiveness of the abolitionists came from their faith in the rightness of their cause. Like the Civil Rights activists in the Sixties, abolitionists believed that their actions would have an effect upon history. They fought against a great evil that they

---

* "Peculiar Institution" was a euphemism slaveholders, most famously of which was John C. Calhoun, used to refer to slavery. Kenneth Stampp's book, *The Peculiar Institution*, is a detailed description of U.S. Slavery from 1830-1860, which achieved its most horrible and unique form during that period.

knew may not be defeated in their lifetime. They did so out of pure faith in the rightness of their cause or because they believed that they were part of a stream of history in which future generations could possibly succeed on the foundations of their actions. Either way, it was faith that allowed them to risk their livelihood and their lives.

Another important tradition that Civil Rights activists drew upon (at least as a tactic if not a way of life) was nonviolent direct action. Principles of nonviolence had been developed by Henry David Thoreau and Gandhi. Both Thoreau and Gandhi drew upon Hindu scriptures and their own experiences to develop philosophies of life that included a moral imperative to oppose unjust laws. Thoreau opposed slavery and the Mexican-American War. Gandhi spent the better part of his life opposing the imposition of British rule in South Africa and India. Martin Luther King revealed the influence of these men's philosophies on his own thinking when he explained why *breaking* the law while simultaneously *respecting* the law was not really a contradiction.

> Much has been made of the willingness of [Civil Rights activists] to break the law. Paradoxically, although they have embraced Thoreau's and Gandhi's civil disobedience on a scale dwarfing any past experience in American history, they do respect law. They feel a moral responsibility to obey just laws. But they recognize that there are also unjust laws. . . . In disobeying such unjust laws, the students do so peacefully, openly and non-violently. Most important, they willingly accept the penalty, whatever it is, for in this way the public comes to re-examine the law in question and will thus decide whether it uplifts or degrades man.[1]

An important note: Gandhi's theory of nonviolence is currently referred to as "principled" nonviolence to distinguish it from "pragmatic" nonviolence. The Reverend Martin Luther King, Jr. was an adherent to principled nonviolence, which included the belief that such strategies and tactics were intended to transform those who opposed racism and all its manifestations through a dramatic and disciplined appeal to their humanity. Most Civil Rights organizers were pragmatic or practical adherents of nonviolence, seeing it as an effective strategy against those who had a monopoly of the use of force and violence. Either way, nonviolence has proved to be an effective strategy from Gandhi's time to today.

1.A   William Lloyd Garrison: Abolitionism

Questions to help you adopt a critical stance while reading the section below:

1. *What is abolitionism?*

2. *How can you explain Garrison's passionate campaign not only against slavery but against racism? Why would a northern white man not devote his life, nor risk his life for such a cause? How can you explain why most northern white men chose not to follow Garrison's path?*

3. *What are the implications for black/white collaboration given the instant fame of the LIBERATOR after Nat Turner's rebellion?*

Further Information:

The Constitution of the American Anti-Slavery Society is at douglassarchives.org/ aass_a58.htm, Garrison's essay "The Governing Passion of my Soul" is at douglassarchives.org/garr_a27.htm

ABOLITIONISM

The "myths" and stereotypes that the Freedom School Curriculum challenged had their origins in colonial America. The racist stereotypes that Americans continue to live with today were man-made. This can be seen, for example, in Britain's first successful colony, Jamestown, Virginia (1607). Jamestown was founded by its investors to make money. It was the first colony to purchase African American slaves in 1619. Nevertheless, it was only after Bacon's failed Rebellion in 1676 that the Virginia state government began to legally transform slavery into an institution whose form would become so grotesque by 1830 that even its ardent supporters would call it "peculiar." In 1676, fifty or so African laborers joined several hundred European laborers in an attempt to overthrow the harsh rule of the plantation owners. The rebellion may have succeeded, except that several heavily armed supply ships from Britain sailed into the Jamestown harbor just when the laborers had defeated the planter elite.

The reinstated plantation owners wanted to do everything they could to make sure an alliance between blacks and whites would never happen again. To prevent new alliances, the state legislature passed laws during the following decades that made as many distinctions as possible between whites and blacks. In this way, the color line was drawn.*

---

* See chapter 2 in Howard Zinn's *A People's History of the United States* for an explanation of how this happened generally.

After the American Revolution, many who opposed slavery believed it would die a natural death. This may, indeed, have happened if the cotton gin had not been invented. Others, however, were not willing to leave the fate of the peculiar institution to historical forces. The first national convention of abolitionist societies convened in Philadelphia in 1794 (including representatives from Maryland and Virginia). Under the influence of Quakers, Pennsylvania had become the first state to abolish slavery in 1780. Besides lobbying state legislatures to abolish the institution of slavery, the early abolitionists focused on helping freed blacks find jobs, provide schools and to protect them from being seized and sold back into slavery. The federal government opposed these actions and passed the Fugitive Slave Act of 1793, which seemed to encourage such kidnapping.

But at the same time as they were abolishing slavery, northern state governments were creating poll (head) taxes and other methods to discourage freed blacks from voting. The status of blacks in the north continued to deteriorate during the period following the American Revolution as segregation of public transport, accommodations and schools became customary. A National Negro Convention Movement emerged by 1830 to combat the increasing racism in the country. This movement had its roots in the many local conventions of black leaders who met throughout the 1790-1830 period. During this period, these Americans of African descent were fighting both the segregation and disenfranchisement (no vote) in the north as well as slavery in the south. The members of these early, local conventions also provided the backbone for the abolitionist societies that emerged in full force during the 1830s.

Before 1830, most white abolitionists believed that the solution to slavery was colonization, a term used by those who believed the solution to slavery was to send African Americans back to Africa or to other countries in which blacks lived. Most black abolitionists opposed colonization. This as well as other issues caused a great deal of tension and strife between white and black abolitionists. By 1830, the United States became engulfed by a full fledged social reform movement. Long time proponents of temperance, peace, women's rights, school and insane asylum reform finally had followers. No group benefited more than the abolitionists from this widespread momentum for change. Abolitionists from wealthy families pumped needed money into the movement and were able to create national structures within which the long-standing local groups gathered. White abolitionists split into two camps. One camp believed that emancipation should be gradual and was not ready to disavow colonization. But the other, younger camp, epitomized by David Walker and William Lloyd Garrison now called for immediate abolition.

WILLIAM LLOYD GARRISON

"Hisses are music to my ears."[2]

In the power of the press, William Lloyd Garrison discovered his primary weapon against slavery. Apprenticed to a printer at an early age, by the age of twenty-three Garrison became the editor of *The Genius of Universal Emancipation,* a journal produced in collaboration with the Quaker abolitionist Benjamin Lundy. After a particularly biting editorial in an 1829 issue of *The Genius,* Garrison was sued for libel, and because he was unable to pay the fine, imprisoned. "I am in prison," he commented, "for denouncing slavery in a free country."[3] In *The Liberator,* whose first issue appeared on January 1, 1831, Garrison pledged to be "harsh as truth," and his ability to offend those in power never wavered. On the paper's front page, Garrison invoked the Declaration of Independence, holding "these truths to be self-evident—that all men are created equal. . . . My language is exactly such as suits me; it will displease many, I know—to displease them is my intention." In an early editorial, Garrison challenged the validity of a United States Constitution that condoned slavery, claiming, "No body of men ever had the right to guarantee the holding of human beings in bondage. . . . It was not valid then—it is not valid now."

In 1831, Garrison and his fiery editorials were blamed for inspiring the slave rebellion led by the black minister Nat Turner, an uprising which left fifty-seven whites dead and spread fear among slave holders. Because of Turner's rebellion, Garrison went from obscurity to infamy overnight. In 1832, he organized the New England Anti-Slavery Society, saying to its few members, "Our numbers are few and our influence limited, but mark my prediction. . . . We shall shake the nation with their mighty power!"[4] In 1833, Garrison participated in the founding of the American Anti-Slavery Society. Its *Declaration of Sentiments*, which he composed, demanded immediate emancipation of slaves. In this *Declaration*, Garrison found the grievances that had led Americans to rebel against England in 1776 trivial in comparison to those suffered by slaves. "Our fathers were never slaves—never bought and sold like cattle—never shut out from the light of knowledge and religion—never subjected to the lash of brutal taskmaster." The *Declaration* rejected prejudice based on race and resolved to win not only emancipation for the "colored population" but all rights and privileges that belong to them as men and as Americans. . . . The paths of preferment, of wealth, of intelligence should be opened as widely to them as to persons of white complexion."[5]

In October 1835, while working in his office, Garrison was seized by an irate mob of well-dressed Bostonians armed with tar and feathers. A rope was tied around Garrison's waist and he was dragged through the streets. The mayor succeeded in placing Garrison in prison for his own protection. While imprisoned, Garrison wrote on the wall of his cell:

> Wm. Lloyd Garrison was put into this cell on Wednesday afternoon, October 21, 1835, to save him from the violence of a 'respectable and influential' mob, who sought to destroy him for preaching the abominable and dangerous doctrine 'that all men are created equal'. . .'Hail Columbia!'[6]

Gradually, however, the abolitionist cause became more acceptable. The murder of abolitionist editor Elijah Lovejoy in 1837 created support for the protection of the press. Garrison's response to the Fugitive Slave Act of 1850, which required the return of escaped slaves, was to burn publicly the despised act along with the United States Constitution, which he termed "a blood-stained document."[7] Offending both black and white abolitionists in the American Anti-Slavery Society, Garrison suggested that they, like he, should refuse to vote. Legislative efforts to end slavery heartened Garrison, and finally, with the passage of the Thirteenth Amendment in 1865, he considered his work done. He closed *The Liberator,* but retained his vigilance about the excesses of government. In 1865, speaking at the flag-raising exercises at Fort Sumter, Garrison stated,

> I have not come here with reference to any flag but that of freedom. . . If your Constitution does not guarantee freedom for all, it is not a Constitution I can subscribe to. . . . And now let me give the sentiment which has been, and ever will be, the governing passion of my soul: "Liberty for each, for all, for ever!"[8]

Document 1.1   William Lloyd Garrison: First Editorial from "The Liberator"[9]
Assenting to the "self evident truth" maintained in the American Declaration of Independence, "that all men are created equal, and endowed by their Creator with certain inalienable rights—among which are life, liberty and the pursuit of happiness," I shall strenuously contend for the immediate enfranchisement of our slave population. In. . .1829. . .I unreflectingly assented to the popular but pernicious doctrine of gradual abolition. I. . .make a full and unequivocal recantation. . .for having uttered a sentiment so full of timidity, injustice and absurdity. . . .

I am aware, that many object to the severity of my language; but is there not cause for severity? I will be as harsh as truth, and as uncompromising as justice. On this subject, I do not wish to think, or speak, or write, with moderation. No! No! Tell a man whose house is on fire, to give a moderate alarm; tell him to moderately rescue his wife from the hands of the ravisher; tell the mother to gradually extricate her babe from the fire into which it has fallen; —but urge me not to use moderation in a cause like the present. I am in earnest—I will not equivocate—I will not excuse—I will not retreat a single inch—AND I WILL BE HEARD. The apathy of the people is enough to make every statue leap from its pedestal, and to hasten the resurrection of the dead.

It is pretended, that I am retarding the cause of emancipation by the coarseness of my invective, and the precipitancy of my measures. The charge is not true. On this question my influence,—humble as it is,—is felt at this moment to a considerable extent, and shall be felt in coming years—not perniciously, but beneficially—not as a curse, but as a blessing; and posterity will bear testimony that I was right. . . .

1.B   Frederick Douglass: The Fugitive Slave Act

Questions to help you adopt a critical stance while reading the section below:

1. *How does Douglass (Document 1.2) explain the need for a newspaper owned and operated by blacks only? Do you agree with his argument? Why or why not? Are the arguments relevant to today?*

2. *How could the Baptist Church argue that Anthony Burns violated the law of both man and God? Compare Burn's response to the Baptists' argument with the arguments of the transcendentalists against the Fugitive Slave Act.*

3. *Why would Douglass, Garrison and the other male abolitionists support the nascent women's suffrage movement?*

4. *After emancipation, many former slaves expected payment for their exploitation in the form of help for their economic independence (slogan "forty acres and a mule"). This economic help never materialized. Should the U.S. pay reparations for the descendents of slavery today?*

Further Information:

Douglass' essay "What to the Slave is the Fourth of July" is at douglassarchives. org/doug_a10.htm

FREDERICK DOUGLASS

"What to the American slave is your Fourth of July? I answer a day that reveals to him more than all other days of the year, the gross injustice and cruelty to which he is the constant victim. . . . There is not a nation on earth guilty of practices more shocking and bloody than are the people of these United States at this very hour."[10]

Born into slavery, Douglass understood, even as a child, the role the enforced ignorance of the slave played in his oppression. When he was seven years old, his mistress began teaching him to read, but ceased her efforts when her husband ordered her to do so. "If you give a nigger an inch, he will take an ell. A nigger should know nothing but to obey his master—to do as he is told to do. Learning would spoil the best nigger in the world." These words created in Douglass an understanding that slavery was consciously created and maintained for the benefits of slaveholders and that knowledge was the means of challenging oppression. "From that moment," he wrote in his autobiography, "I understood the pathway from slavery to freedom. . .Mistress, in teaching me the alphabet, had given me the *inch,* and no precaution could prevent me from taking the *ell*"[11] Douglass continued his education by carrying a book with him always and by persuading white boys he encountered to assist him. Disguised as a sailor, Douglass escaped from slavery and later earned enough money to purchase his freedom. At the risk of being returned to slavery, he published his autobiography in 1845.

As a young man, Douglass had refined his skills as a speaker and debater as a member of the East Baltimore Mental Improvement Society, a secret group of free blacks committed to study and debate. In 1838, Douglass encountered Garrison's *The Liberator* and began reading it faithfully. In 1841, Douglass heard Garrison speak, and was so impressed by him that he called him "the Moses raised up by God, to deliver His modern Israel from bondage."[12] Three days later, Douglass delivered a speech attended by Garrison, who invited Douglass to lecture under the aegis of the American Anti-Slavery Society. As part of their campaign of "moral suasion," the Garrisonians sponsored speaking engagements by former slaves, who joined the white abolitionists on the platform and whose testimonies served to demonstrate the horrors of slavery. "'Tell your story, Frederick,' would whisper my then revered friend, William Lloyd Garrison, as I stepped upon the platform. . . . It did not entirely satisfy me to narrate wrongs; I felt like denouncing them."[13]

Even before the Civil War, the fight against segregation in public transportation in the north was a cause embraced by both black and white abolitionists. In June of 1841, African American David Ruggles refused to vacate a "whites only" section of a Nantucket-bound steamer. Ruggles soon carried his protest to the New Bedford railway, filing suit after being forcibly ejected from the white car. After the judge found in favor of the railroad, Garrison, Douglass, and a group of fellow abolitionists held an anti-slavery meeting on the "Negro deck" of the steamer from which Ruggles had been ejected, prompting similar acts of protest throughout New England.[14] Douglass performed such acts of civil disobedience even when traveling alone. While traveling on a railroad in Massachusetts, Douglass was ordered to leave the first-class coach for which he had purchased a ticket. He protested, and "half a dozen fellows of the baser sort" were enlisted to remove him. "I refused to move," he wrote, "they clutched me, head, neck, and shoulders. But, in anticipation of the stretching to which I was about to be subjected, I had interwoven myself among the seats. In dragging me out, on this occasion, it must have cost the company twenty-five or thirty dollars, for I tore up seats and all."[15]

Recognizing the need for blacks to plead their own case, Frederick Douglass started his own newspaper, *The North Star,* on December 3, 1847. Douglass' decision to publish his own paper was seen by many Garrisonians as the first sign of dissension. Douglass later wrote that his relationship with Garrison had been "like that of a child to a parent."[16] However, philosophical differences between Garrison and Douglass, as well as Douglass' increasing awareness of paternalism and racial bias within the white abolitionist movement, prompted Douglass to claim greater independence as a speaker and activist. The relationship between the two men became increasingly strained and was ultimately severed. Until his death in 1895, Douglass remained an outspoken advocate of rights for women, an unsparing critic of racial oppression throughout the world, and an ardent opponent of lynching. To Douglass, "The real question, the all-commanding question, is whether American justice, American liberty, American civilization, American law and American Christianity can be made to include and protect alike and forever all American citizens in the rights which. . .have been guaranteed to them by the organic and fundamental law of the land."[17]

Document 1.2   Frederick Douglass: Editorial from the North Star (1847)[18]
We solemnly dedicate *The North Star* to the cause of our long oppressed and plundered fellow countrymen. May God bless the undertaking to your good! It shall fearlessly assert your rights, faithfully proclaim your wrongs, and earnestly demand for you instant and even-handed justice. Giving no quarter to slavery at the South, it will hold no truce with oppressors at the North. While it shall boldly advocate emancipation for our enslaved brethren, it will omit no opportunity to gain for the nominally free complete enfranchisement. Every effort to injure or degrade you or your cause— originating wheresoever, or with whomsoever—shall find in it a constant, unswerving and inflexible foe.

Remember that we are one, and our cause is one, and that we must help each other if we would succeed. We have drunk to the dregs the bitter cup of slavery; we have worn the heavy yoke; we have sighed beneath our bonds and writhed beneath the bloody lash;—cruel momentos of our oneness are indelibly marked on our living flesh. We are one with you under the ban of prejudice and proscription—one with you under the slander of inferiority—one with you in social and political disfranchisement. What you suffer, we suffer; what you endure, we endure. We are indissolubly united, and must fall or flourish together. . . .

It is scarcely necessary for us to say that our desire to occupy our position at the head of an Anti-Slavery Journal has resulted from no unworthy distrust or ungrateful want of appreciation of the zeal, integrity or ability of the noble band of white laborers in this department of our cause; but, from the sincere and settled conviction that such a Journal, if conducted with only moderate skill and ability, would do a most important and indispensable work, which it would be wholly impossible for our white friends to do for us.

It is neither a reflection on the fidelity, or a disparagement of the ability of our friends and fellow-laborers, to assert "what common sense affirms and only folly denies," that the man who has suffered the wrong is the man to demand redress, —that the man STRUCK is the man to CRY OUT—and that he who has endured the cruel pangs of Slavery is the man to advocate Liberty. It is evident we must be our own representatives and advocates— not exclusively, but peculiarly—not distinct from, but in connection with our white friends. In the grand struggle for liberty and equality now waging it is meet, right, and essential that there should arise in our ranks authors and editors, as well as orators, for it is in these capacities that the most permanent good can be rendered to our cause. . . .

ANTHONY BURNS AND THE FUGITIVE SLAVE ACT

In 1850, a second Fugitive Slave Act was passed to strengthen the 1793 law. This new law made assisting and sheltering fugitive slaves a criminal act and required private citizens to assist the government in the tracking down of runaways. The passing of the act galvanized many abolitionists into action. Even the reserved Ralph Waldo Emerson responded with outrage. Speaking for many northern moderates, he cried, "By God, I will not obey it!"[19] Garrison's *Liberator* published suggestions for vigilante committees to prevent slave-hunters from returning slaves to bondage. "Whenever they go out," advised *The Liberator,* "two resolute, unarmed men should follow each of them wherever he goes, pointing him out from time to time with the word SLAVE-HUNTER. . . . He should not have a moment's relief from the feeling that his object is understood, that he cannot act in secret, that he is surrounded by those who loathe his person and detest his purpose. . . ."[20]

The case of Anthony Burns demonstrated the extent of resistance in Massachusetts to the Fugitive Slave Act. While employed at a clothing store in Boston, Burns was arrested as a fugitive and, while imprisoned, spoke briefly to Colonel Charles Suttle, his former master, acknowledging that he had never been beaten and admitting that Suttle had given him "twelve and a half cents, once a year." A crowd of irate Bostonians, led by abolitionist Thomas Higginson, made an unsuccessful effort to rescue Burns from custody. Defended by the writer, lawyer, and abolitionist Richard Henry Dana, Burns was convicted on the evidence of his initial brief conversation with Suttle; the judge ruled that Burns had acknowledged the master/slave relationship and was therefore guilty of violating the Fugitive Slave Law. Twenty companies of militia were required to maintain order as Burns was escorted through the streets to the ship that would return him to Virginia and a life of slavery.[21] Windows along the route and American flags were draped with black mourning crepe. "From the window opposite Old State House was suspended a black coffin on which were the words, 'The Funeral of Liberty'. . .The solemn procession was witnessed by fifty thousand people who hissed, groaned, and cried, 'Kidnappers! Kidnappers! Shame! Shame!'"[22] Of the protest, Burns commented, "There was a lot of folks to see a colored man walk down the street." After this display of resistance, Chief Justice Shaw of the Massachusetts Supreme Court commented, "No law can stand another such strain."[23] Purchased for thirteen hundred dollars by Boston supporters, Burns finally obtained his freedom. He was awarded a scholarship and studied for the Baptist ministry at Oberlin College.

In 1855, Anthony Burns, in a letter protesting his excommunication by the Baptist Church, expressed sentiments like those expressed by Thoreau in "Civil Disobedience." The Church had charged that the "said Anthony Burns absconded from the service of his master, and refused to return voluntarily—thereby disobeying both the laws of God and man. . . ." Burns replied,

> I admit that I left my master (so called), and refused to return; but I deny that in this I disobeyed either the law of God or any real *law* of men. Look at my case. I was stolen and made a slave as soon as I was born. No man had any right to steal me. That man stealer who stole me trampled on my dearest rights. God made me a *man*—not a *slave;* and gave me the same right to myself as he gave the man who stole me to himself. . . . You charge that, in escaping, I disobeyed God's law. No, indeed! That law which God wrote on the table of my heart, inspiring the love of freedom, and impelling me to seek it at every hazard, I obeyed, and by the good hand of my God upon me, I walked out of the house of bondage.[24]

I.C   Henry David Thoreau: Civil Disobedience

Questions to help you adopt a critical stance while reading the section below:

1. What are the intellectual origins of transcendentalism? Why would transcendentalism lead one logically to oppose slavery as well as justify resistance to it?

2. How does Thoreau define civil disobedience? What would qualify as civil disobedience today?

3. What is the relationship between ideology, belief and action? Does one need reasons to act on one's beliefs? Do reasons to act ensure effective action? Is passion and intuition enough? Does "intellectualizing" a problem paralyze action?

4. Does Thoreau's defense of John Brown support the ideals and strategy defined by Martin Luther King Jr. at the beginning of this chapter?

5. How does Thoreau's characterization of John Brown compare to modern historical accounts such as that of Bruce Catton or Eric Foner? How can you explain the differences and their significance?

6. "Passivity means complicity." What does that mean to you in your life?

7. What modifications might Amnesty International, the organization that fights human rights abuses, make to the statement, "they do not know by how much truth is stronger than error, nor how much more eloquently and effectively he can combat injustice who has experienced a little in his own person?"

HENRY DAVID THOREAU

"Law never made a man a whit more just, and, by means of their respect for it, even the well-disposed are daily made the agents of injustice."[25]

For most of his life, Henry David Thoreau was a man of contemplation, not of action. He accomplished little of the work the world admired; many of those who knew him considered him a failure. As Emerson said of him, he "studied no profession, wanted no marriage, attended no church, never voted, refused to be taxed, abstained from wine and tobacco, renounced meat, hated guns and traps."[26] In pursuit of a life of contemplation, Thoreau spent two years in relative solitude on the banks of Walden Pond where he wrote *Walden; or, Life in the Woods,* his best-known work. However, his influence on thinkers and political activists, in America and throughout the world, has been profound. Gandhi termed Thoreau's work "so convincing and truthful" and claimed that it had "greatly influenced (his) movement in India."[27] Martin Luther King called Thoreau "more alive today than ever before."[28]

Thoreau was primarily a student, and he found in Transcendentalism a philosophy that saw Nature as the ultimate teacher and the manifestation of Divinity. Born of the Reform Movement of the 1830s, Transcendentalism offered the belief that each person could derive wisdom from the Universal Intelligence, which the Transcendentalists termed "The Oversoul," a force manifest in Nature and in the individual conscience. "The Transcendentalists believed that man possesses an intuitive faculty, an innate moral sense, through which a person directly identifies his inner, central self with God and thereby experiences a sense of oneness with the world."[29] Influenced by the Hindu Scriptures, Ralph Waldo Emerson, one of the primary creators of the philosophy, saw the inner life, as a reflection of the Oversoul, a source of truth that transcended the finite conventions of society. As Emerson wrote in "Self Reliance," the individual possessed an "internal ocean" more vast than a "cup of water" drawn from "the urns of other men."[30]

CIVIL DISOBEDIENCE

In his essay "[On the Duty of] Civil Disobedience," Henry David Thoreau argued that the individual conscience provided a law more compelling than the laws of the state. Most at home in nature, "the hermit of Concord" was seldom drawn into political causes. However, the abolitionist cause, particularly the extension of slavery by the war in Mexico, the passage of the Fugitive Slave Act, and the execution of John Brown, prompted Thoreau into action. In 1846, Henry David Thoreau was jailed for one night for refusal to pay a poll tax, a tax that would be used to support a war of aggression against Mexico, in which the United States government showed its willingness to serve the interests of the planters by annexing more of Mexico as slave territory. The passage of the Fugitive Slave Act in 1850 was to Thoreau so great an injustice that passivity would have meant complicity. Thoreau's mother was an active member of the Anti-Slavery Society of Concord, and he had on more than one occasion assisted his family in the sheltering of fugitives from slavery. The Fugitive Slave Law made such an action criminal and required private citizens to assist the government in the tracking down of runaways. In "Life Without Principle," Thoreau wrote, "The law will never make men free. It is men who have got to make the law free."

Both Emerson and Thoreau publicly supported John Brown's unsuccessful raid on Harper's Ferry. Upon hearing that Brown's lawyers planned to enter a plea of insanity, Emerson commented that Brown was "the rarest of heroes, a pure idealist, with no by-ends of his own. He is therefore precisely what lawyers call crazy, being governed by ideas, and not by external circumstance."[31] In his journal, Thoreau wrote of Brown,

> He was a superior man. He did not value his bodily life in comparison with ideal things. He did not recognize unjust human laws, but resisted them as he was bid. . . . No man in America has ever stood up so persistently and effectively for the dignity of human nature, knowing himself for a man, and the equal of any and all governments. In that sense, he was the most American of us all.[32]

The ordinarily reticent Thoreau, determined to voice publicly his support for Brown, delivered "A Plea for Captain John Brown" in Concord to a small and somewhat hostile audience. He repeated the address to a larger and more receptive crowd in Boston. As he had in "Civil Disobedience," Thoreau defended the individual conscience over the laws written by an unjust state. "The only government that I recognize—and it matters not how few are at the head of it, or how small its army—is that power which establishes justice in the land, and not that which establishes injustice," he argued.

> I hear many condemn these men because they were so few. When were the good and the brave ever in a majority?. . .His company was small indeed, because few could be found worthy to pass muster. Each one who there laid down his life for the poor and oppressed was a picked man, culled out of many thousands, if not millions; apparently a man of principle, of rare courage and devoted humanity; ready to sacrifice his life at any moment for the benefit of his fellow-man. . . . These alone were ready to step between the oppressor and the oppressed. Surely they were the very best men you could select to be hung. . . [33]

Document 1.3   Henry David Thoreau: Essay on the Duty of Civil Disobedience[34]
(Excerpts)

Under a government which imprisons any unjustly, the true place for a just man is also in prison. The proper place today, the only place which Massachusetts has provided for her freer and less desponding spirits, is in her prisons, to be put out and locked out of the state by her own act, as they have already put themselves out by their principles. It is there that the fugitive slave, and the Mexican prisoner on parole, and the Indian come to plead the wrongs of his race, should find them; on that separate but more free and honorable ground, where the state places those who are not <u>with</u> her but <u>against</u> her—the only house in a slave state which a free man can abide with honor.

If any think that their influence would be lost there, and their voices no longer afflict the ear of the state, that they would not be as an enemy within its walls, they do not know by how much truth is stronger than error, nor how much more eloquently and effectively he can combat injustice who has experienced a little in his own person.

Cast your whole vote, not a strip of paper merely, but your whole influence. A minority is powerless while it conforms to the majority; it is not even a minority then; but it is irresistible when it clogs by its whole weight.

If the alternative is to keep all just men in prison, or give up war and slavery, the state will not hesitate which to choose. If a thousand men were not to pay their tax bills this year, that would not be a violent and bloody measure, as it would be to pay them, and enable the state to commit violence and shed innocent blood.

This is, in fact, the definition of a peaceful revolution, if any such is possible. If the tax gatherer or any other public officer asks me, as one has done, 'But what shall I do?' my answer is, 'If you really wish to do anything, resign your office.' When the subject has refused allegiance and the officer has resigned his office, then the revolution is accomplished. . . .

Must the citizen ever for a moment, or in the least degree, resign his conscience to the legislator? Why has every man a conscience, then? I think that we should be men first, and subjects afterwards. It is not desirable to cultivate a respect for the law so much as for the right. The only obligation which I have a right to assume is to do at any time what I think right. It is truly enough said, that a corporation has no conscience; but a corporation of conscientious men is a corporation *with* a conscience.

Law never made men a whit more just; and, by means of their respect for it, even the well-disposed are daily made the agents of injustice. A common and natural result of an undue respect for law is that you may see a file of soldiers, colonel, captain, corporal, privates, powder-monkeys, and all, marching in admirable order over hill and dale to the wars, against their wills, aye, against their common sense and consciences, which make it very steep marching indeed, and produces a palpitation of the heart. They have no doubt that it is a damnable business in which they are concerned; they are all peaceably inclined. Now, what are they? Men at all? or small movable forts and magazines, at the service of some unscrupulous men in power. . . .

The mass of men serve the state thus, not as men mainly, but as machines, with their bodies. They are the standing army, the militia, jailers, constables, posse comitatus, etc. In most cases there is no free exercise whatever of the judgment or of the moral sense; but they put themselves on a level with wood and earth and stones; and wooden men can perhaps be manufactured that will serve the purpose as well. Such command no more respect than men of straw or a lump of dirt. They have the same sort of worth only as horses and dogs. Yet such as these even are commonly esteemed good citizens. . . .

A very few, as heroes, patriots, martyrs, reformers in the great sense, and <u>men</u>, serve the state with their consciences also, and so necessarily resist it for the most part; and they are commonly treated as enemies by it. . . .

Freedom School Curriculum Link:

Nonviolence in American History

www.educationanddemocracy.org/FSCfiles/C_CC7e_NonviolenceInAm Hist.htm

This article, written for the Freedom Schools, shows that nonviolence has a long tradition in American History too.

I.D   Mohandas Gandhi: Nonviolence

Questions to help you adopt a critical stance while reading the section below:

1. *Is there a "common interest" to which Gandhi appeals in his letter to Lord Irwin? What are the common interests that all humans share?*

2. *What is the most striking part to you of Gandhi's "Letter to Lord Irwin?"*

3. In the "Letter to Lord Irwin," Gandhi states he will use nonviolence but does not explain why it will work. Why did Gandhi choose to explain the inequities of British rule rather than explain how nonviolence will prove triumphant? Would Gandhi have used violence if it would have been successful (see Saul Alinsky's view of nonviolence as a tactic in his Rules for Radicals)?

4. Compare the role jail plays in Thoreau's strategy with that of Gandhi's. Are there circumstances under which being arrested may not produce "revolution"?

5. Does the scene of the demonstrations at the Dharsana Salt Works described by United Press reporter Miller "shake [your] faith. . .that love is the supreme and only law of life?" How does Gandhi argue that it doesn't shake his own faith?

6. What do you imagine Gandhi's response to Thoreau's defense of John Brown to have been? Would Gandhi have defended John Brown's raid on Harper's Ferry? Can Thoreau's ideas on civil disobedience be reconciled with his defense of John Brown?

7. Compare the Salt March and the demonstrations at the Dharsana Salt Works to the modern day protests at World Trade Organization meetings (for example, 1999 in Seattle). The choice of salt as an issue galvanized a movement because of what it symbolized for people. What might the issue be today around which a social movement on the scale of the Civil Rights Movement could spring?

Further Information

Very extensive information on Gandhi and his influence, and many of his essays are at www.mkgandhi.org/index.htm

Recommended Film

A Force More Powerful (Documentary; 6 x 30 min, 2000; produced and directed by Steve York). This is a six-part documentary series on one of the 20th century's most important and least known stories—how non-violent power overcame oppression and authoritarian rule. The documentary covers nonviolent movements in Nashville, India, South Africa, Denmark, Poland, and Chile.

MOHANDAS GANDHI

"None of us knew what name to give to our movement. I then used the term 'passive resistance' in describing it: I did not quite understand the implications of 'passive resistance' as I called it—I only knew that some new principle had come into being. As the struggle advanced, the phrase 'passive resistance' gave

rise to confusion. . . . I thus began to call the Indian movement 'Satyagraha,'
that is to say the Force which is born of Truth and Love or nonviolence."[35]

Early in his life, Gandhi had been an admirer of the British and wished nothing more than to become an English gentleman. In time, he was to become one of the most formidable opponents ever faced by the British Empire. His method of resistance—ahimsa, or nonviolence—ultimately resulted in the withdrawal of the British from India, the "jewel in the crown" of their far-flung Empire.

As a young man and a law student in London, Gandhi supported the British and their Dominion in India. "I wanted to invoke in the Indian breast the same loyalty to the British crown that there is in the breast of an Englishman."[36] He later recalled his efforts at physical transformation during his student days in London in 1888.

> I undertook the all too improbable task of becoming an English gentleman. The clothiers after the Bombay cut that I was wearing were, I thought, unsuitable for English society, and I got new ones. . . . I wasted ten pounds on an evening suit made in Bond Street, the center of fashionable life in London. . .while in India, the mirror had been a luxury permitted on the days when the family barber gave me a shave. Here I wasted ten minutes every day before a huge mirror, watching myself arranging my tie and parting my hair in the correct fashion. My hair was by no means soft, and every day it meant a regular struggle with the brush to keep it in position.[37]

Influenced by Thoreau, Gandhi began to question the right of government to impose controls that supported not justice but exploitative power relationships. After suffering discrimination while practicing law in South Africa, Gandhi began demonstrations against British rule and began to formulate his method of nonviolent protest, which he termed "satyagraha."* In 1913, during his efforts on behalf of Indian laborers in South Africa, Gandhi led

---

* *Satyagraha.* Power or firmness of truth, love, or nonviolence. The nonviolent demonstrator seeks to elevate the understanding of his oppressor and thus transform the conflict. Gandhi created this term by combining the word satya (truth) with agraha, producing a word which means "clinging to the truth" or "firmness in truth." The term satyagraha also refers to a specific political action, such as a march or demonstration, undertaken as a means of manifesting the principle.

a march of more than two thousand to protest repressive legislation and to prompt negotiation with General Jan Smuts. Upon his return to India in 1914, he began to organize non-cooperation protests against British rule, including a boycott of cloth manufactured in British mills in 1920. During this time, Gandhi organized the All India Spinners Association, a movement which encouraged the manufacture of homespun cloth, or khadi, as a means of economic autonomy and protest. Gandhi himself spun cloth daily, an effort that was both practical and symbolic. As he became more identified with the struggles of the peasants in India, Gandhi later chose the simple garb of the Indian peasant to symbolize his political solidarity with his people. Such simple dress prompted Winston Churchill to dismiss him as a "half-naked fakir."

NONVIOLENCE

One of his most dramatic illustrations of the principle of satyagraha was the Salt March in 1930. Gandhi led the march, gradually joined by thousands of protesters, to the sea to acquire natural salt in defiance of British law. The march was undertaken to protest the tax defined in the British Salt Act of 1882, which granted the British government a monopoly on the manufacture of salt and the right to impose a salt tax on India's already impoverished peasant population. Gandhi hoped that the Salt March would begin a process of civil disobedience which would result in India's independence.

"The aim in satyagraha," writes historian Dennis Dalton, "is not merely to prevail but to transform the conflict in such a way that all parties may be uplifted in the process by being brought closer to a sense of their common interest . . . . The dynamics of conflict resolution should humanize rather than degrade the participants. When this happens, the means are consistent with the end and one moves toward swaraj."[38] In keeping with this position, Gandhi wrote a detailed letter to Lord Irwin, the British Viceroy in India, carefully explaining his position.

Document 1.4   Gandhi's Letter to Lord Edward Irwin[39]
Dear Friend,

Before embarking on Civil Disobedience and taking the risk I have dreaded to take all these years, I would fain approach you and find a way out. I cannot intentionally hurt anything that lives, much less human beings, even though they may do the greatest wrong to me and mine. Whilst, therefore, I hold the British rule to be a curse, I do not intend harm to a single Englishman or to any legitimate interest he may have in India. . . . And why do I regard the British rule to be a curse? It has impoverished the dumb millions by a system of progressive exploitation and by a ruinous expensive military and civil administration which the country can never afford. It has reduced [Indian peasants] politically to serfdom. It has sapped the foundations of our culture. . .I fear. . .there has never been any intention of granting. . .Dominion status to India in the immediate future.

The entire system of revenue would have to be revised so as to make the peasant's good it's primary concern. But the British system seems to be designed to crush the very life out of him. Even the salt he must use to live is so taxed as to make the burden fall heaviest on him . . .The tax shows itself still more burdensome on the poor man when it is remembered that salt is the only thing he must eat more than the rich man. The drink and drug revenue, too, is derived from the poor. It saps the foundations of their health and morals.

The iniquities sampled above are being maintained in order to carry on a foreign administration demonstrably the most expensive in the world. Take your own salary. It is over 21,000 rupees (about $7,000) [$84,000 in 2006 US dollars] a month, besides many other indirect additions. . . . You are getting over 700 rupees a day (approximately $233) [$2,800 in 2006 US dollars] against India's average income of less than two annas (four cents) [$.50 in 2006] a day. Thus you are getting much over five thousand times India's average income. The British Prime Minister is getting only ninety times Britain's average income. On bended knee, I ask you to ponder this phenomenon. I have taken a personal illustration to drive home a painful truth. I have too great a regard for you as a man to wish to hurt your feelings. I know that you do not need the salary you get. Probably the whole of your salary goes to charity. But a system that provides such an arrangement deserves to be summarily scrapped. What is true of the Vice-regal salary is true generally of the whole administration.

Nothing but organized nonviolence can check the organized violence of the British government. . . . This nonviolence will be expressed through civil disobedience. . . . My ambition is no less than to convert the British people through nonviolence, and thus make them see the wrong they have done to India.

I respectfully invite you to pave the way for the immediate removal of these evils, and thus open a way for a real conference between equals. But if you cannot see your way to deal with these evils and if my letter makes no appeal to your heart, on the eleventh day of this month I shall proceed with such co-workers of the Ashram as I can take, to disregard the provisions of the Salt Laws. . . . It is, I know, open to you to frustrate my design by arresting me. I hope that there will be tens of thousands ready, in a disciplined manner, to take up the work after me.

THE SALT MARCH

In spite of Lord Irwin's support for a roundtable conference to discuss dominion status for India, the British government remained opposed to any form, however limited, of Indian independence. So, Gandhi proceeded with the Salt March. On March 12, 1930, Gandhi set out from his ashram accompanied by a small group of followers. One observer noted:

> The road outside the ashram gate was cleared of the crowds, and the little group collected in disciplined order, all clad in white khadi and with nothing but a satchel slung over one shoulder—except for the music pundit, who carried his stringed instrument. Here was an army such as had never before been seen, devoid of all physical arms, only eighty strong, and marching off in joyous confidence to overthrow the greatest empire in the world.[40]

Gandhi and his followers, soon numbering in the thousands, reached the tiny village of Dandi on the coast of India on the evening of April 5. Gandhi addressed his followers and declared the place and the coming event sacred. The next morning, Gandhi requested that the marchers purify themselves by bathing in the sea, and thousands followed him into the water. Then, in a public act of civil disobedience that served both as symbol and as example, Gandhi picked up a handful of natural salt and declared, "With this, I am shaking the foundations of the British Empire."[41] Gandhi's example prompted a massive campaign of civil disobedience. Along the seacoast of India, peasants waded into the sea and manufactured salt in open defiance of British authority. Soon, Lord Irwin had arrested more than sixty thousand political demonstrators.

Irwin, however, hesitated to arrest Gandhi despite his open defiance of the law. An Indian newspaper concisely expressed Irwin's dilemma.

To arrest Gandhi is to set fire to the whole of India. Not to arrest him is to allow him to set the prairie on fire. To arrest Gandhi is to court a war. Not to arrest him is to confess defeat before the war is begun. . . . In either case, Government stands to lose, and Gandhi stands to gain. . . . That is because Gandhi's cause is righteous and the government's is not.[42]

Later, Irwin wrote, "I am anxious to avoid arresting Gandhi if I can do so without letting a 'Gandhi legend' establish itself that we are afraid to lay hands on him."[43] One British police officer expressed a growing distaste for his responsibility to quell demonstrations. When called upon to disperse demonstrators, the policeman "felt a severe physical nausea which prevented me from taking food until the crisis was over. . . . I was at a loss to understand why I should be physically affected by it. . . . I thought then, and I still think, that I was largely influenced by the feeling that. . .the policy of our Government in dealing with it was wrong."[44]

As the weeks passed and it became evident that Gandhi's example had prompted massive demonstrations whose participants began to fill the jails, the British government's hesitancy vanished. On May 4, police found Gandhi sleeping under a mango tree in his camp near Dandi and arrested him. He was neither tried nor sentenced, but confined to prison under a law that allowed Indians to be held "at the pleasure of the government."[45] Gandhi's confidence that his followers would be able to continue the campaign during his imprisonment was justified by a demonstration held on May 21 at the Dharsana Salt Works. Led by Mrs. Sarojini Naidu, over two thousand demonstrators attempted a raid on the works, a raid observed and made famous by reporter Webb Miller of the United Press. Miller's account focused world-wide attention on the struggle in India. The Dharsnana Salt Works Satyagraha brought the people of India one step closer to independence.

In complete silence the Gandhi men drew up and halted a hundred yards from the stockade. A picked column advanced from the crowd, waded the ditches, and approached the barbed wire stockade. . . . Suddenly, at a word of command, scores of native policemen rushed upon the advancing marchers and rained blows on their heads with their steel-shod lathes. Not one of the marchers even raised an arm to fend off the blows. They went down like tenpins. From where I stood I heard the sickening whack of the clubs on unprotected skulls. The waiting crowd of marchers groaned and sucked in their breath in sympathetic pain at every blow. Those struck down fell sprawling, unconscious or writhing with fractured skulls or broken shoulders. . . . The survivors, without breaking ranks, silently and doggedly marched on until struck down. . . .

They marched steadily, with heads up, without the encouragement of music or cheering or any possibility that they might escape serious injury or death. The police marched out and methodically and mechanically beat down the second column. There was no fight, no struggle; the marchers simply walked forward till struck down.

The police commenced to savagely kick the seated men in the abdomen and testicles and then dragged them by their arms and feet and threw them into the ditches. One was dragged to a ditch where I stood. The splash of his body doused me with muddy water. . . . Hour after hour stretcher-bearers carried back a stream of inert, bleeding bodies. . . . By 11 A.M., the heat had reached 116 degrees, and the assault subsided.[46]

The Salt March was an inclusive effort, which made it an important example for Freedom Summer. Gandhi's march had covered two hundred miles, its path passing through dozens of villages. By sending supporters to these villages beforehand, Gandhi had learned of local concerns and held numerous public meetings along the way to the sea. The Salt March appealed to students, who supported Gandhi with letters from the announcement of his intention. "We are determined to join your campaign, but we are disallowed by our parents," wrote the members of an Indian Youth League. "So we have come to a definite conclusion that our holy nation's call is to be responded to more than our parents' wish. We are under a firm belief that our service to humanity will outweigh the sin of disobeying our parents. . . .Please allow us to join your volunteer corps." Another youth wrote Gandhi, offering his services. "If we could only establish the truth of our way in the public mind with our own blood," he wrote, "we will have achieved our end."[47] The upper class women of India, confined by tradition to the home, astonished the British by appearing in public and manufacturing salt. An official government report remarked, "Thousands of them many being of good family and high educational attainments suddenly emerged from the seclusion of their homes and in some instances actually from the purdah (veil)."[48] The march's focus on a common household item was seen as inviting the women's participation and expanding the appeal of the march. Historian Madhu Kishwar commented, "Salt is one of the cheapest of commodities which every woman buys and uses as a matter of routine. . . . To manufacture salt in defiance of British laws prohibiting such manufacture, became a way of declaring one's independence in one's own daily life and also of revolutionizing one's perception of the kitchen as linked to the nation."[49] Salt, found everywhere, became charged with moral, political, and spiritual significance. "Salt suddenly became a mysterious word," said Jawaharlal Nehru, "a word of power."[50]

The people of India bestowed on Gandhi the title "Mahatma"—Great Soul. The admiration he frequently won from his former adversaries, the British, demonstrated the power of *ahimsa* (nonviolence). Louis Mountbatten, the last British viceroy to serve in India, presided over the transfer of power from the British to the newly independent India. Mountbatten said, "Mahatma Gandhi will go down in history on a par with Buddha and Jesus Christ."[51] Efforts to unite Muslim and Hindu elements in India resulted in continued conflict after the end of British rule. Gandhi, himself a Hindu, was assassinated in 1948 by a Hindu zealot protesting Muslim influence in the emergent government.

Questions based on Document 1.5 below:

1. *How does this document compare to the principles of CORE or to NAACP tactics?*

2. *Of all of Gandhi's writings and of all that has been written about Gandhi by 1964, why did the Freedom School Curriculum contain the specific selection it did, why choose this piece over any of the others? (Or, what would you need to know in order to test your hypothesis/answer to this question?)*

Document 1.5   Mahatma Gandhi: My Faith in Nonviolence[52] (Excerpt)
"I have found that life persists in the midst of destruction and, therefore, there must be a higher law than that of destruction. Only under that law would a well-ordered society be intelligible and life worth living. And if that is the law of life, we have to work it out in daily life. Whenever there are [fears?], wherever you are confronted with an opponent, conquer him with love. . .that does not mean that all my difficulties are solved. I have found, however, that his law of love has answered as the law of destruction has never done."

"Nonviolence is a weapon of the strong. . . ."

"Practically speaking there will be probably no greater loss in men than if forcible resistance was offered; there will be no expenditure in armaments and fortifications. The nonviolent training received by the people will add inconceivably to their moral height. Such men and women will have shown personal bravery of a type far superior to that shown in armed warfare. In each case the bravery consists in dying, not in killing. Lastly, there is no such thing as defeat in nonviolent resistance. That such a thing has not happened before is no answer to my speculation. I have drawn no impossible picture. History is replete with instances of individual nonviolence of the type I have mentioned. There is no warrant for saying or thinking that a group of men and women cannot by sufficient training act nonviolently as a group or nation. Indeed the sum total of the experience of mankind is that men somehow or other live on. From which fact I infer that it is the law of love that rules mankind. Had violence, hate, ruled us, we should have become extinct long ago. And yet the tragedy of it is that the so called civilized men and nations conduct themselves as if the basis of society was violence. It gives me ineffable joy to make experiments proving that love is the supreme and only law of life. Much evidence to the contrary cannot shake my faith. Even the mixed nonviolence of India has supported it. But if it is not enough to convince an unbeliever, it is enough to incline a friendly critic to view it with favor."

(From the selection "Readings in Nonviolence" in the Freedom School Curriculum)

Freedom School Curriculum Link:

Nonviolence in American History

> *www.educationanddemocracy.org/FSCfiles/C_CC7e_NonviolenceInAmHist.htm*
> *This article, written for the Freedom Schools, shows that nonviolence has a long tradition in American history, too.*

TWO

National Association for the Advancement of Colored People (NAACP)

Questions to help you adopt a critical stance while reading the section below:

1. *What are the characteristics of the NAACP in terms of history, strategy, and membership?*

2. *What is the meaning of Jim Crow; Separate but Equal; and Segregation?*

THE NAACP IS IMPORTANT not only because the participation of its members was crucial to the success of the 1964 Freedom Summer Project but also because it is part of the history of courageous resistance to unjust laws. When the federal government withdrew its protection of freed slaves in the South after 1876, the old planter elite intensified their violent intimidation tactics. Lynching and race riots were used to not merely deprive African Americans of their property and lives but also to inhibit resistance to daily exploitation by establishing a reign of terror. These tactics were not confined to the South. The 1908 Springfield, Illinois race riot prompted reformers to organize nationally against the injustices of African Americans. The journalist William English Walling wrote an article for *The Independent* describing the Springfield riot. He ended with the appeal:

Either the spirit of the abolitionists, of Lincoln and of Lovejoy, must be revived and we must come to treat the Negro on a plane of absolute political and social equality, or Vardaman [Governor of Mississippi] and Tillman [Senator of South Carolina] will soon have transferred the race war to the North. . . . The day these methods become general in the North every hope of political democracy will be dead. . . . Yet who realizes the seriousness of the situation, and what large and powerful body of citizens is ready to come to their aid?[1]

One of the readers of Walling's article was Mary White Ovington, granddaughter of Brooklyn abolitionists. Seeing in Walling's challenge the opportunity to continue the work of her grandparents, Ovington wrote to him offering her services. Walling, New York lawyer Henry Moskowitz, and Ovington met. They issued "The Call"—a statement of the intention to form an organization to address the injustices against blacks.

"The Call" united progressives from the Labor Movement, the College Settlement Movement, and the educational reform movement. Signers of the call included educational philosopher John Dewey; Jane Addams, founder of Hull House; Labor leader Leonora O'Reilly; journalist and activist Ida B. Wells-Barnett; and Atlanta University professor and outspoken leader W.E.B. DuBois. Combining their efforts with the newly formed Niagara Movement, which had been established in 1905, they formed the NAACP in 1910.

The NAACP launched an anti-lynching campaign in 1911 and also began the long series of successful legal challenges to segregation upon which the nonviolent action of the 1950s and 1960s was based. The strategy of the NAACP was to work toward justice for African Americans through existing legal institutions. During the Civil Rights Movement, this strategy often created tensions with those who favored nonviolent, but direct action tactics. Yet, as Medgar Evers believed, a coalition of forces was crucial for success. Four significant tactics of the NAACP were:

1. To educate the public through its journal *The Crisis* and other pamphlets using well researched factual material and passionate prose.

2. To use test cases to challenge unjust laws and to demand the enforcement of existing laws.

3. To lobby in Congress for the interests of African Americans.

4. To create a network of local branches connected to a central office.

THE SILENT MARCH

The NAACP's tactics included legal challenges to segregation and cultural challenges to the mythology that justified the enforced second-class citizenship of African Americans. But these were not the only tactics used. In organizing the Silent March, the NAACP drew upon a rich tradition of nonviolent direct action (see the Salt March in Chapter 1).

On July 2, 1917, East St. Louis erupted in a riot which resulted in the killing of several hundred black residents. After a Congressional investigation, Missouri's Congressman Leonidas Dyer reported to the House of Representatives a scene of shocking brutality. Summarizing an interview with a black veteran, Dyer said,

> He saw this mob go to the homes of these Negroes and nail boards up over the doors and windows and then set fire and burn them up. He saw them take little children out of the arms of their mothers and throw them into the fires and burn them up. He saw the most dastardly and most criminal outrages ever perpetrated in this country. . . .[2]

On July 28, 1917, the NAACP conducted a Silent March through the streets of New York City. To the sound of muffled drums, hundreds of men, women, and children marched to protest the conditions of law enforcement in urban as well as rural areas. "The parade," wrote James Weldon Johnson, "moved in silence and was watched in silence."[3] Carrying signs which read, "Mother, Do Lynchers Go to Heaven?" and "Treat Us so That We May Love our Country," demonstrators marched as Boy Scouts distributed pamphlets explaining their cause.

> We march because we want to make impossible a repetition of Waco, Memphis, and East St. Louis, by rousing the conscience of the country and bringing the murderers of our brothers, sisters, and innocent children to justice. We march because we are thoroughly opposed to Jim-Crow Cars, Segregation, Discrimination, Disenfranchisement, LYNCHING,

and the host of evils that are forced on us. . . . We march because we want our children to live in a better land and enjoy fairer conditions than have fallen to our lot.[4]

THE "SOUTHERN EMPIRE"

A strong public advocate of the rights of African Americans, the poet, educator, musician, and activist James Weldon Johnson became the first black field secretary of the NAACP in 1916. In 1919, he was promoted to be the first black executive secretary for the NAACP. Johnson created what the organization later termed its "Southern Empire." He observed that few NAACP branches existed in the South, and yet it was in the South that such branches were most needed. The NAACP could not, according to Johnson, "reach its goals by hammering at white America." Ultimately, the NAACP "would have to awaken black American to a sense of its rights."[5] Johnson wrote personally to prominent black Americans in Southern cities, requesting that each gather at least twenty-five persons willing to speak to him about the NAACP. From such meetings, nineteen branches were opened in Southern cities from Richmond, Virginia, to Tampa, Florida.

Johnson investigated lynchings for the NAACP, traveling South and speaking to sheriffs, newspaper reporters, and local African Americans. While investigating a particularly gruesome lynching in Tennessee, Johnson felt, "I tried to balance the sufferings of the miserable victim against the moral degradation of Memphis, and the truth flashed over me that in large measure the race question involves the saving of black America's body and white America's soul."[6]

2.A   Ida B. Wells: The Anti-Lynching Campaign

Questions to help you adopt a critical stance while reading the section below:

1. *Does any of the information given here about Ida B. Wells suggest possible explanations as to why she may have found the NAACP "too conservative"? Would you consider Wells an "extremist"?*

2. *Full text of "A Red Record" is at www.gutenberg.org/etext/14977, "Lynch Law in Georgia" by Wells-Barnett is at afroamhistory.about.com/library/blidabwells_lynchlawinamerica.htm*

Further Information:
> *"Strange Fruit" is a song about lynching made famous by Billie Holliday. See www*
> *.pbs.org/independentlens/strangefruit/film.html*

Recommended Film
> Ida B. Wells: A Passion for Justice *(Documentary; 53 min, 1989; produced and*
> *directed by William Greaves).* A Passion for Justice *documents the dramatic*
> *life and turbulent times of the pioneering African American journalist, activist,*
> *suffragist and anti-lynching crusader of the post-Reconstruction period.*

IDA B. WELLS

"Our work has only begun. Our race—hereditary bondsmen—must strike the blow if they would be free."[7]

In Holly Springs, Mississippi, where Ida B. Wells was born, her father, a former slave, was known as a "race man," an African American who was proud of his race and refused to bow to white intimidation. When her parents died in a yellow fever epidemic, Wells was the sole supporter of her five younger siblings at the age of fourteen. By concealing her age, she secured her first teaching position at age fifteen, riding a mule to school each week and returning on weekends to take care of her brothers and sisters. At eighteen, when relatives in Memphis assumed care of the family, she moved to Memphis where she continued her teaching career and her education at Fisk University. While riding a train from Memphis to Woodstock, Tennessee, Wells experienced first-hand the end of the Federal government's legal protections of Reconstruction (1865–1877) and the beginning of the state government's "black codes" or Jim Crow. When she was ordered to relinquish her seat in the train's "Ladies Coach," she refused, resisting the conductor who tried to remove her by force by biting him on the hand. It took three men to remove Wells, who was under five feet tall, from the car. She brought suit and won her case, a victory that a local paper announced with the headline: "Darky Damsel Obtains a Verdict for Damages Against the Chesapeake and Ohio Railroad."[8] Wells later learned that she was the first American to challenge the 1883 nullification of the Civil Rights Bill. Her case suffered a devastating reversal in the Tennessee Supreme Court.

Wells expressed her disillusionment through a series of articles in an African American newspaper. Her column, written under the pen name "Iola" attracted attention in the black press, and her columns were soon printed in other papers. Growing respect for her writing led to her election as secretary of the National Afro-American Press Association. Fired from her teaching position for exposing inadequate facilities in the Memphis school system, Wells began her career as a journalist and soon became an owner of *The Memphis Free Speech.*

Wells began her uncompromising and lifelong campaign against lynching after Thomas Moss, Calvin McDowell, and Henry Stewart were lynched near Memphis, Tennessee in 1892. The three men had been partners in a business called the People's Grocery, a store which had become a meeting place for blacks in Memphis. Capital to start the business had been supplied by Moss, a postman and the first black Federal employee in Memphis. Armed whites attacked the store on a Saturday evening, and were repelled by a group of armed black men. Three whites were shot during this incident. The three business owners were arrested along with a hundred other blacks and charged with conspiracy. The three men were removed from prison and lynched a mile outside of Memphis. Thomas Moss' last words were, "Tell my people to go West. There is no justice for them here."[9]

Moss and his wife had been personal friends of Wells, who was the godmother of their first child. Her editorial in *The Memphis Free Speech* condemned the act. "The city of Memphis," she wrote, "has demonstrated neither character nor standing avails the Negro if he dares to protect himself against the white man or become his rival."[10] At first, she suggested that blacks heed Moss' final words and "Save our money and leave a town which will neither protect our lives and property, nor give us a fair trial in the courts, but takes us out and murders us in cold blood."[11] Wells helped to organize a boycott of the city's trolley lines, threatening the transportation company with bankruptcy. She further suggested that blacks arm themselves against possible white retaliation. Determined to "sell my life as dearly as possible," she purchased a pistol for herself and suggested to her readers that a "Winchester rifle should have a place of honor in every home."[12]

Wells defined lynching as a tactic used to intimidate blacks into subservience and to punish successful blacks, thus maintaining white supremacy by terrorism. In her forceful writing, she challenged the view of the black male as potential rapist, exposing instead the frequent sexual violation of black women by white men. Using her skills as a journalist, Wells conducted investigations and hired private detectives to assist in the gathering of data about lynchings. Further, she concluded that the charge of "rape" was used to explain voluntary relationships between white women and black men. As a result of an 1892 editorial in which she presented this view, a mob attached *The Memphis Free Speech* and destroyed it, forcing Wells to leave Memphis and continue publishing in the *New York Age*. Among her writings on lynching was *The Red Record,* a carefully documented account of her investigations of lynchings throughout the United States.

A founding member of the NAACP, Ida B. Wells soon withdrew, finding the organization too conservative. Her powerful anti-lynching campaign, however, provided a model used by the NAACP in their subsequent work.

ANTI-LYNCHING CAMPAIGN

Wells' anti-lynching campaign became part of the earliest strategy of the NAACP. The brazenness of lynchers was emphasized in 1911, when a postcard was sent to Unitarian minister John H. Holmes in response to an uncompromising anti-lynching speech given by him at an early NAACP meeting. Gathered around the body of a victim, like hunters displaying a trophy, the white men faced the camera calmly. "The men's confidence that no one would dream of prosecuting them was the most striking thing about the card," commented Mary White Ovington.[13]

To focus national attention on lynching, the NAACP launched a campaign which included meetings, pamphlets, and the pages of *The Crisis*. Annual lynching figures were published in *The Crisis* and pamphlets describing the brutality of individual cases were mailed to potential supporters. Evidence gathered by NAACP researchers was used by lawyers to provide legal redress for victims.[14] At an Executive Board meeting in May of 1911, members discussed the brutal lynching of M. Potter, a Black man accused of killing a white man. Dragged by a mob from prison to the stage of the Livermore, Kentucky Opera House, Potter was hanged on the stage while a crowd, who had paid admission to attend the event, were allowed to shoot at Potter's body. The Committee appealed directly to the President, urging them to call "attention to the terrible iniquities and intolerable conditions of Lynch Law, and ask congress to take such action as will save this nation from this foul blot and curse on its civilization."[15]

Questions based on Document 2.1 below:

1. *Who is Wells addressing? What is her argument? Is her argument suited to her audience?*

2. *Does each action item serve the same purpose? Are they different but necessary tactical responses?*

Document 2.1   Ida B. Wells: The Red Record[16]

What can you do, reader, to prevent lynching, to thwart anarchy and promote law and order throughout our land?

1st. You can help disseminate the facts contained in this book by bringing them to the knowledge of every one with whom you come in contact, to the end that public sentiment may be revolutionized. Let the facts speak for themselves, with you as a medium.

2nd. You can be instrumental in having churches, missionary societies, Y.M.C.A.'s, W.C.T.U.'s and all Christian and moral forces in connection with your religious and social life, pass resolutions of condemnation and protest every time a lynching takes place; and see that they are sent to the place where these outrages occur.

3rd. Bring to the intelligent consideration of Southern people the refusal of capital to invest where lawlessness and mob violence hold sway. Many labor organizations have declared by resolution that they would avoid lynch infested localities as they would the pestilence when seeking new homes. . . .

4th. Think and act on independent lines in this behalf, remembering that after all, it is the white man's civilization and the white man's government which are on trial. . .

5th. Congressman Blair offered a resolution in the House of Representatives, August 1894. The organized life of the country can speedily make this a law by sending resolutions to Congress endorsing Mr. Blair's bill and asking congress to create the commission. In no better way can the question be settled, and the Negro does not fear the issue. The following is the resolution:

"Resolved. By the House of Representatives and Senate in Congress assembled, That the committee on labor be instructed to investigate and report the number, location and date of all alleged assaults by males upon females throughout the country and during the ten years last preceding the passing of this joint resolution, for or on account of which organized but unlawful violence has been inflicted or attempted to be inflicted. Also to ascertain and report all facts of organized but unlawful violence to the person, with the attendant facts and circumstances, which have been inflicted upon accused persons alleged to have been guilty of crimes punishable by due process of law which have taken place in any part of the country within the ten years last preceding the passage of this resolution. Such investigation shall be made by the usual methods and agencies of the Department of Labor, and report made to Congress as soon as the work can be satisfactorily done, and the sum of $25,000, or so much thereof as may be necessary, is hereby appropriated to pay the expenses out of any money in the treasury not otherwise appropriated."

The belief has been constantly expressed in England that in the United States, which has produced William Lloyd Garrison, Henry Ward Beecher, James Russell Lowell, John G. Whittier and Abraham Lincoln, there must be those of their descendants who would take hold of the work of inaugurating an era of law and order. The colored people of this country who have been loyal to the flag believe the same, and strong in this belief have begun this crusade.

THE DYER BILL

The NAACP led efforts to prompt Congress to pass a federal anti-lynch law, lobbying the Senate for two years in an effort to gain support for a bill introduced by Missouri's Leonidas Dyer in May of 1920. If enacted, the Dyer bill would make lynching a federal crime distinct from murder, which was a crime subject to state courts. The bill would remove the responsibility for prosecuting lynching from the biased state courts of the South. NAACP research had concluded that lynchings were seldom responses to crimes of rape but a form of terrorism designed to maintain white supremacy. As collusion frequently existed between local law enforcement officials and the white citizens who had elected them, there was little chance of justice for the victim. Dyer, who had investigated the riots in East St. Louis, had introduced the bill into Congress in each session since 1918. Despite a vigorous publicity campaign and extensive lobbying by the NAACP, the Dyer bill, stalled by protests from Southern Senators, never became law.

2.B   W.E.B. DuBois: The Campaign Against "The Birth of A Nation"

Questions to help you adopt a critical stance while reading the section below:

   1. Why do you think the NAACP thought it important to protest against a movie? Are films important for our worldview, do they influence us? Which other films do you know of that people have protested against? Do you know films that are demeaning to certain groups of people?

   2. How was The Crisis *used to call attention and debate to racial injustice in the United States and abroad?*

Recommended Film:

   Color Adjustment *(Documentary, 88 minutes, 1991, directed by Marlon Riggs). Discusses black television images between 1948 and 1988 and the inconsistent portrayal of blacks achieving American equality.*

W.E.B. DUBOIS

"How easy, then, by emphasis and omission, to make children believe that every great soul the world ever saw was a white man's soul; that every great thought the world ever knew was a white man's thought; that every great deed the world ever did was a white man's deed; that every great dream the world ever sang was a white man's dream."[17]

In the late nineteenth and early twentieth centuries, the forceful leadership of W.E.B. DuBois challenged the accommodationist policies of Booker T. Washington. In his conciliatory Atlanta Exposition Speech of 1895, Washington had endorsed the South's segregationist policies by presenting the hand as a metaphor, promising that black and white could remain "as separate as the fingers, yet one as the hand in all things essential to mutual progress." In contrast, DuBois demanded full political and social equality for African Americans. While Washington argued that blacks should be educated for domestic, farm, and industrial work, DuBois created the concept of the "Talented Tenth," an educated black intellectual elite who would lead the transformation of "the race." DuBois believed that organized inquiry into the lives of black people could turn the scientific method into an ally in the struggle for racial justice. While a professor at Atlanta University, DuBois led a series of annual conferences in which the best minds of the nation and the world were brought together to study the question of racial equality.

In *The Souls of Black Folk,* published in 1903, DuBois confronted Washington's policies directly in an essay entitled "Of Mr. Booker T. Washington and Others." DuBois' disagreement with Washington culminated in the founding of the Niagara Movement. In 1905, DuBois arranged a meeting of a "few selected persons" at Fort Erie, Ontario. In its opening sessions, the Niagara Movement stated its intentions clearly. "We want to pull down nothing but we don't propose to be pulled down. . . . We believe in taking what we can get but we don't propose to be satisfied with it and in permitting anybody for a moment to imagine we're satisfied."[18] The first meeting of the Niagara Movement proposed the following objectives:[19]

1. Freedom of speech and criticism.

2. An unfettered and unsubsidized press.

3. Manhood suffrage.

4. The abolition of all caste distinctions based simply on race and color.

5. The recognition of the principle of human brotherhood as a practical present creed.

6. The recognition of the highest and best training as the monopoly of no class or race.

7. A belief in the dignity of labor.

8. United effort to realize these ideals under wise and courageous leadership.

The Niagara Movement proposed a national structure in which state representatives would report to the national office problems faced by local citizens. In this way, it hoped to create a national network to give African Americans access to political power.

The Niagara Movement met annually until 1910, when DuBois urged its members to support the newly formed NAACP. During its tenure, the Niagara Movement created a Civil Rights division to press for greater justice in the courts, attacking Jim Crow laws and demanding the presence of African Americans on juries. This legal division, whose strategy was the sponsoring of test cases, won a victory on appeal in the case of Miss Barbara Pope, an African American woman who had been fined for refusing to enter the Jim Crow car when her train crossed the state line into Virginia.[20] Pope's action and its usefulness would find many echoes later on, not the least of which would be Rosa Parks' refusal to sit in the back of the bus in 1955.

DuBois' vision of a national African American organization with state and local branches was realized in the NAACP. As the first political organization to demand full and equal rights for African Americans, the Niagara Movement not only spawned the NAACP but strongly influenced those groups who followed it. Many of the strategies of the Niagara Movement identified above were able to inspire others because they found their continued expression in the pages of *The Crisis*. DuBois became the founding editor of the NAACP journal *The Crisis,* whose first edition appeared in November 1910. While DuBois was editor, *The Crisis* was his domain, a publication in which DuBois could bring to a wide audience his powerful intellect and uncompromising quest for racial equality. "It goes without saying," read an NAACP report of 1912, "that *The Crisis* must, 1. give reliable information 2. be attractive in make-up, and 3. be frank and fearless in discussion."[21]

THE NAACP CAMPAIGN AGAINST "THE BIRTH OF A NATION"

"The white men were roused by a mere instinct of self-preservation. . .until at last there had sprung into existence a great Ku Klux Klan, a veritable empire of the South, to protect the Southern country."[22]

Early in its history, the NAACP recognized the power of the medium of film in creating and perpetuating racist stereotypes. In 1915, the release of D.W. Griffith's epic *The Birth Of A Nation* challenged the NAACP efforts to raise public awareness about lynching. The film was based on Thomas Dixon's novel and successful Broadway play *The Klansman,* a work that had already been the object of protest in the black press. An editorial in *The Voice of the Negro* in 1905 commented, "Mr. Dixon's two most prominent books, *The Clansman* and *The Leopard's Spots* are both manuals of deviltry and barbarism. They are full of wild, raging mobs and secret bands of marauders. . . . A Negro is shown pursuing a white girl for violent and unholy purposes. . . ." An African American minister who witnessed the play commented, "From the beginning to the end the Negro was represented as a brute, a beast and a demon from hell. . . . It is the forerunner of much bloodshed and anarchy. . . ."[23]

Faithful to Dixon's play, Griffith's story of a family of fallen Southern aristocrats perpetuated the plantation mythology of leering black men preying on helpless Southern white women. The film's hero and founder of the Klan, "The Little Colonel," leads the lynching of Gus, an African American soldier whose pursuit of the Colonel's sister, "The Little Dear One," results in her plummeting to her death from a sheer rock face. The Klansmen triumphantly dump Gus' body on the porch of their nemesis, the Reconstruction Lieutenant Governor. At the film's end, the Ku Klux Klan heroically rides in on horseback to save a cowering white family from a mob of brutal blacks.

In the film's titles, Griffith quoted historian and President Woodrow Wilson, who characterized the Klan as "the organization that saved the South from the anarchy of black rule."* This celebration of the Klan and the perpetuation of the stereotypes used to justify lynching were praised by Woodrow Wilson. "It is like writing history with lightning," he said, after a special showing of the film in the White House, "and my only regret is that it is all too terribly true."[24]

Aware of the great power of the emerging medium of film and of the growing popularity of *Birth Of A Nation,* Mary White Ovington and other NAACP activists launched a campaign against Griffith's film. At a meeting held at Boston's Faneuil Hall, members voted to send to Mayor Curley a resolution calling for the banning of the film. In New York, the NAACP staged "a dignified procession" from Union Square to the Mayor's office to protest the film. Also in New York, five African American protestors, three of whom were ex-soldiers, were arrested for distributing materials protesting the film's depiction of the Ku Klux Klan. Black attorney Aiken A. Pope secured for his clients an acquittal and an affirmation of the right of citizens to distribute propaganda materials.

Ovington, wary of censorship, sought to counteract the film's effect by researching the actual history of Reconstruction, a compulsion equally felt by the authors of the Freedom School Curriculum. Ovington started her research by attempting to locate the sources on which Griffith based the scenes in which unruly blacks in the South Carolina State Legislature leer at white woman visiting in the gallery. Unable to find any historical

* Most school history books in the 1940s and 50s reflected this view. See Kenneth Stampp's *The Era of Reconstruction, 1865–1877* (New York: Knopf, 1965, t.p. 1978) for an analysis of the historiography of Reconstruction.

record of such scenes, Ovington attempted to dispel such mythologizing by writing a pamphlet on the positive legislation of the Reconstruction Period and on the Black Codes. These pamphlets were distributed in cities where the film was shown. "We can only tell history from the other side," said Ovington, "and then let the public weigh the issue."[25] Ovington further felt that a work of art was best countered with another work of art. The NAACP supported efforts to produce a four-reel film to challenge Griffith's version of the Reconstruction South. The proposed film, *Lincoln's Dream,* offered a humane story of a "colored youth and his mother, the boy struggling up from slavery, a fugitive, then a soldier in the 54th Mass., and last an educator in the Reconstruction Days. . . . It tells the story we want told," wrote Ovington, "and it will reach hundreds of thousands where the word we may be able to write will reach so few, and those few not the thoughtless, growing boys and girls who are learning from history through Dixon's eyes."[26] The studio had difficulty raising the necessary funds, and the proposed film was never made.

See Activity 2.1   Emphasis and Omission *in the Appendix*
See Activity 2.2   Facts and Theory *in the Appendix*

2.C Thurgood Marshall: The NAACP Legal Defense Fund

Recommended Film:

> With All Deliberate Speed *(Documentary; 120 min, 2004; directed by Peter Gilbert). In the 1954 Brown vs. Board of Education ruling, the Justices used a four-word phrase that many believe has delayed the process of change for over 50 years: "With All Deliberate Speed." The film explores the history and legacy of this legal decision.*

THE LEGAL DEFENSE FUND

In 1939, Walter White created the NAACP Legal Defense Fund, Inc., soon known as "the Ink Fund," and Thurgood Marshall became its first director. During the twenty-one years Marshall headed the fund, the organization handled most of the major Civil Rights cases in the United States. They worked to overturn legal segregation, established by the Supreme Court decision in 1896 known as *Plessy vs. Ferguson,* and to secure legal rights for African Americans not only in education but in the exercise of basic rights of citizenship.

1896   Plessy vs. Ferguson: Segregation of Schools and Legal Basis for Jim Crow

In 1890, the General Assembly of the state of Louisiana decreed that all railroad companies provide "separate but equal" facilities for white and colored patrons. In 1896, Homer Plessy, an African American described as "seven-eighths" Caucasian, tested the law. Charged with violating the segregation statue after boarding the white car of a train, Plessy argued that the law violated his constitutional rights and sought to prevent the judge, John H. Ferguson, from proceeding with the trial. Plessy appealed the case to the Supreme Court, which upheld the doctrine of "separate but equal." In the ensuing years, legal challenges to segregation were defeated as federal and state judges continued to point to *Plessy vs. Ferguson* as precedent supporting segregation. The body of laws enforcing segregation was known as Jim Crow.

> (See *www.jimcrowhistory.org/history/overview.htm* for a brief history of Jim Crow.)

1944   Smith vs. Allwright: The Unconstitutionality of the White Primary

Disenfranchisement of blacks in the South was accomplished not only by threats of violence but by manipulation of the law. Poll (head) taxes and literacy tests were used throughout the South as ways of keeping blacks from the polls. In 1932, the Texas Democratic Convention adopted the resolution: "Be it resolved that all white citizens of the State of Texas who are qualified to vote under the constitution and laws of the state shall be eligible to membership in the Democratic party and as such are entitled to participate in its deliberations."[27] The Democratic party's candidates were selected in primary elections prior to the general election. Because the South was solidly Democratic at this period, the Democratic Primary was, in practical terms, the general election. Because the Democratic party did not accept black members, blacks were effectively disenfranchised. Marshall brought a suit on behalf of Black Texan Lonnie E. Smith, who had been informed by election judge S.C. Allwright that he was ineligible to vote in the Democratic primary. The court dismissed Smith's suit on the grounds that the Democratic party was a "private institution." Marshall appealed the decision, arguing before the Supreme Court that the primary election "effectively controls the choice" of candidates. In an eight-to-one decision issued on April 3, 1944, the Supreme Court ruled the white primary a violation of the Fifteenth Amendment:

> When primaries become a part of the machinery for choosing officials, state and national, as they have here, the same test to determine the character of discrimination or abridgement should be applied to the primary as are applied to the general election.[28]

With the 1944 decision, blacks began mobilizing for increased voter participation. Jackson, Mississippi businessman T.B. Wilson, secretary of the local NAACP, organized a chapter of the National Progressive Voters League in Mississippi in the mid-forties. When World War II veterans returned determined to claim the rights they had defended, the movement gained momentum.

1954   Brown vs. the Board of Education, Topeka, Kansas: Legal Basis for School Integration

In 1930, the NAACP commissioned a study of the state of civil rights of black Americans, conducted by attorney Nathan Margold. Margold concluded that, since the 1896 decision, *Plessy vs. Ferguson,* the Courts had upheld the concept of "separate" but not the concept of "equal." The most common instance of this was connected with the establishment of separate schools for white and colored children. This practice had been held to be a valid exercise of the legislative power even by courts of states where the political rights of the colored race had been longest and most earnestly enforced.

Despite the precedent set by *Plessy,* the Margold Report offered a strategy for the challenge of legal discrimination. Noting the vastly unequal spending on the education of blacks and whites in the South, Margold reasoned that the demand for equal funding promised by *Plessy* would ultimately prove prohibitively expensive. States would choose the more affordable method of desegregation. Margold's strategy was not to attack segregation as unconstitutional, but to demonstrate that in practice segregation offered unequal facilities to blacks. Such inequality was unconstitutional, based on the Supreme Court's ruling in *Plessy.*

Margold's successor, Charles Houston, and his protégé, Thurgood Marshall, began an assault on legal segregation starting with graduate schools. Houston and Marshall reasoned that inequality was easier to demonstrate at the graduate level, that there would be less resistance to integration of graduate facilities, and that the NAACP could establish legal precedents, which could ultimately be used to build a case against the constitutionality of the entire system of legal segregation. Through this strategy, the NAACP secured desegregation victories in graduate and law schools in such cases as *Murray vs. University of Maryland, Sipuel vs. University of Oklahoma Board of Regents,* and *Sweatt vs. University of Texas.*

On May 17, 1954, the NAACP Legal Defense Fund won its most celebrated victory in *Brown vs. Board of Education of Topeka, Kansas,* a decision that banned segregation in public education. In a unanimous vote, the Supreme Court declared that separate educational facilities are "inherently unequal," thus overturning *Plessy vs. Ferguson* and removing the legal basis for the Jim Crow laws.

THURGOOD MARSHALL

"It is important that the strongest pressures against the continuation of segregation, North or South, be continually and constantly manifested. Probably, as much as anything else, this is the key in the elimination of discrimination in the United States."[29]

Born in 1908, Thurgood Marshall's father was a sleeping car porter and his mother taught school. Marshall grew up in an integrated middle-class neighborhood in Baltimore, Maryland, attending Colored High and Training School. Across the street from the school was the jailhouse. Marshall recalled sitting in his classroom with the windows open, listening to "the police in there beating the hell out of people, saying, 'Black boy, why don't you just shut your god damned mouth, you're going to talk yourself into the electric chair."[30] Marshall graduated a semester early to work as a dining car waiter to earn tuition for college. While attending the nearly all-black Lincoln University in nearby Pennsylvania, Marshall worked at the bakery, successfully rushed a light-skinned fraternity and joined the debate team.[31] During Marshall's second year at Lincoln, he decided to support a crusade to integrate the all-white faculty.[32]

Barred from attending the white-only University of Maryland's law school, Marshall decided to attend Howard University. After graduating from law school in 1933, Marshall joined Charles Houston, the dean of Howard's law school, on tours of the South. These NAACP financed tours allowed the two lawyers to collect data and establish relationships that would lead to future lawsuits. In 1934, Marshall successfully filed his first major lawsuit, which ended the segregation policies of the University of Maryland.[33] This success led the NAACP to hire Marshall as a lobbyist for an anti-lynching bill. The failure of his lobbying efforts reinforced Marshall's belief that the only way to protect blacks was through the court system.[34]

Houston and Marshall, as the principal NAACP lawyers, continued to meet with local NAACP chapter members in the South in order to find legal cases dealing with schools, voting rights and unfair arrests. When Houston left the NAACP in 1938, Marshall took over supervision of NAACP's legal strategies. In addition to responding to requests from black newspaper editors and local NAACP chapters to defend blacks from persecution, Marshall used his office to dissuade U.S. corporations from using derogatory racial epithets. For example, he persuaded Whitman to drop "Pickaninny Peppermints" and the American Tobacco Company to end "Nigger Head" cigarettes.[35]

At the same time that Marshall was directing the fourth attempt to end the white primary in Texas (eventually winning in 1944 with *Smith vs. Allwright*), he oversaw two sensational cases in Oklahoma and Connecticut that made the front pages of black newspapers nationwide leading to a dramatic increase in NAACP membership and fundraising. Marshall revealed that he had learned the value of theatrical law in his letter to Walter White regarding the Oklahoma case—"We've been needing a good criminal case and we have it. . . . The beatings plus use of the bones of dead people will raise money."[36]

During World War II, Marshall was kept busy as black soldiers wrote to the NAACP about mistreatment, black labor unions complained of discrimination, and deadly race riots broke out in northern cities. Marshall used his investigation into the causes of the Detroit race riot of 1943 to help police restrain their responses to similar inflammatory conditions in New York City.[37] At the same time that Marshall and his staff were defending plaintiffs in cases of unfair arrests and gratuitous police beatings, they were looking for test cases with which they could undermine segregation. Irene Morgan presented him with one such case. In 1944, she took a

Greyhound bus from Virginia to Maryland. When Morgan refused to go to the back of the bus, she was arrested and fined 10 dollars. Marshall used the case to persuade the Supreme Court to establish, in 1946 (*Morgan vs. Virginia*), that state segregation laws placed an "undue burden" on interstate commerce.[38] This case would be the basis upon which CORE would develop its Freedom Ride campaigns (see Chapter 3).

In July 1945, Marshall called a national legal conference to brainstorm ways to attack growing housing discrimination.[*] In *Shelly vs. Kraemer* (1948), Marshall used sociological evidence for the first time to successfully argue that ghettos created crime and endangered public health.[39] Marshall simultaneously held a series of brainstorming meetings to define a school integration strategy, seeing the successful argument of the sociological impact of segregation as a potential weapon in this area. As a result of these sessions, local NAACP chapters were charged with finding multiple plaintiffs for a barrage of court cases. In Houston, Lulu White convinced a 33-year-old postman, Herman Maron Sweatt, to apply to the University of Texas Law School. Marshall was able to take Sweatt's case to the Supreme Court in 1950, successfully using a 1946 case (*Mendez vs. Westminster*) to argue that segregation for *any* reason was wrong—another key step in laying the groundwork for overturning *Plessy*. In Clarendon County, South Carolina, the NAACP had lost a case over new buses for black children. The lawyers convinced the plaintiffs to turn the case into one for school integration. Marshall then chose a case from Topeka, Kansas. Wanting a case from Virginia, the heartland of the old Confederacy, Marshall directed his lawyers to turn 16-year-old Barbara John's quest for a new school in Farmville into one for integration. The Supreme Court, knowing that it's next decision on the issue of segregation would be provocative, asked Marshall to find two more cases to bundle together with the three that Marshall had already appealed.[40] On May 17, 1954, the Supreme Court ruled on *Brown vs. Board of Education of Topeka Kansas, et al.* In a unanimous decision, the Court overturned *Plessy vs. Ferguson,* arguing that the five cases before the Court demonstrated "separate is inherently unequal." Marshall then proposed that the Court order full integration by

---

[*] See Kenneth Jackson's "Race, Ethnicity and Real Estate Appraisal" (*American Vistas*, 1983, pp. 163–185) for an analsyis of the federal Home Owner's Loan Corporation's contribution to segregating urban neighborhoods.

the fall of 1956. Instead, the Court decided, a year after its initial ruling, that integration should proceed "with all deliberate speed." This allowed the South to mount effective resistance.

Marshall, deeply disappointed with the vague timeline, nevertheless began work on pressuring Southern school districts to desegregate. Events, however, diverted this work. The NAACP became inundated by calls from those being jailed as a result of a proliferation of non-violent direct action. Marshall, while overtly supportive of direct action, believed that Gandhian nonviolent tactics would "devastate and undermine the progress that had been made" in the courts.[41] Even so, Marshall and his staff continued to defend the new generation of Civil Rights activists while continuing to pressure school districts to desegregate. He won his 19th case before the Supreme Court in 1958 when the Little Rock, Arkansas, school district was ordered to integrate its schools.[42] In 1961, Marshall argued his last case before the Supreme Court, defending the sit-in students in *Garner vs. Louisiana*. Later that year, he accepted the nomination as the first black to serve on the U.S. Court of Appeals. In 1967, he became the first black judge on the Supreme Court.

2.D   Medgar Evers: The Jackson Movement (Mississippi)

Questions to help you adopt a critical stance while reading the section below:
1. *Why was there tension in the relationship between Evers and the NAACP leadership?*
2. *Evers organized the NAACP youth groups; is tension between the young and the old inherent in any organization?*

Recommended Films:

For Us, the Living: The Story of Medgar Evers (Docu-Drama; 84 min, 1984; produced by J. Kenneth Rotcop)
Ghosts of Mississippi (Drama; 131 minutes, 1997; directed by Rob Reiner)

MEDGAR EVERS

"Jackson can change if it wills to do so. . . . We believe there are white Mississippians who want to go forward on the race question. Their religion tells them there is something wrong with the old system. Their sense of justice and fair

*play send them the same message. . . . But whether Jackson and the state choose
to change or not, the years of change are upon us. . . . History has reached a
turning point, here and over the world."*[43]

When Medgar Evers was a child in Mississippi, segregationist Senator
Theodore Bilbo addressed a predominately white audience while Medgar
and his brother Charles listened on the outskirts of the crowd. Bilbo warned
the assembled whites that, if they didn't watch it, soon boys like Medgar
and Charles would be running the state. What Bilbo considered a warn-
ing, the Evers brothers regarded as a challenge. Despite fierce opposition,
Evers was determined to remain in Mississippi and to transform the state
into a genuine home for African Americans. "Why do I live in Mississippi?
The state is beautiful," explained Evers. "It is home, I love it here. A man's
state is like his house. If it has defects, he tries to remedy them. That's what
my job is here."[44] On his twenty-first birthday, Evers set out for the county
courthouse to register to vote. He had completed military service in World
War II, and like many returning veterans in the state, was determined to
exercise the rights for which he had fought. Evers explained:

> I never found out until later that they visited my parents nightly after that.
> First, it was the white. . .and then their Negro message bearers. And the
> word was always the same: "tell your sons to take their names off the books.
> Don't show up at the courthouse voting day." Then, the night before the
> election, Bilbo came to town and harangued the crowd in the square. "The
> best way to keep a nigger from the polls on election day," he told them, "is
> to visit them the night before."[45]

On election day, Medgar Evers, Charles Evers and four friends walked
to the courthouse to vote.

> I'll never forget it. Not a Negro was on the streets, and when we got to the
> courthouse, the clerk said he wanted to talk with us. When we got into
> his office, some 15 or 20 armed white men surged in behind us, men I had
> grown up with, had played with. We split up and went home. Around town,
> Negroes said we had been whipped, beaten up and run out of town. Well,
> in a way we were whipped, I guess, but I made up my mind then that it
> would not be like that again—at least not for me.[46]

Early on, Evers was intrigued by the successes of the MauMau Leader Jomo Kenyatta, and hoped to organize a similar guerrilla band in Mississippi. "I admired the man," he said. "He was intelligent, and he didn't believe in compromise. And while I never cared for brutality, I realized that just as the Africans followed Kenyatta, Negroes might have successfully followed someone like him."[47] Eventually, Evers' religious convictions caused him to reject this idea. After his marriage to the former Myrlie Beasley, Evers settled in the all-black town of Mound Bayou, and began traveling the Delta selling life insurance for Magnolia Mutual, a black-owned company founded by T.R.M. Howard. During these years, he became acquainted first-hand with the poverty in the Delta. When Evers went to work for the NAACP, he applied the skills he had developed selling life insurance to social action. "He was actually a good salesman for the cause," recalled a co-worker. "That's how I viewed him, as a salesman, because he could talk to a group of people and get them to do something."[48] Evers organized branches of the organization in Mound Bayou and Cleveland, and became field secretary of the Mississippi Conference of NAACP branches.

His efforts to achieve equality were unceasing and multi-faceted. He applied for admission to the law school at the University of Mississippi. The names of the plaintiffs in a lawsuit to desegregate the public schools of Mississippi included those of Evers' children Darrell Kenyatta and Reena. "That's what I want for my kids—freedom—right here in Mississippi. And as long as God gives me strength to work and try to make things real for my children, I'm going to work for it—even if it means making the ultimate sacrifice."[49] Evers was aware that his was one of nine names on a "death list," a list on which the name of Rev. George W. Lee had also appeared.*

Evers' increasing use of direct action techniques resulted in tension between him and the more conservative national office of the NAACP. One particularly tense episode occurred at the NAACP's convention in San Francisco in 1956 during which Evers led a group of delegates who called for the organization's immediate endorsement of the Montgomery, Alabama boycott.[50] Preparing a three-page resolution in support of the boycott, Evers found himself at odds with NAACP veterans Roy Wilkins and Thurgood Marshall. Later, Evers attended the founding sessions of the SCLC and was elected assistant secretary of the new organization, which

---

* Lee was murdered in 1955. See Lee's profile in Chapter 6.

stressed direct action. Wilkins advised Evers to "gently ease out of" the new group.[51] A long-time supporter of the NAACP youth groups, from whose ranks he believed must come "the leaders in the future fights,"[52] Evers was sympathetic to the SNCC staffers and their methods. "When the students came along with their spontaneity, with their willingness to be heard and to strike back if necessary, I think it was a kind of turning point for Medgar."[53] Nevertheless, Evers saw the need for Civil Rights organizations to coordinate their objectives and strategy. Evers participated in the planning sessions of COFO* and urged the NAACP national office to support the coalition. Although Aaron Henry of the state NAACP was COFO's president, the national office never officially endorsed the organization.

During the Jackson Movement (described below), Evers became a more visible leader and therefore a more visible target. The last days of Evers' life were consumed with the endless work of coordinating the activities of the Jackson Movement. At Evers' urging, Roy Wilkins of the NAACP had come to Mississippi to picket; Wilkins was arrested with a picket sign in his hand, causing Martin Luther King to chuckle, "We've finally baptized Brother Wilkins!"[54] At a June 7 rally in support of the Jackson Movement, Evers appeared on stage along with comedian Dick Gregory and actress Lena Horne. Evers spoke last. "Freedom has never been free," he said. "I love my children and I love my wife with all my heart. And I would die, die gladly, if that would make a better life for them." On the evening of June 11, returning to his home from a rally, carrying a bundle of t-shirts marked with the slogan, "Jim Crow Must Go," Evers was shot in the back in the driveway of his home by Byron De LaBeckwith, a self-proclaimed "rabid racist" and vocal member of the White Citizens Council. Evers was buried with military honors at Arlington National Cemetery in Washington, D.C. De LaBeckwith was not convicted of murdering Evers until 1994.

THE JACKSON MOVEMENT

At Christmas time of 1962, a group of student activists, led by Tougaloo professor John Salter, organized a holiday boycott of stores on Jackson's Capitol Street. They distributed leaflets listing their demands: integration of facilities such as rest rooms, lunch counters, and drinking fountains;

---

* The Congress of Federated Organizations (COFO) was the umbrella group coordinating the activities of NAACP, CORE, SCLC, SNCC and local citizenship groups in Mississippi during Freedom Summer. See Chapter 7.

the courtesy titles of "Mr." and "Miss" for black customers; service for customers on a first-come, first-serve basis, and equality in the hiring and promotion of black employees. Salter and a group of black students were arrested while picketing Woolworth's; Mayor Allan Thompson, furious, threatened to sue the picketers for a million dollars.

In support of the boycott, Medgar Evers published the following appeal to the Citizens of Jackson in the *Mississippi Free Press:*[55]

Document 2.2   NAACP Appeals to Negro, White Citizens
We want to say thanks to those Negro and White citizens who have decided not to trade on Capitol Street until Negroes are treated with decency, respect, and given employment opportunities like other citizens.

It is our feeling that to ask merchants on Capitol Street to treat all customers alike is not asking the impossible, nor is it asking much. We have asked the merchants on Capitol Street to do this, our request was turned down, inferring that they (the merchants) will go on discriminating against Negro customers in the manner in which they have been for many years. It is apparent, then, the merchants feel that the Negro will continue to trade with them in spite of the mistreatment the Negro receives while trading on Capitol Street. Our only comment here is that Negroes are tired of this mistreatment and will carry their business elsewhere as long as this practice continues.

It is our hope that Negroes who are still shopping on Capitol Street and being discriminated against will cease this practice immediately and join in this campaign to bring greater respect for the Negro People in Jackson and other Mississippi communities. Negroes who continue to shop on Capitol are guilty to helping to maintain segregation, discrimination and the denial of job opportunities to their children and to Negro children yet unborn. Let us strive together for justice and equality—STAY OFF CAPITOL STREET UNTIL PRESENT CONDITIONS HAVE CHANGED.

NONVIOLENT RESISTANCE

In the spring of 1963, a coalition of Civil Rights workers and ministers initiated political action in Jackson, Mississipppi, the state's capitol, hoping to create an organized city-wide campaign modeled on those in Birmingham and Montgomery. They requested from Mayor Allan Thompson a "biracial commission" to study discrimination in the city of Jackson. When the Mayor ignored their requests, the group staged a sit-in at the lunch counter at Woolworth's and a picket line in front of J.C. Penney's. The Jackson establishment still refused to negotiate. In mid-May, a letter signed by John Salter and Medgar Evers was sent to the governor and the mayor. The leaders promised "we shall use all lawful means of protest—picketing, marches, mass meetings, litigation, and whatever other means we deem necessary."[56]

On May 13, Mayor Allan Thompson pledged in a television appearance that he would never negotiate with the demonstrators. Speaking to the black citizens of Jackson, Thompson declared,

> You live in a city, a beautiful city, where you can send your children to modern schools, you live in homes that are clean and neat with all utilities. And I have said, there are no slums as there are in other large cities. . . . You have 24 hour protection by the police department. Just think of being able to call the police any time of the night and say, "Come quick! Someone is trying to get into my house, I need some help!". . .You live in a city where you can work, where you can make a comfortable living. You are treated, no matter what anybody else tells you, with dignity, courtesy, and respect. Ah, What a wonderful thing it is to live in this city!. . .Refuse to pay any attention to any of these outside agitators who are interested only in getting money out of you, using you only for their own selfish purposes."[57]

One week later, Evers delivered a television rebuttal to the Mayor's remarks. Evers' appearance made his friends and family even more concerned for his safety. The speech was a public declaration of principle that brought immediate reprisals. The television station was flooded with angry white callers, many of whom raged at the fact that an African American was speaking, at the content of his speech, and at the pre-empting of the television quiz show *The Price is Right*.

Document 2.3 Remarks of Mr. Medgar Evers
Field Secretary, National Association for the Advancement of Colored People
   Monday, May 20, 1963 8:00 P.M.

For Delivery over WLBT-TV and WJTV-TV

. . . Most Southern white people, whether they are friendly or hostile, usually think of the NAACP as a "Northern outside group." The facts do not bear this out. At least one-half of the NAACP membership is in the South. There have been branches in Mississippi since 1918. . . . Now the Mayor says that if the so-called outside agitators would leave us alone everything would be all right. This has always been the position of those who would continue to deny Negro citizens their constitutional rights. The history of race relations in the South refutes this thesis. Never in its history has the Southern region, without outside pressure, granted the Negro his citizenship rights. . . . All of these gains were obtained through use of the courts, the American way, which has been the policy and practice of the NAACP for 54 years. . . . It is also in the American tradition to demonstrate, to assemble peacefully and to petition the government for a redress of grievances. . .although in Jackson, Negroes are immediately arrested when they attempt to exercise this constitutional right. . . . The NAACP is not subversive. . . . FBI chief, J. Edgar Hoover, in his book, "Masters of Deceit," commended the NAACP for its stand against communism. . . . Tonight the Negro plantation worker in the Delta knows from his radio and television. . .that Willie Mays, a Birmingham Negro, is the highest paid player in the nation. He knows that Leontyne Price, a native of Laurel, [Mississippi] is one of the greatest opera singers who ever lived. He knows about the new free nations in Africa. . . . He sees black prime ministers and ambassadors, financiers and technicians. Then he looks about his home community and what does he see to quote our Mayor, in this "progressive, beautiful, friendly, prosperous city with an exciting future?". . . He sees a city of over 150,000, of which 40% is Negro, in which there is not a single Negro policeman or policewoman, school crossing guard, fireman, clerk, stenographer or supervisor employed in any city department or the mayor's office in other than menial capacities, except those employed in segregated facilities—the College Park Auditorium, Carver Library and the segregated schools. . . . What then does the Negro want? He wants to get rid of racial segregation in Mississippi life. . . . The Negro citizen wants to register and vote. . . . The Negro Mississippian wants more jobs above the menial level. . . . He wants the public schools and colleges desegregated so that his children can receive the best education that Mississippi has to offer. . . . Let me appeal to the consciences of many silent, responsible citizens of the white community who know that a victory for democracy in Jackson will be a victory for democracy everywhere. . . .

ESCALATION

On May 28, one week after Evers' televised speech, Tougaloo students Anne Moody, Memphis Norman, and Pearlena Lewis staged a sit-in at the Woolworth's lunch counter on Capitol Street. An angry mob soon assembled. John Salter joined the group and was assaulted by the crowd as an FBI agent took notes. Moody recalled, "The mob started smearing us with ketchup, mustard, sugar, pies. John Salter joined us, and was hit on the jaw with what appeared to be brass knuckles. Blood gushed from his face and someone threw salt in the open wound. . . . A Negro high school boy sat down. . . . The mob took spray paint and sprayed the word 'nigger' on his white shirt."[58] The demonstration brought national publicity, and Mayor Thompson finally agreed to talk with the demonstrators. During a meeting, he agreed to the hiring of black police and firemen and to the gradual integration of the schools, but later the Mayor denied that such an agreement had been reached.

On May 31, over four hundred black students from Jackson's high schools gathered at the Farish Street Baptist Church for prayer and training in nonviolent resistance. In pairs, many carrying small American flags, the group proceeded toward Capitol Street. They were promptly arrested by the Jackson police. "There was no resistance," recalled the Reverend Ed King. "Each pair simply walked up to the police to replace those who were arrested and beaten in front of them."[59] The police herded some of the demonstrators in a closed garbage truck. From inside the truck, the demonstrators could be heard singing freedom songs. To silence them, the police banged on the sides of the truck. From Capitol Street, the demonstrators were taken to the Fairgrounds, where there were confined in open pens used for livestock. Police placed in each pen barrels of baloney and milk and littered the ground with slices of bread. They sprayed the stockade with clouds of the insecticide used on summer nights in the South to control mosquitoes.[60]

A rally at the Masonic Temple that night drew fifteen hundred people. Among the speakers was nine-year-old Gene Young, already a veteran of demonstrations who had been imprisoned in the stockyards, who raised his fist and exhorted the audience, "Let's march!"[61] During a march the next day, more student demonstrators were arrested and taken to the Fairgrounds stockades, bringing the total of those arrested to nearly seven hundred.

The murder of Medgar Evers on June 11 brought national attention to the protests in Jackson. President Kennedy issued a statement that he was "appalled by the barbarity of the act."[62] Although Evers' battle against racism in Mississippi had frequently been a lonely one, thousands of mourners appeared in the streets of Jackson to bid him good-bye. After the funeral service in the stifling heat of a Mississippi summer, the mourners filed into the streets to express their anger and grief. Mayor Thompson had agreed to a silent march following the funeral cortege. Although the mayor's order had forbidden singing, a young girl in the crowd began "Oh, freedom." Other voices joined hers. Soon someone added a verse:

> *No more killing*
> *No more killing*
> *No more killing over me, over me*
> *And before I'd be a slave*
> *I'd be buried in my grave.*
> *And go home to my Lord and be free*

By the time the crowd reached Capitol Street, the police attacked both marchers and news cameramen with sticks. Several demonstrators picked up rocks, and the police began firing. Fearful of a riot, John Doar of the Justice Department positioned himself between the police and the crowd and urged the demonstrators to go home. After a few uneasy minutes, the crowd dispersed. This event marked the end of mass demonstrations in Jackson.

THREE

Congress of Racial Equality (CORE)

Questions to help you adopt a critical stance while reading the section below:

1. *What is the theory behind CORE's "step-by-step" tactics? How does this compare with the theory and tactics of the NAACP? Would Ida B. Wells (see previous chapter) have found CORE to be "too conservative"?*

2. *Is the theory behind CORE's "jail-in" strategy the same as Thoreau's theory of jail (see Chapter One)?*

3. *What examples of direct action can be defined as civil disobedience and which cannot? How did CORE define "direct action"? Why did CORE avoid civil disobedience and see direct action as a last resort?*

4. *What was CORE's most effective tactic (and define what a tactic is as oppose to a strategy or theory)? If a sit-in is the strategy, what is the theory? What are specific tactics that could be considered implementation of the strategy of a sit-in?*

5. *How would Thoreau (Chapter One) have responded to the statement that non-violence "assumes that it is suicidal for a minority group to use violence, since to use it would simply result in control and subjugation by the majority group"?*

FOUNDED IN 1942, CORE was the first organization to apply Gandhian principles of nonviolence to the problems of race in the United States. The techniques employed by CORE—sit-ins, picketing, public demonstrations, the Freedom Rides—were inspired by Gandhi's methods in India, by the methods of the American labor movement, and by the resistance of conscientious objectors to the draft. The willingness of the participants to be jailed as a public declaration of principle characterized CORE demonstrations.

CORE's basic organizational concept was to establish local CORE chapters composed of trained nonviolent direct-action cadres who fought against specific instances of segregation on behalf of the larger community. CORE was primarily a northern organization built around the CORE chapter. In the mid 1960s, under the influence of the Student Nonviolent Coordinating Committee and out of their experiences with the Freedom Rides, CORE leaders in the South became involved in community-organizing projects. In Mississippi, during Freedom Summer, CORE created community centers to support both the voter registration drives and the Freedom Schools.

Document 3.1   What Then Are the Principles of CORE?[1]

1. CORE believes that racial discrimination in the United States affects *all* Americans adversely. Segregation is a problem that everyone. . .should seek to solve. . . .

2. Because of this principle, CORE locals strive to be interracial. National CORE draws its officers, staff, National Advisory Committee, and its financial support from all groups. Only those Americans whose loyalty is primarily to a foreign power and those whose tactics and beliefs are contrary to democracy and human values are categorically excluded from participation in CORE.

3. CORE believes in *direct action*. . .in opposition to some specific discriminatory practice. . .from restaurants, theatres, amusement parks, swimming pools. . .employment opportunities. . .housing. . .schools. . .voter registration . . .

4. In carrying out the action program, CORE first *investigates* to learn all the facts; second, *discusses* the grievance with those responsible for the practice in an effort to bring about a change of policy; third, *appeal* to the wider public for support in the action; fourth, *publicizes* the unjust racial practice through picketing, leaflets, and press releases; fifth, if all the foregoing fail to end discrimination, uses *direct challenge,* such as sit-ins, standing lines, and boycotts.

5. It is the essence of nonviolence that it proceed step-by-step. . . . Although CORE's distinctive method is direct action, it also employs broad educational techniques, and, occasionally, court procedures.

6. . . .Where CORE members maintain an attitude of persistent good-will. . .often, not only a change in policy results but also the respect and regard of the opposition is gained. Then a change of policy no longer involves loss of face or a sense of defeat for the opponent.

7. . . .CORE, begun in Chicago as a local group, has functioned as a national organization since 1942.

NONVIOLENCE AND DIRECT ACTION

Many of CORE's founding members had belonged to the Fellowship of Reconciliation (FOR), a Christian organization founded in England to promote pacifism during World War I. The first CORE group grew from a "cell," or chapter, of the Fellowship of Reconciliation at the University of Chicago. This cell included James Farmer, graduate of Howard University and student of the African American pacifist Howard Thurman, George Houser, Bernice Fisher, Joe Guinn, and James R. Robinson. The backgrounds of CORE's six founders reflected the diverse strands of activism that came together in the group, which was to become the first chapter of CORE. All were pacifists and, unlike many young pacifists of the 1930s, retained their commitment to nonviolence after the entry of the United States into World War II. Three had served terms in jail or in a Civilian Public Service camp as an alternative to military service. Three of the group were Socialists and all were admirers of the CIO industrial unions who employed direct action techniques such as sit-down strikes. Nonviolence was considered by CORE's founders both an ideal and a practical strategy. Nonviolence "assumes that it is suicidal for a minority group to use violence, since to use it would simply result in control and subjugation by the majority group."[2]

From the Saturday study groups emerged their first direct action project—a challenge to restrictive covenants in the neighborhood surrounding the University of Chicago. Restrictive covenants, in which housing owners signed agreements not to sell or rent housing to blacks, made it difficult for black students to secure housing. The group decided to rent housing to be used for a Fellowship House, a cooperative community modeled on the ashrams Gandhi had begun in India. A group of white CORE members rented an apartment to be used for such a Fellowship House, in which both black and white CORE members set up residence. Following Gandhian principles, the CORE group treated neighbors and building owners with kindness and courtesy; the lease was not contested. CORE's first direct action effort was considered a success.

The Chicago group developed a precise strategy for attacking discrimination. First, the group attempted to convert the opponent by courteous requests and negotiations. If these failed, a form of nonviolent direct action was taken to call public attention to the unlawful discrimination. Civil disobedience was to be undertaken only as a last resort. Acts of civil disobedience, however, were seldom required in CORE's early days, as protestors generally sought observance of existing laws.

The sit-down strike employed by union activists, in which a group of protesters peacefully refuse to relinquish occupancy of a space until their grievances are addressed, was used by an interracial CORE group at Chicago restaurants that discriminated against blacks. CORE's first sit-down or sit-in occurred in May of 1943, at the Jack Spratt Restaurant in Chicago. An interracial group arrived, occupied all available seats, and courteously waited for service. The flustered manager called the police, who informed him that the protesters were in compliance with the law. Two hours after their arrival, the CORE group was served.

CORE groups developed from Fellowship of Reconciliation meetings in Denver, Syracuse, Colorado Springs, Detroit, and New York. These groups organized protests similar to those developed in Chicago, challenging restrictions in restaurants and theaters. Most of these early efforts met with success. CORE was organized in local branches, like the NAACP but, unlike the NAACP, did not have a strong national office. Throughout its early years, CORE was less a mass movement than a loosely organized confederation of small, dedicated activists deeply committed to ideals that lacked mass appeal. In this, CORE's roots in a religious philosophy are evident. Like early Christians, they cared little for money or conventional success. They did however, want to change the world and believe that this could ultimately be accomplished by moral force.

THE JAIL-IN

Students affiliated with CORE introduced a new strategy modeled on Gandhi's principles—the jail-in. In March of 1960, Tallahassee CORE member and student Pat Stephens organized a sit-in at Woolworth's. Stephens and four other students refused bail, choosing instead to remain in the county jail for sixty days. Demonstrations of students from Friendship Junior College at Rock Hill, South Carolina in February of 1961 also resulted in a CORE jail-in. Demonstrators, given the choice of thirty days of hard labor on a road gang or a one-hundred dollar fine, chose the jail sentence. CORE leader Thomas Gaither explained, "Surprise and shock filled the court room when it became known we had chosen to be jailed in. The only thing they had to beat us over the head with was a threat of sending us to jail. So we disarmed them by using the only weapon we had left . . . jail without bail. . . . It upset them considerably."3 Jail-ins were also used in the New Orleans CORE chapter, the organization's first in the Deep South. The chapter was headed by Rudy Lombard, a thoughtful senior from Xavier University, the city's black Jesuit institution. After attending a CORE training institute, the CORE chapter began a campaign of sit-ins at the city's lunch counters. Despite arrests and a ban from the mayor, the group was undeterred. As Lombard explained, "As chairman of New Orleans CORE, I spent six and a half days in jail to let the nation and world know, that we the citizens of New Orleans are demanding our freedom and are willing to pay the price. No man can imprison the desire to be free."4 Jail-ins would become part of Freedom Summer in Mississippi in 1964. The *Mississippi Summer Project Application Form* asked applicants to "List the names of people to contact for bond."

Freedom School Curriculum Link:
Statements of Discipline of Nonviolent Movements
> *www.educationanddemocracy.org/FSCfiles/C_CC6a_StatementsDiscipline.htm*
> *CORE was only one of many Civil Rights organizations that strictly followed the rules on nonviolence.*

3.A   Bayard Rustin: The Journey of Reconciliation

Questions to help you adopt a critical stance while reading the section below:
1. *Why was the charge of homosexuality so effective in stopping Rustin? Is it comparable to the red-baiting, the charge of communist influence? What other divide-and-conquer techniques are often successful? Have you experienced divide-and-conquer tactics?*
2. *Would charges of homosexuality or of being a communist destroy a career today?*

Further Information:

A report by Rustin on the Journey of Reconciliation is at www.socialdemocrats.org/ jimcrow.html. The website of the Fellowship of Reconciliation is at www.forusa. org/. Bayard Rustin's "From Protest to Politics" is at www.socialdemocrats. org/protopol.html

Recommended Film:

Brother Outsider (Documentary; 83 min, 2002; produced and directed by Nancy Kates and Bennett Singer). Rustin was there at most of the important events of the Civil Rights Movement—but always in the background. Brother Outsider: The Life of Bayard Rustin asks "Why?" It presents a vivid drama, intermingling the personal and the political, about one of the most enigmatic figures in 20th -century American history.

BAYARD RUSTIN

"My activism did not spring from being black. Rather, it is rooted fundamentally in my Quaker upbringing and the values instilled in me by my grandparents who reared me. Those values were based on the concept of a single human family and the belief that all members of that family are equal."[5]

Bayard Rustin's political activism began in high school, when he protested segregated seating in local movie theaters and organized fellow black members of his football team into refusing Jim Crow accommodations during out-of-town games. In 1938, Rustin moved to New York City, where he enrolled as an evening student in CCNY and sang in the chorus of the all-black Broadway musical *John Henry* with Paul Robeson. At City College of New York, Rustin joined the Young Communist League, a group that attracted him because of its support of The Scottsboro Boys, seven young black men arrested for rape in Alabama, and because of its strong position against racism. Rustin was assigned by the League the task of protesting segregation in the American military. When the Communist Party changed its position on the American entry into the war and began advocating a Soviet-American alliance, the challenge to Jim Crow in the military was abandoned. Disillusioned, Rustin realized that "the communists' primary objectives were not with the black masses but with the global objectives of the Soviet Union. . . ."[6] Rustin left the Party, later becoming an outspoken critic.

In 1941, Rustin joined A. Philip Randolph's March on Washington Movement, an effort to organize a mass demonstration to challenge racial discrimination in the munitions factories gearing for the war effort. In the face of Randolph's planned demonstration, Roosevelt issued Executive Order 8802, which stated that "there shall be no discrimination in the employment of workers in defense industries or government because of race, creed, color, or national origin."[7] Randolph then cancelled the march, but the youth organizers of the march, including Rustin, felt that Randolph had done so prematurely, feeling that Randolph should press for full desegregation of the military. Although the 1941 march did not occur, Rustin later regarded the plan as "the symbolic inauguration of the modern Civil Rights Movement."[8]

When the United States did enter World War II, Rustin's pacifist convictions prompted him to choose a prison term rather than military service. Rustin had become involved in the Fellowship of Reconciliation, and there met George Houser and James Farmer, who were later to found CORE. At FOR, Rustin was mentored by FOR leader A.J. Muste, a radical pacifist, who appointed Rustin field secretary for youth and special affairs. In the early forties, Rustin traveled for the Fellowship, spreading its message of pacifism and opening chapters throughout the United States. In a letter to his draft board, Rustin wrote, "Though joyfully following the will of God, I regret that I must break the law of the State. I am prepared for whatever may follow."[9] Rustin was sentenced to three years in prison. Rustin continued his activism in prison, often subjected to solitary confinement for initiating hunger strikes against segregated seating in the prison dining hall. After receiving an appointment to the prison's education department, Rustin conducted classes in English, drama, and music for the prison's sketchily educated white inmates. He also staged a powerful version of Eugene O'Neill's *The Emperor Jones*. In 1947, he was one of the eight members of CORE's Journey of Reconciliation.

In 1953, while speaking on behalf of the Fellowship of Reconciliation, Rustin was arrested on a "morals" charge, after being discovered in a parked car with two young men who had attended his lecture. Colleagues in the Fellowship of Reconciliation had been aware of Rustin's homosexuality and of Rustin's acceptance of his sexual orientation. One of his former lovers recalled, "He had no shame at all about being gay, and that was very strengthening to me. . . . Bayard felt he had a right to be who and what he was."[10]

A.J. Muste, however, had requested that Rustin keep his sexual conduct separate from his work with FOR, and felt that Rustin's arrest had compromised him as a representative for the organization. Muste requested and received Rustin's resignation. "Bayard was not ashamed of his homosexuality," recalled his friend Tom Kahn, "but was quite out front about it. He had a strong ego, so that he was willing to put himself out on the line. A part of him said, 'I'm also a child of God. I also have a soul and a personality made in the image of God.' That side of him could not accept Muste's condemnation."[11]

Rustin served as an advisor to Martin Luther King during the Montgomery bus boycott (1955–6). Having traveled to India in 1948 as a delegate from the American Friends Service Committee to an international convention of pacifists, Rustin helped King reconcile Gandhian philosophy with Christianity. The seven Working Papers drafted by Rustin for the Southern Christian Leadership Conference's initial conference became the foundation of the SCLC's philosophy and strategy. In 1960, King requested that Rustin be made associate director of the organization that he had been instrumental in founding. Rustin was reluctant to accept, fearing the questions about his sexual orientation would be raised. "Hasn't a vicious cycle been created," a friend asked Rustin, "whereby you have calculatedly avoided real public prominence in order not to expose yourself and others to attack?"[12] Rustin accepted the position, but later resigned at the request of King when Adam Clayton Powell threatened to state publicly the false allegation that King and Rustin were having a homosexual relationship. Explaining his position in an article in the black weekly New York Courier, Rustin said, "Those who have worked with me during my twenty years in the movement know that I have never sought high position or special privilege, but have always made myself available to the call of the leadership. . . . Nonetheless, Congressman Powell has suggested that I am an obstacle to his giving his full, enthusiastic support to Dr. King. I now want to remove that obstacle. I have resigned as Dr. King's special assistant, and have severed relations with the Southern Christian Leadership Conference."[13]

Rustin's remarkable talents as an organizer and as a builder of coalitions proved invaluable to the Civil Rights Movement both before and after his resignation. In 1957, Rustin was the primary organizer of the Prayer Pilgrimage to Washington, D.C., a joint venture of the NAACP and the SCLC. In 1963, he negotiated around obstacles that seemed insurmountable and helped make the March on Washington a reality. Planned to exert pressure on Congress to pass the pending Civil Rights Act, the March was initially conceived as a large-scale act of civil disobedience. This plan was cancelled, as both the Urban League and the NAACP refused to participate in such a demonstration. President Kennedy opposed the March, fearing that it would hinder the passage of the Civil Rights Act. At a planning meeting in July, Roy Wilkins of the NAACP expressed the fear that Rustin's presence would jeopardize the effectiveness of the effort, citing his prison record as a pacifist, his former Communist affiliation, and his sexual orientation. A. Philip Randolph, convinced that Rustin's skills were essential to the success of the March, refused to withdraw his support; King sided with Randolph and Rustin. Wilkins retorted that King was "politically naive." John Lewis, representing SNCC, described what ensued as a "nasty scene. It took A. Philip Randolph to restore some peace and civility." A compromise was suggested: that Randolph present himself as the director of the March, but that he could appoint any assistants he chose. "But I want you to know," Randolph informed the other leaders, "that my choice will be Bayard."[14] Randolph's faith was more than justified, as Rustin pulled off a feat most had termed impossible—organizing a mass march in a mere seven weeks. Quickly establishing an office headquarters, Rustin and his staff arranged for details from sandwiches to water coolers to transportation to emergency medical care. The March succeeded beyond its organizers' expectations, drawing two hundred thousand demonstrators to hear speeches by Randolph, John Lewis, Roy Wilkins, and Martin Luther King, whose "I Have A Dream" speech took its place in American history. At the end of the day, as the demonstrators filed away, Rustin found his mentor Philip Randolph, then in his seventies, standing alone. "I said to him," Rustin remembered, "'Mister Randolph, it seems that your dream has come true.' And when I looked into his eyes, tears were streaming down his cheeks."[15]

THE JOURNEY OF RECONCILIATION

In 1947, FOR undertook its most ambitious project, the Journey of Reconciliation. An interracial group sponsored by CORE planned to travel together by bus through the Upper South. For years, blacks traveling on interstate buses had staged individual acts of protest against illegally segregated seating on interstate buses. In 1946, the Supreme Court ruled that it was illegal for carriers to enforce segregated seating in buses on interstate travel. Individual black travelers, however, discovered that bus companies ignored the ruling.

In planning the Journey of Reconciliation, CORE leaders saw an opportunity to create a national campaign, which would call attention to their cause. Sixteen men, eight white and eight black, left Washington on April 9, 1947. Among the group were CORE founder George Houser and Bayard Rustin. For a week before their departure, they had trained intensively in role-playing techniques that allowed them to anticipate possible forms of retaliation. During the two-week trip, the group traveled to Virginia, North Carolina, and Kentucky, with half of the group traveling on Greyhound and half traveling on Trailways. The group's challenge was not to the segregated public facilities in bus stations but to the segregated seating on buses.

On the first day, one group member was arrested for refusing to vacate a seat at the front of the bus and released on a twenty-five dollar bond. Black group members Andrew Johnson and Bayard Rustin were arrested on the third day for occupying seats at the front of the bus; white member James Peck stepped forward during their arrest and stated, "If you arrest them, you'll have to arrest me too, for I'm going to sit in the rear."[16] The group was arrested without being charged. In Cargill, North Carolina, the group first encountered violence and threats, as Peck was attacked by a group of angry white cab drivers in the bus station.

The riders discovered that most drivers and passengers were unfamiliar with the law they were testing, and that white passengers were generally "apathetic" rather than violent. Rustin and Houser noted that black passengers, at first nervous at the riders' actions, on occasion moved forward when they observed the interracial pairs riding together at the front of the bus. Houser and Rustin claimed the ride as a victory for CORE's direct action principles.

When the student sit-ins began in Greensboro in 1960, CORE saw the potential for establishing the mass movement based on Gandhian principles, which had long been CORE's intention. As CORE leader Charles Oldham stated, "We must widen and deepen the understanding of nonviolent direct action so that soul force, the Satyagraha of Gandhi, develops and transforms our society."[17]

3.B   David Dennis: The Freedom Rides

Questions to help you adopt a critical stance while reading the section below:

1. *What was the difference between the Journey of Reconciliation and the Freedom Rides? Why was the reaction to the Freedom Rides so violent?*

2. *What role did theory and songs play during the Freedom Rides? What role did they play during the activists' incarceration in Parchman Prison?*

Recommended Film:

Ain't Scared of Your Jails *(Documentary; Vol.3 of Eyes on the Prize; 55 min, 1987 and 2006; produced by Henry Hampton). As the movement's front lines moved from the courts to confrontations in daily life, college students led the way. This program zeroes in on four related stories: the lunch counter sit-ins of 1960; the formation of the Student Nonviolent Coordinating Committee, SNCC; the impact of the movement on the 1960 presidential campaign; and the Freedom Rides of 1961.*

THE FREEDOM RIDES

In December of 1960, the Supreme Court, in *Boynton vs. Virginia*, extended the ban on discrimination aboard buses traveling interstate to include facilities in bus terminals. Despite this, Jim Crow was enforced in waiting rooms, restaurants, and restrooms serving passengers on buses traveling through the South. James Farmer, who assumed leadership of CORE in February of 1961, announced that CORE would apply direct action techniques to the desegregation of facilities at bus terminals to pressure the Federal government into enforcing existing laws. "What we had to do was to make it more dangerous politically for the federal government *not* to enforce federal law than it would be for them to enforce federal law . . ." explained James Farmer. "We felt we could count on the racists of the South to create a crisis."[18]

CORE field secretary Gordon Carey recalled that the idea for reviving the Journey of Reconciliation actually came to him as he and fellow CORE worker Tom Gaither were riding a bus back from a nonviolent training workshop in Rock Hill, South Carolina. Stranded in a snowstorm on the New Jersey Turnpike for twelve hours, Carey found that his only reading material was Louis Fisher's biography of Gandhi. "Tom and I were reading and talking about it, and a combination of sitting on the bus, the recent Supreme Court decision, and reading about Gandhi's march to the sea got us talking about an analogous march to the sea in the South. . . . We planned to go to New Orleans because that was the ocean and that was analogous to Gandhi's salt march to the sea."[19]

Although the Freedom Rides were modeled on the Journey of Reconciliation of 1947, they extended the objectives of that effort in several ways. Their plan included desegregation not only of seating on buses but of bus station facilities; they would travel all the way to New Orleans, challenging the most resistant areas of the Deep South, and they would pledge to remain in jail without bail if arrested along the way. Half of the group would ride a Greyhound bus, half a Trailways bus, just as the 1947 action did. The group that assembled in Washington, D.C. to begin the Freedom Rides included seven black and six white activists. The CORE group included James Farmer and James Peck, who had made the 1947 Journey of Reconciliation. Twenty-one-year old John Lewis decided to forego his college graduation to make the journey. Aware that they might be risking their lives, the group assembled for dinner at a Chinese restaurant in Washington, D.C. on the eve of their departure. John Lewis recalled, "It was my first time having Chinese food. Growing up in the South and going to school in Nashville, I'd never had it before. To me this meal was like the Last Supper, because you didn't know what to expect going on the Freedom Ride."[20]

As intended, the Freedom Rides provoked the confrontation between state and federal authorities. In Anniston, Alabama, the tires of a Greyhound bus were shot out by a mob following the bus. An incendiary bomb tossed through one of the windows of the stalled bus destroyed it. A dramatic photograph of the flaming bus was picked up by newspapers and shown throughout the world. When the Trailways bus arrived in Birmingham, the riders were assaulted by a mob armed with lead pipes, baseball bats, and chains. When asked why no police protection had been given the riders, Birmingham Chief of Police "Bull" Connor explained that, because it was Mother's Day, his department was understaffed.

Shaken by their assault and unable to locate a driver to continue the ride to Montgomery, the first group of Freedom Riders was flown to New Orleans. They were soon replaced by a second group of Student Nonviolent Coordination Committee (SNCC) students, coordinated by Diane Nash, ready to face retaliation in the deep South. To continue the rides, CORE formed a coalition with SNCC and the SCLC. The new alliance, The Freedom

Ride Coordinating Committee, determined to "fill the jails of Montgom-ery and Jackson in order to keep a sharp image of the issue before the public."[21] In Montgomery, the riders were again attacked. "The Freedom Riders emerging from the bus were being mauled," recalled Presidential aide John Seigenthaler. "It looked like two hundred, three hundred people all over them."[22] Martin Luther King, in Montgomery to address a rally in support of the Rides at Rev. Ralph Abernathy's church, was trapped with the congregation inside the building as an angry mob swarmed outside. The mob was finally dispersed by Alabama state troopers under orders, however reluctantly given, by Governor John Patterson.

The Freedom Riders were headed for Mississippi. "If Alabama had been purgatory," commented James Farmer, "then Mississippi would be hell."[23] Some Freedom Riders began writing final messages to their parents, which the men stuffed into their pockets and the women into their bras. Crossing the Mississippi border, the riders uneasily read a sign reading "Welcome to the Magnolia State." Reporters covering the event received word that the bus was to be ambushed and destroyed. All but one of the reporters left the bus. Driving through darkened Mississippi woods, with moss-draped live oaks meeting the highway, the Freedom Riders saw armed National Guard troops with rifles drawn in the forest. As the bus approached Jack-son, Farmer recalled, "one of the Freedom Riders broke into song, and this was as it had to be. His words went something like this:

> *I'm a-taking a ride on the Greyhound bus line,*
> *I'm a riding the front seat to Jackson this time.*
> *Hallelujah, I'm a-travelin'*
> *Hallelujah, ain't it fine?*
> *Hallelujah, I'm a-travelin'*
> *Down Freedom's main line.*[24]

On June 24, 1961, in anticipation of the Freedom Riders arrival, the *Jackson Daily News* had run the taunt, "Attention Restless Race Mixers Whose Hobby is Creating Trouble" (see Document below).

Questions based on Document 3.2 below:
   1. What are the threats explicit as well as implicit in this taunt?

   2. *How would you describe the tone of this document? How does the tone compare*
   to that in the CORE Principles? How can you explain the differences?

Document 3.2   Attention Restless Race Mixers Whose Hobby Is Creating Trouble[25]
Get away from your blackboard jungle. Rid yourself of fear of rapists, mug-
gers, dopehead, and switchblade artists during the long, hot summer.

   FULFILL THE DREAM OF A LIFETIME

   HAVE A "VACATION" ON A REAL PLANTATION

   Here's All You Do

   Buy yourself a Southbound ticket via rail, bus, or air.

   Check in and sign the guest register at the Jackson City Jail. Pay a
nominal fee of $200. Then spend the next 4 months at our 21,000-acre
Parchman Plantation in the heart of the Mississippi Delta. Meals furnished.
Enjoy the wonders of chopping cotton, warm sunshine, plowing mules and
tractors, feeding the chickens, slopping the pigs, scrubbing floors, cooking
and washing dishes, laundering clothes.

   Sun lotion, bunion plasters, as well as medical service free. Experience
the "abundant" life under total socialism. Parchman prison fully air-cooled
by Mother Nature.

   (We cash U. S. Government Welfare Checks.)

PARCHMAN PRISON

The Riders were unaware that their fate had been decided in an agreement
between Attorney General Robert Kennedy and Mississippi Senator James
Eastland. Freedom Riders would not be assaulted by a crowd in the state
of Mississippi if they could be taken immediately to prison. The Freedom
Riders commitment to "jail no bail" was seriously tested in the prisons
of Mississippi. When the protestors arrived in Jackson, they were ushered
quickly through an eerily silent bus terminal to the county jail. The stream
of Freedom Riders soon strained the city and county facilities, and the first
group of male Freedom Riders was transferred to Parchman prison. The
female Freedom Riders jailed at the county facility staged a hunger strike
until they, too, were taken to Parchman.

   Parchman, the forbidding Mississippi State prison farm, was the most
feared prison in the South. The Freedom Riders found themselves packed
into army trucks and driven through the Mississippi night. When two white
freedom riders went limp rather than cooperate with the guards removing

them from the truck, a prison sergeant commented, "Ain't no newspaper-men here. Why you acting like that for?"[26] A few days later, the original group of Freedom Riders were surprised to see Mississippi's Governor Ross Barnett escorting visitors through the prison, asking the Freedom Riders, "Are they treating you all right?" Barnett, aware of the publicity surrounding the rides, had instructed that the prisoners not be beaten.

Despite their special status, the group found prison conditions grim. As more Freedom Riders came South to replace those arrested, Parchman received frequent new arrivals. Occupying stifling eight by ten cells, the prisoners were separated by race and sex and spent monotonous hours which lengthened to days. Twice a week, they were allowed to shower. The prisoners were stripped of their clothing, and the men given prison shorts and undershirts, the women striped prison garments. When some of the riders complained, Nashville sit-in veteran James Bevel commented that Gandhi, clad only in a rag, had "brought the whole British Empire to its knees."[27]

The prisoners maintained their spirits and broke the monotony by singing freedom songs, a practice that maddened their captors, who threatened to remove their mattresses. Howard University student and later SNCC field secretary Stokely Carmichael refused to relinquish his mattress, as did his cell mate, Fred Leonard; observers recalled each man clinging tenaciously to his mattress as a guard dragged him down the hall. As he was dragged, Carmichael sang, "I'm Gonna Tell God How You Treat Me."[28] Nashville student leader Bernard Lafayette, who had been nicknamed by Farmer "Little Gandhi," said, "Look, men, we're all worrying about these thin, hard, stupid mattresses, because that's all we've got in this place. But these mattresses ain't nothing but *things*. Things of the body. And we came down here for things of the *spirit*. Things like Freedom and equality and brotherhood. What's happening to us?"[29] Freedom Rider Hank Thomas took to calling to the guards, "Come and get my mattress. I will keep my soul." And the male inmates kept singing, creating a joint chorus with the women housed nearby. After Parchman Deputy Tyson ordered them to be quiet with the threat that they would find themselves "singing in the rain," the group improvised:

> Ole big man Deputy Tyson said,
> I don't want to cause you pain

But if you don't stop that singin' now
You'll be singing in the rain.

Tyson responded by turning the fire hose on their cells.[30] The prisoners were alternately blasted with fans as they froze on the metal frames of their beds at night or confined to the stifling heat with the windows closed.[31]

By the end of the summer, more than three hundred Freedom Riders were confined at Parchman. The first group was released after serving thirty-nine days, the longest sentence a prisoner could serve and still appeal a case. Like Gandhi, they had won sympathy for their cause and survived Parchman Penitentiary, whose reputation was such that many referred to conditions there as "worse than slavery." The Reverend C.T. Vivian, who had been beaten in prison for refusing to call prison guards "sir," remembered,

> The feeling of people coming out of the jail was not that they had triumphed, [but] that they had achieved, that they were now ready, they could go back home, they could be a witness to a new understanding. Nonviolence was proven in that respect. It had become a national movement and there was no doubt about it, for common people in many places in the country. And there was a new cadre of leaders.[32]

DAVID DENNIS

"New leadership is arising and it is not from the white collar man but from the 'down to earth' people. They are people in the rural areas where there is great pressure from the whites. The people are tired. . .and they are beginning to stand up for what they want. It is what I have been dreaming of."[33]

David Dennis was one of the Freedom Riders and became part of the new cadre of leaders. He began his association with CORE while a student at New Orleans' Dillard University. The New Orleans chapter of CORE was strongly grounded in Gandhian principles exemplified by Rudy Lombard and pacifist Jerome Smith. One member recalls, "All the members were prepared to die if necessary. . . . We would not eat and talk for days as a means of acquiring discipline."[34]

David Dennis organized a CORE chapter in his home town of Shreveport, Louisiana shortly after his release from Parchman in the summer of 1961. The CORE chapter suffered serious retaliation from local authorities. After attempting to desegregate the bus terminal lunch counter, chapter members were jailed and the church in which CORE meetings were held was firebombed.

In his first effort as CORE field secretary, Dennis began a direct action campaign in the state capital of Baton Rouge. New Orleans leader Jerome Smith arrived to train local students in nonviolent techniques, and the group began boycotts and sit-ins of downtown dime stores. Dennis, chapter secretary Weldon Rougeau, and twenty-two students were arrested on a newly passed state ordinance prohibiting demonstrations. All refused bail and staged a jail-in. That evening, Ronnie Moore addressed a rally of more than three thousand students from Southern University and announced plans for a downtown march to protest the arrests. However, Moore himself was arrested on charges of operating a sound truck without a permit. Led by CORE field secretary B. Elton Cox, a peaceful march of two thousand students walked to the East Baton Rouge Parish the next day, pledged allegiance to the flag, prayed, and sang "We Shall Overcome." Students inside the jail began singing "Oh, Students, don't you weep, don't you moan"; police responded with tear gas and dogs. Although the Baton Rouge demonstrations had many of the same elements as the later Birmingham events, they attracted far less publicity.

When CORE decided to join COFO, Dennis went to Mississippi. Working alone from June of 1962 to April of 1963 in five Mississippi counties, Dennis was frequently arrested on false charges. On one occasion, he was threatened by a police officer for refusing to say "sir." Dennis, retaining CORE's belief in the transformative power of nonviolence, established something resembling communication with local police.

> The last three times I have been arrested I have also been able to accomplish something greater than anything I can think of. For instance, when the officers arrest me they are always nasty and threatening, but have been able to leave each time with all involved laughing and joking with each other. When I see them on the street, they wave and smile. We have been able to communicate in an understanding manner and to agree on things that would surprise the average person. If each time I am arrested I can accomplish this, then I welcome an arrest every hour of the day.[35]

With funds from the Voter Education Project, Dennis established a CORE base in Canton, Mississippi in June 1963; with a staff of five, he began the arduous work of voter registration, which in retrospect marked one of the beginnings of building the Mississippi Freedom Democratic Party. In his field reports to the national office, he wrote, "During a day I interview about 20 families (canvassing for voter registration), visit leaders in a community, teach voter registration, or speak at assemblies."[36] In heavily black areas in the Delta, Dennis reported,

> We were constantly harassed. . . . Some families who attempted to register were evicted from their homes in Sunflower county by landowners. Several homes were shot into in Ruleville, Mississippi, by hoodlums which resulted in the injury of several people. Threatening phone calls plagued the workers. . . . Some people were threatened by police officers if they attempted to register. Traffic violations against (civil rights) workers climbed steadily.[37]

The Canton base participated in the Freedom Vote of 1963 and attracted support from local activists Annie Devine and C.O. Chinn. The CORE chapter sponsored three Freedom Days in Canton; after the first, over two thousand high school students staged a one-day school boycott to protest inadequate facilities in the local black high school. The CORE office was frequently the target of harassment, and in May, shots were fired into Dennis' office. Dennis' speech on the third Freedom Day in May showed his increasing frustration: "If we want this country to stand up for freedom, we've got to make it that way (ourselves). Right now it's a lie. . . . We know deep in our hearts what we have to do. . . . We've got to sweat, we've got to bleed, a lot of us are going to have to die for it. But you might as well die at once, and get it over with."[38]

In October of 1963, Dennis sent to CORE headquarters a forceful memo, "Mississippi in Motion," calling for a larger staff to expand the Mississippi project. Mississippi "stands as a symbol to segregationists," a symbol that "must be destroyed. . . . We are a part of the great army that has been sent out to destroy this tyrant. Our duty is to hold our front lines at any cost or risk."[39] Among those responding to this charge were Michael and Rita Schwerner. When Chaney, Michael Schwerner and Andrew Goodman were murdered in Mississippi, Dennis was profoundly shaken. His emotional eulogy at Chaney's funeral raised questions about the effectiveness of nonviolence in the face of violent repression. Planning to endorse the CORE philosophy when he rose to speak, Dennis was moved by the sight of Chaney's younger brother Ben in the front row. Abandoning his prepared remarks,* he spoke spontaneously, revealing his pain and growing doubt. "I'm sick and tired of going to funerals of black men murdered by white men. . . . I've got vengeance in my heart tonight. If you go back home and sit down and take what these white men are doing to us. . .if you take it and don't do something about it. . .then God damn your souls. . ."[40]

3.C   Rita Levant Schwerner: Mississippi Community Centers

Questions to help you adopt a critical stance while reading the section below:
1. *Why would a community center help Mississippi blacks "shed the distorting experience of segregation"?*
2. *What is the evidence that organized labor supported the Civil Rights Movement in Mississippi? Why might you find this unexpected?*
3. *Did Rita Schwerner's "Report" end up in the brochure?*
4. *Why would a community center complement a Freedom School rather than make such a school redundant?*

RITA LEVANT SCHWERNER

"My hope is to someday pass on to the children we may have a world containing more respect for the dignity and worth of all men than the world which was willed to us."[41]

With her husband Michael, Rita Schwerner had applied in January of 1964 for CORE posts as advance workers for the coming Freedom Summer Project in Mississippi, positions that paid ten dollars per week. Once they arrived in Mississippi, segregation statues and fear of retaliation made it difficult for the Schwerners to secure housing and basic services. Despite this kind of resistance, Rita Schwerner realized her plans to create a community center for local youths. The Schwerners also participated in efforts to integrate local churches. "We integrated our first white Church last Sunday," Rita Schwerner wrote CORE. "The white minister had invited us, and Mickey and I went with two Negro girls. We were seated without incident, and all we had to endure was some blank and hostile stares. But now the reaction has set in. Members of the congregation have threatened

---

* The entire text of Dennis' eulogy can be found in Aptheker, *Documentary*, vol. 7, page 313, Document 81: "I Am Sick and Tired."

to leave the church, and an effort is under way to oust the minister. A vindictive editorial appeared in the Meridian paper. The gist of the editorial is that outsiders alone are not to blame for integration, but that local people are to blame if they fail to take a stand when members of "another race" invade their church. The paper has urged members of the church to oust the minister and any members who are responsible."[42]

When Michael Schwerner and local CORE worker James Chaney began extending their work into "Bloody Neshoba" County, Rita Schwerner, aware of the danger, stationed herself by the telephone to receive Michael's call in case he was detained. On one occasion before their disappearance, Schwerner and Chaney were two hours late returning from a meeting. "I was frantic," she said, "and at the point of calling the jails, but refrained because I knew that if he had not been picked up, this would inform the authorities of his whereabouts and make the situation far graver. When he and James returned that particular evening, they said that they had been detained in talking with a contact who had no telephone, and that they were fearful of stopping on the road to call in and advise me of their delay."[43]

To help prepare for Freedom Summer, Rita and Michael Schwerner and James Chaney attended the training session in Oxford, Ohio to share their experiences with the summer volunteers. At the end of the first session, Chaney and Schwerner drove back to Mississippi with several volunteers, among them Andrew Goodman. They had heard that the Mount Zion Methodist Church had been burned down, and Schwerner and Chaney were anxious to reassure the congregation that the Freedom School classes would still be held. When the three left that Sunday, they intended to return the same afternoon. They never did.*

Rita Schwerner was still at the training session in Oxford, Ohio, when she received word of her husband's disappearance. Interrupting a lecture by Bob Moses, she urged the volunteers to wire their congressmen to seek a federal investigation. When one volunteer requested the proper spelling of the names of the missing workers, she erased a section of the map of Mississippi Bob Moses had drawn on the blackboard and printed:

James Chaney—CORE staff
Michael Schwerner—CORE staff
Andrew Goodman—Summer Project Volunteer

* See Chapter 8, section C for a more detailed description of the events surrounding the murders of James Chaney, Micheal Schwerner and Andrew Goodman.

Under the names she printed, "Neshoba County—Disappeared."[44] Rita Schwerner then returned to Mississippi to confront Governor Paul Johnson and Neshoba County Sheriff Lawrence Rainey herself. On June 25, accompanied by SNCC field secretary Bob Zellner and the Reverend Edwin King, Schwerner went to the State Capitol building in Jackson in an effort to see Governor Johnson. Rudely rebuffed at the State Capitol, the three proceeded to the Governor's Mansion, where they located Johnson accompanied by Alabama Governor George Wallace. Zellner approached the two Governors, introduced himself, and then introduced Schwerner as the wife of one of the three missing Civil Rights workers. "The moment Johnson heard who I was," said Schwerner, "he turned and bolted for the door of the Mansion. The door was locked behind him and a group of Mississippi highway patrolmen surrounded the three of us."[45] The officers refused to convey her request to Johnson. The next day, her car followed by a pick-up truck with no license plate, Rita Schwerner went to Neshoba County to confront Lawrence Rainey. Rainey denied knowledge of the circumstances of the disappearance. Rainey granted her request to see the burned-out station wagon in which her husband had been riding, and accompanied her to the garage where the vehicle was being kept. "Several young white men, who I believe were workers at the garage, laughed and made screams which are usually referred to as rebel yells when they realized who I was."[46] Rainey's car and an unlicensed blue pick-up followed her to the outskirts of town.

During the days following her husband's disappearance, Rita Schwerner was an outspoken critic of the media attention devoted to the two white Civil Rights workers, attention that was denied Mississippi blacks whose deaths had gone unnoticed for years. Two days after the recovery of her husband's body, she testified, with Aaron Henry, Fannie Lou Hamer, Edwin King, and Martin Luther King, before the Credentials Committee Hearing in Atlantic City.

CORE COMMUNITY CENTERS

Despite the difficulties they had faced in Meridian, Rita Schwerner had been able to create a community center for local youths. She was particularly intent on securing books and beginning to build a library, and was able to report to CORE, "we have several hundred volumes which have been catalogued and arranged on shelves. . . . We have had a small number of teenagers visit the library in the past few days. They seem pleased. . .and now we have about ten books out on loan."[47] These libraries would become crucial resources for the teachers and students at the Freedom Summer Schools. Her report of March 23, 1964, reveals other strategies that the community center pursued that were important in laying the foundation for the successful creation of the Mississippi Freedom Democratic Party.

> In the sewing classes, which began about ten days ago, I believe that we have found one of the programs which we were searching for—an entrance into the Negro community. This program is one which appeals not to the middle class Negro, whom we already have contact with, but to the poor person who can't afford to buy either ready-made clothing or material. . . . I see the sewing classes as serving two specific and important functions. The first is to provide new clothing for people who need it, and this the program is doing. Material is free, and those women who already know how to sew may take what they need and sew at home. Those people who are beginners select their material and receive instruction here. . . . The second function of the program is to provide access for us into the community. We take the name and address of each person who comes for material, and inquire of adults as to whether they are registered voters. We explain our program and ask for their support. Many of these people have already started to use our other facilities, and have brought their friends up to see us. We have received invitations to visit people's homes. . . .
>
> Other classes are also picking up. About four children come daily after school for reading help, the children's story hour is running smoothly and expanding into far more than story reading. . .[for example] how to make puppets. Two nights a week there are classes for people interested in clerks and civil service positions. We do simple math and will in the future have workshops preparing people for the reactions they will receive as first Negro clerks, etc., in the large downtown stores. Teenagers are beginning to show some interest in canvassing and they use the library and teen room constantly.
>
> We do need more staff.[48]

Questions based on Document 3.3 below:
> 1. *Medgar Evers explained in his TV address that the NAACP was not a bunch of "outside agitators." How does the brochure (document 3.3 below) give ammunition to those who would paint CORE as such an organization consisting*

of "outside agitators"? If you were a local CORE member, how would you respond to such an accusation?

2. *What are the theory, strategies and tactics behind the establishment of community centers? What is the "center of communication and influence" in your community? Is there one? If not, what does that say about the nature of "community" today or in the location where you live? How important is community to the development of a movement? If there is center of communication and influence" in your town/neighborhood/city, does it act to empower the people in that community? Or does it act to disempower?*

Document 3.3   Core Community Centers[49]
(Brochure for the Meridian, Mississippi Community Center)

Where a child may not use the local library because he is Negro, where a teenager may not 'hang out' in the local movies or soda joints because he is Negro, where even the dubious sophistication obtainable at a pool hall is forbidden to young men because they are Negro, where the elders and leaders of a community—merchants, farmers, ministers—usually have had limited education and experience because they are Negro, where most families are too restricted economically because they are Negro to afford the weak links to the greater society provided by television and electricity. . . .

It is for these people the CORE Community Centers exist.

In this year, in 1964, a young Negro girl who has come north for an education lives in Harlem. She feels it is somehow immoral to share an apartment with a white girl who lives nearer her college. She finds it difficult to shed the distorting experience segregation has imposed. Even though her wit, intelligence, and charm have opened many doors, she cannot integrate.

But if there had been a CORE Community Center in the town where she grew up. . .? Why, then, she might have seen her parents line up to register at the local court house, she might have grown up knowing the spirit of hope and resistance that has inspired the people of Canton, Mississippi, where the first CORE Community Center opened in 1963. The second CORE center opened in Meridian, Mississippi, early in 1964. Community Centers are desperately needed to destroy the old patterns of segregation. We must not lose another generation of school children to apathy and sullen resentment hidden by cheerful pretense. It is many times easier to find and ship a roomful of books to the south than it is to persuade one brainwashed girl that she has full citizenship in the human race.

WHAT IS A CORE COMMUNITY CENTER?

Ten thousand books, a ping pong table, five sewing machines, half a dozen desks, a typewriter, records and a record player, perhaps a piano and sheet music. . .rooms to put them in, and a few devoted people to give classes in voter registration, sewing, reading, nutrition, remedial courses, arts and crafts.

Not much? A whole new world for those it serves.

Primarily an investment in education, with most of its space and resources devoted to study, books and teaching, every center will try also to have a game room for teenagers to offset the painful effects of recreational limitation as well as those of economic and cultural deprivation.

You'll agree that this is important and worthwhile.

Recently, fabric for 110 dresses was sent by the ILGWU's [International Ladies Garment Workers Union] Local 23–25 to Mississippi. Many of the women who learned to sew by making a dress at the community center had not had a new dress for four or five years. Their involvement in the sewing class encouraged most of them to start voter registration classes. The children who come to the center for books and remedial courses made puppets and toys with every last scrap of left-over fabric. Workers at the center are understandably proud of these results.

Books for CORE Community Centers have been collected by CORE's Southern Educational Project. National CORE has been cooperating with local groups in designing and constructing the centers. Donations of books, money, time (or any useful object) make such centers possible.

Gentlemen:

Here is my contribution of ____toward CORE Community Centers.

My name and address: _____

☐ I am a CORE member.

☐ I would like to join CORE.

☐ I wish to subscribe to the bimonthly paper, CORE-lator.

Please make check marks in the appropriate boxes above, and return to:

CONGRESS OF RACIAL EQUALITY, 38 Park Row, New York, N.Y. 10038

See Activity 3.1 CORE Budgets in the Appendix

FOUR

Southern Christian Leadership Conference (SCLC)

Questions to help you adopt a critical stance while reading the section below:

1. *What are the characteristics of the SCLC in terms of history, strategy, and membership?*

2. *How could one argue that it was inevitable that black churches would be involved in a black rebellion based on Gandhian principles?*

Recommended Film:

Awakenings *(Documentary; Vol.1 of Eyes on the Prize; 55 min, 1987 and 2006; produced by Henry Hampton). The film covers the period from the murder of Emmett Till, the Montgomery Bus Boycott, the formation of the Southern Leadership Conference and the beginning of Dr. Martin Luther King, Jr.'s Civil Rights career.*

THE SCLC WAS ESTABLISHED to nourish and build upon the momentum created by the Montgomery bus boycott of 1955. As an organization of primarily churches, the SCLC added a political dimension to the social and spiritual force of the black church. Long the only place where African Americans could gather, the black church was a crucial means of fostering unity among its members. The sense of unity fostered by the ritual and belief system of the church could be used to build a society more consistent with principles of American justice and Christian charity. The Montgomery bus boycott made clear that the black church could be a powerful agent of social change. The SCLC hoped to use this potential power to encourage nonviolent non-cooperation with unjust laws, adding the power of public demonstrations to the legal foundation laid by the NAACP.

On January 9 and 10, 1957, representatives from ten Southern states met at the Ebenezer Baptist Church in Atlanta to discuss expanding protests beyond bus boycotts. For this conference, Bayard Rustin drafted seven "working papers" that outlined the agenda for the conference, that was entitled "Southern Negro Leaders Conference on Transportation and Nonviolent Integration." Rustin believed that the Montgomery boycott was successful because it had mobilized the residents of Montgomery around a pre-existing shared grievance; the boycott had provided them with a specific means of addressing that grievance. Nonviolence, Rustin believed, "makes humble folk noble and turns fear into courage."[1] Rustin understood that integration on buses was only a first step. The two principal methods necessary to expand the struggle were voting and mass direct action. The SCLC, founded entirely by African Americans, would both work within the existing structures and challenge those structures by nonviolent protest. Rustin acknowledged that, "until the Negro votes on a large scale, we shall have to rely more and more on mass direct action as the one realistic weapon." With the success of the Montgomery boycott, "the center of gravity has shifted from the courts to community action."

It was from the role of the minister in the black church that the founding leadership of the SCLC derived their concept of leadership. "The Negro preacher was 'called' to his office and through his personal qualities achieved a position of dominance. The 'call' was supposed to have come through some religious experience which indicated that God had chosen him as a spiritual leader. . . ."[2] In a letter to the Dexter Avenue Baptist Church, King as a young minister outlined his vision of leadership. He felt that "the pastor's authority is not merely humanly conferred, but divinely sanctioned. . . . Leadership never ascends from the pew to the pulpit, but it invariably descends from the pulpit to the pew."[3]

The Atlanta group met again on the February 14th in New Orleans, where the group elected King as president, Ralph Abernathy as treasurer, and Medgar Evers of Jackson as assistant secretary. At this time, the group changed its name to the Southern Christian Leadership Conference.

Document 4.1   History and Philosophy of the SCLC

On January 10, 1957, more than 100 Southern leaders gathered in Atlanta, Georgia to share and discuss problems of the Southern struggle. This group voted to form a permanent organization that would serve as an agency for groups using the technique and philosophy of nonviolence in creative protest. In 1957 in New Orleans, Louisiana, the Southern Christian Leadership Conference came into being. Dr. Martin Luther King, Jr., was elected president.

The Southern Christian Leadership Conference is made up of organizations all across the South. . . . A large number of ministers have come to the front as leaders in the organization because the Negro ministers in the South have been the community leaders and champions of the Negro's civil liberties.

The Southern Christian Leadership Conference believes in Christian nonviolence. Its activities revolve around two points: the use of non-violent philosophy as a beacon of creative protest, and securing the right of the ballot for every citizen. It has for its aim the achievement of full citizenship rights, equality, and the integration of the Negro in all aspects of American life.[4]

THE CHURCH AS TARGET

Once the Church was recognized as a potential political threat, it became the target of bombings and assaults. In Birmingham, four little girls were killed when a bomb was thrown from a speeding car into the Sixteenth Street Baptist Church. "It is estimated that several hundred churches in the South were bombed, burned, or attacked during the Civil Rights years, with ninety-three of those occurring between 1962 and 1965, with more than fifty in Mississippi alone; the white opposition understood the importance of black churches."[5] SCLC founding member T.J. Jemison stated, "The Negro minister lost his place in the sun with whites when he started leading boycotts, and trying to tear down their social structure."[6]

THE CRUSADE FOR CITIZENSHIP

On Lincoln's birthday, February 12, 1958, the SCLC held mass meetings in twenty-two Southern cities to launch its Crusade for Citizenship. Through the Crusade, the SCLC hoped to use mass direct action applied by local organizations to implement the NAACP's legal gains in the area of voting rights. With the objective of increasing black voter registration throughout the South, the SCLC planned further to politicize black churches by encouraging their use as centers for voter registration. Ella Baker was enlisted as one of the principal organizers of the Crusade, and became the SCLC's acting Executive Director. Although Baker was skeptical of the SCLC's leader-centered style, she saw the Crusade as a means of developing local leadership and organizing communities around a common objective.

> The word Crusade connotes for me a vigorous movement, with high purpose and involving masses of people. . . . To play a unique role in the South, SCLC must offer, basically, a different 'brand of goods' that fills unmet needs of the people. At the same time, it must provide for a sense of achievement and recognition for many people, particularly local leadership.[7]

In information distributed during the Crusade, the SCLC announced, "To mobilize the potential voting strength of Negro population in the South and implement the 1960 Civil Rights Bill, a sustained and vital mass movement must be developed. No legislation is meaningful unless people make proper use of it." The SCLC offered to provide services that would support local voting efforts and to hold training in nonviolent resistance to the inevitable retaliation from segregationists. Through the Crusade, the SCLC hoped to "double the number of qualified Negro voters in the South."[8]

In the Crusade for Citizenship, the SCLC did not challenge fundamental American values but insisted that these principles be applied to African Americans. The preamble to the SCLC Constitution echoes the founding principles of the United States:

> Our nation came into existence as a protest against tyranny and oppression. It was created upon the fundamental assumption that all men are created equal and endowed with inalienable rights. The government exists to protect the life and liberty of all with regard to race, color, or religion. The Federal Government has announced this principle and pledged repeatedly in its basic documents equal protection under the law. The Declaration of Independence, the Constitution of the United States, particularly the Bill of Rights and the 14th and 15th Amendments, the Federal Civil Rights Laws, and many recent decisions of the United States Supreme Court, proclaim

unequivocally that all American citizens shall be accorded full citizenship rights and opportunities without discrimination.[9]

4.A   Martin Luther King: The Montgomery Bus Boycott

Questions to help you adopt a critical stance while reading the section below:
1. *Would any of the SCLC activists disagree with Thoreau's defense of John Brown? How would Thoreau defend Rosa Park's actions?*

2. *How do the Montgomery Bus Boycott demands reveal that a context existed before Mrs. Parks "broke" the law? What implications does the existence of such a "context" have for strategies intended to change the status quo?*

Further Information:
King's *"Letter from Birmingham Jail"* is at thekingcenter.com/prog/non/Letter.pdf
Recommended Film:
Boycott *(Docu-Drama; 113 min, 2002; produced by Preston Holmes, directed by Clark Johnson). Boycott reminds us that Martin Luther King, Jr. was only one of the thousands of ordinary people roused into extraordinary action in the name of equality and social justice.*

MARTIN LUTHER KING

"If you will protest courageously, and yet with dignity and Christian love, when the history books are written in future generations, the historians will have to pause to say 'there lived a great people—a black people—who injected new meaning and dignity into the veins of civilization.' This is our challenge and our overwhelming responsibility."[10]

"It was Martin Luther King who made the contemporary black church aware of its ability to effect change."[11] During his first year of leadership, King proved remarkably effective in adapting the resources of the black church to the demands of a mass political movement. A graduate of Morehouse College, Crozer Theological Seminary, and Boston University's School of Theology, King had expanded intellectually without losing his deep roots in the Southern Baptist Church, translating complex ideas and symbols to his audiences without losing the emotional power of the Baptist pulpit.

It was during the Montgomery Bus Boycott that the Rev. Glenn Smiley, a white Texas-born representative of the Fellowship of Reconciliation

(FOR), visited King to speak to him about the philosophy of nonviolence. Smiley later recalled that he said to King, "I'm assuming that you're very familiar and have been greatly influenced by Mahatma Gandhi." King replied that, from the limited reading he had done, he admired Gandhi, but had to admit that he knew "very little about the man." Smiley was delighted by King's request to learn more. "The role that I played with Martin," recalled Smiley, "was one in which I literally lived with him hours and hours at a time, and he pumped me about what nonviolence was."[12] King's conversations with Smiley helped him reconcile Gandhi's philosophy with Christianity and with pragmatic strategies for achieving social justice in an unjust and violent world.

One of King's many skills as an orator was his ability not only to evoke the Bible stories familiar to his listeners but to make those stories alive in the present, making his congregation one with those who had suffered before them. The story of the Exodus, in which the enslaved people of God are led to the Promised Land through the eloquence and power of a charismatic leader, again emerged in the struggle for freedom. In the words of the traditional spiritual,

> When Israel was in Egypt's land
> Let my people go
> Oppressed so hard they could not stand
> Let my people go
> Go down, Moses,
> Way down in Egypt land
> Tell ole Pharaoh
> To let my people go

During the Montgomery boycott, this story created a moment in which Biblical past and historical present merged. The Israelites, the slaves, and the Montgomery bus boycotters became joined in a moment that transcended history while paradoxically remaining deeply rooted in history. While remaining themselves, the people of Montgomery became the Children of Israel and the suffering slaves. Septima Clark said of King, "As he talked about Moses, and leading the people out, and getting people into the place where the Red Sea would cover them, he would just make you see them. You believed it."[13] According to historian Aldon Morris, "by giving contemporary relevance to familiar biblical struggles through spellbinding oratory and by defining such religious heroes as Jesus and Moses as revolutionaries, King had begun to refocus the content of black religion."[14]

As King evoked the Exodus as another movement of a people against oppression, he also empowered demonstrators with references to the salt *satyagraha* (see chapter 2.) In Albany, Georgia, in 1962, King encouraged the demonstrators by describing Gandhi's Salt March.

> [Gandhi told the Indian people] 'Now we're just gonna march. If you're hit, don't hit back. They may curse you. Don't curse back. They may beat you. . .but just keep [going.]'. . .Just a few men started out, but when they got down to that sea more than a million people had joined in that march. . .and Gandhi and those people reached down in the sea and got a little salt in their hands and broke that law, and the minute that happened it seemed I could hear the boys at Number Ten Downing Street in London, England, say, 'It's all over now.'
>
> There is nothing in this world more powerful than the power of the human soul, and if we will mobilize this soul force right here in Albany, Georgia, we will be able to transform this community.[15]

King's references to Gandhi showed his understanding of the global significance of the boycott. As rooted as the boycott was in local economic and social issues, it linked the people of Montgomery to other people of color who throughout the world were rising against colonization and oppression. "The oppressed people of the world are rising up," King explained. "They are revolting against colonialism, imperialism and other systems of oppression."[16]

Despite his firm dedication to the principles of nonviolence, King on occasion found his role as leader difficult. During the bus boycott, discouraged by his arrest and by the threatening phone calls that plagued him and his family, King began to feel the burden of the role he had undertaken. Late one night, alone in his kitchen, King acknowledged to himself his own fear. "I discovered then that religion had to become real to me, and I had to know God for myself. . . . And it seemed at that moment I could hear an inner voice saying to me, 'Martin Luther, stand up for righteousness. Stand up for justice. Stand up for truth. And lo I will be with you, even until the end of the earth.'"[17]

King's newfound resolve was soon tested by the bombing of his home. While attending the Montgomery Improvement Association's regular Monday night meeting at Ralph Abernathy's church, King received word that his wife Coretta and two-month-old daughter Yolanda had escaped injury as a bomb exploded in the living room of their home. King arrived home to face an emotional crowd, whom he dispersed with advice to remain calm.

A term used frequently by King and throughout the nonviolent movement was "the Beloved Community," a goal in the founding statement of the Southern Christian Leadership Conference. Because the early apostles began their epistles with the term "Beloved," the term "Beloved Community" evoked the early bands of Christians—outnumbered, oppressed, but bound together by a shared spiritual vision and committed to a higher vision of love that transcends social barriers and has the capacity to transform the society which oppresses it. "The end is reconciliation; the end is redemption; the end is the creation of the Beloved Community," King reminded his congregation. "There are great resources of good will in the Southern white man, and we must work to speed up the coming of the inevitable."[18] The Beloved Community was based on *agape,* which King defined as "understanding, redeeming good will for all men, an overflowing love which seeks nothing in return. It is the love of God working in the lives of men."[19] The new "Beloved Community" would be based on the belief that all human beings and the world they inhabit are the creations of God and therefore sacred. In Christian terms, the Beloved Community was "the kingdom of God on earth." But the idea was not limited to Christianity, and encompassed all people. King's metaphor of the "world house" or the "world-wide neighborhood" reflected his belief the Beloved Community could embrace all of humanity.[20]

THE MONTGOMERY BUS BOYCOTT

Rosa Park's act of resistance on a Montgomery bus on December 1, 1955 provided the city's black community with the opportunity to organize its resistance to segregated public transportation. Active with the NAACP, Mrs. Parks had recently returned from a training session at the Highlander Folk School. Word of Mrs. Parks' arrest soon reached E.D. Nixon, a leader in Montgomery's black community and long time member of A. Philip Randolph's Brotherhood of Sleeping Car Porters. With the assistance of white attorney Clifford Durr, Nixon decided, "*This is the case.* We can boycott the bus lines with this and at the same time go to the Supreme Court." Mrs. Jo Ann Robinson, head of the Women's Political Council (WPC), agreed. "We had planned the protest long before Mrs. Parks was arrested," Mrs. Robinson later said. "There had been so many things that happened, that the black women had been embarrassed over, and they were ready to explode. . . . Mrs. Parks had the fiber of character we needed to get the city to rally behind us."[21] With the assistance of members of the WPC and of the students in her English classes at Alabama State College, Mrs. Robinson prepared a leaflet for distribution in the black community.

> Another Negro woman has been arrested and thrown into jail because she refused to get up out of her seat on the bus for a white person to sit down. . . . This woman's case will come up on Monday. We are, therefore, asking every Negro to stay off the buses Monday in protest of the arrest and trial. Don't ride the buses to work, to town, to school, or anywhere on Monday.
> You can afford to stay out of school for one day if you have no other way to go except by bus. You can also afford to stay out of town for one day. If you work, take a cab, or walk. But please, children and grown ups, don't ride the bus at all on Monday. Please stay off all buses Monday.[22]

On Monday morning, the buses were nearly empty. Several hundred supporters appeared at the courthouse that morning to support Mrs. Parks, who, in a trial lasting about five minutes, was found guilty of violating segregation statues and fined ten dollars. Leaving Mrs. Parks' hearing, E.D. Nixon requested a meeting with Martin Luther King and Ralph Abernathy, local ministers who had also appeared to support Mrs. Parks. The three men prepared a proposal to present at the meeting scheduled for that evening. This proposal demanded more equitable seating, courteous treatment from drivers, and the opportunity for blacks to apply for positions as drivers. A new organization, the Montgomery Improvement Association (MIA), was formed, and Martin Luther King, the twenty-six-year-old minister of the Dexter Avenue Baptist Church, was elected president later that day. The boycott continued. The white officials soon used the law as a means of controlling the boycott. Police began following car poolers and issuing traffic citations for trivial or nonexistent offences. After dropping off three boycotters, King himself was arrested for going thirty miles an hour in a twenty-five mile-an-hour zone. This was King's first arrest. Despite continued arrests and harassments, black Montgomerians remained off the city buses.

On November 13, 1956, the Supreme Court upheld an earlier district court ruling declaring racial segregation on Alabama's public transportation unconstitutional. On December 17, 1956, three hundred and eighty two days after it had begun, the boycott ended at 5:45 A.M., as King, Ralph Abernathy, Rosa Parks, and Glenn Smiley boarded a city bus. King and Smiley selected a seat near the front of the bus as photographers recorded the moment. The boycott had lasted more than a year and had involved nearly every member of the black community in a critical struggle, one that resulted in a decisive victory for black Montgomery. Over the course of that year, the attitudes of many black Americans toward social protest and their own power were transformed. As African Americans became aware of their collective economic and political power, the intractable system of Jim Crow no longer seemed invincible. Further, blacks acquired, in King's words, "a new determination to struggle and sacrifice until first-class citizenship becomes a reality. . . . One can never understand the bus protest in Montgomery without understanding that there is a new Negro in the South, with a new sense of dignity and destiny."[23]

After the Supreme Court's ruling that segregation on Montgomery's buses was unconstitutional, FOR's Glenn Smiley and King conducted workshops preparing both blacks and whites for peaceful integration of city bus lines. "It was the biggest nonviolent workshop in history, I guess," recalled Smiley, "because it involved about five thousand people."[24] King and Smiley arranged chairs on a platform to suggest a city bus and engaged workshop participants in various role-plays. King remembered that, "Sometimes the person playing a white man put so much zeal into his performance that he had to be gently reproved from the sidelines. Often a Negro forgot his nonviolent role and struck back with vigor; whenever this happened, we worked to re-channel his words and deeds into a nonviolent direction."[25] Similar workshops were conducted for cooperative white Montgomerians to provide examples for other whites on appropriate behavior. The MIA also distributed throughout the city Smiley's "Suggestions for Integrating Buses," to assist blacks and whites with their new and unfamiliar relationship. Smiley advised black passengers to conduct themselves with a "calm and loving dignity" and to avoid unnecessary confrontations. "Do not deliberately sit by a white person unless there is not another seat," he advised.[26]

After the success in Montgomery in 1956, the SCLC decided to launch a Crusade for Citizenship in 1958. The SCLC hoped to use mass direct action to enforce compliance with the NAACP's legal gains in the area of voting rights. A major objective was to increase black voter registration throughout the South. To this end, the SCLC offered leadership training, training in nonviolent resistance, and launched the Citizenship Education Program. Many of the leaders of these SCLC programs, like some of the leaders of the Montgomery Bus Boycott, had been trained as organizers at the Highlander School. Both Highlander and the Citizenship Education Program would eventually be among the many models from which the architects of the 1964 Mississippi Freedom Schools would look for inspiration.

See Activity 4.1   Montgomery Bus Boycott in the Appendix

4.B   Myles Horton: The Highlander School

Questions to help you adopt a critical stance while reading the section below:

1.   *Compare Myles Horton's statements about following the law to Thoreau's.*

2.   *According to Horton, what is good teaching? What is a good curriculum? Do you agree?*

3.   *Why did Horton fear a well organized school? How does this compare to the way the administration of your school(s) run or ran the school(s)?*

4.   *What contributions did Highlander make to the Civil Rights Movement? What contributions did it make to Freedom Summer?*

5.   *What is your response to the Tennessee state committee's argument that Highlander is "not a school"? Is it important today to argue that Highlander was a school? Why was it important to the Tennessee legislature at the time to deny Highlander the label of a "school"? Is a school not a school when its purpose is to change society (is a school only a school if its purpose is to train students to fit into the society as it exists)?*

6.   *Of what significance is the knowledge that Rosa Parks was part of a network of organizations?*

7.   *Why was music an important part of the Highlander curriculum? Is there a difference between listening to music and singing it?*

8. *What was the purpose of using drama in the Highlander curriculum? Does one learn different things or learn differently if one reads a story instead of watching a dramatization of one? How does the function of drama at Highlander compare to the function of drama at your school? What explanation or theory can account for the differences and similarities?*

Recommended Film:

You Got to Move *(Documentary; 87 min, 1985; by Lucy Massie Phenix & Veronica Selver). A documentary about personal and social transformation, the film records the progress of individuals who, together with Tennessee's legendary Highlander Folk School, founded by Myles Horton, have worked for union, civil, environmental, and women's rights in the South.*

MYLES HORTON

"It is difficult for some people to understand that there are good people, workers, who don't want to imitate the rich, don't even want to be rich. They want to live decently on the basis of their work and don't respect the rich for being rich."[27]

Myles Horton was shaped by two forces—a deep appreciation of the culture of Appalachia and an intense desire for social change. Highlander, the school that Horton founded, was born of this contradiction; Horton did not want improvement of economic conditions to mean destruction of the local culture. At Highlander, he formed from the songs, the tradition of sharing and storytelling, and the religious fervor of the Tennessee Hills a school to teach people how to make social change. Horton's paradoxical impulse to maintain tradition while working for social change originated from a deep belief in the value of the individual. He believed that people had the means to solve their own problems without relying on experts or institutions. What was needed, according to Horton, was the means to share their ideas and work on solutions. Horton himself was grateful that he had had so few good teachers in school. "I'm serious when I say that I probably got a better education by not having good teachers than if I had had teachers who I thought knew things. I would have had to listen to them and learn their opinions, instead of developing my own."[28]

Horton's childhood in rural Tennessee provided a foundation for his later activism. His parents held a range of jobs, from school teaching to factory work to sharecropping. "We didn't think of ourselves as working-class, or poor, we just thought of ourselves as being conventional people who didn't have any money." As a child, Horton learned to respect the keen intelligence of his grandfather, a working man who had never learned to read. From this, Horton "learned to respect people who weren't literate, in the technical sense."[29] To Horton's grandfather, the rich were those "who lived off of somebody else," and he had little respect for the rich.

Horton had his first experience of civil disobedience when he organized a banquet for the statewide YMCA in 1928. Black and white YMCA members arrived at a Knoxville, Tennessee banquet hall to learn that Horton had organized an integrated dinner, which was against the law. Horton asked the hotel what they were going to do with the dinner for one hundred and twenty, which was already prepared. "They fed us," remarked Horton. "In order to act on my beliefs, I had to accept the idea of civil disobedience. I knew that I might have to violate those laws that were unjust, and I made up my mind never to do something wrong just because it was legal."[30] Horton remained an enemy of what he termed "institutionally sanctioned violence." "We live in a violent society, a violent world; that is, a world in which force is a vital mechanism used to keep the economic and social system intact. . . . The laws of the land are supported by the use of violence; that is, the use of physical force to make people obey the law."[31]

His early years studying the culture of his native Appalachia had convinced him that solutions to social problems could come only from the people themselves.

> For generations men and women have been coming to the Southern Mountains to help us. They have put hundreds of thousands of dollars into missionary work and schools. . . . There has been advancement, of course. . .but on the whole, we are still 'poor whites,' waiting to be helped. . . . We must discard our blind faith in the powers that be—whether in manna from heaven, or Red Cross flour.[32]

Plagued by financial troubles, red-baiting, and threats from segregationists, Horton maintained his belief in the values represented by Highlander. In 1954, Horton was called by Mississippi Senator James Eastland, a member of the Senate Internal Security Subcommittee, to answer charges of communism. After refusing to answer the committee's questions, Horton was threatened with a contempt citation. Horton replied, "Let me help you out.

I am in contempt of you and this committee and everything it's trying to do, and I am proud to be in contempt."[33] Eastland informed Horton that his refusal violated the Constitution, but Horton was unimpressed. As he later explained, "If it is against the Constitution, if it is against the law, then that doesn't have any effect on what I'm going to do, because I'm going to do what my conscience and my judgment tell me is the right thing to do. There's absolutely nothing you can do about it. Nothing. The only thing you can do is put me in jail, kill me, but you can't make me do something that I don't want to do."[34] Eastland immediately ordered two U.S. Marshals to seize Horton.

James Bevel, one of the Nashville students who studied at Highlander, said of Horton, "I guess for the first time in my life, I was introduced to a man who reminded me of Socrates. Myles was a guy who'd ask questions about your assumptions. . . . He has arrived at a self-respect and self-appreciation of mankind. He, in that sense, is not a liberal, he's an enlightened man."[35]

THE HIGHLANDER SCHOOL

The Highlander school became a source of renewal and education for the Civil Rights Movement. Pete Seeger noted that, "Highlander was a way to use education to change society. Not to reform the old one cosmetically, but to build a new and more humane society."[36]

The idea of Highlander developed while Horton, the summer before his senior year at Cumberland University in Tennessee, taught classes at a Vacation Bible School in Ozone, Tennessee. His students were the children of mountain people whose rural lives had been disrupted by the coming of the mines upon which they had become economically dependent. Frustrated because the games and stories of the Bible schools weren't connecting with the lives of the people, Horton invited the parents of his students to come in the evening for community meetings, just to talk about their problems. During these sessions, the people of the mountains shared with each other their struggles and their knowledge, and soon began to look for solutions. From this experience, Horton began a quest for "Ozone," which came to him to symbolize a form of education that trusted the wisdom of the people.

In his search, Horton left the mountains for Union Theological Seminary in New York City, where he discovered the theologian Reinhold Niebuhr.

Baffled by Niebuhr's lectures, Horton nearly left the seminar. The young Horton informed Niebuhr, "I'm not going to go back in because I can't understand anything you're saying. I'm not going to waste my time listening to you without understanding because I can go over to the library and read something I can understand."[37] Niebuhr prevailed upon him to stay and became a friend and major influence on Horton's thinking. Reinhold Niebuhr, a Christian Socialist and an outspoken critic of the capitalist system, called control by business an example of "social stupidity."[38] Niebuhr encouraged Horton's idea of a school in the Southern mountains, where the social conflicts he had described in his work were most acute. Horton was also familiar with the work of educator John Dewey. Dewey criticized the "isolation of knowledge and practice" and advocated that education be related to the lives and experiences of the student.

While studying at the University of Chicago, Horton met Jane Addams, founder of Hull House, first of the many settlement houses founded by women to combat urban poverty in the late nineteenth century. After seeing the poverty in urban slums in London, Ms. Addams had returned to the United States and started, in an immigrant neighborhood in Chicago, a neighborhood center to teach immigrants necessary skills and respect for their own cultures and to share music and drama. Addams listened to Horton's idea and supported his notion of what she termed a "rural settlement house." The settlement house was founded on the notion of democracy, which, Addams explained to Horton, means "people have the right to make decisions. If there is a group of people sitting around a country store and there's a problem they're talking about, there are two ways to do it. They can go out and get some official to tell them what to do, or they can talk it out and discuss it themselves. Democracy is if they did it themselves."[39] Addams claims that she had gotten this definition from her father, who had been a friend of Abraham Lincoln's. Horton told Addams that he didn't think this was bad advice at all.

In Chicago, Horton also met Danish-born minister Aage Moller, who encouraged him to learn more about the Danish folk schools. Horton had read about the folk school movement and its role in building a society that was "neither rich nor poor."[40] The folk school movement, founded by Bishop N.S.F. Grundtvig, sought to keep alive the traditions of the farmers and encourage them to struggle against oppressive economic forces. The schools stressed the importance of folk songs, dances, and crafts in retaining culture and building community. With Moller's encouragement, Horton made a trip to Denmark, learning the language and supporting himself with odd jobs as he traveled from school to school. One teacher told Horton the schools sought to create "a picture of reality not as we have met it in our surroundings, but as we ourselves would have formed it is we could—a picture of reality as it ought to be."[41]

Horton returned to the United States with a clearer idea of the kind of school he wanted to create. In Denmark, Horton took notes prompted by his observations of the Danish Folk Schools, notes that he labeled "O" for "Ozone," his "symbol for reality."[42] "Can an idea become organized and still live?. . .The job is to organize a school just well enough to get teachers and students together. AND SEE THAT IT GETS NO BETTER ORGANIZED."[43] In an isolated rural setting, the school could create its own environment. What was taught had to reflect the lived experience of the students. "Go to strike situations and take the students, thus helping labor and education at the same time." Negroes would be among the students who will live in close personal contact with the teacher."

On Christmas night in Copenhagen in 1931, Horton wrote his final notes:

> I can't sleep, but there are dreams. What you must do is go back, get a simple place, move in and you are there. The situation is there. You start with this and let it grow. You know your goal. It will build its own structure and take its own form. You can go to school all your life, you'll never figure it out because you are trying to get an answer that can only come from the people in the life situation.
>
> It all seemed so clear and simple. . . . The way to get started was to start. That Christmas night I had rediscovered Ozone.[44]

With the assistance of Southern radical Don West and a home donated by Dr. Lillian Smith, Horton began his school in 1932. Reinhold Niebuhr agreed to launch Horton's idea with a fundraising letter. "We are proposing," wrote Niebuhr, "to use education as one of the instruments for bringing about a new social order."[45] Niebuhr also served as the chairman of Highlander's Advisory Board, which also included such progressives as socialist and presidential candidate Norman Thomas, First Lady Eleanor Roosevelt, and Riverside pastor Harry Emerson Fosdick.[46]

Document 4.2   Highlander's Statement of Purpose, 1950[47]

We reaffirm our faith in democracy as a goal that will bring dignity and freedom to all; in democracy as an expanding concept encompassing human relations. . . .

Democracy to us means that membership in the human family entitles all to freedom of thought and religion, to equal rights to a livelihood, education and health, to equal opportunity to participate in the cultural life of the community and to equal access to public services.

We hold that democracy is inactive unless workers are given a full voice in industry through unions; or farmers are given a voice in the market place through cooperatives; or where freedom of thought and discussion is limited; that democracy is outlawed by legally entrenched discrimination and segregation; that there must be diversity of approach but each step must be in conformity with the goal, which is dishonored by each undemocratic act.

With a democratic goal, we are in a position to fight anything that gets in the way, whether it be totalitarian communism, or fascism or monopoly-dominated capitalism.

The purpose of the Highlander Folk School is to assist in creating leadership for democracy. . . .

The nature of a specific educational program will be determined by the needs of the students. . . .

The times call for an affirmative program, based on a positive goal. An army of democracy deeply rooted in the lives, struggles and traditions of the American people must be created. By broadening the scope of democracy to everyone, and deepening the concept to include every relationship, the army of democracy would be so vast and so determined that nothing undemocratic could stand in its path.

Approved by the Executive Council, April 3, 1950

FROM WORKERS' RIGHTS TO CIVIL RIGHTS

Highlander's initial focus was on the right to unionize. Highlander grew from Myles Horton's belief that unions could be the training ground for democracy and a vehicle where black and white could work together for a more just and humane society. The coming of industry to the South could, through effective use of unions, teach black and white Southerners to work together toward common economic goals. During Highlander's years of union work, Horton was to learn first hand of the possibility of violent opposition to social change. Horton heard of a strike at Wilder, Tennessee, an impoverished mining town where miners lived in company shacks, were paid script that was redeemable only at the company store. Caught between low wages and high prices at the company store, the miners found themselves sinking deeper into debt. Worker complaints had caused a lock-out. To break the strike, the company had brought in workers at higher wages. Horton arrived, asking questions about the situation to workers themselves, and began a campaign of letter writing and relief in the form of food and clothing for the miners. The strikers' morale was maintained by their forceful leader, Barney Graham, and a song called "The Wilder Blues."

> *Mr. Shivers said if we'd block our coal*
> *He's run four days a week*
> *And there's no reason we shouldn't run six*
> *We're loadin' it so darn cheap*
> *It's the worst old blues I ever had.*

> *I've got the blues*
> *I've shore-God got 'em bad*
> *I've got the blues*
> *The worst I've ever had!*
> *It must be the blues*
> *Of the Davidson-Wilder scabs.*

> *Mr. Shivers told Mr. Boyer*
> *He said, "I know just what we'll do!*
> *We'll get the names of the union men*
> *And fire the whole darn crew."*
> *It's the worst old blues I ever had.*

> *I'd rather be a yeller-dog scab**
> *In a union man's backyard,*
> *Than to tote a gun for L.L. Shivers,*

---

* A "yellow dog contract" between a worker and employer stipulated that the worker would never join a union.

And to be a National Guard
It's the worst old blues I ever had.[48]

Horton himself was arrested by a National Guardsman and charged with "coming here and getting information and going back and teaching it."[49] The Wilder strike ended tragically, with the shooting of Barney Graham and the eviction of the strikers from their homes. Horton and the Highlander staff responded by working with the Tennessee Valley Authority to seek employment for the displaced miners. Horton learned from the Wilder experience that Highlander's teaching had to be deeply rooted in the lives of the people to be meaningful. Although the Highlander staff for years supported the efforts of the CIO to unionize the South's textile industry, the union's increasing bureaucracy and resistance to racial equality strained the relationship between the school and the unions. By the 1950s, the school had shifted its focus to civil rights.

After the 1954 *Brown* decision, Highlander began holding workshops to discuss implementation of school integration in the South. Because Highlander was one of the few places in the South where blacks and whites could socialize and discuss political action, some African Americans left believing for the first time that integration could become a reality. Among those who attended Highlander's workshops was Rosa Parks, who completed a Highlander workshop weeks before her resistance to a bus driver's order sparked the Montgomery bus boycott. As Mrs. Parks recalled,

> At Highlander, I found out for the first time in my adult life that this could be a unified society, that there was such a thing as people of differing races and backgrounds meeting together in workshops and living together in peace and harmony. It was a place I was very reluctant to leave. I gained there strength to persevere in my work for freedom, not just for blacks but for all oppressed people.[50]

Martin Luther King was a keynote speaker at Highlander's twenty-fifth anniversary celebration, on Labor Day, 1957. King spoke of a new spirit among African Americans.

> The Old South is gone, never to return again. . . . The determination of the Negro himself to gain freedom and equality is a most powerful force that

will ultimately defeat the barriers of segregation. . . . He came to feel that the important thing about a man is not his specificity, but his fundament; not the color of his skin nor the texture of his hair, but the texture and quality of his soul. . . . With this new sense of dignity and new self-respect, a new Negro emerged . . .

King also advised his audience to become "maladjusted" to a system based on racism, violence, and economic exploitation.[51]

Typical of Horton's beliefs on education and community were the workshops he held at Highlander for beauticians. Horton saw the political potential of the many beauty parlors in African American communities throughout the South and resolved to work to develop this resource. Beauty parlors and barbershops flourished in African American communities after Emancipation in 1863. They were social as well as commercial gathering places where both ethnic and gender bonding took place. Parlors and barbershops were often economic jumping off places for those who wanted to enter local black leadership.

Question based on Document 4.3 below:

Why was there a need for a "new kind of leadership" in the Civil Rights Movement in 1961? Was the old kind no longer needed or was there a need for a new kind as well as the old?

Document 4.3   Highlander Workshop Announcement

Announcing a Workshop of
NEW LEADERSHIP RESPONSIBILITIES[52]
Highlander Folk School
Monteagle, Tennessee
January 15–17, 1961

Purpose: To explore the opportunities offered in the Beautician's profession, for promoting justice and equality in the South.

Background: The new democratic initiative taken by Negroes in the South is characterized by direct, specific, and immediate public social action.

The requirements now are for a new kind of leadership which is voluntary, and which can speak out openly, hold office in community organizations for integration, and publicly promote the cause.

The Beautician's profession enjoys complete freedom, and has also some unusual opportunities for direct action within its scope of contacts and influence. Someone has said, "The Beauty Salon is a center of communication and influence."

Furthermore, the profession may be considered to represent a new opportunity for leadership of professional women in social action.

Participants: Members of the Beautician's profession only.

4.C   Septima Clark: SCLC Citizenship Schools

Questions to help you adopt a critical stance while reading the section below:

1. *How was a citizenship school different from a conventional public school? Is a citizenship school needed today? Do they exist today? Does your school teach citizenship skills? Would that be important?*

2. *Did SCLC Citizenship Schools brainwash students? Any more so or less than current public schools?*

THE SCLC CITIZENSHIP SCHOOLS

In 1954, Esau Jenkins, a bus driver from Johns Island, South Carolina, attended a Highlander session and sought Horton's advice about literacy training for adults on Johns Island. Jenkins commented on the poor conditions of South Carolina's black schools, conditions that kept large segments of the population illiterate and socially disempowered. If they couldn't read, in short, they couldn't vote. Horton spent six months with Jenkins on Johns Island, asking questions and learning about the community. Using what he learned, Horton helped Jenkins set up the first Citizenship School by partitioning off one corner of Jenkins' small grocery, the Progressive Club Cooperative store. Bernice Robinson, Septima Clark's niece and a local beautician, taught the first Citizenship School. Reading materials included the *UN Declaration of Human Rights* and the State Constitution. At the end of three months, eight of her original fourteen students registered to vote. The original class size more than doubled to thirty-seven students before the first term was completed.

The Citizenship Schools soon started "island-hopping," as requests came from neighborhood islands off the South Carolina coast. The staff at

Highlander decided that only black teachers would be selected, to prevent perpetuation of the idea of white superiority. Also, only "non-teachers" would teach. A Citizenship School teacher could be any local black person who could read and write and who could recruit students. From the start, the program was designed and run by African Americans. The Johns Island project created a network of teachers to instruct residents of the neighboring islands. "Education does not take place in a vacuum," wrote Horton. "It mushrooms when students in one area become teachers in another."[53] In the early 1950s, Horton addressed a black voter registration drive and said, "I hope this will be the last time a white man tells you what to do, how to formulate policy, who should do what and when they should do it. White people should be used as technicians to help you accomplish what you say you want done to end segregation."[54]

Ella Baker, Executive Director of SCLC, encouraged the SCLC to take over the citizenship training program designed by Esau Jenkins, Septima Clark, and Myles Horton. In April of 1960, the SCLC opened a training school in McIntosh, Georgia for citizenship school teachers, and Bernice Robinson's program of "big ideas" continued. The citizenship schools prepared people not only to vote but to understand themselves as citizens with the right to participate. As Septima Clark said,

> You see, people having been living on plantations for so many years, had a feeling that they were afraid to let white people know that they wanted to be a part of the governing body. They were afraid to do that. So, we used to put up a regular form on our blackboard with the government at the head and all the people who would come under. Then on down to the masses, and show how you too can become part of this great governing body, if you will register and vote. In that way they learned that in a country like the United States, they had a right to be a part.[55]

The Citizenship Schools made students feel connected not only to the political process but to the larger Civil Rights Movement. The recruiting materials featured a photograph of Martin Luther King and the statement from Dr. King:

> All over the country there are adults who are not registered to vote, and who generally do not participate in their civic affairs. These persons are not

full citizens. Many of them have not had an opportunity to learn what is required of first class citizens. These people need Citizenship Schools.[56]

The SCLC schools also taught black history, a concept continued in the Freedom Schools. "Our purpose was to see how people could un-brainwash themselves," explained Dorothy Cotton, "and that's a direct quote from one of the people in one of my sessions."[57] The program also continued to teach practical daily skills. "We taught them to make long-distance phone calls. . . . We taught them how to use bank drafts," said Dorothy Cotton. "These were people who, when they got any money, they put it under the mattress. We needed to teach them to use banks. We introduced them to political officials. We wanted to demystify the political process and build a base from which folks could operate."[58]

The evaluation form used by the Citizenship Schools stressed that "graduation" meant taking an active role in the community. Upon completing the program, the Citizenship School student was asked if he or she had encouraged others to vote, had signed petitions, attended community meetings, engaged in demonstrations, served any unselfish cause, or helped others in his or her neighborhood.[59]

SEPTIMA CLARK

"The basic purpose of the Citizenship Schools is discovering local community leaders. . . . It is my belief that creative leadership is present in any community and only awaits discovery and development."[60]

Septima Clark began her teaching career at the age of eighteen, when she was assigned a two-room schoolhouse on Johns Island, South Carolina. In 1955, Mrs. Clark was fired from her job as a Charleston, South Carolina elementary school teacher. An active member of the NAACP and a student at Highlander workshops since 1952, Mrs. Clark had been actively encouraging blacks to vote. Mrs. Clark had offended community standards by socializing with Judge and Mrs. Waites Waring. Waring, a member of an old Charleston family and a federal judge, had been actively enforcing federal law in an effort to bring about integration of Charleston's schools. He and his wife had integrated their social lives as well, much to the disapproval of Charleston society.

At Highlander, Mrs. Clark helped to formulate a program that would adapt itself to the needs and circumstances of the black community in order to teach uneducated blacks the skills they would need to become voters. Clark formulated programs that addressed problems of adult literacy, acknowledged the constraints placed on tenant farmers by the agricultural calendar, and trained teachers to work in such programs. Rosa Parks described her impression of Septima Clark from her 1954 stay at the Highlander Folk School, "I noticed how Septima Clark could organize and hold things together in this very informal setting of interracial living. I had to admire this great woman."[61] Program instructor Dorothy Cotton said of the program Mrs. Clark established at Johns Island, South Carolina, "This education program. . .helped give them give voice to the churning that was inside of them."[62]

On July 31, 1959, during the state's investigation of the school for communism, twenty state troopers and sheriff's deputies raided Highlander in search of illegal alcohol. Mrs. Clark was showing a film as part of a workshop she was conducting on school desegregation. The police insisted that the lights be turned off, and the workshop participants sat in darkness while the place was ransacked by police with guns and billy clubs. Jamila Jones, a teenager attending the workshop, began to sing "We Shall Overcome." The singing continued for nearly an hour while the police ransacked the place. The police found no alcohol on the school property, but discovered in Horton's home an empty whiskey keg and a bottle containing a half-inch of gin. They seized these as evidence and arrested Mrs. Clark, Guy Carawan, and two others. Mrs. Clark was charged with illegal possession and sale of whiskey, and, when she asked to make a phone call, was also charged with resisting arrest. Carawan recalls hearing her singing "We Shall Overcome" from her jail cell.[63]

In 1960, Septima Clark invited Ella Baker to join her on an educational committee at the Highlander folk school, and the two women had the opportunity to express their mutual admiration. "I need your help," wrote Mrs. Clark, "in planning bigger and more vitalizing workshops for the entire South." Miss Baker responded, "I don't think I ever told you, but several years ago, when I first read the thrilling account of your experiences in promoting citizenship schools on the Sea Islands of South Carolina, I yearned for the opportunity to meet you. Little did I dream, at that time, that we would have an occasion to work together here in our beloved Southland. So you see, I have long since been committed to the idea of 'teaming-up' with you."[64] Like Miss Baker, Mrs. Clark supported the right of students to direct the course of their own protests. At the Seventh Annual College Workshop held at Highlander on April 1, 1960, Mrs. Clark said, "Our young have gone out in front, and we must run to keep up with them. We must give them our support, but we must not attempt to wrest the leadership from them."[65]

When the Citizen Education program was transferred from Highlander to the SCLC, Mrs. Clark became its director of teacher education. She conducted workshops and provided inspiration at the Citizenship Education Program at Dorchester. Mrs. Clark visited Citizenship Schools in Mississippi and expressed her indignation about controls on black voting in writing to Louis Martin, a member of the Democratic National Committee.

> I wish you could have been with me last night in Hattiesburg, Mississippi at a Citizenship Education School. There you would have seen men and women 39–70 years of age struggling with the interpretation of the Mississippi Constitution so that they can qualify for registration and be able to vote in an election. This interpretation must be done to the satisfaction of the registrar. How ridiculous can a legislative body be to ask for such a thing. . . . I am asking now for your help in making it easier for Mississippians to move ahead and register to vote. They have no other alternative. If they can't vote, they must demonstrate and present their bodies as living sacrifices against injustice.[66]

Questions based on Document 4.4:

1. *Describe how each of the following ingredients plays a role in the successful achievement of nonviolent direct action: articulate leaders, songs, role-plays, networks, community, experience, research, (anything else?).*

2. *Does the SCLC Citizenship Curriculum explicitly teach these topics in order to empower students to be effective direct action activists?*

3. *Why do you think it was important to look at "Heroes of the Past?" Is your community represented in the stories of heroes in history you were taught? Who are your heroes of the past? Who are your present day heroes? What makes them heroes? Is our society and culture built on their experiences? Should we*

*not have different heroes? Does the study of "heroes" undermine the develop-
ment of local leadership? Do charismatic leaders like Martin Luther King, Jr.
undermine local leadership development, thereby preventing movements from
being sustainable if the leader dies or is murdered?*

4. *How do the following sections of the CEP curriculum encourage voter registration? Black historical figures; handwriting; literacy; block party; songs;
   Citizenship questionnaire; History and philosophy of SCLC; and the first words
   of Jesus' ministry?*

Document 4.4   The SCLC Citizen Education Program [67] *(excerpts)*

REVIEW YOUR READING—IMPROVE YOUR WRITING

For many years Negroes were forced to suffer in broken down school buildings. . . . Now there are more opportunities for young Negroes. Schools are
better and buses are provided. But what of those who went to school prior
to 1960. We still need to know many things to live in the modern world.
Reading is the key to this knowledge. That is why we are going to brush up
on our reading. Writing is also important. Now we have an opportunity to
improve our handwriting. This will help us fill out the blanks to become
Registered Voters. Registered Voters are First Class Citizens.

THE BIBLE AND THE BALLOT

The first words of Jesus' public ministry were:

> The spirit of the Lord is upon me,
> Because he has anointed me to preach
> Good news to the poor.
> He has sent me to proclaim release to the captives.
> To set at liberty those who are oppressed,
> To proclaim the acceptable year of the Lord. (Luke 4:18)

This was Jesus' work and now it is ours. We are to release the captives of
this segregated society, and bring liberty to those who are oppressed. . . .
In America we change things through the ballot. The Constitution allows
each man a vote for what he thinks to be the right way. In 1870 the Fifteenth
Amendment was passed which gave all men the right to vote, regardless

of race, color or previous condition of servitude. Now if we want justice, freedom, peace, and equal wages, we must vote for people who will consider these things important. Every election is a chance to vote. . . .

Discuss the following questions:

1. What would happen in your community if faith in God was put aside and violence took precedence?

2. If you are not registered to vote, do you think you are doing justice to yourself and your fellow man?

3. We have a task which Jesus himself set before us, how can we best accomplish this work?

FIRST RATE HANDWRITING FOR FIRST CLASS CITIZENS

Writing is one way that you share with others the things that are on your mind. It is important to have a handwriting that others can read. A strong, sure handwriting shows that you are a strong sure person. All our First Class Citizens should have a first rate handwriting.

As you improve your writing, new worlds of pleasure will open and old fears will pass away. You will enjoy writing your friends. You will be able to write to your newspaper and express your views on the events of your community. You can write your Congressman or Senator to help him to vote for things that will help our people, and you will not be shy about filling out job application blanks, signing your name to your checks or registering to vote. . . .

THE POWER OF NON-VIOLENCE

When Jesus said, "If a man smite thee on one cheek, turn to him the other also," he was introducing mankind to a new way of life—a way of life which overcomes evil through love. This simple New Testament truth was put into practice by Mahatma Gandhi in India. Under his leadership, the Indian people won their freedom from the British without firing a shot. Their weapon was moral force, or truth force as Gandhi called it.

The idea of non-violence first received widespread attention in the United States when a young Baptist minister, the Rev. Martin Luther King, Jr., led the people of Montgomery, Alabama in a non-violent protest against discourtesy and segregation on the busses of that city. . . .

When we don't fight back, they are forced to think about why we don't. This is the beginning of understanding. Understanding is the stepping stone to true brotherhood.

THINGS TO DO
Answer these questions by filling in the blanks:

1.   The weapon used to gain freedom in India was_____.

2.   _____ led the first non-violence movement in Montgomery. . .

DISCUSS THE FOLLOWING QUESTIONS:

1.   What would happen in your town if minority groups used violent means to solve their problems?

2.   What happens when nothing is done to overcome community problems?

3.   How can non-violence be used in your community?

NEW WORDS TO STUDY
Introduce, younger, person, call, first, woman, clearly, new

ONE HUNDRED YEARS FROM SLAVERY
The first African slaves were brought to America in 1619. This was only a few years after the first white settlers. These strong young men were stolen from their tribes in Africa. They were needed to clear the trees to make farm land and roads. They planted and harvested the crops.

These slaves were chained and crowded into ships under animal conditions. Many died of sickness. Others jumped overboard determined to die rather than be enslaved. Still others planned revolts and attempted to fight for their freedom. Some escaped to freedom, others were returned to slavery, but their spirits remained free. The sound of freedom came out of their hearts, and gave us the Negro spirituals.

Slavery was a degrading experience for the Negro but the progress of the last one hundred years and the rugged determination to be free makes our heritage glorious.

In the twentieth century, we see the fruits of this longing for freedom. The new Negro in America is standing up, demanding first class citizenship.

In Africa and Asia new nations are being born as people of color everywhere are demanding the freedom to decide their destiny.

HEROES OF THE PAST

Crispus Attucks. This man was one of our first freedom fighters. America was only a colony. It had not yet become a country. England made the laws. England made the colonies pay taxes but would not let them be represented in the government. This is very much like the Negroes problem of voting in parts of the South today. England said to the people "You just pay the taxes, you can't tell us what to do with the tax money." This made the people angry. . . . It was on a cold winter night in Boston. . . . Leading the people was Crispus Attucks, a tall handsome Negro, big as a giant. He had worked on a whaling ship and knew the docks well. He shouted to the people, "The way to get rid of the soldiers is to attack the main guard! Strike at the root! This is the nest!" As the people with sticks, clubs and snow balls went toward the soldiers, the soldiers fired their guns. The first shot killed Crispus Attucks. He was the first man to die for our country's freedom.

THINGS TO DO

Put the correct answers in the blanks:

1. Before America became a country, the laws were made by _____
   _____.

2. We can help bring freedom by _____
   _____.

QUESTIONS TO DISCUSS

1. What is a colony?
2. How was the problem of taxes like Negroes' problem of voting?
3. Why did Crispus Attucks lead the people when the soldiers had guns?
4. What does July 4th mean?

Sojourner Truth. Even though she was born in New York, Sojourner suffered as much as her Southern sisters. She slept in a cellar which had a floor of loose boards on the ground. In winter the water that settled turned to ice, her bed was made of straw and a blanket. She was sold into slavery many times before she was even 12 years old. . . . She ran away early one morning with her small son, Peter. . . . She said the Spirit called her and she must go. She roamed all over, speaking against slavery and its evils. . . . She also spoke up for the rights of women. . . . She strongly believed in the power of the ballot as well as in ownership of land, and education in agriculture and the trades. She did all she could to help her people. . . .

THINGS TO DO
Make a list of words in the story ending in -ly, -ing, -ed, -s and find out what they mean.

QUESTIONS TO DISCUSS
1. Why do you think Sojourner spoke against slavery?

2. In what ways did she help her people?

3. Is the ballot still powerful?

PLANNING A VOTER REGISTRATION CAMPAIGN
A good citizen must be a registered voter. But the job does not stop there. We cannot rest until every citizen is a registered voter. You have been helped to register through this citizenship course. It is now your turn to help your neighbors. Plan a registration drive for your neighborhood or community:

1. Select a site (neighborhood or town) _____

2. What is the size of the Negro population? _____

3. Number of Registered Voters _____

4. Number of Negroes of Voting age _____

5. How many can we get to register? _____

6. During what period of time? (state dates) _____

7. Area of Concentration _____

8. Number of Volunteer Workers needed to cover area _____

9. Organizations to take part in the drive (churches, voter's leagues, youth groups, clubs) _____

SUGGESTED STEPS FOR A BLOCK PARTY

Have a meeting at your home to help your neighbors to understand the importance of voting, how to register, and where to register.

1. Invite every adult on your street, from corner to corner (In rural communities, select all houses within walking distance) to come to your home for an evening of information and fellowship.

2. Have Voter Registration information and material on hand.

3. Have someone there who can talk on why, how and where to register.

4. Following speaker, have a discussion on some of your community problems and how voting can help solve them.

5. Tell why your block should have 100% voters.

6. Plan a meeting for the next week to give help to each other. (If possible, arrange to start a Citizenship School.)

7. Plan trips to take people down to register when they are ready.

8. Have someone contact the persons who did not show up at the meeting.

FREEDOM SONGS TO READ AND SING [LYRICS ORIGINALLY INCLUDED]

We Shall Overcome
Oh Freedom
Woke Up This Morning
Keep Your Eyes On The Prize
The Hammer Song
Didn't My Lord Deliver Daniel
Done Made My Vow To Be Free
We Are Soldiers In The Army

Southern Christian Leadership Conference Citizenship School Questionnaire 1965 (excerpts)

- Are you registered?
- Have you ever voted?

- Are you working?

- Where are you working?

- What type of work do you do?

- How much money do you earn? Day $____ Week $____

- Are you married?

- If you have children, how many?

- How many sisters and brothers do you have? ____Sisters ____ Brothers

- How many of your sisters and brothers have left your home area? Where did they go? Why do you think they left?

- How many of your children have left home?

- Where did they go? Why do you think they left?

- If you are not working, but have a family, how do you support your family?

PROBLEMS

In what way do you believe Negro people could be helped to become first-class American citizens?.

What would be most helpful? (Check four of the most important ones in order 1, 2, 3, 4)

- Guaranteed minimum-wage by government

- Adult-literacy classes

- Pre-kindergarten preparatory schools

- Adult-retraining schools

- Medical clinics

- Federal registrars—poll watchers

- Legal help and lawyers provided to communities upon request

- Child-care clinics for working mothers

- Economic aid to provide school children with clothes, spending money, etc.

Who are the strong Negro leaders in your community? (You don't have to mention them by name, check) Ministers, Teachers, Businessmen, Local People, Other

What conditions seem to bother you the most?

- How can these conditions be changed?
- Has the workshop been helpful to you? Explain.
- How can the workshop be improved?

See Activity 4.2 Heroes of the Past in the Appendix

1964 Freedom School Curriculum Links:

Unit III: Examining the Apparent Reality (Myths about the Negro)

www.educationanddemocracy.org/FSCfiles/C_CCl_Units1to6.htm#Unit3

Guide to Negro History

www.educationanddemocracy.org/FSCfiles/C_CC3a_GuideNegroHistory.htm

Development of Negro Power

www.educationanddemocracy.org/FSCfiles/C_CC3f_DevelopmOfNegroPower. htm. In the Freedom School in Mississippi in 1964, Negro history became a favorite of the students, because it was the first time they heard about their own history.

4.D Annelle Ponder:
The Citizen Education Program in Mississippi

Questions to help you adopt a critical stance while reading the section below:

1. *Why do Septima Clark and Annelle Ponder think that it is important to read and write?*

2. *The evaluation form of the SCLC Citizenship School says "graduation" meant taking an active role in the community. Does your school support that model? If playing an active role in the community were a requirement for graduation, would you be (have been) able to graduate?*

CITIZENSHIP EDUCATION PROGRAM

The SCLC Citizenship Schools served as direct support for the voter registration process in Mississippi and for Freedom Summer. Annelle Ponder, a recent college graduate employed by the SCLC to start the Citizenship Education Program (CEP) in Mississippi, arrived in Greenwood in February of 1963. Ponder was assisted in organizing early classes by James Bevel, SCLC representative in Cleveland. Having arrived four days after the shooting of SNCC worker Jimmy Travis, Miss Ponder immediately became aware of the fear "which gripped the Negro community, almost totally immobilizing the middle class who would have nothing to do with the movement."[68] Her efforts were further frustrated by the threatened withdrawal of commodities on which local sharecroppers were dependent during winter. Violent assaults and official harassment were constants. "Yet in spite of these problems, the workers and the people of the Delta continue steadfast and hopeful," she reported. "And I write about them, because it is from them, working day after day, early and late, that I have received the inspiration, the will, and the hope which have helped to make possible the realization of a citizenship program in the area. . . ."[69] Ponder considered the CEP part of the general voter registration work in the Delta. The classes were significant because they stressed the concept of "first class citizenship," the "motivations toward freedom and human dignity which the adult citizens bring with them to the program."[70]

In memos to CEP teachers, Ponder indicated that she regarded the Citizens Education Program, the voter registration drive, and Freedom Summer part of a single effort. In an April 2, 1964 memo, she wrote, "I know that you are aware of the fact that Negroes will be running for office during the summer months. I hope that you and CEP participants will support the candidates and the Freedom Summer Program in every way possible (canvass for registration, serve as deputy registrars, provide housing for out-of-town workers, continue to attempt bonafide registration at your County Court house, etc."[71] On June 1, she encouraged CEP teachers to assist with conducting precinct workshops, securing deputy registrars for freedom registration, finding buildings for community centers and Freedom Schools, and locating housing for summer volunteers. "One additional suggestion," she wrote,

> Try to work with the Freedom Schools to form a Freedom baseball team. We will try to arrange for transportation and have a Freedom league, Batesville and Leake County already have these teams and others are organizing. This is a very promising direction for the COFO program. Please encourage any kind of contact between the young people of different towns. It's worth a lot of work to build up a group of young people across the state who know each other and work together.[72]

The importance of the experience became clear in letters from teachers and writings by students. One retired school teacher was among the first to respond to the need to train Mississippians for "first class citizenship." One of the 'best teachers in the Mississippi Delta,' she began active participation in the Mississippi Freedom Democratic Party (MFDP), soon applying to run for mayor of the city of Greenwood on the MFDP ticket. Of her work, she wrote to the SCLC office, "I get joy out of so doing, as the more difficulties one has in life, the greater his success. I do not mind the expense of travel, for I know there is a reckoning day ahead."[73] Another teacher listed her activities for a two-week period: "On Mondays and Fridays evening, I worked with the youth group. Tuesdays and Thursdays canvassing, Wednesdays, Fridays, and Saturday mornings, take groups to register. Thursdays and Friday nights, citizenship class." She also reported a boycott of a local white store whose manager was rude to black customers. "Shot a Negro woman for speaking about him discourteous," she reported. An elderly woman, too ill to teach, offered her large house to the citizenship school program if they would pay utilities.[74]

Students and teachers shared their views of the citizenship schools and some of their poetry in newsletters. "I think this is about the best movement that has come to Greenwood on behalf of the Negro race," wrote one student. "If people can come from distant places trying to help us why can't we try to help ourselves? So please go to the courthouse and register to vote." Another wrote, "I have gotten 14 members of my class to go down and register to vote, and they are very happy over it. Many people have planned to register but are afraid of the officers. I wish that every teacher who hasn't voted would go down and register."[75]

See Activity 4.3   The Role of Teachers in the Appendix

ANNELLE PONDER

"After the beating Annelle Ponder's face was swollen and she had a black eye. She could barely talk, but she looked at me and whispered, 'Freedom.'"[76]

The SCLC Citizenship Program was one area of the early Civil Rights Movement in which women exercised considerable authority. Under the leadership of Septima Clark, Dorothy Cotton, and Andrew Young, the program was administered by able field supervisors like Annelle Ponder. Despite threats of violence and economic reprisals, Ponder recruited eight citizenship school teachers, all of them women, "ranging in age from nineteen to well over sixty." The eight "braved the jeers and criticism of their neighbors who would take no part in the 'mess' which we were stirring up, worked hard to master the course, and received their certificates at a mass meeting on March 25," wrote Ponder. This early group consisted of one retired school teacher, four housewives, one elderly woman who supplemented her social security with work as a domestic, and two young women in their late teens or early twenties. Many opened their homes to CEP classes because public facilities were closed to them. One landlord threatened a 65 year-old female tenant with eviction if she continued holding classes in her home. The tenant told the landlord that she

> was going to continue her meetings, she said she hoped to [increase the participation from 5 to] ten people at the next meeting and he could put her out if he wanted to. (In the face of this courage and determination, the landlord backed down and has not bothered this teacher anymore.)[77]

The women who taught in the Citizenship Schools were subject to the same threats and intimidation as the voter registration workers in SNCC, yet they continued, successfully, to teach and to work toward increased voter registration. "In spite of all the harassment's, reprisals, and intimidations," wrote Ponder, "over 1300 Negroes in Leflore County have attempted to register to vote since the beginning of March." Teachers not only held classes but they canvassed communities, helped to organize block parties, worked at voter registration headquarters, went to jail, signed property bonds for other's bail, and walked voters to the polls.[78]

It was while returning from a CEP training session in Charleston, South Carolina, that Mrs. Fannie Lou Hamer, Annelle Ponder, and their companions were arrested and beaten in Winona, Mississippi. When the group reached Winona, they attempted to desegregate the facilities at the bus station. Annelle Ponder remembers:

> Three or four of us got off the bus and went in the cafe to be served, and we sat down at the lunch counter and when we sat down there were two waitresses

back of the counter and one of them just balled up her dishcloth. . .and threw it against the wall behind us. She said, "I can't take no more," and so right after she said that, the chief of police and the highway patrolman came from the rear area of the cafe and came around and tapped us on the shoulder with the billy clubs. Said, "Ya'll get out. Get out."

Ponder responded, "You know it's against the law to put us out of here, don't you?" The patrolman replied, "Ain't no damn law, you just get out of here!"[79]

The women were taken to cells and then removed for questioning. Ponder was ordered to call the police officer "Sir." When she responded that she didn't know him well enough to call him "Sir," she was beaten "by at least three of them. . .with blackjacks, a belt, fists, open palm and at one point the highway patrolman hit me in the stomach. . . . They really wanted to make me say 'yes, sir,' and that's one thing I wouldn't say."[80] Concerned that some members of the party had not phoned in as usual, SNCC worked diligently for information as to the whereabouts of the missing women, finding out they had been jailed. Visitors were allowed to see the prisoners the day after their arrest. One reporter noted that Annelle Ponder's face "was swollen and she had a black eye. She could barely talk, but she looked at me and whispered, "Freedom.'"[81] The group was released from prison after three days.

FIVE

Student Nonviolent Coordinating Committee (SNCC)

Questions to help you adopt a critical stance while reading the section below:

1. *What are the characteristics of SNCC in terms of history, strategy, and membership?*

2. *Why did the Nashville students begin their protests by sitting down at "white" lunch counters? What is the theory determining such a strategy?*

3. *What factors caused African American college students to become involved in direct action in the early 1960s? What do you think their parents thought? Did nonviolence serve to heal divisions within African American life as well as between blacks and whites?*

Recommended Film:

February One: The Story of the Greensboro Four *(Documentary; 55min, 2005; produced by Rebecca Cerese). On February 1, 1960, four college students staged a sit-in at a Woolworth's lunch counter in Greensboro, North Carolina, a pivotal event leading to the formation of SNCC.*

THE STUDENT NONVIOLENT COORDINATING COMMITTEE developed out of two grassroots movements from 1959–1960—the Greensboro Sit-Ins and the Nashville Movement. From the founding conference of SNCC at Shaw University in 1960 to it's central role in mobilizing to create the Mississippi Democratic Party in 1964, SNCC promoted a concept of leadership that differed significantly from that of CORE and SCLC. Ella Baker articulated SNCC's concept of leadership as "group-centered" in contrast to the "leader-centered group pattern of organization" of the more established groups. This concept of leadership influenced the evolution of the organization. When SNCC leaders left their campuses and local communities to become full-time organizers (called "freedom fighters" by the communities in which they worked), they did not do so with the intention of creating SNCC local chapters, as CORE did, nor offer support to already established organizations, as SCLC did. Instead, SNCC activists focused on building grassroots leadership and indigenous organizations that would carry on the struggle after SNCC organizers moved on. Hoping to create organizations that represented the majority of a community and not just the elite, SNCC organizers recruited and trained leaders from the bottom rather than the top of black society. SNCC organizers were instrumental in creating the local organizations that eventually knitted together the Mississippi Freedom Democratic Party as well as creating organizations that advanced the political and economic interests of the tenant farmers, sharecroppers, maids, and laborers.

While SNCC's concept of leadership and organizational strategy were distinctive, the direct action tactics used by the Greensboro and Nashville students in 1960 were not invented by them. The young SNCC organizers who employed the tactics of sit-ins, jail-ins, kneel-ins and similar nonviolent tactics throughout the Civil Rights era were using the same tactics that both the labor movement and the women's suffrage movement had used in the past. The Industrial Workers of the World experimented with both the sit-down strike, jail-ins and slowdowns. The Woman's Party in 1917 employed the tactic of silent pickets and hunger strikes. The labor, feminist and Civil Rights movements, as they developed, experienced tensions between a leadership that felt uncomfortable with direct action and grassroots leaders who felt impatient with the slow pace of working within the political system. But an honest appraisal of how social movements happen indicates that both direct action and the slow and tedious work of canvassing, lobbying, and filing law suits are all needed in order to produce fundamental change.

THE GREENSBORO SIT-INS

In the fall of 1959, four students at the North Carolina Agricultural and Technical College (NCA&T) sat in their dormitory rooms at night discussing the central contradiction of their lives. What good were the ideas they were learning in college, when their ambitions were so arbitrarily limited by the laws of the Jim Crow South? One of the students, Ezell Blair, Jr., whose father was a member of the NAACP, had recently been intrigued by a television documentary on Gandhi. The four young men decided on a course of action: they would sit-in at a local segregated lunch counter.

At four-thirty P.M., on February 1, 1960, the students entered the local Woolworth's, purchased school supplies, and requested receipts. Resolved to be courteous but firm, the four—Blair, David Richmond, Joseph McNeill, and Franklin McCain—seated themselves at the store's "white" lunch counter. Blair politely attempted to place an order. The students were refused, but remained seated. Responses from white patrons ranged from fury to encouragement; the four young men were ignored by the management and the police. Although they were not served, they remained until the store closed. The next day, twenty NCA&T students joined the original four; white students joined the protest on the third day. The movement spread rapidly, prompting demonstrations first in other North Carolina communities and then throughout the South.

Of the sit-ins, Lillian Smith, white Southern author and long-time critic of segregation, wrote,

> For me, it is as if the *No Exit* sign is about to come down from our age. It is the beginning of new things, of a new kind of leadership. If the white students will join in ever-increasing numbers with these Negro students, change will come; their experience of suffering and working together for what they know is right; the self-discipline, the refusal to act in violence or think in violence will bring a new spiritual life not only to our region but to our entire country.[1]

THE NASHVILLE MOVEMENT

Under the tutelage of minister and activist James Lawson, a group of students in Nashville also had begun preparing for direct action in the fall of 1959. Lawson conducted training workshops in nonviolence in the basement of Clark Memorial Methodist Church on Tuesday nights, workshops that attracted students from Fisk, Meharry Medical College, and American Baptist Theological Seminary. Among these students were John Lewis, James Bevel, Bernard Lafayette, and Diane Nash. In addition to teaching the workshops, Lawson had visited churches and community centers to ask local people which specific form of segregation troubled them most. Most named segregation in lunch counters located in stores where most black Nashville residents shopped. So, on November 28, 1959, the students made their first test of Jim Crow in Nashville. Diane Nash led a racially mixed group of well-dressed, orderly students to Harvey's, a popular downtown department store, where they made a small purchase, establishing themselves as store patrons. The students proceeded then to the lunch counter and seated themselves. Nash, the appointed spokesperson for the group, requested service. When she was refused, she asked to speak to the manager, who also refused the group service. Nash requested service for the white students, and was told that, because they were accompanying the black students, they could not be served. Nash thanked the manager and the group left the store. The following Saturday, a group of eight students approached the lunch counter at Cain-Sloan, another Nashville store, and met with a similar response.

"These tests," explained John Lewis, "were a prelude to a massive assault, a series of sit-ins that would involve hundreds of students. How many sit-ins for how long a time would depend on the response of the stores and the city. We would not stop until the policy of segregation at those counters was ended. It was that simple."[2]

During the month of January, attendance at Lawson's workshops increased, and both black and white students trained in techniques of non-violent resistance. After hearing of the Greensboro sit-ins, the Nashville students became even more impatient for their first real demonstration. The week after the events in Greensboro, during a meeting attended by more than five hundred students at Fisk University, Lawson asked for volunteers for a massive sit-in effort in all of Nashville's department stores. On February 13, 1960, a group of one hundred and twenty five students marched to downtown Nashville occupying several lunch counters. Although the counters were immediately closed, the students remained, reading or doing homework quietly until 6 P.M. The following Saturday, three hundred and forty students sat in. The store owners requested a moratorium on sit-ins until they could draft a proposal; Lawson granted their request. The store owners failed to produce a proposal, but the police chief announced that all participants in sit-ins would be arrested. In spite of hecklers, the students resumed the sit-ins.

Because the ranks of student volunteers were growing rapidly, John Lewis and fellow ABT student Bernard Lafayette typed up a list of guidelines for the new recruits:

DO NOT:

1. Strike back or curse if abused.

2. Laugh out.

3. Hold conversations with floor walker.

4. Leave your seat until your leader has given permission for you to do so.

5. Block entrances to stores outside or the aisles inside.

DO:

1. Show yourself friendly and courteous at all times.

2. Sit straight; always face the counter.

3. Report all serious incidents to your leader.

4. Refer information seekers to your leader in a polite manner.

5. Remember the teachings of Jesus Christ, Mahatma Gandhi, and Martin Luther King. Love and nonviolence is the way.

MAY GOD BLESS EACH OF YOU.[3]

When the demonstrations resumed, the protestors were greeted with taunts, attacks, and ridicule. Some had ketchup and mustard poured on their heads, and a white demonstrator was pulled from his seat and beaten by a group of whites. The contrast between the orderly demonstrators and the jeering, grimacing crowds of hecklers was noted even by newspapers who endorsed segregation.

Here were the colored students, in coats, white shirts, ties, and one of them was reading Goethe and one was taking notes from a biology text. And here, on the sidewalk outside, was a gang of white boys come to heckle, a ragtail rabble, slack-jawed, black-jacketed, grinning fit to kill, and some of them, God save the mark, were waving the proud and honored flag of the Southern states in the last war fought by gentlemen. Eheu! It gives one pause.[4]

The first group of students was arrested in Nashville on February 27. These were immediately replaced by another group, which was also arrested. This process continued until eighty-one students were arrested that day. "We hadn't been in jail more than a half hour," said Paul La Prad, "before food was sent into us by the Negro merchants. A call for bail was issued to the Negro community and within a couple of hours there was twice the amount needed."[5]

At the students' trial, the judge found them guilty on charges of disorderly conduct. Members of the group were fined fifty dollars and court costs, and several were rearrested on charges of "conspiracy to obstruct trade and commerce."[6] More student demonstrators were arrested after sitting-in at Nashville Greyhound and Trailways bus stations.

Because a network camera crew was filming the demonstrations, Tennessee Governor Buford Ellington charged that the sit-ins were "instigated and planned by and staged for the convenience of the Columbia Broadcast System."[7] A committee appointed by the Mayor continued to negotiate with the demonstrators. On April 5, the committee suggested that stores "make available to all customers a portion of restaurant facilities now operated exclusively for white customers" and that charges against demonstrators be dropped.[8] The students rejected this proposal. "The suggestion of a restricted area," they replied, "involves the same stigma of which we are earnestly trying to rid the community. The plan presented by the Mayor's Committee ignores the moral issues involved in the struggle for human rights."[9]

On April 11, the students resumed their demonstrations. The black community of Nashville, maintaining their Easter Week boycott, flexed their economic power by seriously damaging the downtown merchants during one of their most profitable seasons. On April 19, the home of African American attorney Z. Alexander Looby was bombed. In response, a group of nearly two thousand students and local citizens marched on City Hall to confront Mayor Ben West.

"You all have the power to destroy this city," the Mayor told the demonstrators. "So let's not have any mobs."

After stating that he had no power to force restaurant owners to serve anyone they did not want to serve, West suggested, "Let's all pray together." Someone in the crowd shouted, "How about *eating* together?"

Diane Nash stepped from the crowd and asked the Mayor to use "the prestige of your office to appeal to the citizens to stop racial discrimination."

"I appeal to all citizens," he replied, "to end discrimination, to have no bigotry, no bias, no hatred."

"Do you mean that to include lunch counters?" Nash asked.

"Little lady," West retorted, "I stopped segregation seven years ago at the airport when I first took office, and there has been no trouble there since."

"Then, Mayor," Nash continued. "Do you recommend that the lunch counters be desegregated?"

"Yes," replied West.[10]

The next night, Martin Luther King arrived in Nashville and addressed an audience that had filled the Fisk University gym to capacity. "I came to Nashville not to bring inspiration," King said, "but to gain inspiration from the great movement that has taken place in this community. . . . No lie can live forever. Let us not despair. The universe is with us. Walk together, children. Don't get weary."[11] On May 10, 1960, Nashville lunch counters served meals to black customers for the first time in the city's history.[12]

THE FOUNDING OF SNCC

The Nashville students were not the only young people moved by the Greensboro sit-ins. Similar demonstrations spread rapidly throughout the South—Raleigh, Durham, and Fayetteville, North Carolina; Chattanooga, Tennessee; Atlanta, George; Montgomery, Alabama; and Tallahassee, Florida, among other places. In New York and New Haven, sympathizers picketed Woolworth's to exert pressure on the store chain. Ella Baker, an NAACP and SCLC veteran decided that it was time to organize these many efforts, and at the same time saw an opportunity to develop leadership "among other people." In a letter to all major protest groups, signed by herself and King, she asked them to send representatives to a meeting at her alma mater, Shaw University in Raleigh, North Carolina, April 16–18, 1960.

Baker and King assured the youthful activists that "Adult Freedom Fighters will be present for counsel and guidance, but the meeting will be youth-centered."[13] A week before the conference, Ella Baker requested the individual stories of student activists planning to attend the Shaw Conference. "We need—YOUR STORY!" began her letter. "Write the story up in your own way," she advised, "but we suggest that you will, no doubt, want to cover the following questions:"

1. How, when, and by whom were your demonstrations started?

2. What was the reaction of (1) student body, (2) parents, (3) faculty, (4) President and governing board?

3. How have the police and public officials reacted?

4. How has the white community reacted?

5. Have any efforts been made to set up bi-racial or student committees to negotiate with businesses and others involved?

6. Have any businesses or public facilities changed their discriminatory practices?

7. What are your plans now?[14]

The students arrived at Shaw University on Friday April 16, 1960. On Saturday, the students led a panel discussion followed by workshops. Suggested topics for workshop discussions were:

1. Advantages and Disadvantages: of Mass Demonstrations of Small Sit-ins.

2. "Jail vs. Bail". . .Going to Jail with a Purpose.

3. Where Picketing and Economic Pressure are Useful.

4. Dangers, Limitations, and Potentials of the Legal Approach.

5. Philosophy and Techniques of Nonviolence.[15]

A Saturday evening discussion session was led by Martin Luther King, and the students ended their meeting with a luncheon and press conference early Sunday afternoon. With Ella Baker's support, they created the "Student Nonviolent Coordinating Committee."

At the organization's founding conference at Shaw University, students also established a newspaper, *The Student Voice*. From the beginning, the students in SNCC understood the power of the press. Media coverage of the sit-ins helped create a mass movement. From Diane Nash's dramatic confrontation with Mayor Ben West to the assault of Tougaloo College students and faculty at the Woolworth's lunch counter in Jackson, Mississippi, the press captured moments that defined, recorded, and extended the sit-in movement. When SNCC extended its activities into the Deep South, embattled field workers hoped that journalists could bring public attention to injustice, which had thrived on secrecy. Directed by Julian Bond and Mary King, SNCC's communications department issued press releases and produced SNCC's newspaper. Bond brought to *The Student Voice* skills as both a journalist and a poet. The newspaper's first issue, published in June 1960, featured one of Bond's poems:

> *I, too, hear America singing*
> *But from where I stand*
> *I can only hear Little Richard*
> *And Fats Domino.*
> *But sometimes,*
> *I hear Ray Charles*
> *Drowning in his own tears*
> *or Bird*
> *Relaxing at Camarillo*
> *or Horace Silver doodling,*
> *Then I don't mind standing a little longer.*[16]

See Activity 5.1 Convene a Student Conference in the Appendix

Freedom School Curriculum Link:
Unit VII, Part 1, Freedom Rides and Sit-Ins
www.educationanddemocracy.org/FSCfiles/C_CC7_UnitVII.htm
This unit of the Citizenship Curriculum tells the story of the new Southern Civil Rights movement.

5.A Ella Baker: Developing Leadership

Questions to help you adopt a critical stance while reading the section below:
1. Of what importance was Baker's experience with the NAACP? Can networks be created without bureaucracy? Can there be political movements without networks?

2. Do you have any personal experiences (or second hand knowledge) that either support or contradict Ella Baker's critique of leaders?

3. How did each of the four major Civil Rights organizations define leadership?

4. Do you have activities at school that are student run? How much influence do the students have in your school's "student-run" clubs, groups or activities? What kinds of student-run activities do you think the school administration would not allow to exist?

5. Why does the statement "If we forget the importance of means, then we shall not obtain goals" connect to the specific organizational structure of SNCC?

Recommended Film:

Fundi: The Story of Ella Baker (Documentary, 48 minutes, 1986; directed by Joanne Grant)

ELLA BAKER

"I have always felt it was a handicap for oppressed peoples to depend so largely upon a leader, because unfortunately in our culture, the charismatic leader usually becomes a leader because he has found a spot in the public limelight. It usually means he has been touted through the public media, which made him, and the media may undo him. . . Such people get so involved with playing the game of being important that they exhaust themselves and their time, and they don't do the work of actually organizing people."[17]

Born in Virginia in 1905, Ella Baker learned early the principles that she would apply in her work for civil rights. Baker believed strongly in communities who achieved self-sufficiency through sharing; throughout her life, she remained skeptical of the type of leadership that robbed people of their initiative and right to act autonomously. It was this vision she communicated to the young people in SNCC; in this way, she served as a bridge between the visions of community of the rural south and the political activism of the SNCC workers. Historian Charles Payne wrote, "The young activists of the 1960s trying to work within the organizing tradition were bringing back to the rural Black South a refined, codified version of something that had begun there, an expression of the historical vision of ex-slaves, men and women who understood that, for them, maintaining a deep sense of community was itself an act of resistance."[18]

After graduating from Shaw University, Baker went to New York during the Depression to work as a community organizer, joining the Young Negroes Cooperative League, a consumer group that hoped to establish cooperative buying practices among African Americans. "With the Depression," she said, "I began to see that there were certain social forces over which the individual had very little control. . .I began to identify. . .with the unemployed."[19] Later, she became assistant field secretary for the NAACP, traveling frequently through the South to organize work at local branches. "At that time, the NAACP was the leader on the cutting edge of social change. I remember when NAACP membership in the South was the basis for getting beaten up or even killed."[20] Although Baker questioned the bureaucratic style of leadership in the NAACP, through her field work she was able to establish a network of relationships that proved invaluable in later civil rights work. Sent by the NAACP to assist at a meeting of the newly formed SCLC in 1958, Baker stayed to organize the SCLC's headquarters in Atlanta. Because of her questions about King's style of charismatic leadership, Baker was considering resigning from this position. "There would never be any role for me in a leadership capacity with SCLC. Why? First, I'm a woman. Also, I'm not a minister. And second. . .I knew that my penchant for speaking honestly. . .would not be well tolerated."[21] When the student sit-ins arose, Baker felt that experienced activists should offer their support without assuming control. "I believe in the right of people to expect those who are older, those who claim to have had more experience, to help them grow."[22]

Among the local activists Baker had met during her years traveling for the NAACP was Amzie Moore. Baker was one of the founders of In Friendship, an organization that raised money to provide economic assistance to activists in the South suffering economic reprisals, which included the failure to distribute federal food aid to the poor if they registered to vote. In Friendship was able to assist Moore and to provide clothing for distribution to the poor in Mississippi. Believing that it was crucial for activists like Amzie Moore to remain in Mississippi, Baker arranged speaking engagements for Moore outside of the South, so that he could share his experiences and help to end the isolation of civil rights workers in Mississippi.

In the summer of 1964, Baker played a significant role in the organization of the Mississippi Freedom Democratic Party (MFDP). In her address to the MFDP state convention in August, she described the party as "a demonstration of the people of Mississippi that they are determined to be a part of the body politic of Mississippi. We are here to demonstrate the right of the governed to elect those who govern, *here,* in *this* state. . . . It has never been true that the Negro people were satisfied. It was never true even in the darkest days of slavery."[23]

After her speech at the MFDP convention in Jackson, Mississippi, Baker moved to Washington to help the MFDP prepare for their attempt to be seated, that is, to be acknowledged as the official representatives of Mississippi Democrats by the national Democratic Party at the National Convention in Atlantic City in August. She expressed her hope that "hundreds of Democrats" would join forces and "face up to the fact that only a renegade democratic party exists in Mississippi which enjoys the benefits of national affiliation but spurns all responsibilities and can only continue to bring disgrace to the National Democratic Party."[24] Baker later argued that if the debate over seating had been brought to the convention floor instead of decided behind closed doors, the MFDP would have had a chance of being seated. "But I knew enough about political chicanery to know that if a vote is likely to go against the powers that be, they try to find ways of keeping those things from coming to a vote. And so, this is what they did."[25]

Throughout her many years of activism, Baker remained a staunch advocate of inclusiveness within the movement and of the inherent value of every individual. "We need to penetrate the mystery of life and perfect the mastery of life and the latter requires understanding that human beings are human beings."[26]

DEVELOPING LEADERSHIP

Baker organized SNCC's founding conference, held at Shaw University, April, 1960. She was unwavering in her encouragement of the students' autonomy and resisted their co-optation by one of the established Civil Rights organizations. What Baker felt was needed in social movements was "the development of people not who are interested in being leaders as much as in developing leadership among other people."[27] "And after SNCC came into existence, of course, it opened up a new era of struggle. I felt the urge to stay close by. Because if I had done anything anywhere, it had been largely in the role of supporting things, and in the background of things that needed to be done for the organizations that were supposedly out front."[28]

Although the more established and influential Civil Rights organizations hoped to appropriate the fledgling student group as a youth branch, Ella Baker insisted on the right of the students to maintain their autonomy. SNCC resisted the bureaucratic structure of the established adult groups, preferring instead loose organization and a consensus style of decision making. The students established an organization that was very different from the established groups. Baker described that difference as one of "group-centered leadership" versus "leader centered group pattern of organization." A SNCC pamphlet in 1960 warned its members of the dangers that organizations fall into, one of which was that leaders tend to become more interested in perpetuating their own leadership rather than keeping the focus on the goals of the organization.

Document 5.1   Ella Baker: "Bigger than a Hamburger" [29]

RALEIGH, N.C., June 1960—The Student Leadership Conference made it crystal clear that current sit-ins and other demonstrations are concerned with something much bigger than a hamburger or even a giant-sized coke. . .it is important to keep the movement democratic and to avoid struggles for personal leadership.

It was further evident that desire for supportive co-operation from adult leaders and the adult community was also tempered by apprehension that adults might try to "capture" the student movement. The students showed willingness to be met on the basis of equality, but were intolerant of anything that smacked of manipulation or domination.

This inclination toward *group-centered leadership,* rather than toward a *leader centered group pattern of organization,* was refreshing indeed to those of the older group who bear the scars of the battle, the frustrations and the disillusionment that come when the prophetic leader turns out to have heavy feet of clay.

However hopeful might be the signs in the direction of group centeredness, the fact that many schools and communities; especially in the South, have not provided adequate experience for young Negroes to assume initiative and think and act independently accentuated the need for guarding the student movement against well-meaning, but nevertheless unhealthy, over-protectiveness.

Here is an opportunity for adult and youth to work together and provide genuine leadership—the development of the individual to his highest potential for the benefit of the group. . .

MEANS AND ENDS

A SNCC document of October 1960 states: If we forget the importance of means, then we shall not obtain goals. If we use the movement as an abstract cause, as a way to quick glory, as a dramatic device to manipulate—then we cheat. If our concern is that we, as chairman of such and such a group, be re-elected chairman, be given publicity, be asked to speak all over the nation—then we, too, are victims of the same kind of fear that has built segregation. . . . The using of the movement for personal security is a very present danger. This must not happen. . .because it would kill the movement and forever prevent the reaching of being and the redemptive community.[30]

5.B   Bob Moses: Voter Registration

Questions to help you adopt a critical stance while reading the section below:
1. *Why did Moore and Moses agree that voter registration should be the focus of SNCC's organizing in Mississippi? Was voter registration as a tactic consistent with SNCC's concept of leadership development?*

2. *Why is it important to vote? Why did people risk their lives to be allowed to vote? Do you think people would do the same today?*

Further information:
The current Federal Voting Rights Law is at www.usdoj.gov/crt/voting/intro/intro. htm

Recommended Film:
Freedom Song (Docu-Drama; 110 min, 2000; directed by Phil Alden Robinson). The story of the Civil-Rights Movement as seen through the eyes of a teenage Owen Walker growing up in bigotry laden Mississippi in the 1960s at a time when Jim Crow segregation laws were legal. Based on accounts of Student Nonviolent Coordinating Committee members who worked in Mississippi, and featuring trainings in nonviolence.

BOB MOSES

"This is a tremor from the middle of the iceberg—from a stone that the build-ers rejected."[31]

Robert Parris Moses was a philosopher who tested his convictions in the crucible of rural Mississippi. The son of a Harlem janitor, Moses was a graduate of Stuyvesant High School, Hamilton College, and Harvard University. Moses was teaching math at the Horace Mann School in the Bronx when he read of voter registration struggles in Mississippi in the early 1960s. During his summer vacation, he took the bus to Mississippi and began investigating abuses in voter registration.

Moses' philosophical connection to nonviolence was not Christianity but existentialism, particularly the work of Albert Camus. In 1964, he commented during an interview:

> When I was in jail this last time I read through *The Rebel* and *The Plague* again. The main essence of what he [Camus] says is what I feel. . .closest to. It's not a question that you just subjugate yourself to the conditions that are and don't try to change them. The problem is to go on from there, into something that is active and yet the dichotomy is whether you can cease to be a victim any more and also not be what he calls an executioner. The ideal lies between these two extremes—victim and executioner.[32]

Nonviolence offered a way of social transformation through elevated understanding rather than violent struggle. The vote transformed society through an orderly political process. Both methods were consistent with Moses' search for ways of gaining power without compromising his ethi-cal base. Both offered blacks the opportunity to cease being victims while refusing to become executioners.

Strongly influenced by Ella Baker, Moses embodied the SNCC style of consensus leadership and of participation in local communities. While canvassing for votes, Moses' adopted the denim overalls and white t-shirts of the rural blacks and gradually gained the confidence of potential vot-ers. When asked at a news conference how to involve local people in voter registration, Moses replied, "By bouncing a ball." "What?" "You bounce a ball. You stand on a street and bounce a ball. Soon all the children come around. Before long, it runs under someone's porch and you meet the adults."[33] Amzie Moore described him as "quiet, unassuming, a deep thinker. . .very seldom expressed himself unless asked."[34] During the debate in Atlantic City over the proposed compromise, Fannie Lou Hamer sought Moses' advice. Characteristically, he declined to give it. She recalled that he said, "You grown, you make your own decision."[35]

Moses' reflective style was coupled with remarkable physical courage. After the Greenwood SNCC office was broken into by the Klan, Moses arrived with fellow worker Willie (now Wazir) Peacock who later recalled the moment.

> So we made it there at about 2:00 A.M. We just walked in and Bob Moses went ahead of me into the office. He didn't see anything ruffled up or anything of that nature, so Bob turned the light on in the office, let the couch out and put the covers on, turned the fan on, which makes a lot of noise and went to bed. I was very—I was scared. I just didn't understand what kind of guy this Bob Moses is, that could walk into a place where a lynch mob had just left and make up a bed and prepare to go to sleep, as if the situation was normal. So I guess I was learning and I said, well, if Bob can go to sleep, I can go to sleep, so I guess about five minutes after I got into the bed I was asleep.[36]

Moses imagined that the movement could create a genuine alternative, a movement of rational people who could place themselves beyond the questions of race. By serving as a model, the movement could become the microcosm of a world that transcended race and contained the potential to transform the moral and spiritual bankruptcy of society. His embittering experiences with the brutality and poverty of the lives of rural blacks in Mississippi, coupled with politics of compromise and complacency at the National Democratic Convention in Atlantic City, caused him to question whether this vision could ever be realized. Democratic national leaders like President Lyndon Johnson, Hubert Humphrey and Walter Mondale were able to turn away the MFDP challenge at the Convention, in large part, because too many national delegates were able to be bribed with or threatened by loss of promotions and appointments.

VOTER REGISTRATION

After its founding in 1960, SNCC expanded its activities beyond demonstrations; SNCC workers began moving into rural areas of the South to work with local people to facilitate change. In the summer of 1960, Bob Moses, at the suggestion of Ella Baker, met with Amzie Moore to discuss a strategy for making a permanent change in the state of Mississippi. Impatient with the time-consuming legal approach of the NAACP, Moore welcomed the youth and the commitment of the SNCC workers. Although Moses shared the SNCC philosophy that local leadership should be cultivated, he believed that the degree of oppression suffered by local blacks required the help of outsiders to teach them to demand their rights. Moore and Moses agreed that voter registration should be the focus of SNCC's campaign in Mississippi. Believing that most blacks in Mississippi were too poor to benefit from direct action campaigns to integrate public accommodations, Moore expressed his belief that the ballot box, rather than demonstrations, was the key to addressing the problems of Mississippi's blacks. At the time, only five percent of Mississippi's blacks were registered to vote. The Civil Rights Act of 1957 had established a Commission to ensure protection of voting rights. "The Commission shall," read the law, "investigate allegations in writing under oath that certain citizens of the United States are being deprived of their right to vote. . .by reason of their color, race, religion, or national origin." Further, the 1957 Law provided for prosecution of whites who attempted to interfere with black voters. "No person, whether acting under color of law or otherwise, shall intimidate, threaten, or coerce any other person for the purpose of interfering with the right of such other person to vote or to vote as he may choose. . . ."[37] Supported by the possibility of Federal protection, Moore and Moses formulated the SNCC strategy: empower local blacks by organization, conduct voter education classes, get more voters registered, and seek federal assistance to override local law enforcement. Blacks could then gain the vote and change the local power structure.

However, the SNCC strategy required time, and reprisals for resistance in the South were often immediate and violent. These reprisals, the most feared of which was lynching, had created and maintained the existing system. Victims of Mississippi's shamefully inadequate school systems, Mississippi blacks needed literacy and political education to claim their right to vote.

And when would they receive this training? After working from dawn to dusk (or "cain" see to "cain't" see) in fields or in white people's kitchens? In addition, sharecroppers and domestic workers were economically dependent on whites. Resisters could be fired and even starved. How could they survive during the lengthy period required for education and for voting to take effect? And what about violence? Was the Federal Government willing or able to provide the needed protection? Would the short-term crises prompted by direct action, with its accompanying publicity and demand for immediate intervention, be a more effective tool for creating protection for disenfranchised blacks in rural Mississippi?

With local activists, C.C. Bryant and Webb Moore, Moses established the pattern SNCC used to build voter registration drives in Mississippi. First, SNCC workers moved outward from initial contacts with local leaders. While NAACP efforts had often concentrated on the middle class, SNCC workers approached the entire community. Moses and his small group of canvassers set out for the country, bringing with them voter registration forms. "What do you tell somebody when you go to their door?" wrote Moses. "Well, first you tell them who you are, what you're trying to do, that you're working on voter registration. You have a form that you try to get them to fill out. . . ."[38] At first the SNCC field workers dressed in coats and ties, as had the students in the Nashville sit-ins. When this style proved impractical for trekking through rural areas and seemed to intimidate farm workers, Bob Moses began dressing in t-shirts and overalls, establishing an example, which other canvassers soon followed.

In addition to canvassing, this small number of SNCC workers began holding classes on nonviolence. These activists were routinely arrested on various charges, from disturbing the peace to interfering with the police. On August 7, Moses began holding voter registration classes at the local Masonic temple. At these classes, Moses went over the twenty-one question form and the sections of the Mississippi constitution most likely to appear on the test.[39]

On August 15, Moses accompanied three local citizens to Liberty to register. Although, after delays, the three were allowed to register, they were stopped by a highway patrolman on their way home. At the police station, the patrolman and County Prosecuting Attorney charged Moses with interfering with an officer in the discharge of his duties. Moses was sentenced to serve ninety days in jail. In jail, he phoned the Justice Department, collect, and stated that he was arrested while assisting local citizens with voter registration. Somewhat intimidated, the local authorities suspended his sentence.

After succeeding in adding the names of six black voters to the registration rolls, Moses was invited to conduct similar classes in Amite and Walthall counties. Moses agreed, aware that the SNCC workers were moving into some of Mississippi's most violent counties. "The problem is that you can't be in the position of turning down the tough areas because the people then, I think, would simply lose confidence in you; so, we accepted this."[40] On August 22, in Liberty, Mississippi, he was attacked by a relative of the local sheriff, receiving a head wound, which required eight stitches. Hoping to challenge the use of violent intimidation to discourage black voters, Moses pressed charges. His assailant was acquitted as a crowd of about one hundred whites formed outside of the courthouse.[41] Despite the beating, however, by the end of August, the dozen SNCC organizers at work in southwest Mississippi returned to Liberty to try to register more voters. "We felt it was extremely important that we try and go back to town immediately so the people in that county wouldn't feel that we had been frightened off by the beating and before they could get a chance there to rally their forces," wrote Moses.[42]

SNCC's methods of organizing in the South placed it at odds with more established civil rights groups. According to James Forman, SNCC "believed in sending its staff to work with the most wretched of the earth while some of the organizations thought this a waste of time. It believed in the absolute right of freedom of association while other organizations acted as fearful as McCarthy of communism. It argued for a basic revolution in American society. . .while others always advocated change within the present system."[43]

Questions based on Document 5.2 below:
   1. *How does Guthrie Hood's testimony reveal the limitations of legal solutions to the problem of unequal political participation? What are the obstacles inhibiting Thomas' ability to vote? Which of these obstacles could Hood reasonably deny direct involvement in?*

2. *At what point in each testimony are the commissioners asking for hearsay evidence? For conjecture? Why does a court of law not allow hearsay evidence or conjecture on the part of witnesses? Why does the commission ask for these kinds of evidence? Is the hearsay evidence or conjecture given in these hearings as legitimate or persuasive as the eyewitness testimony?*

3. *How does the framing or nature of the questions asked by the commissioners reveal their biases? Give some examples of such questions and explain what bias(es) are revealed in your selection. Do such biases affect their ability to get at the facts? the truth? Would there be bias if these questions were reworded to sound objective?*

4. *Compare the Bilbo Hearings (Chapter 6) with the 1965 Commission Hearings (document below). How can you explain the differences and similarities? Suggested criteria for comparison:*

   a. *Committee members' attitudes towards witnesses representing the power structure and those outside the power structure.*

   b. *The nature and scope of the complaints to which the committees are listening.*

   c. *The relationship between those complaints and your understanding of the conditions out of which those complaints emerged.*

   d. *Why the hearings were being held.*

Document 5.2   Testimony Before the U.S. Commission on Civil Rights, 1965
TUESDAY MORNING SESSION, FEBRUARY 16, 1965

[The seven members of the Commission represented prominent newspapers, universities and the federal government]

TESTIMONY (EXCERPTS) OF GUTHRIE HAYES HOOD, CIRCUIT CLERK AND
    REGISTRAR, HUMPHREYS COUNTY, MISSISSIPPI

MR. TAYLOR Well, the figures that were given here this morning were that about 68.3 percent of the 3,344 voting age whites were registered to vote and that zero percent, no Negroes of the 5,561 voting age Negroes are registered to vote. Do you have any reason to believe that those figures are incorrect?

MR. HOOD I couldn't answer that, sir. I don't know.

MR. TAYLOR How many Negroes have applied to register during your term of office? About how many?

MR. HOOD During my term of office? About 16.

MR. TAYLOR About 16?

MR. HOOD Yes, sir.

MR. TAYLOR How many of these have succeeded in registering, Mr. Hood?

MR. HOOD None have passed the test.

MR. TAYLOR Has any Negro made any request for a copy of his application?

MR. HOOD Only one has made a request for a copy of his application.

MR. TAYLOR Did you furnish the copy?

MR. HOOD I told him to bring me a written request and the State law allows me $1.50 for a certified copy, and I would be glad to furnish it to him.

MR. TAYLOR If he paid $1.50?

MR. HOOD Yes, sir.

MR. TAYLOR Were you aware at the time that on various occasions police have photographed Negroes outside the door of your office after they applied to register?

MR. HOOD No, sir; I could not answer that because I was trying to run my own office. . . .

MR. TAYLOR Have you heard of any of the testimony given by other witnesses concerning your activities as registrar?. . .

MR. HOOD I heard Mary Thomas and Alene Hunter; yes, sir.

MR. TAYLOR Did you in October of 1964 say anything to the effect—to Mrs. Thomas—that she would be sorry if she came down to register?

MR. HOOD I don't recall saying that; no, sir. . . .

MR. TAYLOR Did you toward the end of October 1964, say to Mrs. Daisy Griffin and Mrs. Mary Oliver Welsh, who came to register, words to the effect that if they registered you would stop their commodities?

MR. HOOD No, sir, I did not.

. . .

COMMISSIONER HESBURGH . . . But I would guess that the way tests are administered, it is possible for no one to ever pass a test. Do you remember a Negro ever passing a test in this State—I mean in your county, rather?

MR. HOOD I cannot answer that. I can only say in my own time since I've been in there.

COMMISSIONER HESBURGH In your own time?

MR. HOOD Yes.

COMMISSIONER HESBURGH There hasn't been a single Negro?

MR. HOOD No, sir; there hasn't been a single one. My blanks there stand up for themselves. I don't have to deny that.

. . .

COMMISSIONER GRISWOLD I hand you a copy of section 182 of the Mississippi constitution. Would you please make a reasonable interpretation of section 182 for the Commission?

(PAUSE). . .

MR. HOOD Well, it means that the power to tax corporations, their property, shall never be surrendered or abridged by any contract. And—

COMMISSIONER GRISWOLD I didn't ask you to read it, Mr. Hood. I asked you to interpret it.

MR. BRIDGES *(Aside to Mr. Hood.)*

COMMISSIONER GRISWOLD Mr. Chairman, I think it should be the witness' interpretation; not his counsel's.

MR. BRIDGES If you please, gentlemen, the conference between the witness and his attorney had nothing to do with the question. It was a question whether he was to answer it or not.

MR. HOOD Which I will not.

MR. BRIDGES Which he will not.

. . .

CHAIRMAN HANNAH Mr. Hood, when a white man comes in to register, do you give them the same section of the constitution, whatever is the next number up?

MR HOOD I do, sir.

CHAIRMAN HANNAH And you ask for an interpretation just the same for the whites?

MR HOOD I do.

CHAIRMAN HANNAH And you believe that the standards of grading, as to whether or not they have given a satisfactory interpretation, you apply alike?

MR HOOD To the best of my ability; yes, sir.

. . .

MR. TAYLOR I would just like to ask one question, Mr. Hood. Do I understand that if a Negro citizen of Humphreys County comes into your office
to register in the future, he can do so without fear of being questioned
about why he's there or without any other—

MR HOOD I have never questioned him why he's there, Mr. Taylor.

MR. TAYLOR And he has nothing to fear about it in the future?

MR HOOD No, sir. . .

TESTIMONY (EXCERPTS) OF MRS. MARY THOMAS, HUMPHREYS COUNTY,
MISSISSIPPI

MR. TAYLOR Have you ever attempted to register to vote?

MRS. THOMAS Yes, I have.

. . .

MR. TAYLOR Can you tell us what happened, Mrs. Thomas, when you got
to the registrar's office?

MRS. THOMAS Well, when we got to the registrar's office, we walked in and
one of the COFO workers stepped in behind, and the chancery clerk
looked up and saw he was in the room and he demanded that he leave
the room, and so he did. And then he asked us what did we want, and
I stepped to the desk and told him that I came down to register to vote.
And he asked me my name, my address, how old I was, and how long
had I lived in Mississippi. And I told him.

MR. TAYLOR And then what happened?

MRS. THOMAS Then he said why did we come down; why did we let those
boys bring us down. We didn't say anything. He said, "Well, why didn't
you come alone?" We still didn't say anything. So then he opened the
desk and got the blank and a card with the 66th amendment of Mississippi, and he told me to come on around the desk and go in there and
have a seat. And then when he had finished with the other lady, she
got in, he said, "Well, haven't we all been good to you all?" He said,
"We've always given you commodity, and any time you say you wanted
money or needed money, we would give it to you." So we didn't say
anything. Then I decided I would read my blank and start filling in my
questions. And he sat at the end of the table and steadily picked on the
table until we were finished.

MR. TAYLOR What happened after you finished?

MRS. THOMAS Well, after we finished we passed our blanks in and he told us that he would have to run our name in the Banner for 2 weeks and then he would let us know if we passed.

· · ·

MRS. THOMAS Yes, I guess about 15 minutes after I arrived home from the courthouse, the deputy sheriff came in and told me he had a warrant for my arrest.

MR. TAYLOR Did he say what he was arresting you for?

MRS. THOMAS Yes. He said he had a warrant for my arrest for selling beer without a license.

MR. TAYLOR Did you have a license to sell beer?

MRS. THOMAS Yes, I had the city license, the State permit, and the Federal stamp. And I live within the city limits, and I had been operating for about 8 years or longer, and I had never bought a county license. So I didn't know about county license, so that's what I was fined for: County license.

MR. TAYLOR Did the sheriff know that you had been involved with Civil Rights workers before your arrest?

MRS. THOMAS Yes, I would say that he did.

· · ·

MR. TAYLOR What happened to you after you were arrested?

MRS. THOMAS Well, after I was arrested, the deputy carried me on down and he opened the cell door and I stepped in, and he turned the key on the door. He told me "Your bond is $1,000 if you want to get out."

MR. TAYLOR Did someone raise your bond for you?

MRS. THOMAS Well, yes. The next day I got out about 2:00—something after 2:00.

MR. TAYLOR And what happened after you were released from jail?

MRS. THOMAS Well, after I was released from jail, they held court that following Monday, and I was fined $365.71 and suspended from selling beer for 1 year.

MR. TAYLOR Have you since gotten your license to sell beer?

MRS. THOMAS Yes. I got my license Friday.

MR. TAYLOR This past Friday?

MRS. THOMAS This past Friday, in February.

. . .

COMMISSIONER HESBURGH Did you ever get word whether or not you were registered, Mrs. Thomas?

MRS. THOMAS Well, no, I didn't. Everyone else went down and they didn't pass. So I didn't want to be intimidated any more, so I just assumed I didn't pass, because I didn't want to be seen any more to have anything else to happen.

COMMISSIONER HESBURGH You didn't have any official word from them, from the registrar, as to whether you passed or failed?

MRS. THOMAS No.

. . .

COMMISSIONER HESBURGH No one had said anything about this county beer license before?

MRS. THOMAS Well, no. I had received a card stating that I was late for some license, but I didn't understand it. It didn't say for what license. And in August, my permit and my federal stamp all was due around that time, and I had sent them off. But they hadn't got back. And so I just thought maybe that was it. . . .

COMMISSIONER FREEMAN Mrs. Thomas, how long have you lived in Mississippi?

MRS. THOMAS All of my lifetime.

COMMISSIONER FREEMAN You have been in business for 8 years?

MRS. THOMAS Or longer. Since my husband's death.

COMMISSIONER FREEMAN Have you ever had occasion before the summer of 1964 for the sheriff or the deputy sheriff to enter your place of business?

MRS. THOMAS Well, no.

COMMISSIONER FREEMAN Had they, at any time in this period, asked you about a county license?

MRS. THOMAS No, they had not.

. . .

COMMISSIONER GRISWOLD Mrs. Thomas, do you know whether other places which sell beer in Belzoni or Humphreys County have a county license?

MRS. THOMAS Well, they do now. But during the same time that I didn't have any, they didn't have any.

. . .

VICE CHAIRMAN PATTERSON Mrs. Thomas, you say you have lived in Mississippi all your life. But you didn't try to register to vote until 1964; is that right?

MRS. THOMAS That's right.

VICE CHAIRMAN PATTERSON What moved you to try to register to vote in 1964?

MRS. THOMAS Well, I had begun to understand business a little more and I was in business alone and I was straining paying my taxes. And then I wasn't a citizen. I didn't have no voice. So that made me want to go register.

VICE CHAIRMAN PATTERSON Did anyone encourage you to go and register?

MRS. THOMAS Well, yes. The COFO workers asked me if I would go down. So I agreed that I would go.

See Activity 5.2   Registering to Vote (Role Play) in the Appendix

Freedom School Curriculum Link:

Voter Registration Laws in Mississippi

*www.educationanddemocracy.org/FSCfiles/C_CC7c_VoterRegistrLawsInMS.htm
The COFO research staff wrote this case study to explain how the laws in Mississippi made it nearly impossible for African Americans to register to vote.*

5.C   Herbert Lee: Nonviolent High

Questions to help you adopt a critical stance while reading the section below:

1. *How does the concept of nonviolence relate to the death of Herbert Lee? Would Lee have survived if he had tried to defend himself? How would the others have reacted, the blacks and the whites?*

2. *What is direct action? How does it compare to civil disobedience?*

Further information:

A.J. Muste's essay "Nonviolence and Mississippi" is at www.mkgandhi.org/gandhi his%20relevance/chap17.htm

Recommended Film:

Deacons for Defense *(Docu-Drama; 99 min, 2003; produced by Mark Little and Nick Grillo, directed by Bill Duke). In Bogalusa, L.A., a group of harassed Afro-*

Americans had decided they'd had enough and took up arms to defend themselves and force the white power structure to listen to them. This took place during "Freedom Summer," 1964, right after the Civil Rights Act had become law.

HERBERT LEE

"The growing power of SNCC was not a power of numbers or financial resources or friends in high places. It was the power of an idea whose time had come, the power of a reawakening people."[44]

—*James Forman*

On September 25, 1961, Herbert Lee was shot dead by his neighbor, Mississippi State Representative E.H. Hurst outside of the cotton gin in Liberty, Mississippi. Lee was a local farmer and the father of nine children. Being illiterate he was not eligible to register to vote, but Lee had driven SNCC workers around rural areas in his pick-up truck. A day before he was shot, Bob Moses was told that Lee and two others had been threatened by Hurst. After Lee had been shot, Moses spent days tracking down the witnesses to establish what had happened:

> Essentially, the story was this: they were standing at the cotton gin early in the morning and they saw Herbert Lee drive up in his truck with a load of cotton, E.H. Hurst following behind him in an empty truck. Hurst got out of his truck and came to the cab on the driver's side of Lee's truck and began arguing with Lee. He began gesticulating towards Lee and pulled out a gun which he had under his shirt and began threatening Lee with it. One of the people that was close by said that Hurst was telling Lee, "I'm not fooling around this time, I really mean business," and that Lee told him, "Put the gun down. I won't talk to you unless you put the gun down." Hurst put the gun back under his coat and then Lee slid out on the other side, on the offside of the cab. As he got out, Hurst ran around the font of the cab, took his gun out again, pointed it at Lee and shot him.[45]

The witnesses also told Moses that they had been forced to testify that Hurst had killed Lee in self-defense, that Lee had tried to hit Hurst with a tire tool. While Lee was left lying on the ground for hours because nobody dared to touch him, Hurst was driven away by the sheriff and acquitted the next day of all charges by a local jury. As Moses later wrote,

Hurst was acquitted. He never spent a moment in jail. . . . I remember reading very bitterly in the papers the next morning, a little short article on the front page of the *McComb Enterprise Journal,* said that the Negro had been shot in self-defense as he was trying to attack E. H. Hurst. That was it. You might have thought he had been a bum. There was no mention that Lee was a farmer, that he had a family, that he had nine kids, beautiful kids, that he had been a farmer all his life in Amite County and that he had been a very substantial citizen. . . . Now we knew in our hearts and minds that Hurst was attacking Lee because of the voter registration drive, and I suppose that we all felt guilty and felt responsible, because it's one thing to get beat up and it's another thing to be responsible, or to participate in some way in a killing.[46]

Some time later, Louis Allen, another black local resident, informed Bob Moses that he had witnessed Hurst shoot Lee in cold blood. Moses informed the Justice Department but was told that if Allen testified, he could not be protected.[47] Several months later, the deputy sheriff beat up Allen and made clear that he knew that Allen had contacted the Justice Department. Allen decided to leave the state and was shot dead just as he was locking up his house, a year and a half after Lee was murdered.[48]

Lee's murder solved a dispute that had been simmering for a while within SNCC. In the summer of 1961, while Moses and a small group of workers initiated voter registration and education in Mississippi, SNCC members debated the direction of the organization at a workshop held at the Highlander Folk School. Since the Justice Department and foundations that could supply funds, would support such efforts, some SNCC members endorsed concentrating their future efforts on voter registration. The direct action group, mostly from Nashville, saw voter registration as a "safe" activity, which took the focus off the streets where they thought the struggle belonged.[49] A compromise was proposed by Ella Baker, who suggested that SNCC work on both objectives, forming one branch to concentrate on direct action and another to work on voter registration.

Lee's murder sent a clear message to blacks in Mississippi that the penalty for resistance was death. SNCC workers now understood fully the risk that they were asking local residents to assume. The SNCC conflict between direct action and voter registration seemed resolved in Mississippi—they were one and the same. Attempts to register to vote prompted the same violent reprisals as direct action. Arrests of voter registration workers, according to James Forman, would "dramatize to the nation and to the world that the black man does not even have the right to try to be an American citizen in some parts of our so-called democracy."[50] SNCC worker Reginald Robinson later stated, "If you went into Mississippi and talked about voter registration, they're going to hit you on the side of the head, and that's as direct as you can get."[51]

NONVIOLENT HIGH

Lee's death and the protests against it spurred more action in Mississippi. SNCC workers Charles Sherrod and Marion Barry went to McComb, Mississippi, to plan direct action assaults on the city's segregated facilities. Local youths Curtis Hayes and Hollis Watkins were thwarted in their efforts to enter the "membership only" McComb Public Library when the doors were locked against them. On their way back to the movement office, they sat-in at the lunch counter at a local Woolworth's. The two young men were arrested on charges of "conduct calculated to provoke a breach of the peace" and "failure to move at the order of an officer." Hayes and Watkins spent the weekend in the McComb County Jail and on Monday were found guilty on all counts. Each received the maximum jail sentence and fine. Three other McComb students, fifteen-year-old Brenda Travis, Ike Lewis, and Robert Talbert, Jr., entered the Greyhound Bus Terminal on August 30, purchased tickets for New Orleans, and seated themselves in the Whites-Only waiting room. The three were arrested, and Travis and Lewis, who pleaded "not guilty," were given jail sentences and fines. Travis, Lewis, Hayes, and Watkins were not released from jail until September 30, when appeal bonds were posted by the NAACP, SCLC, and the Yale Freedom Fund for Southern Students.

On October 4, 1961, one hundred and fifteen high school students marched to protest Lee's death and the expulsion of Brenda Travis and Ike Lewis from Burgland High School after their arrest. Nine SNCC staffers including Bob Moses were arrested and jailed for joining the students in this protest. The student demonstrators were suspended for three days and allowed to return to school on the condition that they sign an affidavit acknowledging that they would be expelled if they attempted another demonstration. Many of the demonstrators returned to school with their unsigned affidavits, expecting expulsion. That afternoon, more than a hundred students walked out, issuing a statement explaining their action.

We, the Negro youth of Pike County, feel that Brenda Travis and Ike Lewis should not be barred from acquiring an education for protesting an injustice. We feel that as members of Burgland High School they have fought this battle for us. To prove that we appreciate their having done this, we will suffer with them any punishment they have to take. In the schools we are taught democracy, but the rights offered by democracy have been denied us by our oppressors; we have not had a balanced school system; we have not had an opportunity to participate in any of the branches of our local, state, and federal government; however, we are children of God, who makes the sun shine on the just and the unjust. So, we petition all our fellowmen to love rather than hate, to build rather than tear down, to bind our nation with love and justice with regard to race, color, or creed.[52]

The SNCC staffers, released on bond, opened Nonviolent High, a school for the student protesters. The school's objectives were not only to teach academic subjects but to keep alive the spirit awakened by the demonstrations. Nonviolent High accommodated fifty to seventy-five students in a single room. Bob Moses taught English and math, Charles McDew handled history, and Dion Diamond taught physics and chemistry. Chuck McDew was shocked at "how systematic the school system is in messing up the minds of children." One student asked if they were going to learn about "the war for Southern Independence," the term he had been taught for the Civil War. Joe Martin, one of the organizers of the walk-out, was impressed that Nonviolent High escaped the class consciousness that had existed at Burgland. "It wasn't like in the public schools that this was Mr. So-and-so's Daughter. If you had a good idea, it was accepted regardless of what your social status was."[53] Because the fire laws forbade occupancy by more than thirty-five in their room at the Masonic Lodge, they moved to the Church next door closing Nonviolent High less than a month after it was opened. Campbell Junior College opened its doors to the expelled students, and Nonviolent High closed as its teachers faced sentencing.

On October 30, 1961, Bob Moses, along with SNCC staffers Charles McDew, Bob Zellner, and local high school students were sentenced to four months in jail for their participation in the student protests. They were warned by the judge of the dangers of their intended course of action.

You have caused a very bad relationship to exist in this town. Through the years, and up until this past August, we have gotten along very well. It was then that this outsider Bob Moses came into the area to have a campaign to register 'Nigra' voters. . . . Some of you are local residents. Some are outsiders. Those of you who are local residents are like sheep being led to the slaughter. If you continue to follow the advice of outside agitators you will be like sheep and will be slaughtered.[54]

See Activity 5.3 Nonviolence and/or Self-defense *in the Appendix*

Freedom School Curriculum Links:
A. J. Muste: Rifle Squads or the Beloved Community
 www.educationanddemocracy.org/FSCfiles/C_CC7b_RifleSquadsBelComm.htm

Readings in Nonviolence
 www.educationanddemocracy.org/FSCfiles/C_CC7a_ReadInNonvNoKing.htm

5.D Amzie Moore: SNCC in Mississippi

A question to help you adopt a critical stance while reading the section below:
 What general principle(s) of movement creation can one establish with the evidence of Moses' relationships with Henry, Moore and Evers?

Further information:
The transcript of an interview with Amzie Moore is at the Digital Archives of the University of Southern Mississippi, anna.lib.usm.edu/%7Espcol/crda/oh/ohmooreab.htm.
This interview gives a good background on the situation in Mississippi and the early work of the NAACP and the Civil Rights Movement in the 1960s

AMZIE MOORE

"I found that SNCC was for business, live or die, sink or swim, survive or perish. They were moving, and nobody seemed to worry whether he was going to live or die."[55]

As a child, Moore experienced first-hand the poverty and powerlessness of blacks in Mississippi. Moore was first exposed to the Freedom Movement in 1942, when he attended a rally of more than ten thousand African Americans at Delta State Stadium. Before leaving for the service, Moore began questioning Christianity. "You're standing there and you hear the word, the message, and you believe in it but you're wondering about whether God believes in it."[56]

In 1942, Moore was drafted, and later said, "Here I'm being shipped overseas, and I been segregated from this man whom I might have to save or he save my life. I didn't fail to tell it."[57] Moore and the other men in his unit kept wondering, "Why were we fighting? Why were we there? If we were fighting for the four freedoms that Roosevelt and Churchill had talked about, then certainly we felt that the American soldier should be free first."[58] Because the Japanese were broadcasting programs designed to demoralize African American soldiers by reminding them of the racism within the United States, Moore was given the task of delivering pro-American lectures to black servicemen. "We were promised that after the war was over, things would be different, that men would have a chance to be free. Somehow or another, some of us didn't believe it, others did."[59]

When Moore returned to Mississippi, he discovered a climate of increased repression. News photographs of German women sitting on the laps of African American soldiers had angered white Mississippians. "For at least six to eight months, at least one Negro each week was killed." In 1950, Moore, Dr. T.R.M. Howard, and a group of black Mississippians founded the Regional Council of Negro Leadership in the all-black town of Mt. Bayou, Mississippi. The purpose of the council was to encourage "first-class citizenship"—voting, office holding, and property owning. The organization, whose rallies were attended by thousands, began a campaign, which included encouraging boycotts of service stations where blacks couldn't use the restrooms and political pressure on the state to equalize public facilities. After the *Brown* decision* and the formation of the White Citizens Councils, Moore sensed a movement to drive blacks from the Delta, because the whites sensed that otherwise blacks "might dominate them politically, and. . .that," according to Moore, "is really the beginning of our trouble."

---

* In 1954, the U.S. Supreme Court overturned *Plessy vs. Ferguson* (1896) with the *Brown vs. Board of Education of Kansas City et al.* (five different cases were considered as one). The *Brown* decision established that segregated schools were "inherently unequal." White Citizens Councils were created to resist any attempts to enforce the *Brown* decision.

In 1955, Moore was elected President of the Cleveland branch of the NAACP, a group of eighty-seven members. Moore, with the support of Medgar Evers, soon expanded the branch to include 564 members, but soon violence against blacks in the Delta escalated. The murders of Dr. George W. Lee and Emmett Till, followed by Dr. T.R.M. Howard's decision to leave the state, thwarted efforts to enforce the political gains promised by *Brown*. Moore noted a "great exodus of leaders from the state due to the pressure that was being brought on by white organizations bent and bound on maintaining slavery."[60] In 1956, the fourteen blacks who attempted to vote in the East Cleveland precinct were greeted at the ballot box by a man armed with a .38 Smith and Wesson, who ordered them to place their ballots in a brown envelope. Moore went to the telephone to inform the Justice Department that the group had been prevented from voting. Moore continued to carry on his isolated battle to enfranchise blacks, printing up copies of the Constitution and opening citizenship schools. His ability to build connections outside of the state offered him not only personal friendships with activists like Ella Baker, but economic support from Baker's organization In Friendship.

In 1960, frustrated by the bureaucracy of the NAACP, Moore attended a meeting of SNCC in Atlanta, Georgia, and invited Bob Moses and the voter registration drive to Mississippi. Moses' first impression of Moore is that he was a man "who lives like a brick wall in a brick house, dug into this country like a tree beside the water."[61] Moore often accompanied Moses on his early trips to encourage voter registration among rural blacks, sharing with Moses his connections throughout the state. Once the SNCC workers arrived in Mississippi, Moore's home served as an improvised Freedom House. Moore recalled that he "used to have sleeping in my house six and eight and ten, twelve, who had come. I bought a lots of cheese, and always we'd eat cheese and peaches, and sometimes we would get spaghetti and ground chuck or ground beef and make a huge tub of meatballs and spaghetti to fill everybody up."[62]

Moore agreed with Bob Moses about the difficulties voter registration was facing.

Because of "Hitlerism" tactics that are employed by whites in the Delta, it is extremely difficult to go into a community and start registering people.

First, they must lose all the fear that now grips the hearts and minds of 99 percent of the Negro people.

Secondly, they must regain their self-respect and self-reliance. This can be done by teaching them the philosophy of non-violence.

Thirdly, they must be taught how to endure suffering because if there are any changes in the immediate future, there will undoubtedly be a lot of suffering among the people who attempt to exercise their constitutional rights.

These things must be taught before a voter registration program in the Delta can be successful.[63]

Moses termed Amzie Moore his "father in the movement."[64] To Moses, Moore "was what I like to think an organizer should be—working behind the scenes, helping to set up things. . . . He didn't have a formal education; he still had his common roots, which didn't have that sort of institutional stamp a university can put on you. On the other hand, he had a very special analytical and well-read mind. So he could talk to the people and he could talk to the powerful."[65]

SNCC IN MISSISSIPPI: "FOOD FOR THOSE WHO WANT TO BE FREE"

Threats of physical violence and school expulsions were not the only serious obstacles to voter registration. There was also the threat of economic violence. Sharecroppers could be starved. Barely surviving on the meager return for their grueling labor, a sharecropper owned little, neither land nor tools, and owed a portion of his crop to his landlord. A poor crop meant a deeper plunge into the debts that kept him bound to an endless struggle for survival. In November 1962, SNCC field secretaries Charles Cobb and Charles McLauren conducted a survey on the condition of the Negro farmers in Ruleville, Mississippi.[66] Their report, based on talking with people in Ruleville at the close of the cotton season, demonstrated the economic dependencies in the Mississippi Delta.

Questions relating to Document 5.3 below:
   1. What are the characteristics of sharecropping? Can you imagine living on the property of your (your parent's) employer? Would that affect your social life, your political life, or what you say? Are there current examples of economic dependencies comparable to sharecropping?

2. *Compare commodities to food stamps. Who controls food stamps? Do food stamps "encourage dependency?" Should the government provide food for those in need? What are the alternatives to food stamps (what needs to happen to eliminate the need for food stamps)?*

Document 5.3   *The Economy of Ruleville, Mississippi*

The cotton picking season in the Mississippi Delta lasts from the middle of August until the middle of December. At the end of the season, all of the debts incurred by the Negro sharecropper during the year are totaled up by the plantation owner and deducted from the money that the sharecropper has made during the cotton picking season. The sharecropper plays no part in the totaling up of debts which include: cost of raising cotton crop, rent, food, and miscellaneous bills such as doctor's bills, cost of buying a car, etc.

The agreement between sharecropper and plantation owner is that the sharecropper will raise a crop of cotton, and split it 50–50 with the plantation owner. But the cost of raising the cotton crop is paid entirely by the sharecropper. All of the cotton is sold by the plantation owner, who in turn tells the sharecropper how much the cotton was sold for. The fact that all finance is handled by the plantation owner makes the sharecropper subject to all sorts of financial chicanery from the plantation owner. In fact, several sharecroppers and day workers have reported that they have had to pay out Social Security even though they have no Social Security number. Mrs. Irene Johnson of Ruleville, who is active in the voter registration drive there, reports that even her ten-year-old son has had Social Security taken from him.

Mrs. Willie Mae Robinson, who sharecrops on a plantation near Ruleville, picked twenty (20) bales of cotton this season; yet she only cleared three dollars ($3.00) for the entire year. (There are approximately 550 lbs. in a bale cotton; and the current selling price per pound of picked cotton is $.34. Simple arithmetic shows that before deductions, Mrs. Robbinson should have made $3,740.00.) It is true that she had to split her gross with the plantation owner, and pay for her yearly expenses, but as one man told us in reference to the plight of this lady, "I know that she hasn't eaten what would have come out of ten bales."

We cannot report in much detail on settlements, because most won't be made until after Christmas.

The average amount of money made by sharecroppers for the year is between $300–400. The average amount of money made by day laborers for the year is between $150–160.

The general opinion among the Negro community in Ruleville is that they "won't make anything much" and will need commodities.

Commodities are surplus government foods given out to people on welfare and farming people in need of them. The commodities are usually meal, rice, flour and dry milk. Last year it was announced in Ruleville's paper that butter, peanut butter, and canned meat would be given out; but several people have told us that they never get any.

Before this year, all one had to do in order to receive commodities was to go to City Hall, and sign up. This year, however, there is a registration form to be filled out before anyone becomes eligible. This form has to be signed by the applicant and countersigned by his boss, or a responsible person (which usually means a white person). Due to the voter registration drive that has been and is being carried on in Ruleville, the "responsible people" are not particularly inclined to do favors for the Negro.

Mrs. Mary Burris of Ruleville went to City Hall to sign up to receive commodities. As she approached City Hall, she met several Negro citizens coming out. They told her that all persons with their own homes now had to go to the Welfare Department in Indianola (county seat) to sign up for commodities. When she got there, the lady in charge asked her why she hadn't signed up in Ruleville. Mrs. Burris explained that she was told to come to Indianola. She was then told to take a seat. After about two hours, another lady came out and told Mrs. Burris that her papers (registration for commodities) were not filled out properly. Mrs. Burris was told that she would have to go to every person she had picked for, and bring back something showing how much she had earned from each of them. She was given until 9 A.M. the next morning to do this. Mrs. Burris has been receiving commodities for the past three years, and she says that this is the first time this has happened. She said that this is also the first time that she has had to fill out papers to get food. . . .

At this point, I would like to bring to your attention something Mayor Dorrough said a month or two ago in reference to Negro participation in the voter registration drive in Ruleville: "We gonna see how tight we can make it—gonna make it just as tight as we can—gonna be rougher, rougher than you think it is."

When Mrs. Leona McClendon, a day laborer, went to sign up to receive commodities, she was told that she could not get the food because she had a job, and had earned $15.00 per week. Mrs. McClendon says, "I did not earn $15.00 the whole year."

Grocers in Ruleville have always objected to commodities being issued there.

Commodities are the only way many Negroes make it from cotton season to cotton season. If this is taken from them, they have nothing at all; and the success of our voter registration program depends on the protection we can offer the individual while he is waiting for his one small vote to become a part of a strong Negro vote. It doesn't take much to tide over the rural Mississippi Negro, but the commodities are vital.

The mechanical cotton picker is still imperfect; but it is being used more and more. Essentially what makes the mechanical picker disliked by the plantation owner is that it chops the cotton as it picks, giving a shorter fiber, and thereby lowering the value of the cotton.

Still, Negroes tell us that the machines were used with increasing frequency this year: "cotton picking machines used all the way this year." Where cotton grew in greatest quantity this year, the machines were used. More cotton was picked by machine than by hand.

Mrs. Anderson runs a small grocery store, and is full of ideas and gossip. She had something to say on where Ruleville stands economically. "People haven't made anything this year. . . . Folks don't have any money now."

FROM RESEARCH TO RESULTS

To help the local farmers maintain their resolve, SNCC held mass meetings in the Delta. These gatherings served as an "energy machine,"[67] a place for blacks to share their fears and gain strength from each other as they had traditionally done in Church.[68]

> They use the time to 'testify': to talk about whatever troubles their minds—mostly the absence of food, money, work, and the oppressiveness of the police. They talk about loss of credit, eviction, and voting, three things which form an inseparable unity in the Delta. . . . In the meetings everything—uncertainty, fear, even desperation—finds expression, and there is comfort and sustenance in 'talkin' 'bout hit.'[69]

Economic pressure was increased when, in October of 1962, the Leflore County Board of Supervisors voted to discontinue all participation in the distribution of surplus food to the poor of Mississippi. This withdrawal of support affected some twenty-two thousand black residents of the county.

SNCC started a food distribution program, "Food for those who want to be free." SNCC acknowledged the necessity of providing economic assistance to those engaged in voter registration work. According to Moses, the food distribution program helped SNCC acquire "an image in the Negro community of providing direct aid, not just 'agitation.'"[70] The program also gave SNNC the opportunity to talk about basic rights like voting. "Whenever we were able to get a little something to give a hungry family, we also talked about how they ought to register," said Moses. The food became "identified in the minds of everyone as food for those who want to be free, and the minimum requirement for freedom is identified as registration to vote."[71] Local officials attempted to interfere with SNCC's food distribution efforts. SNCC workers and Michigan State students Ivanhoe Donaldson and Benjamin Taylor were arrested on drug charges as they attempted to deliver food and medicine to Aaron Henry's drug store. In late February of 1963, Moses observed,

> Nine thousand pounds of food arrived February 19, by truck from Chicago. That night four buildings, including a community center and a store, were burned down. At least one worker received an anonymous phone call gloating that no food would be distributed the following day. But they missed the storage place and food was distributed to six hundred people.[72]

DICK GREGORY AND THE POWER OF CELEBRITY

During this time, SNCC experimented with another form of power— borrowing the power of the black celebrity. Prominent African Americans could bring with them material resources, influence, and the power of the press. Moses' letter to SNCC supporters lists actor Harry Belafonte, writer James Baldwin, and comedian Dick Gregory, among others. Because of his fame, Gregory brought the outside press to Mississippi and potentially the power to make injustice visible. Local authorities were often told not to interfere with Gregory, as there could be reprisals.

Dick Gregory did not avoid the topic of race in his comedy routines. Humor became his primary means of expressing rage. In *Nigger,* his autobiography, Gregory recalls hearing the testimony of an elderly voter registration worker at a rally in Jackson, Mississippi, in November, 1962.

> I didn't mind going to jail for freedom; no, I wouldn't even mind being killed for freedom. But my wife and I was married a long time, and, well, you know, I ain't never spent a night away from home. While I was in jail, my wife died.[73]

"That destroyed me," Gregory recalled. "I sat there, and my stomach turned around, and I couldn't have stood up if I had to. . . . This man bucked and rose up and fought the system for me, and he went to jail for me, and he lost his wife for me." A personal friend of Medgar Evers, Gregory realized that his celebrity status did not exempt him from social obligation. "There was a battle going on, there was a war shaping up, and somehow writing checks and making speeches didn't seem enough. Made in the shade? As long as any man, black or white, isn't getting his rights in America, I'm in danger. Sure I could stay in the night clubs and say clever things. But . . . I wanted a piece of the action now, I wanted to get in this thing."[74]

Gregory participated in the food drive in Greenwood, Mississippi, demonstrated in the streets, and was harassed and arrested by the white police. He also participated in the Jackson demonstrations with Medgar Evers and attended Evers' funeral.

See Activity 5.4   Connecting Parental Income and High School Test Scores *in the Appendix*

1964 Freedom School Curriculum Links:

Unit I: Comparing the Students' Realities with Others
   www.educationanddemocracy.org/FSCfiles/C_CCI_UnitsIto6.htm#UnitI
Statistics on Education, Housing, Income etc.
   www.educationanddemocracy.org/FSCfiles/C_CCIa_StatisticsOnEducEtc.htm
Unit II: North to Freedom?
   www.educationanddemocracy.org/FSCfiles/C_CCI_UnitsIto6.htm#Unit2
The Poor in America

In the Freedom Schools, the students learned to analyze the causes and the effects of poverty.

www.educationanddemocracy.org/FSCfiles/C_CC1c_ThePoorInAmerica.htm

Triple Revolution

www.educationanddemocracy.org/FSCfiles/C_CC2a_TripleRevolution.htm

One of the documents students in the Freedom School were encouraged to read is a letter sent to President Johnson regarding the connection between civil rights and economic opportunities.

SIX

The Challenge of Mississippi

Questions to help you adopt a critical stance while reading the section below:

1. *How did the state, local and federal governments work together to create and support the power structure in Mississippi in 1964?*

2. *Why is it important to understand who exerts power and how power is structured?*

3. *Who has the power in your town, your state? Do ordinary citizens have power? What is the influence of lobbyists and campaign contributions?*

Recommended Film:

Fighting Back *(Documentary; Vol. 2 of* Eyes on the Prize; *55 min, 1987 and 2006; produced by Henry Hampton). Covers period from 1957–62. Emphasizes the critical 1954 Supreme* Court Brown vs. Board of Education *decision and the resistance to it.*

THE POWER STRUCTURE

When the first SNCC field workers entered Mississippi in 1961, they faced opposition from a power structure that was complex and long-established. "The Southern Way of Life" was buttressed by a social mythology commonly referred to as the "Plantation Myth." This myth permeated every level of government. The myth was used by both government officials and private citizens to justify the use of every weapon from economic reprisals to terrorism to maintain their power. In its resistance to desegregation, the white power structure was united. Cultural institutions promoted a Plantation Myth that encouraged white southerners to see themselves as defenders of the gracious and aristocratic Southern Way of Life. Mississippi's elected officials—Senator James Eastland, Governor Paul Johnson, Jackson Mayor Allan Thompson—staked their political futures and reputations on an uncompromising defense of segregation. The Mississippi State Sovereignty Commission launched a campaign of surveillance against political activists. With regards to local law enforcement, SNCC workers found themselves harassed rather than protected by local police. Two private organizations were significant parts of the Power Structure's "interlocking series of cliques." In response to the 1954 *Brown vs. Board of Education* decision, the White Citizens Council was formed to insure the continuation of the Southern Way of Life. Nicknamed "The White Collar Klan," the Citizens Council organized business and economic interests against changes in the status quo. Evoking images of Yankee occupation during Reconstruction, the Ku Klux Klan revived its campaign of terrorism.

The white power structure of Mississippi, consisting of interlocking networks of public and private institutions, was reinforced by federal policy and programs. Federal law enforcement, particularly the FBI but also all other federal agencies, worked hand-in-glove with southern law enforcement to enforce segregation laws and to criminalize or stigmatize as "reds" anyone who resisted or opposed segregation. The crucial Agriculture Stabilization Conservation Service subsidized the plantation economy and allowed local agents to use its federal food commodities program to punish communities who resisted segregation and exploitation by withholding the distribution of food aid to the poor in that area. Federally-funded health care services and hospitals accommodated segregation. To varying degrees military installations and bases in the South supported, enforced, or accommodated segregation and Jim Crow customs. Federal housing projects were operated on a strictly segregated Jim Crow basis with white oversight and control of black housing projects.

In 1961, freedom fighters in Mississippi faced the most powerful and deadly white power structure in the nation. With courage, cooperation, intelligence and patience, local Mississippians were able to work with outside volunteers to effect a crack in the system by 1964. To do so, they needed to understand what they were up against.

1964 Freedom School Curriculum Link:
Unit IV: Introducing the Power Structure
   www.educationanddemocracy.org/FSCfiles/C_CCI_Units1to6.htm#Unit4

THE PLANTATION MYTH

"Like other Southerners, Mississippians are obsessed by their sense of the past, but this does not insure the accuracy of their historical picture; they see legend rather than history."[1]

The foundation of this power structure was the Plantation Myth, a set of romanticized beliefs which had served to glamorize slavery and conceal the violence which supported it. The South's humiliating defeat in the Civil War had served not to destroy but to strengthen this ideology. In this mythology, the romanticized Plantation South became a Paradise Lost, destroyed by Northern invasion and proudly remembered by an impoverished but unde-feated aristocracy. Central to the Plantation Myth was white supremacy. African Americans were seen as grateful for the civilizing influence of white planters and as loyal as children to their paternalistic white masters, with-out whose control they would revert to savagery. In this myth, the black male is a particularly contradictory figure—a childlike servant on the one hand and a constant sexual threat on the other. Such mythology offered a justification for the racial terrorism of lynching. That the mythology had little factual basis did not diminish its power.*

   It was not only in the South that such legends were found. The Plantation South was frequently presented by Hollywood as a romantic lost utopia. It was this mythology, presented in D. W. Griffith's *The Birth of a Nation*, that the NAACP had protested as part of its anti-lynching campaign. Another example is in one of Hollywood's most successful films—*Gone with the Wind*. In the opening of this celebrated film, images of contented slaves and fertile fields are presented with the words:

> There was a land of Cavaliers and Cotton Fields called the Old South. . . .
> Here in this pretty world Gallantry took its last bow. . . .

---

* The Plantation Myth has morphed into more sophisticated versions since the Civil Rights Movement successfully challenged it. Perpetuation of this myth at the time and the persistence of its modern forms helps dull whatever consciousness white people might have about their racism. Conversely, portrayal of all whites as Klan members undermines the development of multiracial coalitions.

Here was the last to be seen of Knights and their Ladies Fair, of Master
and of Slave. . . .
Look for it only in books, for it is no more than a dream remembered. . . .
A civilization gone with the wind. . . .
—*From the opening of the film,* Gone With the Wind

In the Freedom Schools, students were encouraged to examine carefully
the social myths which distorted their experience. They were particularly
encouraged to examine films which glorified the Southern Way of Life and
perpetuated notions of white supremacy.

Question: What do these movies teach us? What is taught in the schools
and through other media? The myths of our society (enumerate) and what
the effect of these myths is on the Negro (and other Americans) and what
purposes these serve?
—*From Unit III, Freedom School Curriculum*

For white Southerners, resistance to desegregation was frequently
couched in terms of the Civil War and Reconstruction. The heroes and
villains of the Civil War and of the Plantation Myth re-emerged in force
during the resistance to the Mississippi Summer Project. Frederick Sullens,
editor of the Jackson *Daily News,* wrote, in an editorial entitled *Blood on
the Marble Steps,*

The United States Supreme Court decision abolishing segregation in the public
schools of our nation, even when equal but separate facilities are provided,
is the worst thing that has happened in the South since the carpetbaggers
and scalawags took charge of our civil government in reconstruction days.
It is even worse. It means racial strife of the bitterest sort. It can conceiv-
ably lead to bloodshed and loss of life. . . .
Mississippi will never consent to placing white and Negro children in the
same public schools. The white people and the thinking Negro people did
not want that to happen. Both look on the decision as a calamity. Every
possible human effort will be made to prevent it from happening.[2]

See Activity 6.1   The Movies *in the Appendix*

White resistance to changes demanded by decisions such as *Smith vs. Allwright* (discussed earlier) took the form of harassment and political grandstanding by Mississippi Senator Theodore G. Bilbo. Bilbo was so outspoken a defender of white supremacy that *Time* magazine had dubbed him "The Prince of the Peckerwoods." In 1946, a group of Mississippians led by T. B. Wilson filed a petition claiming that Senator Bilbo had stirred racist sentiment in Mississippi by encouraging whites to keep blacks, newly empowered by *Smith vs. Allwright*, away from the polls. Joined by the NAACP and some labor organizations, T. B. Wilson and company urged the Senate to refuse to seat Bilbo. The challenge was unsuccessful.

The following documents are taken from testimony filed and recorded before the U.S. Senate's Special Committee on Senate Campaign Expenditures by an investigative committee hired to effect the impeachment of Senator Theodore G. Bilbo (D-Mississippi). According to the *Complaint*, Senator Bilbo was accused of having ". . . Engaged in and inspired systematic continuous attacks upon the Negro race [which] took the form of vituperative, insulting, abusive, and slanderous statements. . .acts of violence and intimidation against the Negro people of Mississippi. . . . Except for the fraud. . .the [recent] election would have resulted in the defeat of Senator Theodore G. Bilbo. . . ."

Questions based on Documents 6.1 and 6.2 below:

1. *What is ideology? Was Bilbo's testimony ideologically consistent? Was it logically consistent? For example, which parts of the "Complaint" does Bilbo challenge in his testimony? Which parts of the "Complaint" does Bilbo accept? (Can ideology be inconsistent?) Is there a difference between ideology and theory? When someone accuses another of being "ideological," what do they mean by that? Are they using the word as the dictionary defines it?*

2. *To what degree did the excerpts from the testimony before the Committee support your understanding of the investigators' report? To what degree did they support Senator Ellender's understanding of the report? How do you explain the difference between your understanding of the report and Senator Ellender's?*

3. *What biases are revealed by the transcripts of the hearing? Answer the question for each of the committee members and witnesses. For example, did the*

record of Senator Ellender's questions reveal a desire to generate only evidence in opposition to the Complaint?

Document 6.1   *The Bilbo Hearings: Complaints*

THE UNITED STATES SENATE SPECIAL COMMITTEE TO INVESTIGATE SENATORIAL CAMPAIGN EXPENDITURES, 1946[3]

The committee. . .had compiled evidence of Senator Bilbo's inflammatory remarks:

- From Jackson, Mississippi *Daily News*, June 23, 1946: Citizens of Mississippi were again called on here Saturday by Senator Theo. G. Bilbo "to resort to any means" to keep Negroes from the polls in the June 2 Democratic Primary. "And if you don't know what that means, you are just not up on persuasive measures," said Senator Bilbo as he completed a week of stump speaking in South Mississippi.

- From Jackson *Daily News*, May 28, 1946: "The poll tax," he said has nothing to do with the Negro not voting in the State; the real thorn in their imaginary crown—placed there by the Negro lovers of the North—is section 244 of the State's Constitution, which provides that before anyone can register he must be able to read, or explain after it is read to him or her, the provisions of this Constitution.

- From Jackson, Mississippi *Daily News*, May 25, 1946: . . . . Senator Theo. G. Bilbo said here Monday "anyone caught in the act of negro-organizing, Communist-supporting, racial-antagonizing acts should be horse-whipped, tar-and-feathered and chased out of our beloved Southland."

FROM INTERVIEW ON MUTUAL BROADCASTING CO., MEET THE PRESS PROGRAM, AUGUST 9, 1946:

QUESTION: If you don't believe in lynch law, I wish you would explain in very simple terms to all of us what you meant by the statement that was several times attributed to you as having been made in campaign speeches down there, that the way to stop Negroes from voting was to start from the night before.

BILBO: I said the best time to keep a nigger away from a white Primary in Mississippi was to see him the night before.

QUESTION: Wasn't that in effect to intimidate any Negroes who might have differed with your interpretation of the law and to keep them from the polls?

BILBO: You can call it what you may.

EXCERPTS FROM INVESTIGATORS REPORT [ACCOMPANIED "COMPLAINT"]

October 31, 1946: This preliminary survey and report is predicated upon a complaint dated September 16, 1946, received by the committee from Mr. T. B. Wilson. . .[The following information concerning registration and voting statistics for selected counties in Mississippi was gathered through interviews and statements]

COUNTY	WHITE POPULATION	COLORED POPULATION	TOTAL REGISTRATION	NEGRO REGISTRATION	NEGROES VOTED
Adams	10,344	16, 883	3371	147	0
Harrison	40,742	10,946	11,000	340	12
Hinds	51,826	55,445	27,386	414	196
Leflore	14,394	38,970	4,345	26	0
Sunflower	17,465	43,477	7,715	35	0

[QUALIFIED ELECTORS WHO WERE] PREVENTED FROM REGISTERING OR VOTING BY ACTS OF VIOLENCE:

- Varnado R. Collier . . . Thrown out of building.

- John T. Hall, Jr. . . . Assaulted by unknown white man. . . .

- Lusta Prichard . . . Also arrested, but not assaulted. . . .

- Richard E. Daniel . . . Beaten by two unidentified white men at polls. Then arrested by same two men and Officer Williams. . . .

- Joseph Parham . . . aged 79 . . . pushed off sidewalk. . . .

- Etoy Fletcher . . . taken for ride by four white men, into woods 4 miles away, clothes removed, and flogged mercilessly by four men with large cable wires. All four took turns beating him until they were tired.

[QUALIFIED ELECTORS WHO WERE] NOT PERMITTED TO REGISTER TO VOTE BECAUSE OF ACTION OF PUBLIC OFFICIALS

- Mayor threatened deponent with loss of his Federal position for his Negro franchise organization activities. . . .

- Circuit clerk informed him that no matter how well he answered questions, he could not let him register. . . .

- Statements of town marshal, circuit court clerks, etc., threatening, advising, counseling, or discouraging them from registering and voting. . . .

- Had poll-tax exemption certificates, but not permitted to vote because of erroneous decision of circuit clerk that any veteran discharged prior to January 15, 1946, was considered disqualified unless he held in addition a receipt for 1945 poll tax. As a result 71 Negroes and 9 white men were ruled out with notation. "Discharged prior to January 15, 1946, poll tax for 1945 not paid. . . ."

[QUALIFIED ELECTORS WERE NOT PERMITTED TO VOTE BECAUSE THEY WERE] UNABLE TO INTERPRET FEDERAL AND STATE CONSTITUTION TO SATISFACTION OF CIRCUIT COURT CLERKS

Sample questions asked:
- What is habeas corpus?
- State law regarding slavery?
- Quote portion of the Constitution?
- Who is Secretary of Labor?
- What is ipso facto and ex post facto law?
- How is the President of the United States elected. . . ?
- Who is the Vice President?
- How many men does it take to constitute the Cabinet?
- Name the Cabinet members.

- Name the Lieutenant Governor . . . of the state of Mississippi.

- How is the country run?

It will be noted that most of the above questions related to matters other than those pertaining to the Mississippi Constitution, while section 244 of the Constitution of the State of Mississippi reads "Shall be able to read any section of the constitution of this State, or he shall be able to understand the same when read to him, or give a reasonable interpretation thereof."

WE FOUND:

. . . That while it is true that potential Negro witnesses will have the force of law on their side, their situation may be likened to the case of a pedestrian in any typical American city or community, attempting to cross the street with a green light and the law in his favor, but who, nevertheless, is seriously injured or killed in the process.

Document 6.2   The Bilbo Hearings: Testimony

THE UNITED STATES SENATE SPECIAL COMMITTEE TO INVESTIGATE
SENATORIAL CAMPAIGN EXPENDITURES, 1946

[Excerpts from Minutes, Fifth Meeting, November 16, 1946, Special Committee to Investigate Senatorial Campaign Expenditures]

Senator Ellender (Louisiana) stated that he had studied the [above report] and found . . . there was no evidence that Senator Bilbo had personally prevented Negroes from voting. . .he pointed out that under the Mississippi law, the election officials were acting within their legal rights in not permitting Negroes to vote because it was strictly a white primary, under existing State laws. He stated that he believed in white supremacy and pointed out that all of the other candidates in Mississippi were of the same view. . . . He commented that while the Supreme Court had declared unconstitutional a Texas statute involving primary elections in the Allwright case, in his opinion the statute in Mississippi was law until the question of its validity was adjudicated by the Supreme Court. . . .

SENATOR ELLENDER: Do you think. . .that the clerk was at fault in requiring you to produce your [original copy of your] discharge certificate [in order to receive your veteran's poll-tax-exemption certificate]?

MR. [NAPOLEON B. LEWIS *of McComb, Miss.*]: Yes; because when I was discharged from the Army they told me that my photostatic copy would be sufficient; that I wouldn't have to carry my original discharge around with me . . .

SENATOR ELLENDER: Evidently [the clerk] misunderstood you, because it says here, "because I could not furnish a photostatic copy of my Army discharge." There was no question of the original.

MR. LEWIS: I beg to differ with [the clerk] in my statement.

SENATOR ELLENDER: (asks to see the original statement and examines it) Evidently when the copy was made, there was an error committed. . . . You are correct in what the original says.

MR. LEWIS: Thank you, sir.

. . .

MR. [SHELBY S. STEELE, *of Greenwood, Miss.*]: . . . [A]long about 3 weeks before the primary there seemed to be quite an unrest among the nigger population; and was with certain elements of white men. . . . As long as I can remember we never had a nigger in that county to offer to vote in a Democratic primary. . . .

SENATOR ELLENDER: And you feared if they were permitted to vote at that primary, trouble would occur?

MR. STEELE: . . . As you know, we have an element in all cities of that size that is pretty tough, and they were just ready at any moment to start trouble, so our advice to the niggers was to let it alone. . . . We want you to use your own judgment. You have a right to vote. We won't disturb you or stop you. . . but I say this personally: I can't protect you if there is trouble. . . .

SENATOR ELLENDER: But you and Mr. Johnson and the Mayor did advise them—that is, you did tell these two colored men to advise these thirty-some-odd colored people—

MR. STEELE: Well, we believed—

SENATOR ELLENDER: That it might be better not to vote?

MR. STEELE: To decide for themselves, but we couldn't say that there would not be trouble. . . .

SENATOR ELLENDER: Well, now, what caused this, if I may say, undue excitement or trouble. . . .

MR. STEELE: Well, there are a good many niggers up there that have been voting in the general election all the time, and the returned veterans had the desire to register and vote; and it was an unemployed element right after the war just to stir, and the tendency was to go around and register and vote in a Democratic primary. . . .

SENATOR BILBO'S ATTORNEY: Is it not true that there is and has been for the past 50 years the very best racial relationship in LeFlore County and no race riots or disturbances?

MR. STEELE: Yes, sir.

SENATOR ELLENDER: Is it not true that even if Senator Bilbo had not been running there might have been violence if Negroes had attempted to vote in the primary election?

MR. STEELE: Well, the chances are there would have been. . . .

. . .

TESTIMONY OF SENATOR THEODORE G. BILBO, UNITED STATES SENA-TOR FROM THE STATE OF MISSISSIPPI. . . . AFTER READING A PREPARED STATEMENT IN WHICH HE DENIED THE CHARGES AGAINST HIM, SENATOR BILBO WAS QUESTIONED BY SENATOR HICKENLOOPER FROM IOWA.

SENATOR HICKENLOOPER: Referring to the last paragraph in the Collier's story. . .is that a substantially accurate reporting of your statement?

SENATOR BILBO: Yes, except they left out the qualifying phrases I always use in my speech, "use all the power, the legal power, lawful power and persuasion." You know, the Negro is a very persuasive person, and the relationship there seems—of white people and Negroes in Mississippi has been very, very fine, until we had the scourge of [labor organizer] Sidney Hillman, CIO-PAC, Eleanor Roosevelt, and so on. They have gotten great ideas in their heads. I know a lot of these veterans from the war; they were also poisoned by the courses of orientation that were written by some of the students of Dr. Boax of Columbia University. You know, we stopped 50,000 copies of the book entitled, "Races of Mankind" from being scattered in the armed forces. We stopped social equality. But they slipped around and hired the editors of that paper to write the orientation courses that were taught in the Army. That's where some of these niggers [sic] got the wrong idea about their proper status. . . .

SENATOR HICKENLOOPER: There is a series of excerpts at the bottom of page 4 from an interview on the Mutual Broadcasting Co. "Meet the Press" program, August 9, 1946 [see Document 6.1 above]. . . . . Would you say that the questions and your answers there are accurately stated as they were made on that broadcast?

SENATOR BILBO: Except the newspaper boy there in propounding his question—. . .[he] tried to make me say that "Visit the nigger the night before" was a form of intimidation, which it was not. . . . [On Meet the Press] I thought I was having a conversation with four newspapermen. . . . So I was sitting up there talking to four little dummies, and the nigger back out in Howard College had prepared those questions. You see, what is behind that program was a bunch of nigger lovers and Communists. . . . If I could have legally prevented [blacks] from voting, there wouldn't have been one voted.

SENATOR HICKENLOOPER: Well, is it your contention that they cannot vote legally in the Democratic primary in Mississippi?

SENATOR BILBO: Yes, sir; under the law they cannot; therefore, they cannot qualify under section 3129. . . . They could vote in the November election. . . . Well, under the Fourteenth and Fifteenth Amendments of the Constitution of the United States and the laws of the State and the Constitution and the Supreme Court decision, they are legally and can be legally qualified to vote in November. . . . The fact of the business is, I agree with Abraham Lincoln. He said they ought not to be permitted to vote or hold office or to serve as a juror, and I think Abraham Lincoln is a pretty good authority for a Democrat to quote. (Laughter)

SENATOR HICKENLOOPER: I refer to this statement you made in which you said: The poll tax won't keep 'em from voting. What keeps 'em from voting is section 244 of the constitution of 1890. . . .

SENATOR BILBO: Purposely that amendment was written by Senator George and adopted by the legislature in 1890. . . . I did not want any of them to vote. Would you? Would you want somebody to vote that you knew was going to vote against you? (Laughter). . . I said nothing that would cause the nigger to be afraid. . . . [I have said that the best way to prevent a black from voting is to visit him the night before.] In the North I guess they consider that an announcement that we will go and take the nigger out and beat him up the night before and tell him he had better not come. . . . But that is not what I had in mind, because I know the Mississippi nigger and I know the white people. . . . I called on my opponents to join me, and "let's you and I ask the nigger not to vote." It was a persuasion, and the best time to do it is the night before. I stick to it.

1964 Freedom School Curriculum Link:
Power of the Dixiecrats
   _www.educationanddemocracy.org/FSCfiles/C_CC4b_PowerOfTheDixiecrats._
   htm

6.A   James Eastland: The White Citizens Council

Questions to help you adopt a critical stance while reading the section below:
   1. _Why was segregation important to the whites in Mississippi—what were the fears?_

   2. _What influence did segregation have on the power of poor whites and poor blacks?_

   3. _How would you desegregate schools? Would busing work? If so, why, or why not? What else would you do?_

Further information:
   The transcript of an interview with M.W. Hamilton is at the Digital Archives of the University of Southern Mississippi, anna.lib.usm.edu/%7Espcol/crda/oh/ ohhamiltonmb.htm
   Mr. Hamilton was a founding member of the Citizens Council in Hattiesburg, and the interview also covers Freedom Summer.

JAMES EASTLAND, UNITED STATES SENATOR FROM MISSISSIPPI
"To resist is the only answer I know. Southern people will not surrender their dual school system and their racial heritage at the command of this crowd of radical politicians in judicial robes."[4]

James Eastland was a native of Sunflower County, home also to Fannie Lou Hamer. His family was one of the oldest and most powerful families of planters in the region, and Eastland's commitment to Southern traditions never wavered.

Eastland's response to the _Brown vs. Board of Education_ decision was swift: On the floor of the Senate, Eastland charged that the Supreme Court Justices had been "indoctrinated and brainwashed by left wing pressure groups."[5] On May 27, 1954, Eastland stated, "Segregation is not discrimination. Segregation promotes racial harmony.... There is no racial hatred in the South. The Negro race is not an oppressed race."[6]

While campaigning for the Senate in 1954, Eastland urged the attorneys of Mississippi to offer their services for free in law suits to maintain racial segregation in the South. In 1955, Eastland and other Mississippi officials joined other Southern states in passing a resolution of interposition. By this doctrine, a state government could interpose itself between the citizens of the state and an "unconstitutional" order issued by the federal government. To a crowd in Senatobia in August of 1955, Senator Eastland urged, "On May 17, 1954, the Constitution of the United States was destroyed because the Supreme Court disregarded the law and decided integration was right. *You are not required to obey any Court which passes out such a ruling.* In fact, you are obligated to defy it!"[7]

As Chairman of the powerful U.S. Senate Judiciary Committee, Eastland was a force to be reckoned with. He boasted publicly of his ability to kill any civil rights legislation, and U.S. Presidents had to bargain with Eastland for appointments. John Kennedy, eager to appoint Thurgood Marshall to a federal judgeship, found Eastland a major obstacle. Eastland, considering the two open benches on the court, offered Attorney General Robert Kennedy his deal: "Tell your brother if he'll give me Harold Cox, I'll give him the nigger."[8] Cox, a college roommate of Eastland's, was an outspoken segregationist who had once insulted a group of African American plaintiffs by calling them "a bunch of niggers. . .acting like a bunch of chimpanzees."[9] The Kennedys accepted the deal, placing Marshall on the bench but creating in Cox a barrier for civil rights cases in the South. The Kennedys again negotiated with Eastland when the Freedom Riders arrived in Mississippi. Eager to avoid bloodshed, the President accepted Eastland's offer: the Freedom Riders would be protected from the mob, if they could immediately be imprisoned on charges of "inflaming public opinion."[10]

In 1965, Eastland addressed the U.S. Senate in an effort to demonstrate that civil rights activity in Mississippi, particularly Freedom Summer and the Freedom Democratic Party, were communist-inspired efforts to destroy the American way of life. "The state of Mississippi has been subjected to an invasion which the communists regard as only the opening maneuver in the coming Negro revolution," argued Eastland.

> The people of Mississippi understand. . . . They know what they face; they
> know what they are fighting for—not only to protect their own way of life
> and their own freedoms, but to turn back the concentrated and focused

power of the world Communist conspiracy and all its helpers, witting or unwitting, on what the Communists themselves have termed a critical testing ground.

The people of Mississippi did not ask for this critical struggle. They did not want it or seek it. But they will not shirk it; they will not run from it; they will not compromise with the enemy!

Mr. President, there is no compromise with death![11]

In 1956, Eastland had joined eighteen other Senators and seventy-seven members of the House of Representatives from the South in voicing their resistance to *Brown vs. Board of Education:*

Document 6.3   The Southern Manifesto, 1956 [12]

DECLARATION OF CONSTITUTIONAL PRINCIPLES

. . . The Founding Fathers . . . framed this Constitution . . . to secure the fundamentals of government against the dangers of temporary popular passion or the personal predilections of public officeholders.

We regard the decision of the Supreme Court in the school cases as a clear abuse of judicial power. . . . The original Constitution does not mention education. Neither does the 14th Amendment nor any other amendment. The debates preceding the submission of the 14th Amendment clearly show that there was no intent that it should affect the systems of education maintained by the States . . . in *1927, in Lum v. Rice,* that the "separate but equal" principle is "within the discretion of the state in regulating its public schools and does not conflict with the 14th amendment." This interpretation restated time and again became a part of the life of the people of many of the States and confirmed their habits, customs traditions, and way of life. . . .

This unwarranted exercise of power by the Court . . . is destroying the amicable relationships between the white and Negro races that have been created through 90 years of patient effort by the good people of both races. . . .

Outside agitators are threatening immediate and revolutionary changes in our public-school systems. . . .

Even though we constitute a minority in the present Congress, we have full faith that a majority of the American people believe in the dual system of Government which has enabled US to achieve our greatness and will in time demand that the reserved rights of the state and of the people be made secure against judicial usurpation.

We pledge ourselves to use all lawful means to bring about a reversal of this decision. . . .

THE WHITE CITIZENS COUNCIL

Politicians like Eastland and Bilbo could base their support on a number of private organizations committed to a segregated South. Shortly after the *Brown vs. Board of Education* decision, in July of 1954, a group of thirteen white Mississippi businessmen, led by Delta planter Robert Patterson, met in Indianola to form the White Citizens Council. The "White Collar Klan" set out to organize resistance to school desegregation and to make such resistance respectable. "We want the people assured that there is responsible leadership organized which will and can handle local segregation problems," explained one member. "If that is recognized, there will be no need for any 'hot-headed' bunch to start a Ku Klux Klan. If we fail, though, the temper of the public may produce something like the Klan."[13] Patterson distributed a letter that read,

> Dear Fellow Americans. . .it seems a great danger is hanging over the heads of our children—mongrelization. . . . A lot of people are resigning themselves to seeing their children crammed into schools and churches with children of other races and being taught the Communist theme of all races and. . .mongrelization. . . . I gathered my children and promised them that they would never have to go to school with children of other races against their will, and this is my solemn vow and pledge. If every Southerner who feels as I do, and they are in the vast majority, will make this vow, we will defeat his communistic disease that is being thrust upon us. . . . If we are bigoted, prejudiced, un-American, etc., so were George Washington, Thomas Jefferson, Abraham Lincoln, and our other illustrious forebears who believed in segregation.[14]

Less than six weeks after its founding, the Council had branches in over seventeen counties. By November, the organization was coordinated state wide through the Associated Citizens Councils of Mississippi and claimed over 25,000 members.[15] The pamphlet *Black Monday*, written by Mississippi circuit judge Tom Brady, became a manifesto for the White Citizens

Council. "*Black Monday* belongs in every home, every school, every library," declared an ad in *The Citizen*, a publication of the Citizens Council. "At $1 per copy, it's a collector's item. . .and at $10 per dozen, you'll want copies for distribution!"[16] The pamphlet contained undocumented conclusions about the racial inferiority of African Americans, the communist conspiracy underlying the Civil Rights Movement, and the necessity for the maintaining of segregated schools to prevent "race mixing." The book's title refers to May 17, 1954, the date of the *Brown vs. Board of Education* decision. This small book crystallized for many Mississippians their resistance to *Brown* and gave them confidence that their stance was not only justified but legally defensible. "Race Mixing," according to Brady, lead inevitably to the degeneration of civilization.

> Whenever and wherever the white man has drunk the cup of black hemlock whenever and wherever his blood has been infused with the blood of the Negro, the white man, his intellect and his culture have died. This is as true as two plus two equals four. The proof is that Egypt, India, the Mayan civilization, Babylon, Persia, Spain and all the others, have never and can never rise again.[17]

Brady further held that communist forces had inspired the *Brown* decision.

> Though it is yet largely underground, it is rampant in our nation. The Communist masses of Russia and Red China must have howled with glee on 'Black Monday.' They know the unanimous decision of the Supreme Court abolishing segregation. . .was an illegal usurpation of the legislative prerogative of those State Legislatures and of Congress. The hoards of Russia and Red China know that another deadly blow has been dealt our Constitution.[18]

The Citizens Council, official newspaper of the organization, evoked images of the Civil War and Reconstruction to present white resistance against school desegregation as heroic. The white Southerner was depicted as a member of a beleaguered band resisting the destruction of a threatened way of life. Slogans like "Forgit, Hell!" and "Unreconstructed Rebel" and displays of the Confederate flag were seen as signs of loyalty to the past.

In an article entitled "The Gentle Weapon," Southern women were advised to join the resistance to desegregation.

> It is an undisputed fact that in Nashville, Tennessee's capital city, a handful of misguided white women—and men—are meeting with Negroes, eating with them, and apparently, according them full social recognition. . . . If the forces of radicalism succeed in duping gullible women who may head your organizations, you will soon find yourself sitting next to Negro women at luncheon or standing in receiving lines with them at your teas. Do you want this? Is it for your good—or theirs? Only you can decide. And, assuming that you do not want it, what can you do?
>
> Here are a few of the things:
>
> (1) You can look for spiritual, as well as practical guidance, to the women of the South during the dark days of Reconstruction. . .as a leading Southerner, who had been a Captain in the Confederate Army testified, the ladies took things into their own hands. 'Our women say that during the war when we men were shot at we had a chance to shoot back again, but that they were compelled to endure in silence the indignities and depravations. . . .'
>
> (2). . .You can, quietly and privately, or publicly, join hands with thousands of Southern women who are now reviving this gentle weapon—social ostracism—to defend their way of life. . .do not attend meetings or other gatherings in which integration is either advocated or practiced. . . .
>
> Racially, there are three major groups in the South—the whites, the mixed, and the Negroes.
>
> To which will you and your children's children belong?[19]

In an early issue, *The Citizens Council* introduced a feature entitled, "A Manual for Southerners," to be used in the education of white children.

Document 6.4   A Manual For Southerners[20]

Lest our friends in other sections of the country feel that we are becoming too ardent "Confederates," let us hasten to say that we are not. The truth is that for too long Southern children have been "progressively educated" to scorn their origins and the reasons for our bi-racial society.

"A Manual for Southerners" seeks to correct this.

The portion appearing in this issue is for use in grades 3 and 4. However, there are many adults who might benefit from a review of these fundamental truths.

God Made Four Races God made all of the people in the world. He made some of them white. He made some of them black. He made some of them yellow. And He made some of them red.

God Put Each Race By Itself God put the white people off by themselves. He put the yellow, red, and black people by themselves. God wanted the white people to live alone. And He wanted the colored people to live alone. That is why He put them off by themselves.

White Men Built America Some white people came to America. America is where you live. It is your country. The white men built America for you. They want you to have a free country that you can grow up in.

America Is The Land Of Freedom Do you know what the name of your country is? It is called the United States of America. We love the United States. It is the land of freedom.

You Make Your Rules Freedom means that you can choose your own rules. We have to have rules to live by. Do you help make rules in your classroom? You and your friends help make the rules you use in school.

White People Like To Be Free White people built the United States so they could make their rules. They could not make their rules in the country they came from. So they built America and make their own rules. They wanted to be free.

America Was Made Strong The red man is the Indian. You know what Indian is. The red man fought the white man. But the white man won. He worked and worked. He wanted you to have a strong free country. It was not easy to build.

Whites And Negroes Live Apart The black man is the Negro. You have seen Negroes all of your life. The Negro came to our country after the white man did. The white man has always been kind to the Negro. But the white and black people do not live together in the South.

Whites, Blacks Different Races Do you know why the white and Negro people do not live together? It is because we are two different races. You will ask, "What are races?" You may know already. Races of men are different colored men. God made the different races. He made a White race, a

Black race, a Red race, and a Yellow race. And he put the races in different lands. Your Bible tells you all about the races of man.

It Is Wrong To Live Together Most of the Negroes in our country live in the South. They know the white men in the South are their friend. White people live in peace with Negroes in the South. But white and black people do not live together in the South. We do not believe God wants us to live together. It is wrong to live together and mix our races.

The Races Like To Live Alone Negro people like to live by themselves. They like to go to Negro doctors. They like to go to Negro schools. They like to live with their own race. And white people like to live with their own race, too.

We Do Not Mix Races In The South Negroes and white people do not go to the same places together. We live in different parts of town. And we are kind to each other. This is called our Southern Way of Life. We do not mix our races, but we are kind to each other.

See Activity 6.2   Race Mixing and Communism *in the Appendix*

1964 Freedom School Curriculum Link:

Mississippi Power Structure

www.educationanddemocracy.org/FSCfiles/C_CC4a_MSPowerStructure.htm

6.B   Emmett Till: The Ku Klux Klan

Questions to help you adopt a critical stance while reading the section below:

1. *"Now I felt like a fool." Do raised hopes dashed provide the fuel of revolution?*

2. *How was the lynching of Emmett Till similar to thousands of those who committed before? Why was the effect so different?*

Further information:

The transcript of an interview with Edward L. McDaniel is at the Digital Archives of the University of Southern Mississippi, www.lib.usm.edu/%7Espcol/crda/ oh/mcdanieltrans.htm

Mr. McDaniel was a member of the White Knights of the Ku Klux Klan.

Recommended Film:

The Murder of Emmett Till (Documentary; 53 min, 2003; directed by Stanley Nelson)

EMMETT TILL

"Before Emmett Till's murder, I had known the fear of hunger, hell, and the Devil. But now there was a new fear known to me—the fear of being killed just because I was black."[21]

Fourteen-year-old Emmett Till was visiting relatives in Mississippi from Chicago in the summer of 1955. Responding to a dare from his friends, Till entered Roy Bryant's store in Money, Mississippi and, as he left the store, said "Bye, baby," to Bryant's wife Carol. Four days after the incident, Bryant and his brother-in-law J.W. Milam arrived at the home of Moses Wright, Till's great-uncle, at 2 A.M. The two white men demanded to see the boy and drove away with him. On August 31 (three days later), Till's body was recovered from the Tallahatchie River. Till had been badly beaten and shot once through the head. A seventy-pound cotton-gin fan had been tied with barbed wire around his neck. Moses Wright identified his nephew's decomposed body at the riverside by the silver ring, which had been Till's father's.

The body was taken to Chicago for burial. Mamie Bradley, Till's mother, insisted upon an open casket, insisted that the world see her son's mutilated body. A photograph of the body appeared on the cover of *Jet* magazine. Lynching, which had thrived on secrecy and silence, was exposed to the scrutiny of the international press. Defying Southern custom and placing his life in jeopardy, Till's elderly uncle Moses Wright publicly identified one of the two men who had abducted Till from his home, pointing his finger in the courtroom and testifying, "Thar he." Nineteen-year-old Willie Reed, a local black resident, also testified to hearing the sound of "some licks" coming from Milam's barn and seeing Milam leave the barn wearing a pistol.[22]

The local sheriff, in the course of his investigation, had offered his opinion that "the killing might have been planned and plotted by the NAACP."[23] In its closing statement, the prosecution argued, "There was no justification for killing Emmett. The most he needed was a whipping if he had done anything wrong."[24] The defense claimed that the body was not Till's, but a body brought to Mississippi by "outsiders" attempting to discredit Mississippi's system of justice. In his summation to the jury, one attorney said that "there are people in the United States who want to destroy the customs of southern people. . . . They would not be above putting a rotting, stinking body in the river in the hope he would be identified as Emmett Till."[25] The defense attorney, in his final words to the jury, was

"sure every last Anglo Saxon one of you has the courage to free these men."
Another warned the jurors that if they returned a guilty verdict, "your fore-
fathers will turn over in their graves."[26] Bryant and Milam were promptly
acquitted by an all-white, all-male jury, exposing not only the brutality of
lynching but the ineffectiveness of local courts in securing justice. Once
acquitted, Bryant and Milam sold their story to *Look* magazine, describing in detail how they had kidnapped, beaten, and murdered Till. "What
could I do?" one of the killers asked the reporter. "He thought he was as
good as any white man."[27]

The Till case prompted a generation of young Mississippi blacks to
political action. Joyce Ladner, a young SNCC worker, referred to herself
as a member of the "Till generation." "I can name you ten SNCC workers
who saw that picture in *Jet* Magazine, who remember it as the key thing
about their youth that was emblazoned in their minds. . . . One of them
told me how they saw it and thought that one day they would avenge his
death."[28] For writer Anne Moody, fifteen at the time of Till's murder, the
crime prompted a new awareness and fear of the racial mores of Mississippi. "Before Emmett Till's murder," she said,

> I had known the fear of hunger, hell, and the Devil. But now there was a
> new fear known to me—the fear of being killed just because I was black.
> This was the worst of my fears. I knew once I got food, the fear of starving
> to death would leave. I also was told that if I were a good girl, I wouldn't
> have to fear the Devil or hell. But I didn't know what one had to do or not
> do as a Negro not to be killed. Probably just being a Negro period was
> enough, I thought."[29]

Another black youth affected by Till's death was John Lewis, the future
SNCC leader and Congressman. "I was fifteen, black, at the edge of my
own manhood just like him. He could have been me. *That* could have
been me, beaten, tortured, dead at the bottom of a river. It had been only
a year since I had been so elated at the *Brown* decision. Now I felt like a
fool."[30] The Till case, however, received a level of publicity unheard of in
Mississippi history. "Whites had been killing blacks for years," said Aaron
Henry, "and there was not any real outcry about it. Emmett Till's slaying
came simultaneously with the advent of nation-wide television, and the
story was well covered."[31]

Question based on Document 6.5 below:

"M Is For Mississippi And Murder" was issued by the NAACP shortly after the murder of Emmett Till in 1955. It was part of their national anti-lynching campaign. Does the pamphlet suggest any change in approach by the NAACP since it's founding?

Document 6.5   M Is For Mississippi And Murder[32]

BACKDROP FOR MURDER

A Few Killings—An Associated Press dispatch written by Sam Johnson and datelined from Jackson, Miss., September 9, 1954, says in part: ". . . One [state legislator said a] 'few killings' would make certain that the people would approve the amendment [to abolish public school] and 'would save a lot of bloodshed later on,' he added."

Obligated to Defy—. . . Press-Scimitar reports a rally of the Citizens Council at Senatobia, Miss., August 12, 1955, and quotes United States Senator James O. Eastland (Democrat, Miss.) as saying: "On May 17 the Constitution of the United States was destroyed. . . . You are not required to obey any court which passes out such a ruling. In fact, you are obligated to defy it."

Gun and Torch—Although he said it was "abhorrent," John C. Satterfield, president of the Mississippi Bar Association and a member of the board of governors of the American Bar Association, in a speech at Greenville, Miss., nevertheless listed "the gun and torch" as one of the three methods of continuing segregation. . . .

White Man's Problem—In a front page editorial August 22, 1955, the Jackson, Miss. *Daily News* describes Dr. A. H. McCoy, state president of the National Association for the Advancement of Colored People, as "Insolent, arrogant and hot-headed" and says, "The fanatical mouthings of McCoy have reached the limit. If not suppressed by his own race, he will become the white man's problem. . . ."

In the climate of opinion which derides the courts and the rule of law, which harps on violence, sometimes nakedly and sometimes through the device of repeated disavowal, three persons were murdered in Mississippi between May 7 and August 28, 1955.

GETTING AWAY WITH MURDER

Rev. Lee was the first of his race to register to vote in Humphreys County and he had urged others to register. He had told a friend on the afternoon of his death day that he had been ordered to remove his name from the registration list. He had refused to do so.

No arrests have been made.

The Sheriff said the lead pellets in Rev. Lee's jaw and neck "could have been fillings from his teeth."

In the broad daylight of Saturday afternoon, August 13, Lamar Smith was shot dead in front of the courthouse at Brookhaven, Miss. He had been active in getting voters out for the primary election August 2 and was working on the run-off primary scheduled for August 23. . . .

A grand jury on September 21, 1955, failed to return an indictment against the three men arrested in connection with the Smith murder.

The District Attorney is reported in a United Press dispatch as accusing the Sheriff of refusing to make an immediate arrest "although he knew everything I know" about the slaying. In another dispatch the District Attorney is quoted as saying: "The Sheriff told me he saw Noah Smith (one of the accused men) leave the scene of the killing with blood all over him. It was his duty to take that man into custody regardless of who he was, but he did not do it."

Sometime after 2 A.M. on August 28, Emmett Louis Till, 14 who had come to the town of Money, Miss., from Chicago to visit his great-uncle, Moses Wright, was kidnapped at gun point, beaten, shot and thrown into the Tallahatchie River.

Two half brothers, J. W. Milam, 36, and Roy Bryant, 24, were tried for murder in Summer, Miss., in Tallahatchie County where the body was found. The two admitted taking the Till boy from his uncle's cabin because he allegedly "wolf-whistled" at Mrs. Bryant three or four days earlier, but said they released him unharmed a short time later. Moses Wright identified Milam from the witness stand as the man who had come to his home with a drawn gun, demanded the Till boy, took him from his bed and pushed him into a waiting car.

An all-white jury (only voters may serve on juries and none of the county's 19,000 Negroes is permitted to vote) took only one hour and seven minutes to acquit the two defendants who were released on bail pending the facing of a kidnap charge in neighboring LeFlore County later in the fall or winter.

The Sheriff said the body was not that of the Till boy, but was part of a plot by the National Association for the Advancement of Colored People.

John C. Whitten, one of the five attorneys defending Milam and Bryant, in addressing the jury said: " I am sure every last Anglo-Saxon one of you has the courage to free these men. . . ."

The Jackson (Miss.) *Daily News* said editorially, September 25, 1955: "It is best for all concerned that the Bryant-Milam case be forgotten as quickly as possible. It has received far more publicity than should have been given."

This is Mississippi.

These were not murders of passion, or for profit, but futile, cold, brutal murders to bolster a theory of superiority based upon skin color.

It is the people who make a state. . . . This is Mississippi. . . .

THE KU KLUX KLAN

"Mississippi's vocabulary of violence is varied and old," wrote Mississippi-born journalist Frank Trippett. "Almost before he learns to spell the words, a white Mississippi boy masters the braggadocio of racial conflict. "A nigger gets smart with me I'll be on him like white on rice and turn that nigger every way but loose." And he utters these words as clarion proof of his masculinity.[33] In such a climate, the Ku Klux Klan, promoted as heroic defenders of white womanhood, offered license for and glamorized images of racial violence. The "vocabulary of violence" emerged, in part, from the valorizing of the Ku Klux Klan in novels and films of the Plantation School. Founded in 1866 by six Confederate veterans in Pulaski, Tennessee, the organization derives its name from "kuklos," a corruption of the Greek word for "circle" and from "klan," the designation of family groups in Scotland. In *Gone With the Wind*, Margaret Mitchell describes Scarlett O'Hara's response to the Reconstruction South:

> Now she knew what Reconstruction meant, knew as well as if the house were ringed about by naked savages, squatting in breech clouts. . . . The Negroes were on top and behind them were the Yankee bayonets. She could be killed, she could be raped, and, very probably, nothing would ever be done about it. And anyone who avenged her would be hanged by the Yankees,

hanged without benefit of trial by judge and jury. . . . "What can we do?" she thought, wringing her hands in an agony of helpless fear.[34]

In the novel, Southern men, including the novel's heroes Ashley Wilkes and Rhett Butler, seek redress in the Ku Klux Klan, an organization defined as the only hope for justice for Southern whites. "If the Ku Klux handles many more Negroes," Rhett Butler informs her, "the Yankees are going to tighten up on Atlanta in a way that will make Sherman's conduct look angelic. . . . They mean to stamp out the Ku Klux if it means burning the whole town again and hanging every male over ten."[35]

One of many secret organizations that emerged during Reconstruction, the Klan employed tactics of threats, burnings, and lynching in a effort to restore white political supremacy threatened by the presence of Federal troops. The organization splintered into many groups throughout its history. On February 15, 1964, in Brookhaven, Mississippi, Samuel Bowers, a self-proclaimed minister and owner of the Sambo Amusement Company, founded The White Knights of the Ku Klux Klan in Mississippi. The rhetoric of the White Knights was characterized by religious fervor and a strong sense of mission. In his "Executive Lecture," Bowers argued that only two forces compete in the world—God's "spiritual force" and Satan's "materialistic force of destruction."[36]

Believing that the Klan was called by God to eliminate "heretics," Bowers distributed recruiting pamphlets, which described the new organization and offered potential members twenty reasons to join. Among these reasons were:

> The administration of our National Government is now under the actual control of atheists who are Bolsheviks by nature. As dedicated agents of Satan, they are absolutely determined to destroy Christian Civilization and all Christians. . . . (Our) members are Christians who are anxious to preserve not only their souls for all Eternity, but who are MILITANTLY DETERMINED, God willing, to save their lives, and the Life of this Nation, in order that their descendants shall enjoy the same full, God-given blessings of True Liberty that we have been permitted to enjoy up to now.
>
> We do not accept Jews, because they reject Christ, and through the machinations of their International Banking Cartel, are at the root-center of what we call "communism" today.

We do no accept Papists, because they bow to a Roman dictator, in direct violation of the First Commandment and the True American Spirit of Responsible, Individual Liberty.

We do not accept Turks, Mongols, Tartars, Orientals, Negroes, nor any other person whose native background of culture is foreign to the Anglo-Saxon system of Government by responsible, FREE, Individual Citizens.

The issue is clearly one of personal, physical SELF DEFENSE for the American Anglo-Saxons. The Anglo-Saxons have no choice but to defend our Constitutional Republic by every means at their command, because it is LITERALLY their life. They will die without it.[37]

If you are a Christian, American Anglo-Saxon who can understand the simple Truth of this Philosophy, you belong in the White Knights of the Ku Klux Klan in Mississippi. We need your help right away. Get your Bible out and Pray! You will hear from us.[38]

The Mississippi Summer project was seen as a gauntlet tossed down, prompting the Klan to defend its principles. On June 7, 1964, Bowers, in a sermon to his followers, announced his intention to combat the enemy invasion represented by the Mississippi Summer Project.

This summer, within a very few days, the enemy will launch his final push for victory here in Mississippi. This offensive will consist of two basic salients. . . .

One. Massive street demonstrations and agitation by blacks in many areas at once, designed to provoke white militants into counter-demonstration and open, pitched street battles, resulting in civil chaos and anarchy to provide an "excuse" for:

Two. A decree from the communist authorities in charge of the national government, which will declare the State of Mississippi to be in a state of open revolt, with a complete breakdown of law and order, and declaring martial law, followed by a massive occupation of the state by Federal troops, with all known patriotic whites placed under military arrest. . . . We will, of course, resist to the very end, but our chance of victory will undoubtedly end with the imposition of martial law in Mississippi by the communist masters in Washington. . . .[39]

See Activity 6.3 Lynchings Today? *in the Appendix*

6.C   Elected Officials: State and City Government

Questions to help you adopt a critical stance while reading the section below:

1. *How do Eastland, Johnson and Thompson perpetuate the Plantation Myth? How do they use it?*

2. *What reason might explain Mayor Thompson's adamant opposition to federal economic and educational aid to his city?*

3. *How do politicians and elected officials today use race in their political campaigns and again, when they are in office? Do they play different communities against each other?*

4. *Do different communities work against each other in your town?*

Further information:

The transcript of an interview with Horace H. Harned, Jr. is at the Digital Archives of the University of Southern Mississippi, www.lib.usm.edu/%7Espcol/crda/ oh/harnedtrans.htm

Mr. Harned is a former Mississippi state legislator and member of the Mississippi State Sovereignty Commission. The interview covers the interplay between the commission and the Citizen's Council and the influence on politics. Note especially the remarks regarding communist influence in the Civil Rights movement, including the added statement at the end.

Recommended Film:

The FBI's War on Black America (Documentary; 50 min, 1989) The film offers a thought provoking look at a government-sanctioned conspiracy, the FBI's counter intelligence program known as Cointelpro.

PAUL JOHNSON, GOVERNOR OF MISSISSIPPI

"Integration is like prohibition. If people don't want it, a whole army can't enforce it. People who want to force integration in Mississippi had better think nine hundred thousand times. The white people of Mississippi know that the vast majority of colored people of this state have turned their backs on the motley crew of invaders of our state. We will not permit ourselves to subvert our people and our rights."[40]

Paul Johnson had been Lieutenant Governor under Ross Barnett when James Meredith was the first African American student admitted to the University of Mississippi in 1962. In the minds of white Mississippians, Meredith's admission under the guard of United States troops was a federal invasion, a second Civil War. Cast in the role of defenders of the Southern "way of life," Governor Ross Barnett and Lieutenant Governor Paul Johnson, like many Mississippi politicians before them, staked their political futures on their resistance to racial equality.

Barnett had pledged in his 1959 campaign to maintain segregation at all costs. His slogan was "Roll with Ross," and lyrics to his campaign song were a paean to the Southern Way of Life. "For segregation one hundred percent; he's a moderate like some other gent. He'll fight integration with forceful intent. . . . Roll with Ross, roll with Ross; he's his own boss."[41] "The good Lord was the original segregationist," Barnett assured his supporters. "He put the Negro in Africa, separated him from all other races."[42]

"I do, hereby, finally deny you admission to the University of Mississippi," Barnett had informed Meredith. "I do so politely!"[43] When it became clear that he could no longer prevent Meredith's admission to the University of Mississippi, Barnett attempted to salvage his public image, asking the Kennedys if a Federal Marshall could draw a gun on him and appear to secure his compliance only under force of arms. Then, worried that a single gun would not convince his constituents that he had adequately resisted, Barnett requested an entire squad. "We'll have a big crowd here and if we all turn away because of one gun, it would be embarrassing," Barnett complained.[44] Kennedy refused, offering instead a single drawn gun, while a squad of federal marshals patted their holsters. The two men failed to reach an agreement on the appropriate theatrics, and the plan was abandoned.[45]

When Paul Johnson, who was photographed as Lieutenant Governor resisting a Federal officer with clenched fist, ran for governor, he evoked images of his "stand" at the University of Mississippi with the slogan, "Stand Tall with Paul." His inaugural address seemed moderate to outsiders, however, and there was hope that a new level of co-operation could be reached. "I would point out to you that the Mississippi economy is not divisible by race, color, or creed," Johnson promised. "As of this hour, Paul Johnson is working for everybody with every resource at his command. I will say to you that you and I are part of this world, whether we like it or not. We are Americans as well as Mississippians. Hate or ignorance will not lead

Mississippi while I sit in the governor's chair."[46] Despite these statements, however, Johnson took an uncompromising stance toward the activities of Freedom Summer.

On July 2, 1964, President Lyndon Johnson signed into law a new Civil Rights Act, which the Supreme Court declared constitutional five months later.* Many areas of the South announced their intention to comply. A group of businessmen in Saint Augustine, Florida, scene of a recent jailing of Martin Luther King when he had attempted to integrate a local restaurant, agreed to abide by the "law of the land." When asked what would happen if King returned, one local businessman replied, "He will be served."[47] Mayor Beverly Briley of Nashville promised that local citizens "not only will abide by the law of the land, but will continue to co-operate voluntarily in solving the complex problems that are of this generation."[48]

Mississippi's Governor Paul Johnson, on the other hand, predicted "some real trouble." "I think a lot of people would go out of business rather than try to comply with the law." When asked if he thought Mississippians should obey the ruling, Johnson replied, "I don't think they should."[49]

Document 6.6   1965 Voting Rights Hearings
U.S. Commission on Civil Rights[50] (excerpt)
STATEMENT OF HON. PAUL B. JOHNSON, GOVERNOR OF THE STATE OF
MISSISSIPPI

GOVERNOR JOHNSON: My statement is entitled "Mississippi, the State of Law and Order." The Civil Rights Act of 1964 as passed by the Congress is the law of the land, and Mississippi knows it. Most Mississippians do not like the new law. They are convinced that its passage was unwise and unnecessary. Some of them will challenge its constitutionality in the courts, as is their right. But resistance will be confined to such accepted legal processes. Law and order will be maintained in Mississippi by Mississippians. . .all law violators being dealt with equally. . . . The unfavorable and in many instances the false image of Mississippi that has been created by the few in our State who have committed unpardonable criminal acts has been exploited by unfriendly national news media. . . . Mississippi now asks those who have criticized our former position and

---

* The new law established the Equal Employment Opportunity Commission (EEOC) and Community Relations Service to handle bias complaints. Johnson appointed an advisory committee, and asked Congress for increased funding to insure enforcement of the new law.

actions to get off of our back and to get on our side. With your help, I predict that from this turbulent time will be born expanding opportunities for the disadvantaged people, white as well as nonwhite, of our potentially wealthy or rich State, increasing productivity through which we can earn a standard of living closer to the national average. . . . In my inaugural address I said to the people of Mississippi. . .that as long as I sat in the Governor's office, that there would be no prejudice, no ignorance that would control the Governor's office. . . . And I say to this Commission that I am delighted that you are here; that you will be a real fact-finding committee. We believe in Mississippi that the facts will show, or will bear out to a great extent the statement which I have read. . . . I believe that people on the local levels and on State levels can solve their own problems. . . . I have this morning enunciated the golden dawning of a grander day for all our people. Thank you.

ALAN THOMPSON, MAYOR OF JACKSON, MISSISSIPPI

Before the arrival of the Freedom Summer volunteers in 1964, Jackson Mayor Allan Thompson armed his city as if for war. Proud of his successful defiance of the Jackson movement, Thompson adopted a similar posture toward the "invaders." The Jackson police department acquired an armored vehicle dubbed a "Thompson Tank," which had room inside for ten men and fourteen vents from which to fire rifles or tear gas. The police added to their fleet of paddy wagons, which could be outfitted with wire cages for transporting prisoners, and arranged for the renovation of two large buildings at the Mississippi State Fair grounds to hold up to five thousand prisoners.

In 1965, Thompson testified before the United States Commission on Civil Rights, an investigation into alleged abuses of voting rights in Mississippi:

> We have spent $30 million on our school construction alone. . . . We do not want Federal money put into our educational system. . .this excellent school system. . . . The city of Jackson has no slums. We do not have any Federal urban renewal. . . . This is another way that we are protecting the civil rights of the people of this city. . . . I fought [the 1964] civil rights law probably more than any other mayor in the United States. . .but Congress passed it, and as long as it is on the books, we are going to obey the law.

Now, the thing that worries me, though—and I want to get this point over—is not so much the civil rights law, but the pressure groups who [say:] we are going to intimidate, we are going to threaten, we are going to bring violence by nonviolence, we are going to tear up your city unless you do everything that we say. . . . [O]ne of the hardest things we have ever had to endure was the invasion of the COFOs last summer. . . . Second, another inexcusable thing to me. . .is the acceptance of the so-called Freedom Democrats. . . . Then next, the threat of a boycott of Mississippi worries a great many people. It doesn't worry me, because I know when people find out about it, they will say that is un-American. . . . No matter what is said, the citizens of Jackson, both white and colored. . .are guaranteed equal protection under the law in Jackson, and in Mississippi.[51]

THE STATE SOVEREIGNTY COMMISSION

In the wake of the *Brown vs. Board of Education* decision, the Mississippi State Legislature created the State Sovereignty Commission. The bill, which created the agency, stated that its purpose was to prevent "federal usurpation of states' rights."[52] The State Sovereignty Commission funded a speaker's bureau; advocates of segregation from Mississippi toured other parts of the country in an effort to clarify and explain Mississippi's resistance to desegregation. An investigative branch reported to the Commission the activities of "subversives" and outsiders to the state, in an effort to rid the state of what were believed to be communist influences. COFO's activities were reported in detail to the Commission.

Document 6.7 Excerpts from Reports of the Mississippi State Sovereignty Commission[53]

TITLE: Sunflower County—Negro Voter Agitators—Robert Moses, Samuel Block, John O. Hodges, Albert Garner, Charles R. McLauren, Lafayette Burney (a 17 year old Negro boy)

DATE OF INVESTIGATION: September 7, 1962

INVESTIGATED BY: Tom Scarbrough, Investigator

DATE OF REPORT: September 11, 1962

Upon my arrival [at Indianola, Mississippi], I contacted Sheriff Woodley Carr and Chief of Police Will Love. I learned from these two gentlemen that the trial of five Negro males who were charged with handing out literature without a city permit would be held at 7:30 A.M. I spent the remainder of the night in Indianola and returned to the Mayor's Office the next morning around 7:00 to attend the trial of the five Negroes, namely,

Robert Moses, 17 West 139th Street, New York, New York. I am advised that his address is located two doors from the Communist Party's newspaper, *The Daily Worker.*

Samuel Theodore Block, Jr., 206 Washington Street, Cleveland, Mississippi. This Negro has been getting benefits through the State Vocational Rehabilitation. He graduated from the East Side Negro High School in 1959. This is the same Negro on whom I made an investigation in the early part of August in Greenwood, Mississippi.

John O. Hodges, who is President of the Student Body of the Greenwood, Mississippi, High School.

Albert Garner, who is a student at Greenwood, Mississippi, and the leader of a Negro high school band in Greenwood.

Charles R. McLauren, who gave his address only as Jackson, Mississippi, and a Negro youth who was released from his charges by the name of **Lafayette Burney,** seventeen years old, address, Greenwood, Mississippi.

These same Negroes were tried in City Court in Clarksdale, Mississippi the week before on similar charges. At this trial so many Negroes crowded into the courtroom to lend their moral support to these agitators it was impossible for a white man to get a seat. The situation at this trial in Indianola went in complete reverse to their trial in Clarksdale the previous week, as there were at least a hundred good, substantial white citizens in the Mayor's Court, which completely filled up the courtroom before any of the defendants arrived for trial. . . . All of the defendants, as well as their attorney, appeared to be very much set back by the fact that so many white people were in the courtroom who were interested in hearing the trial of this bunch of agitators. . . . The Mayor found everyone guilty as charged and fined each one $100.00 or thirty days in jail. . . .

It is my thinking that Moses is the brains behind all of the group of voter agitator registrants which is going on in the Delta at this time, and it is highly possible Moses is affiliated with the Communists. Moses was asked in Indianola if he is acquainted with Carl Braden, who has been labeled a Communist and who also is up in the same area as Moses at this time. Moses replied that Carl Braden is a good friend of his. . . . Further investigation revealed that Norman Kurland and Edgar Brown, two white males who are U.S. representatives on Civil Rights out of Washington,

D.C., were active in this area at the same time all of these agitators were busy regimenting Negroes, bringing them into the Circuit clerk's office to register to vote. Also, James Bevel and his wife, Diane Nash. . .are busy insisting on Negroes going to the courthouse in Indianola, Greenwood and Cleveland to register to vote. . . . The following is a list of the names, ages, and addresses of the Negroes whom this bunch of agitators have excorted [sic] to the Circuit Clerk's Office in Indianola, Mississippi, during this voters' drive by Negroes in Sunflower County: [There follows a list of 29 residents of Indianola and Ruleville, ranging in age from 24 to 75. Included in the list is Fannie Lou Hamer.]

I examined all of the applications which have been filled out by both Negroes and Whites for the month of August up to the 7th day of September in Sunflower County, and it is my thinking that not more than two out of the group that took the examination came close to passing the test to qualify to vote. More investigations will be pursued over the area where these agitators are now at work. . . . It is my opinion that almost anything can happen in the Delta at this time and it will be brought about by the activities of these known communist-associated agitators.

INVESTIGATION OF THE FIREBOMBING OF THE HOME OF HARTMAN TURNBOW

TITLE: Holmes County

DATE OF INVESTIGATION: May 10, 1963

DATE OF REPORT: May 14, 1963

INVESTIGATED BY: Tom Scarbrough, Investigator

Deputy Smith advised me. . .that the Justice Department had received a report from Hartman Turnbow that the home in which he was living was fired into by two white men that morning and further that the home was set on fire by bottles filled with lighted gasoline being thrown through the window. Deputy Smith stated that 30 minutes later he was on the scene at Hartman Turnbow's home and that when he arrived, Robert Moses was already there and was busy taking pictures. . . . Deputy Smith stated he arrested Moses and charged him with interfering with an officer. He further stated that Lee Vone Hampton, Zack E. Ball, and Hollis Watkins all Negroes, were on the scene and appeared very much interested in what had taken place at the Turnbow home. The above trio, he stated, were arrested for questioning. All three of these Negroes are known racial agitators believed to be trained by Robert Moses in the field of agitation. . . .

Hollis Watkins told Investigators that Hartman Turnbow, his wife and daughters came to his house on the morning of May 9 about 6:00 and advised him as to what had happened at the Turnbow residence several hours previously and further requested Watkins to call the Justice Department and let them know what had taken place. He stated that he thought the best thing to do was to call Robert Moses the ring leader of all Negro agitation and advise him first as to what Turnbow had told him. He stated Moses assured him that the Justice Department would be notified by him immediately as to the firing into Turnbow's home and setting it on fire. . . .

It was generally concluded because of the physical facts pertaining to the bombing and shooting at the Turnbow home and because of conflicting statements the five Negro agitators gave, that Turnbow himself set his home on fire and that the entire incident was bogus and further that Turnbow did all the shooting which he alleged white people did, or else he had knowledge as to whom did do it. It is possible that Turnbow was assisted by Lee Vone Hampton, Zack Ball, and Hollis Watkins, and possibly Robert Moses in framing up and implementing the shooting and burning of Turnbow's home in order to create more interest in the Negro voter registration drive in which all of these five Negroes have been the principal leaders in trying to put across the drive among the Negroes of Holmes County. It seems that Holmes County Negroes had decided for themselves that no good could come from anything these five Negroes were advocating and supporting.

Immediately after the aforementioned five Negroes were jailed. . .the Justice Department has filed in federal district court a suit seeking immediate release of all five of the Negroes who were suspected of being involved in the shooting and burning of Turnbow's home on the grounds that Holmes County authorities had made false charges against them to intimidate and place the defendants under duress for the purpose of preventing them from making progress in the field of voter registration work among the Negroes and from obtaining their constitutional rights.

Apparently the voter registration drive has flopped in Holmes County as local Negroes feel that agitators like the ones mentioned in this report are doing much harm to the Negroes in Holmes County and are not responding by trying to register to vote. Only seven Negroes, which makes a total of 36, have applied to register to vote in Holmes County since my last report. . . .

It is my personal thinking that unless the group of Negro agitators receive more support through the Justice Department and if they cannot create some sensational incident by which they can obtain the interest of more Negroes that the voter registration drive in Holmes County will flop.

Since this incident cited above, Lawrence Guyot, a mulatto Negro voter registration worker, from Atlanta, Georgia, has been going from house to house in the city of Lexington among the Negroes trying to get them to go to register to vote, but so far as is now, Guyot has not been able to influence anyone inside of Lexington to apply to vote. The vast majority of Holmes County Negroes would like very much for this group of outside Negro agitators to leave Holmes County and let them alone.

More investigation will be done in Holmes County concerning these Negro agitators as needed.

TITLE: Leflore County

DATE OF INVESTIGATION: June 20, 21, 26, and 27, 1963

DATE OF REPORT: July 2, 1963

INVESTIGATED BY: Tom Scarbrough, Investigator

Upon my arrival in Greenwood, I was advised by Sheriff John Ed Cochran that 58 Negroes were arrested the night before about 10:30 or 11:00 P.M. for demonstrating and throwing bricks through the windshields in some used cars. . . . Seventeen of the group between the ages of 12 and 17 were turned over to the youth court for trial. Twenty-eight adults were tried and found guilty before Justice of the Peace Joe Russell. They were given $500.00 each and sentenced to six months on the county farm. Seventeen Negro women were fined $200.00 and four months on the county farm. . . .

On June 26. . .Negro agitators. . .assembled at the courthouse with their lunches just outside of the Circuit Clerk's office and were told by the officer that the Circuit Clerk's office was closed. They were scattering papers in which their lunches were wrapped around the front of the courthouse. When told to disperse some of them did but later re-grouped and renewed their demonstration. The Negroes claimed that they were waiting for the clerk to return. . . . They were told more than one time to disperse. Guyot began to jump up and down and stomp his feet and told the officers they had no right to tell him what to do; that he was well within his constitutional rights. This was when the officers moved in and arrested the entire group who were left. . . . One of the youths who was arrested told authorities the reason they did not disperse when officers told them to was they were instructed by their leaders to pay no attention to authorities but to follow the advice and leadership of the Negro agitator leaders. . . . He said he did not know what part he had in the movement other than to follow the leaders and to try to help his people. He did not say how other than by adding his presence. . . .

A Jewish lawyer by the name of Rothenburg and another lawyer by the name of Martin with the Civil Rights Division of the Justice Department were. . .trying to get them released from the county farm. There were also some out of state reporters in the clerk's office. . . . The Justice Department has already filed suit against John Frazier, County Attorney, the sheriff and other officials of Leflore County requesting the release from the county farm of all agitators mentioned in this report. This hearing is scheduled before Federal Judge Claude Clayton. It is my thinking that the petition for release of most of these agitators will be denied by the federal court because of the fact civil rights were not involved for many of those who were found guilty by the courts.

6.D George W. Lee: Local Law Enforcement

Questions to help you adopt a critical stance while reading the section below:

1. *What incidents occurred that reveal that the power structure was continuing to use both legal as well as illegal violence to hold onto its power? Why would the power structure believe that such violence is effective? Under what conditions would it be? Under what conditions might it not be?*

2. *How do you look at the police in your town, in your neighborhood? Is that different in other your communities or ethnic groups? Do you think the police are on your side?*

GEORGE W. LEE

"We respectfully ask that you will at this time endorse and support our efforts to become full-fledged citizens in this county."[54]

The Reverend George W. Lee was a minister, grocer, and owner of a small printing press in Belzoni, Mississippi. As president and co-founder of the local chapter of the NAACP, Lee produced pamphlets encouraging participation in the NAACP and in voter registration efforts. Lee was alternately cajoled and threatened by local whites in an effort to suppress his activities and finally murdered. His widow recalls that the local power structure "knew that he couldn't be bought."[55] In 1955, after a year of intense effort, Lee and Gus Courts had convinced ninety-two people to try to register to vote.

Shortly before Lee's death, Congressman Charles Diggs of Detroit had been the featured speaker at a rally. Diggs had told the assembled crowd of several thousand that "the time for segregation is running out in Mississippi." Lee had also spoken to the crowd, and made a strong impression on journalist Simeon Booker. Booker wrote,

> One of the most unusual men at the meeting was the Reverend George W. Lee. 'Pray not for your mom and pop,' he urged the crowd. 'They've gone to heaven. Pray you can make it through this hell. . .' Unlike his brethren, he preached well beyond the range of Bible and Heaven and the Glory Road. As one of the vice presidents of the Mississippi Council of Negro Leadership and a member of the NAACP, he sermonized about voting and eventually electing a Negro congressman—an idea that caused whites to fear such a political triumph because of the predominant Negro population.[56]

Gus Courts, a local Mississippian encouraged by Lee to register to vote, recalled:

> Two hours before (Rev. Lee) was killed, he called me over to his store and he showed me a letter that . . . was sticking in his screen door, and it said, 'Preacher, instead of you preaching the Gospel, what you say you were called to do, you are preaching to Negroes here in Humphreys County to register and vote. You had better do what you claim that you were called to do, that is, preach the Gospel.'[57]

On May 7, 1955, the Saturday evening before Mother's Day, Lee was driving home from the dry cleaners where he had just picked up his "preaching suit." Someone drove up beside him in a car and shot him through the window with a shotgun. The blast tore off one entire side of his face. A sheriff's investigation ruled that Lee had died in an automobile accident, and that the lead pellets removed from his jaw were probably dental fillings.

Lee's neighbors did not accept the verdict and attempted to notify officers of the NAACP. The NAACP sent Medgar Evers to investigate Lee's death. At first, Evers had difficulty convincing witnesses to testify. After the FBI entered the investigation, one witness was flown to Illinois, where it would be safer to make a statement.

Lee's shooting was typical of the intimidation tactics used for years to discourage NAACP participation and voter registration. By the time of the funeral several days later, many who had known Lee were angry. The crowd attending Lee's funeral was so large that it overflowed the church, indicating a new resistance to intimidation. Lee's casket was set for display on an open truck which was also used as a rostrum. Several of the mourners took the opportunity of Lee's funeral to whisper information about the killing to Evers. Dr. A. H. McCoy had noticed the local sheriff hovering near the service. "Instead of frightening us," said McCoy, "this shocking tragedy has served as a stimulus. Sheriff Shelton is sitting outside that door right now; he and his boys... The Sheriff says that the Reverend Lee's death is one of the most puzzling cases he's ever come across. The only puzzling thing is why the Sheriff doesn't arrest the men who did it."[58]

Of Lee, Roy Wilkins said, "Rev. Lee did not just tell the people what they ought to do. He gave them an example. He fought for equality and first class citizenship and asked them to follow him."[59] In concluding the service, Dr. T. R. M. Howard said, "Reverend Lee was a warrior, and he was murdered because he refused to put down his arms in this civil rights battle. He was murdered because there are people in this state who oppose our having every advantage of citizenship. Reverend Lee did not die as a cringing coward but as a hero. His death will be long remembered in this Delta land. He did not die in vain."[60]

LOCAL LAW ENFORCEMENT

The action of the police after Lee's death was not unusual. Local police in Mississippi failed to enforce laws protecting persons and property of civil rights workers as well as actively intimidating the workers. COFO was so concerned about this double defiance that they kept detailed records of incidents.

Document 6.8 COFO, Running Summary of Incidents[61] (excerpts)

JUNE 24

Drew: Thirty volunteers, staff workers engaged in voter registration meet open hostility from whites. Weapons shown.

Canton: Civil rights car hit by bullet.

Collins: 40 M-1 rifles 1,000 rounds of ammunition stolen from National Guard armory.

JUNE 25

Ruleville: Williams Chapel firebombed. Damage slight. Eight plastic bags with gasoline found later outside building.

Jackson: Two separate arrests of volunteers on minor traffic charges. Seven questioned in one case; charges dropped in other.

Phil: Southern newsman's car deliberately rammed by local citizen. Newsman gets two tickets.

Itta Bena: Two volunteers working with local Negro, handing out literature for voter registration rally, taken to gas station–bus stop by four white men who tell them: "If you speak in town tonight, you'll never leave here."

Greenville: Federal building demonstration. No harassment.

Durant: Civil rights worker's car stopped on highway for repairs. Driver charged with illegal parking. $60 bond paid.

JUNE 26

Hattiesburg: Hatred literature from whites: "Beware, good Negro citizens. When we come to get the agitators, stay away."

Columbus: Seven voter registration workers arrested for distributing literature without a city permit. Bond: $400 each.

Itta Bena: FBI arrests three local residents for June 25 incident. Two are released on $2,000 bail, one on $1000.

Clinton: Church of Holy Ghost arson. Kerosene spilled on floor, lit after local white pastor speaks to Negro Bible class. (Fifth firebombing in 10 days.)

Holmes County: Two staffers detained for illegal parking, no Mississippi permit. One arrested. Bond $60.

Holly Springs: Harassment: beer cans tossed at volunteers, car tires slashed.

THE CHALLENGE OF MISSISSIPPI 197

Greenwood: Freedom House call: "You'd better not go to sleep or you won't get up." Voter registration worker picked up by police, released after questioning.

Jackson: CORE field secretary beaten at Hinds County jail while a federal prisoner. Third beating of a civil rights worker at same jail in two months, second of federal prisoner.

Canton: Two volunteers picked up by police, told all out-of-town visitors must register with them. Registered, released.

Belzoni: Three arrested for disturbing the peace. Two released without charges, third held on $100 bond.

JUNE 27

Batesville: Local person helping voter registration gets obvious harassment: ticket for illegal parking outside courthouse.

Vicksburg: Threatening call: "We're going to get you."

Philadelphia: Local Negro contact has bottle thrown through window of home. Threatening note attached.

Greenwood: Several phone harassments; bomb threat.

Doddsville: Highway Patrol kills 34-year-old Negro with history of mental illness. Local deputy who knew Negro with patrolman. Mother asks to see body. Police reply: "Get that hollering woman away." Ruled "justifiable homicide" in 17 hours.

Jackson: Two phone threats: "We're going to kill you white SOBs."

JUNE 28

Jackson: Civil rights worker held 8–1/2 hours without charges; stopped for no reason while driving near COFO office. (Mississippi law permits holding for 72 hours "for investigation.")

Vicksburg: High school girl tells friends COFO "going to get it."

Canton: Threatening calls throughout the night.

Ruleville: Mayor tells visiting white Methodist chaplain he cannot attend white Methodist services: "You came here to live with Negroes, so you can go to church with them, too." He does, with three volunteers.

Batesville: Report local Negro man beaten, missing.

Jackson: "Hospitality Month" in Mississippi: white volunteer kicked over from behind, slugged on arrival from Oxford at local train station.

JUNE 29

Hattiesburg: Two cars owned by volunteers shot by four whites in pickup truck at 1 AM. No injuries, $100 damage to each car. Three witnesses. (Owners were sleeping two blocks away.)

Columbus: Six carloads of whites drive up on lawn of Freedom House. Five flee before police arrive. Police question, release two men in sixth car.

Hattiesburg: Civil rights worker charged with reckless driving, failure to give proper signal. Held overnight, paid fine. Phone rings. Volunteers hears tape recording of last 20 seconds of his previous conversation. Someone Goofed!

Biloxi: Volunteers in White Community Program turned away from hotel.

Columbus: Restaurants serving volunteers threatened.

JUNE 30:

Vicksburg: Negro woman threatened for registering to vote.

Ruleville: Man loses job for housing white volunteer.

Jackson: Car circles office with gun, threatens teenager: "Want to shoot some pool, nigger?" Volunteer charged with reckless driving. Fine $34. (He moved from one traffic lane to another in integrated car.)

Holly Springs: White teenagers scream profanities, throw rocks at office from passing car.

Hattiesburg: Whites in pickup truck with guns visible drive past office several times. FBI checks June 29 car shooting.

Holly Springs: SNCC staff worker jumped by local white who threatens to shoot both him and his office with 12-gauge shotgun.

Harmony: Freedom School teachers arrive. School superintendent announces first Negro summer school in memory of local residents.

Document 6.9   Report on Beatings in McComb, June 8, 1964[62]
SNCC
6 Raymond Str. NW
Atlanta 14, Ga.
Three men, ages 22, 24 and 29 all white (from New York, Chicago and Waltham, Mass) were traveling from New Orleans to Jackson. They stopped in McComb about 2 pm Monday June 8th to have some food at a drive-in. As soon as they entered the town (the car has Massachusetts plates), a

police car spotted them and radioed the chief of police. Within 3 minutes the police chief arrived at the drive-in and demanded to know what they were doing in McComb. They answered that they were doing some free-lance writing on Mississippi and the South and were interested in seeing some of the city officials. The police chief detained them for another 4–5 minutes asking if they were planning to stay in McComb and, if not, why had they stopped in McComb. Again the men (one is a recent student, one a writer and the other a lawyer) answered that they were writing about the South and just traveling through. (They were on a two-week tour of the South and were not connected with the movement directly). Then the police chief took them to the City Hall where they spoke with the mayor of McComb for about two hours. (The mayor is the past president of the White Citizen's Council in that area.) Then they talked with the police chief again who told them that McComb was "ready for the summer and prepared to meet the Northern agitators who were coming down." The chief then asked if they were leaving McComb and they answered that they would visit a few more people in town before going on to Jackson. They left the city hall and visited several Negroes in town but were followed by the police the entire time.

During their conversations with the police chief he was extremely proud of his "efficient" police force; then the three men said that if the police force was so good then they expected that their rights would be well protected in McComb, too. Upon leaving McComb (about 8 PM) they were escorted to the city line by a police car that was tailed by an unmarked car. At the city limits a police car turned off and the unmarked car continued to follow them. Beyond Summit, Mississippi—about 5–8 miles out of McComb—the unmarked car passed them and slowed down. Another car pulled up behind them and the third car pulled out from a side road and forced them over to the edge of the road. Nine men jumped out of the three cars and at least three were armed with rifles. One had a pistol which he placed at the driver's head, and forced him (the driver) out of the car. He said: "you guys are going to get blown sky high." Meanwhile the other men with brass knuckles began to beat the two fellows left in the car. The one in the front seat (the lawyer) had a broken nose and jaw and smashed face as a result while the fellow in the back seat suffered head cuts. They were beaten continuously for 7 minutes. The man with the gun at the driver's head said this was only a taste of what outsiders would get in McComb and that they were sick and tired of having Northern agitators around. He then asked the driver which Negroes they had seen in town and the driver replied that they knew as well as he since the police had followed them all day. Suddenly the men stopped beating the three and drove off— apparently because several cars had passed and they were worried about being seen. The three then drove on to Jackson to the COFO office where hospital treatment was required for the two who were beaten. Protests were lodged with the FBI, the Justice Department and with the McComb police department.

See Activity 6.1   Segregation Under Attack *in the Appendix*
See Activity 6.2   Role Play: What Really Happened? *in the Appendix*

1964 Freedom School Curriculum Link:

Behind the Cotton Curtain
   www.educationanddemocracy.org/FSCfiles/C_CC7g_BehindCottonCurtain.htm
   This is an account by a SNCC field secretary about the repression in Mississippi

SEVEN

Toward Freedom Summer

Questions to help you adopt a critical stance while reading the section below:

1. *What role did each organization (NAACP, CORE, SCLC, and SNCC) play in the Mississippi Freedom Summer Project?*

2. *To what degree does this chapter support the following hypothesis: The NAACP may have seemed bureaucratically slow and maddeningly middle class to the young activists in the 1960s. Nevertheless, the organization made the Mississippi Freedom Summer Project possible in two important ways. One, the NAACP was the only functioning Civil Rights organization by 1960 that allowed activists to circumvent local authorities. Two, the NAACP had provided the legal foundation from which the strategies and tactics upon which the Freedom Summer architects depended.*

Recommended Film:

Mississippi: Is this America? (Documentary; Vol.5 of Eyes on the Prize; 55 min, 1987 and 2006; produced by Henry Hampton). Central to the Civil Rights Movement was the fight for the right to vote. This video chronicles the voting rights efforts of activists like the NAACP's Medgar Evers, and the pivotal Freedom Summer of 1964. Michael Schwerner, Andrew Goodman, James Chaney, Robert

Moses, Fannie Lou Hamer, and others are featured. Profiles of the NAACP, SCLC, SNCC and COFO are provided. The role of Northern whites and their participation in the Freedom Summer of 1964 is also highlighted.

THE STORY OF MISSISSIPPI FREEDOM SUMMER is one of cooperation. In the years before 1964, many organizations worked to promote social justice for African Americans. Many times such efforts were hampered because the leadership of these organizations had trouble working together. To avoid the conflict of egos and competition for funds, the freedom fighters in Mississippi formed a coalition in 1962 by creating the Council of Federated Organizations (COFO), made up of members from NAACP, CORE, SCLC, and SNCC. While the leadership often jealously guarded the independent identities of their associations, many of the rank-and-file of each of the participating organizations in COFO did not always see themselves in competition with one another. The membership of each association often overlapped or people moved from one organization to another. For example, Rosa Parks worked as secretary for the NAACP while she participated in workshops at Highlander and initiated the events leading to the Montgomery Bus boycott and the formation of the SCLC. Ella Baker was assistant field secretary for the NAACP, organized the SCLC's headquarters in Atlanta and became instrumental in the founding of SNCC. Throughout the story of Freedom Summer, COFO provided the support for the people, who shared the same vision and passion and cooperated regardless of tensions among the leadership of the four organizations—NAACP, SCLC, CORE and SNCC.

COFO emerged organically out of many ad hoc meetings and conversations between and among those who were working to oppose the white power structure in Mississippi. COFO was the name recognized by Mississippians as responsible for Freedom Summer. Nevertheless, within COFO, SNCC was to be the driving force of the Summer Project, and the vast majority of those who were working in Mississippi in the summer were the young members of SNCC, even though the organization was receiving the smallest portion of the funds that was being distributed through COFO. For example, when the Council for United Civil Rights Leadership (CUCRL) was set up on July 17, 1963, to distribute $1.5 million in corporate funding to the four major Civil Rights groups, SNCC received "by far the smallest share."[1] The project was divided into the five Mississippi congressional districts, and SNCC staffed and financed four of the districts, with 78 of the 100 project staff members, while CORE staffed one district. Bob Moses of SNCC was Program Director for COFO and served as director of the Summer Project, while Dave Dennis of CORE was Assistant Program Director.[2] Although Aaron Henry of the NAACP was president of COFO, the national leadership of the NAACP was a reluctant COFO ally. In spite of internecine struggles, however, an informal albeit fragile coalition survived to support the growing movement in Mississippi.

The Freedom School Curriculum described the history and purpose of COFO:

> QUESTION: What is COFO?
>
> ANSWER: COFO is the Council of Federated Organizations—a federation of all the national Civil Rights organizations active in Mississippi, local political and action groups and some fraternal and social organizations.
>
> QUESTION: How did COFO get started?
>
> ANSWER: COFO has evolved through three phases in is short history. The first phase of the organization was little more than an ad hoc committee called together after the Freedom Rides of 1961 in an effort to have a meeting with Governor Ross Barnett. This committee of Mississippi Civil Rights leaders proved a convenient vehicle for channeling the voter registration program of the Voter Education Project, a part of the Southern Regional Council, into Mississippi. With the funds of the Voter Education Project, COFO went into a second phase. In this period, beginning in February 1962, COFO became an umbrella for voter registration drives in the Mississippi Delta and other isolated cities in Mississippi. At this time COFO added a small full-time staff, mostly SNCC and a few CORE workers, and developed a voter registration program. The staff worked with local NAACP leaders and SCLC citizenship teachers. . .as a committee with a staff and a program until the fall of 1963.
>
> The emergence of the Ruleville Citizenship Group, and the Holmes County Voters League, testified to the possibility of starting strong local groups. It was felt that COFO could be the organization through which horizontal ties could develop among these groups. . . . During this second phase we began to feel more and more that the Committee could be based in a network of local adult groups sprung from the Movement as we worked the state.

The third phase representing the present functioning of the organization began in the fall of 1963 with the Freedom Vote for Governor. This marked the first state-wide effort and coincided with the establishment of a state-wide office in Jackson and a trunk line to reach into the Mississippi Delta and hill country. The staff has broadened to include more CORE and SNCC workers and more citizenship schools.

—From Unit VII, Part 2(I), Freedom School Curriculum

SNCC's decision to move to Mississippi can be seen as the culminating decision of many that led to Freedom Summer. Its decision to focus on voter registration in Mississippi in 1960 led ultimately to the Freedom Vote of 1963 and the Freedom Days of 1964. The success of these efforts inspired the creation of a state-wide alternative party to challenge the entrenched political power of the Mississippi Democrats on the national stage. But to register voters in Mississippi, even for an alternative party, required that the institutions that supported the white power structure be undermined with a wide range of tactics. White northern volunteers were needed to provoke federal intervention. NAACP legal defense lawyers were needed to rescue jailed protesters and demand enforcement of existing federal laws. And an educational program was needed to instill the confidence and provide the skills needed to organize and vote. CORE community centers and SCLC citizenship schools provided the foundation upon which the Freedom Schools would be built. At the end of 1963, Charles Cobb proposed having Freedom Schools. In a March 1964, meeting in New York City, the Freedom School Curriculum began to be written. Shortly after that, the call went out for volunteers to come down to Mississippi to help teach in the schools and work in community centers. Nearly a thousand people would answer the call. Roughly 650 volunteers, mostly white college students from 37 states, came for the whole summer, and hundreds of ministers, nurses, doctors, lawyers and artists lent their professional support for a few weeks.[3]

See Activity 7.1   Taking Action: A Hypothetical Case in the Appendix

1964 Freedom School Curriculum Links:
Prospectus for the Mississippi Freedom Summer
    www.educationanddemocracy.org/FSCfiles/B_01_ProspForMSFSummer.htm

This prospectus was sent out by COFO to explain the Freedom Summer and invite
  people to join the project.
COFO Flyer: Freedom Summer
  www.educationanddemocracy.org/FSCfiles/B_02_FlyerFreedomSummer.html
  This Flyer was distributed in Mississippi.

7.A   Aaron Henry: Freedom Vote and Freedom Days

Questions to help you adopt a critical stance while reading the section below:
  1. *How did the "protest vote" work? Why did the organizers ask white students*
     to come and help with the campaign? Why did the organizers set up a bi-racial
     ticket: the black pharmacist Aaron Henry for Governor and the white chaplain
     Ed King for Lieutenant Governor?
  2. *Is it important for blacks to vote for black candidates? What are "minority*
     voting districts," and is it important to have them?

Further information:
  The transcript of an interview with Aaron Henry is at the Digital Archives of the
  University of Southern Mississippi, anna.lib.usm.edu/%7Espcol/crda/oh/
  ohhenryab.htm

AARON HENRY
"The sharecropper is dependent. The cottonpicker is dependent. The school-
teacher is dependent. And the public employees are dependent. Any step which
will bring a Negro into the public view, in an effort to register to vote, will
increase the likelihood that an employer, or a creditor, or landlord will deprive
him of the economic necessities of life. . . . To take an economic risk in Missis-
sippi is to risk life itself."[4]

Like Medgar Evers and Amzie Moore, Aaron Henry was a veteran of World
War II who returned to Mississippi determined to change things. Henry
grew up in a sharecropping family near Clarksdale, Mississippi, where he
was encouraged to join the NAACP by a high school teacher. A successful
pharmacist and businessman, Henry, often referred to as "Doc," started out
as a shoeshine boy and porter at the Cotton Bowl Court Hotel in Clarksdale.[5] A local chapter of the NAACP was formed in Clarksdale after a case
involving the rape of two black teenaged girls by local white men resulted in
an acquittal. Opposition to Henry's political activities by whites increased

after the 1954 *Brown v. Board* decision, which Henry publicly supported. He then began to suffer economic reprisals and threats.

A friend of Medgar Evers, Henry appreciated the importance of a national organization to challenge the isolation of blacks in Mississippi. Although Henry became state president of the NAACP by 1960, he frequently questioned the organization's opposition to direct action. At his acceptance speech, Henry called for Mississippi blacks to confront their status directly: "Our actions will probably result in many of us being guests in the jails of the state. We will make these jails Temples of Freedom."[6] Under his leadership, the black community in Clarksdale organized and maintained a boycott against local businesses. The boycott began in November of 1961, when the newly elected mayor, a vocal segregationist, cancelled the longstanding tradition of including the marching bands from the local black high school and junior college in the annual Clarksdale Christmas parade. The angry students, perhaps inspired by the recent student demonstrations in McComb, planned a march on City Hall, but were dissuaded by Henry. "There were too many students and too much bond money involved to go into this without it being well-planned," explained Henry. Henry suggested a boycott to exert pressure on the Chamber of Commerce. The boycotters adopted the slogan, "If we can't PARADE downtown, should we TRADE downtown?"[7] The students were a significant factor in the boycott's success. When local authorities began harassing Henry with specious legal charges and fired his wife from her teaching job, he requested help from the national office of the NAACP and from the SCLC. Martin Luther King spoke to an audience of over a thousand in Clarksdale, urging them to "stand in, sit in, and walk in by the thousands."[8] However, local officials still refused to negotiate, hoping to wait out the boycotters and harass the group's leadership. Both Henry's home and his pharmacy were bombed. Picketers and demonstrators were arrested, and the Clarksdale jails were filled with the sounds of freedom songs so galling to local law enforcement. Henry himself was arrested and assigned to work detail on a garbage truck.

Henry headed COFO in Mississippi, and the creation of COFO helped to ease somewhat the tension between the traditional NAACP and SNCC staff. During the Freedom Vote of 1963, Henry was elected Governor of Mississippi. As a campaigner, Henry proved to have a clear grasp of issues combined with an engaging stump-speaker style of oratory. While on the campaign trail, he frequently joked with his audiences. "Now white people will tell us that they have to have segregation because they don't want us fooling with their white women. I just wish the white men were as satisfied with their women as we are with ours."[9] Henry opposed the state legislature's efforts to increase spending in Mississippi's segregated black schools and spoke forcefully on the necessity of integrating schools as a means of equalizing educational facilities for blacks and whites.

THE FREEDOM VOTE

By spring of 1963, Bob Moses realized that, despite SNCC's efforts, only five percent of the eligible black population in Mississippi was registered. SNCC was open to new strategies. In July of 1963, Moses met Allard Lowenstein, a white activist who had come to Mississippi to participate in demonstrations following the death of Medgar Evers. Lowenstein, author of a book entitled *Brutal Mandate* about his experiences in Africa, found Mississippi "like South Africa, only a little bit better."[10] Basing his suggestion on the day of mourning called by black South Africans to protest their disenfranchisement, Lowenstein suggested a protest vote for the black population of Mississippi. Among the first white student volunteers in Mississippi were a group of law students doing research in Jackson. They uncovered a Mississippi state law under which voters who felt that they had been unfairly excluded from the official election could cast votes that would be set aside until their protest had been investigated. Applying this law in 1963, COFO workers began to organize a protest vote for the August Democratic primary. Many disenfranchised blacks were able to file protest votes at polling places in Jackson and Greenwood without suffering violent reprisals.[11]

Nevertheless, the Voter Education Project (VEP), a non-profit organization that had been distributing funds to the four COFO organizations, continued to indicate that it was going to withdraw much of its financial support from the state, claiming that the failure to officially register black voters did not justify the expense. Further, the risk to all concerned seemed too great. VEP Director Wiley Branton stated that the project "was very concerned about the failure of the federal government to protect the people who have sought to register and vote or who are working actively in getting others to register."[12]

To demonstrate to outsiders like Branton that their withdrawal would be premature, Bob Moses, with the assistance of Allard Lowenstein, planned a Freedom Vote for the November general election. Moses believed that a parallel, non-official election would create political solidarity among Mississippi's disenfranchised black population while simultaneously proving their desire to vote. By building on the protest votes cast in the August Democratic primary, with the Freedom Vote, blacks could demonstrate their willingness to be involved in the political process without the violent reprisals suffered by those trying to enter the entrenched Mississippi system. James Forman described the purposes of the Freedom Vote:

> The time had come for us to expand our voter registration work in separate communities into active political organizing on a statewide basis. And we felt ready to do so in Mississippi. The Freedom Vote Campaign. . .aimed to bring about that consolidation and expansion.
>
> The Freedom Vote had two other purposes. One was to demonstrate that, if black people could vote, they would, and in great numbers. And they would not vote for bigots. . .The second purpose was to make a further breakthrough in the fear and self-doubts of black people, to provide them with a forum for speaking out their own political ideas.[13]

To facilitate the process of publicizing and organizing the November Freedom Vote, Lowenstein, who had been a student at Yale and a dean at Stanford, contacted about one hundred Northern white students to work in Mississippi for the month before the election. These white volunteers could help assist in the massive organizational task to be completed in a brief period of time; they could also gather ballots wherever the voters were—at work, at home, or in the fields. With the assistance of Yale and Stanford students recruited by Lowenstein, Moses and the SNCC staffers organized the Freedom Vote to coincide with the fall election.

On October 6, 1963, the Freedom Vote officially began with a state-wide convention held in the Masonic Temple in Jackson. Aaron Henry, head of the Mississippi NAACP, was selected as the candidate for governor; Ed King, white chaplain at Tougaloo College, was later chosen as his running mate. The Freedom Vote gave blacks the opportunity to express political ideas forbidden in the official election. The platform was a call for justice in education, employment, and voting rights. The convention challenged literacy as a prerequisite for voting in Mississippi, arguing that a state that offered black children substandard schools could not rightfully demand that voters could read and write. The platform argued for progressive farm measures, an increase in the minimum wage, and protections for labor unions.[14] According to campaign literature,

The platform of these candidates advocates:

1. Immediate establishment of universal suffrage.

2. Desegregation of all schools by 1965.

3. A crash program begun immediately to improve all phases of the educational system.

4. Establishment of a State Fairness Commission to insure non-discrimination in jobs, public places, public accommodations, and equal justice under the law.

5. That the following steps be taken to insure full and fair employment in Mississippi:

    a. An extensive public works system

    b. A job retraining program

    c. A just minimum wage

6. The repeal of anti-labor laws, particularly those preventing the right to organize unions.[15]

Campaign organizers were encouraged to work with the resources available in local communities. In late October, District Managers and Field Workers received a memo that stated, "With only a week left in the campaign, it might be advisable to spend most of the remaining time in trying to get as many places as possible to serve as polling places. . . . In the cases of taverns and restaurants, you might try to find someone who hangs around most of the time who will really work out or else get the owner to pitch in as much as possible. In the case of churches, it may only be necessary to have someone there on Sunday—though you may want to keep the church open for the entire three-day voting period." Campaign workers were told that it would be necessary to work with whatever materials were available. "We will not have standardized ballot boxes, so you will have to improvise," they were instructed, "i.e., use shoe boxes, hat boxes, and small cardboard boxes, etc. You should seal all boxes with tape, leaving only a slit on top large enough for the insertion of the ballots. The boxes should be marked "Freedom Ballot Box."[16]

More than 80,000 blacks voted for the Henry/King ticket while 13,000 voted for the regular, all-white Democratic candidates.* The dramatic increase in voting by blacks during the Freedom Vote brought renewed energy to voter registration work in Mississippi. According to Ivanhoe Donaldson, the Freedom Vote,

> showed the Negro population that politics is not just 'white folks' business, but that Negroes are also capable of holding political offices. It introduced a lot of Negroes, for the first time, to the idea of marking ballots. For the first time, since Reconstruction, Negroes held a rally on the steps of the Courthouse, with their own candidates, expressing their own beliefs and ideas rather than those of the 'white folks.' There was less fear in the Negro community about taking part in civil rights activities.[17]

According to Lawrence Guyot and Mike Thelwell, the Freedom Vote "extended beyond activities affecting a single town, county, municipality or electoral district, and placed us in the area of state-wide organization."[18]

Shortly after the election, an effort was made to use the Freedom Vote as a basis for challenging the legitimacy of the Mississippi general election. On November 5, Freedom Vote for Governor headquarters announced its plans to challenge the results of the Mississippi governor's race in the Federal Courts. Henry's campaign manager Bob Moses said that

> arrangements were presently being made to file suit to oust Governor-elect Paul Johnson. The suit would be based on a federal statute passed during Reconstruction which allows a candidate defeated in a state or federal election to challenge the outcome of the vote on the basis that the persons supporting him were unlawfully denied the right to vote because of race. 'Clearly,' Mr. Moses said, 'The results of the Freedom Vote indicate that there are at least eighty thousand people who would have voted for Aaron Henry if they had not been disenfranchised.'[19]

---

* The total of 93,000 represented many more than were officially registered to vote. In 1954, for example, only 22,000 of a total of 440,000 voting-age blacks were registered. Little had changed in the following decade.

The Freedom Vote also proved that white Civil Rights workers were susceptible to harassment by local authorities. While canvassing, workers were arrested and fined for distributing leaflets without a permit, for breaking curfew, for purse snatching, and for violating traffic laws. Integrated groups attempting to attend church services were also arrested and faced a year in jail and a fine of one thousand dollars. A Yale Divinity student was arrested on "suspicion of auto theft" and charged with "interfering with a police officer" after asking if the police searching his car had a proper warrant.[20]

Efforts were made to inform the Federal Government of harassment of workers. A telegraph sent to both President Johnson and the U.S. Attorney General stated,

DEMAND IMMEDIATE DISPATCH OF FEDERAL MARSHALLS TO PROTECT CAMPAIGN WORKERS FROM GROWING HARASSMENT THROUGHOUT MISSISSIPPI STOP OVER 200 INCIDENTS INVOLVING POLICE VIOLATION OF CONSTITUTIONAL RIGHTS HAVE OCCURRED IN LAST TEN DAYS STOP . . . POSSIBILITY OF FURTHER SHOOTINGS LEADING TO DEATH AS WELL AS WHOLESALE INFRINGEMENTS OF BASIC RIGHTS MAKE IMMEDIATE ACTION ON YOUR PART IMPERATIVE.[21]

> Aaron Henry, Ed King, Bob Moses, David Dennis,
> Charles Evers, R.F.T. Smith, and Allard Lowenstein.

FREEDOM DAYS

Freedom Days were attempts to follow up on the success of the Freedom Vote. The Freedom Day was both a direct action demonstration and a voter registration effort. On Freedom Days, large groups of African Americans converged on the county courthouse, symbol of segregation's stronghold, using the strength of the group and of potential publicity to pressure local officials to allow blacks to register to vote. The first Freedom Day was held January 21, 1964, in Hattiesburg, the stronghold of the notorious county registrar Theron Lynd. Lynd, a former football player and member of the White Citizens Council, had prompted a lawsuit by the Federal Government in 1961 (*U.S. vs. Lynd*) when he refused to allow examination of his files. When they were finally brought to light, it was discovered that only twenty-five of the county's nearly eight thousand eligible blacks were registered to vote. While Lynd had placed 1,836 whites on the voter roll without requiring that they fill out applications or interpret sections of the constitution, he had refused to tolerate every effort to register on the part of blacks. After the 1961 federal lawsuit, Lynd did administer the test to members of Hattiesburg's black community, testing David Lewis, a science teacher with a masters degree, and David E. Roberson, a biology teacher and recipient of a National Science Foundation grant to do graduate study at Cornell. Both were deemed unfit to vote.[22]

The Hattiesburg Freedom Day was attended by John Lewis, James Forman, Aaron Henry, and Ella Baker, in addition to members of the local community. Ella Baker stressed economic problems in her address to those convened at a rally:

> Even if segregation is gone, we will still need to be free; we will still have to see that everyone has a job. Even if we can all vote, if some people are still hungry, we will not be free. . . . Singing alone is not enough; we need schools and learning. . . . Remember, we are not fighting for the freedom of the Negro alone, we are fighting for the freedom of the human spirit, a larger freedom that encompasses all mankind.[23]

The next day, a group of about two hundred, including many clergymen from out of state, converged on the courthouse. Local police attempted to disperse the crowd, but took no action when the crowd continued to march on the courthouse. Historian Howard Zinn attended the Hattiesburg Freedom Day as both an observer and a participant. He wrote that "something unprecedented was taking place in. . .Mississippi: a black and white line of demonstrators was picketing a public building, allowed to do so by police."[24]

It was on this Freedom Day that Moses announced plans for a "Freedom Registration," the beginning of the creation of a viable alternative political party, the Mississippi Freedom Democratic Party (MFDP), which would challenge the legitimacy of the entrenched white Democratic Party. The MFDP was open to voters of all races; its intention was not to replace the Democratic Party but to replace illegally elected delegates with legally elected delegates. The existing whites-only Democratic Party was not the real Democratic Party, according to the MFDP, as it was not operating in accordance with the law or the stated principles of the Democratic Party.

Freedom Days were held throughout Mississippi. They were one of the many streams that would flow into the river of Freedom Summer.

7.B James Forman:
The Debate Over the Use of White Volunteers

Questions to help you adopt a critical stance while reading the section below:
1. *Did James Forman represent proof of Ella Baker's theory about leaders and movements (see beginning of Chapter 5)?*

2. *What were the issues that prompted a debate over whether to invite white students down?*

THE DEBATE OVER THE USE OF WHITE VOLUNTEERS

The success of the Freedom Vote suggested that it would be useful to ask again for volunteers to come to Mississippi for the Freedom Summer Project. This extension of the use of white volunteers proved very controversial among the local SNCC staff and was discussed extensively over the next months. Many within SNCC felt that Federal intervention was essential, and that such intervention would be brought about by the crisis created by the presence of hundreds of privileged white students. But others opposed that concept. "Yes, they said, those eighty white kids who had come down the previous November had created a lot of press, a lot of attention," John Lewis later wrote.

> But almost all that attention was focused on *them*. Dozens of magazine and newspaper stories featured Suzy Jones from Stanford or Jimmy Smith from Yale, working alongside poor, nameless, faceless blacks, as if those black people *had* no names or faces. That caused a lot of resentment. There was a strong current of feeling running through the SNCC membership that, 'Hey, we've been down here all these months, all these *years,* working our butts off day in and day out, and these white kids come down and stay a week or two and they get all the headlines, they get all the credit.' At an even more basic level, there was the question of perpetuating the image of racial dependence, that somehow black people need whites to get anything done. . . . Even more troubling was the tendency of some white SNCC

members to thrust themselves into leadership roles, pushing black members aside in the process.[25]

Hollis Watkins feared that SNCC's gains in terms of developing local leadership would be lost. "For the first time, we had local people who had begun to take the initiative themselves. . . . Local indigenous people knowing that most of the students would be more educated than themselves. . .would become complacent, they would feel inferior and fall back into the same rut."[26] SNCC staffer Willie Peacock commented that the local blacks might cooperate with the white students for reasons that had nothing to do with freedom. "I know that if you bring white people to Mississippi and say 'Negro, go vote,' [they will respond] 'Yassuh, we'll go try and register and vote.' I know that's not permanent. . . . When the one who looks like the oppressor comes and tells them to do something, it's not commitment. It's done out of that same slavery mentality."[27]

Fannie Lou Hamer however supported the idea: "If we're trying to break down this barrier of segregation, we can't segregate ourselves."[28] Bob Moses insisted that the issue was not one of race, but one of "rational people against irrational people." SNCC's plan was "an annealing process. Only when metal has been brought to white heat, can it be shaped and molded. This is what we intend to do in the South and in the country, bring them to white heat and then remold them."[29] Moses argued that SNCC workers had the potential to challenge within SNCC the racist system they were protesting:

And the only way you can break that down is to have white people working alongside of you—so then it changes the whole complexion of what you're doing, so it isn't any longer Negro fighting white, it's a question of rational people against irrational people. . . . I always thought the one thing we could do for this country that no one else could do is to be above the race issue.[30]

The press coverage of the Freedom Vote had revealed the media's color and class bias; their coverage had centered on the presence of the Yale and Stanford students. One article on the Freedom Vote began, "Bruce Payne is a white, blond-haired, twenty-one-year-old graduate student in political science at Yale." Mendy Samstein noted that "during the Freedom Rally in Jackson which concluded the (Freedom Vote) Campaign, TV men from NBC spent most of their time shooting film of the Yalies and seemed hardly aware of the local people and the full-time SNCC workers." According to Allard Lowenstein, "The bitterness of the SNCC workers was understandable and intense."[31] SNCC worker Lawrence Guyot noted that, during the brief period the Yale and Stanford students were in Mississippi, "wherever those white volunteers went, FBI agents followed." Stokely Carmichael observed, "While these white volunteers are here, national attention is here. The FBI isn't going to let anything happen to them. They let the murderers of Negroes off, but already men have been arrested in Itta Bena just for *threatening* white lives."[32]

At a November 14 staff meeting not attended by Moses, SNCC staffers agreed to involve whites on the condition that their role and influence were limited. They could not serve as project directors, write party platforms, or operate long distant phone lines. Then an event took place that altered the framework of the discussion. In January 1964, the SNCC staffers received word that Louis Allen, the Mississippi resident who had requested federal protection to testify against the murderer of Herbert Lee, had been found shot in his front yard the night before he was to have left the state of Mississippi for good. Once more SNCC field workers were reminded of the great risk they were asking the rural poor of Mississippi to assume. Greater Federal intervention, prompted by the arrival of the white volunteers, with their accompanying power and publicity, seemed the only answer. Bob Moses felt, "I had to step in and make my weight felt in terms of this decision about the Summer Project. . . . We couldn't guarantee. . .the safety of the people we were working with. . . . And so that's how the decision was made to actually invite the students down for the summer of '64."[33]

Questions based on Document 7.1 below:

    1. *Should the SNCC staff invite the white students to come to Mississippi for an intensive summer program, expanding on Allard Lowenstein's use of Yale and Stanford students to assist with the Freedom Vote?*

    2. *Why did some SNCC staffers object?*

    3. *What were the potential hazards?*

    4. *Who were the primary supporters of the Freedom Summer plan?*

5. *Why did they feel that the Volunteers would help SNCC's agenda more than they would hinder it?*

Document 7.1: Some Aspects Of Black-White Problems As Seen By Field Staff[34]
(SNCC internal document)

1. Fears (that Negroes have of being associated with an inter-racial group in Mississippi. Thing varies per area and depends upon the sex of the whites in some areas).

2. Insecurities (skilled vs. unskilled—whites tend to have superior educational background and tend to get in command posts).

3. Deep feelings (past racial incidents that still are 'bugging' people. Very deep, emotional, not easily gotten at by talking, etc.) Some problems in staff—trying to get white staff members to understand these feelings—and the whites' inability to do so.

4. Growing up hating white people. *Many* people have grown up *in* isolated communities where the whites have killed their friends and relatives and have seen only whites beating or interrogating Negroes.

5. Role of whites *in* the movement—Do you want whites visible in places where people have not learned to trust Negro leadership? Question of where you want white people in the movement. Missionary attitudes are really resented.

6. Do I have competent black leadership which I can aspire to and emulate and admire? What does it mean for a white person to come down and work on projects? White people do come down without grappling with their own feelings about Negroes.

7. Obsession of Negroes with whites (the problem).

8. Conflicts between hating whites and having to cooperate with them, knowing that much of the movement depends upon them—and having to differentiate between good whites and bad whites.

9. Sometimes whites are an unnecessary risk. Other places where they can be better used.

10. Problems the whites in the movement feel.

11. Sexual problems that racism produces.

12. Different motivation between white and black being in the movement.

13. Public Relations Aspects.

14. White's reactions to Negroes feelings about whites.

15. Degrees of experience.

16. Who sets the rules—use of facilities, etc.

17. Whites who try to become Negroes? Motivations, etc. for being in the movement.

18. Field Staff Problems . . .

19. Learning from Negro community. . .

20. White community needs to be changed first.

SNCC MOVES TO MISSISSIPPI

Once the decisions had been taken to accept white volunteers, SNCC put its full weight behind Freedom Summer. On June 12, 1964, SNCC Chairman John Lewis issued a statement announcing SNCC's plans to shift its national headquarters to Mississippi. "We believe the nation is not sufficiently informed, nor the federal government sufficiently aroused, about the possibility of violent reprisal to the Summer Project," wrote Lewis. "An upsurge of white terrorist activity throughout the state in the past few months, and the passage of six new laws by the state legislature designed to halt the summer's activity, gives grounds for concern." SNCC would commit the "bulk of its resources" to the Mississippi Summer Project. After the training session in Ohio, Lewis, Executive Secretary James Forman, and Communications Director Julian Bond, editor of SNCC's official newspaper *The Student Voice,* planned to proceed to Mississippi as well.[35] Within COFO, SNCC was to be the driving force of the Summer Project.

Questions based on Document 7.2:

1. On what issues or tasks was there a consensus or the likelihood of consensus? Over what issues did those who attended the meeting fundamentally disagree? Was "projection" an important issue for the staffers?

2. What were the factors undermining people's commitment to nonviolence? What factors supported people's commitment to nonviolence?

3. Do you think this was an important meeting?

4. Was the meeting conducted in a manner consistent with the SNCC theory of how decisions should be made? Does the dialogue of the meeting explain why SNCC decided to move its headquarters to Mississippi? Is there any indication that the move was not unanimous?

5. Which staffer do you identify with the most?

6. What does the discussion teach you about the "do's" and "don'ts" of organizing? Can you talk about this in terms of theory, strategy and tactics?

7. Does the discussion give you any insight as to how "messy" a movement is? Is such an insight significant? Useful?

Document 7.2: Notes (excerpts) from the Third Organizational Meeting of SNCC, June 10, 1964[36]

Forman: . . . Wilkins said that national NAACP is not part of COFO. NAACP is only part of COFO because they have an individual as President who is part. He has misgivings about the project, having 1000 people go down and be exposed to Mississippi society. He is also concerned about the potential for embarrassing the President and the Justice Department. There is also potential for furthering the aims of a Goldwater. . . .

[Mary] King: raised the question of reconciliation. The Summer Project is the most creative thing in the movement. . . .

King: despite the above discussion suggested that CUCRL could still give money to the Summer Project.

Young: was against giving money to something which they couldn't participate in.

Forman: pointed out that $3000 had been voted to the Leadership Conference on Civil Rights which CUCRL didn't participate in. Aaron Henry had earlier stated that all projects would raise money off of Mississippi and all had a responsibility to the state.

Wilkins: Mississippi hurts, rather than helps NAACP; it uses rather than raises money. NAACP was the first organization in Mississippi. . . .

Ella Baker: notes that the pamphlet says that the NAACP state conference helped to organize COFO. We have the responsibility to push them for financial support since they'll ride the summer out otherwise.

Forman: if they disclaim active involvement it gets them off the hook as far as any responsibility.

Moses: when questioned as to his own commitment to SNCC and COFO, his commitment is basically to SNCC. COFO isn't a source of energy for change. SNCC is committed to develop groups like COFO, which is similar to the Albany and Cambridge movements. . . .

Cobb: . . .Amzie Moore was told by a white that he, Mrs. Hamer, Moses, and Aaron Henry were slated to be killed. The feeling is that violence this summer will be directed at black staff members and leaders and not at white summer volunteers. Staff members felt they would be killed. They got guns for the house and the office with the idea of self defense. . . .

Peacock: County people. . .have set up a self defense structure. . . . The FBI was unwilling to track down the guilty parties in the shooting last year. That means the whites are sure they can kill a Negro and get away with it . . . when he and the other four were beaten in jail in Starksville that they could have been taken to the county farm without anyone knowing it. . . .

Peacock: What Frey said of Greenwood is true. People are frustrated because of lack of money. Machines need repairs: cars, mimeos, etc. They feel that everything takes priority over Leflore County. . . . When they were beaten in Starksville no one knew and no one cared. . . .

Ruby Doris: We have personnel and staff problems in all projects. People are irresponsible because we've allowed them to be so and left them in the projects. . . .

Courtland: To the extent that we think of our own lives we are politically immobilized. We volunteer for this situation knowing what's happening and we must accept the implications. Self defense can only maintain the status quo, it can't change the existing situation.

Cobb: We will be living on a farm with a man who has guns. What would happen if someone attacked his house and he shot back. If Charlie were there would SNCC stand by him, even though SNCC advocates nonviolence?

Blue: It's very difficult to define our situation. We don't know how far we will let the man push us before we defend ourselves. It's a personal thing.

Prathia Hall: Nothing said so far has been invalid. No one can be rational about death. . . . When I discovered I was dead already I decided that I'd die to gain life. We must improve our communications so that we won't lose a man without knowing it. . . . When the kids in Birmingham were killed I wanted to pick up a gun until I realized that by destroying lives we don't preserve them. . . . Concerning funds, when we came down we knew we didn't have a dime, and if we think the country will give us money to turn it upside down we're crazy. When we started raising Cain in Atlanta the next week the money began to stop coming in. We're idealistic if we think that people will give us money to take it out of their pockets.

Ruby Doris: If we must operate off the land like guerrillas we must function that way. . . .

MacLaurin: When are we going into the white community with the idea of nonviolence?

Mendy Samstein: Ed Hamlett is developing programs with about 25 southern whites. It's difficult to develop such a program. Note that when the whites hit McComb they were immediately beaten.

MacLaurin: When whites come down they rush into the Negro community. That's why they're beaten. Whites should develop within the white, not Negro community. . . .

Moses: . . . Wilkins has said Miss[issippi] should be isolated and that the NAACP isn't interested in participating in a confederation of groups. SCLC has given $2000 a month through its citizenship teachers. They have the largest bulk of cit. teachers in Miss. However, the same relationship does not exist between SCLC workers and the COFO offices as exists between the workers of other organizations (SNCC and CORE) and COFO. We should begin to consider what COFO is and how the staff relates to it. Perhaps specific problems might be discussed in this context. . .

Cobb: Local Mississippians don't identify with any organization (COFO or SNCC). I like COFO on one level—it gives Negro Miss. an organization with which to identify (a very important fact since it is they who must change Miss.) Have always thought that COFO should be set up as a strictly Miss. organization—not as a coalition of national groups working in Miss. . . .

Garman: Problem of COFO only takes place in-state in terms of organization back-stabbing. . . .

Moses: . . . The problem which is as yet unresolved is one of press releases. Can't have duplication or contradiction in press releases coming from different organizations. . . .

Moses: Part of the fund-raising problem is that the national organizations want to project their organizations while working within COFO. . .

Barry: . . . People led to believe that SNCC activities are being done by COFO . . .

Moses: Can't control what people think and must realize that press is basically unfriendly and will try to ignore SNCC when it can. . . . SNCC will always have pockets of people who know what's happening.

Hayden: How do we interpret the SNCC move to Miss. when the Summer Project is supposed to be a COFO project?. . .

Cobb: SNCC's move to Miss should be projected as part of its program to push COFO as a local organization and to give impetus to local leadership. . . .

Mary: . . . Julian would be in Jackson since he can deal with the press there more easily; Dotty Zellner will be in Greenwood with help of Betty as northern co-ordinator. . . .

Baker: . . . Image of SNCC-COFO relationship will probably be limited to summer. After summer other national organizations will want to become more involved in the decision-making procedures . . .

Moses: The Negro kids [identify with COFO and] don't identify with SNCC because they don't know much about it. Also we can't ask that all northern students identify with SNCC because other national organizations would become irate. . . .

Garman: What if SNCC-prone person is assigned to CORE project?

Moses: Students will be asked their preference. But volunteers should not be called SNCC volunteers automatically. . . .

Mitch: CBS is doing a documentary on SNCC.

Moses: This documentary is focusing on Miss. and is being done by Bill Peters' Organization. His projects will depend upon the field project he chooses to focus on. Intends to follow a northern Negro down and then focus on local people. Must remember that if the Summer Project is successful, America will be so very busy patting itself on the back, SNCC will be ignored.

Dona: Bob thinks you should air your decision concerning the film with the group. Peters wanted to interview Johnson and then Moses. Bob rejected the proposal.

Moses: Rejected the proposal because didn't want myself projected as leader as would be if set next to Johnson. Concept of group leadership more important to get across. Decided we'd focus on a group which was representative not necessarily of the decision-making group in COFO but of COFO itself. . . .

Don: You've said 75% of our energy, money, and other resources are being expended in Miss. with a minimum of projection possibilities. Yet other projects where SNCC projection is more possible are receiving no support. Exec. gave us a mandate to expand but no money. Have no indication of how many people will be coming to S.W. Ga. nor how they will be supported. . . . Rick spent 30 days in jail; wouldn't have if had important post in SNCC. . . . If you're not going to support us then tell us. . . .

Betty: . . . Problem with funds is that no system of priority has ever been set up. . . . Albany office should never have gone three months with no phone. Administration breakdown somewhere. . . .

Stearns: Selma project has had no director—that isn't a matter of funds. . . .

Harris: Wouldn't say anything if S.W. Ga. wasn't working. But we are: just recently got shirt factory in Americus integrated. . . .

Ivanhoe: . . . We only talk about structural weaknesses and never do anything about them. When the national office is moved to Greenwood, these weaknesses will be isolated. . . .

Ruby: Need a mobile staff person to travel to project areas to determine their needs. This can't be determined from a desk in the Atlanta office.

Harris: No one could develop the program Bob has because they don't have the skilled people Bob has. Other projects also find it impossible to get the contacts Bob has in the North. . . .

Frank:. . .Reason Miss. hasn't fallen into same trap S.W. Ga. has is Miss. didn't depend on Atlanta—it did things for itself. Function of office will be more acute in Miss. . . .

Moses: . . . I don't share your concern about these problems, possibly because I have a very limited idea of what we'll be able to accomplish. . . . Questions of priorities is a key question. . . .

Forman: Suggest that we discontinue the Alabama and Arkansas projects temporarily for the summer in order to concentrate on Miss. and S.W. Ga. . . . we should begin to view the MSP as a pilot project. . . .

Ruthie Ha.: If we leave [Ark] now we'll be set back a year. . . .

Smith: Learning process go through in Miss. this summer maybe more valuable than any other we've ever experience. . . .

Ruthie: Can learn same lessons from Ark. We've got beatings and murders in Ark., too, you know. . . .

Forman: Labor unions want us to work in the 3rd congressional district [S.W. Ga.] so they can follow us and organize labor there. . . .

Harris: In Thomasville [S.W. Ga.] we want to avoid demonstrations. In Americus, as a result of the REDBOOK article, three teachers from white high schools wanted and held a meeting with us. We now have rapport with about 15 whites, including the county attorney. . . . Americus is small and could be broken by strengthening the white liberal elements. . . . Negroes in Americus intend to demonstrate and they look to us for leadership. . . .

Ella Baker: Don [Harris] should formulate and write out his role of the reconciliatory role of the white community, and these ideas should be used in other projects. . . . We must reach the white community at their level of readiness to work with us. . . .

Financial Report: We have $11,600 in the bank, but we have $17,600 in bills . . . at one point during the spring we had a debt of $40,000. We should try to clear our present debt before incurring additional expenses. Priorities for payment of bills are that companies we do large business with are paid first so they won't discontinue service. . . . RE the $40,000 debt: about half of it was bills from the Gregory tour—the money from the tour hadn't come in at that point, but it is coming now. We have received $28,000 to date. . . . We now believe that we will net between $6–10,000 from the tour. . . .

Jack Minnis: RE sending summer people into the white community: the people we recruited for the summer were recruited on the basis of their commitment to civil rights. It takes more political sophistication to understand the problems of politics and economics for the poor whites who don't have the white man to focus on as the cause of their troubles, nor do they have the Negro to focus on. Working in the white community requires preparation that we have not done . . .

Forman: We must question our relation to the other civil rights groups on a national level as demonstrated by their attempts to undercut us on the [Dick Gregory] tour. . . .

Mitchell: . . . CORE picketed the ticket agency that was handling tickets for the concert the day before they were to begin selling. They were picketing about employment, but they knew we were going to be selling tickets for the Gregory concert [and NAACP held events the same evening as a Gregory concert forcing the Gregory people to cancel that performance] . . .

Guyot: Are we concerned that whites are taking over SNCC or would take over SNCC? Is the real fear one of lack of trust?

MacLaurin: What are we trying to do, develop Freedom Schools and work on voter registration or get the federal government involved and open the eyes of the nation? If the latter is our goal perhaps we should send whites into new communities where violence will occur.

Cobb: I don't believe that the federal government will move in any case. We must try to be mobile therefore and make our efforts at organizing successful. . . .

Emma Bell: We have the students, there is no use in saying now that we won't work with them in one place or another. We'll have to work with them so we might as well quit complaining.

JAMES FORMAN

"What we needed in the United States, as black people, were committed souls to assist in the development of organizations that would survive the organizer. We did not need charismatic leadership, for this most often led to a disintegration once the charismatic leader was gone. My goal was to build structures that would perpetuate revolutionary ideas and programs, not personalities."[37]

Forman spent his early childhood in rural Mississippi near the Tennessee border, in his grandmother's farm house, heated by a wood stove. While a student in Chicago, Forman sold the Chicago *Defender,* and for the first time encountered a newspaper that made the concerns of black people central. His awareness was heightened by "the call of Dr. DuBois for young black people to get an education, including higher education, for the use of their people."[38] He attended church meetings called by A. Philip Randolph for the proposed march on Washington in 1941.

In 1947, Forman enlisted in the Air Force and learned the injustices of Jim Crow in the military. While a student at Roosevelt University, Forman saw in the Montgomery bus boycott the possibility of effective mass action. After teaching elementary school in Chicago, Forman decided to join SNCC to work on direct action. SNCC's structure had changed with the forming of a staff of some sixteen full-time workers, and Forman was asked to join the staff.

Forman played a crucial role in SNCC's transition from a coalition of protest groups based on college campuses to a small group of full time activists attempting to penetrate the racist structures of the Deep South. Forman drove into the Delta in August of 1962 to help organize the voter registration drive initiated by "Bob Moses and his band of guerrilla fighters."[39] "They were writing history with their lives," commented Forman. After SNCC's third general conference, held in Atlanta in 1962, Forman took over the position of Executive Secretary and the task of reorganizing SNCC to accommodate full time workers who would be paid subsistence wages.

> One of the most important values to be changed was that a person should work for money. These students were saying that they were more concerned with human rights than with money. . . . They were against the profit system, which placed them against capitalism. And they were willing to demonstrate this with their lives. They were willing to build a community of brothers and sisters who would take care of each other insofar as possible and by their very actions demonstrate that money—the making of money—should not be the highest value in 'the American way of life.'. . . I felt that if this idea could grow among young black people, it could usher in revolutionary change.[40]

Forman himself was arrested during the protests in Greenwood, Mississippi in the spring of 1963.

During Forman's tenure as Executive Secretary, SNCC changed not only structurally but philosophically. Its religious roots in the Nashville Movement were replaced by political pragmatism. Nonviolence became a political strategy, not a religious conviction. Forman also stressed the importance of precise reporting of events in *The Student Voice*. Forman combined strong administrative skills with a willingness to perform any necessary task. One SNCC worker recalled arriving at the SNCC office in Greenwood and finding Forman scrubbing the bathroom. Forman spoke of the need to "involve the people themselves, individually, personally, in the struggle for their own freedom."[41]

7.C   Andrew Goodman: The Volunteers

Questions to help you adopt a critical stance while reading the section below:

1. *Can you draw any conclusions about the spirit of the time? How did the applicants perceive themselves as a "generation"? What factors defined the generation who volunteered for Freedom Summer? What was their race? their class? their motives for joining the Summer Project?*

2. *What was Goodman's understanding of the relationship between theory and practice? How does this compare with your understanding of the relationship between theory and practice?*

3. *Why did Andrew Goodman want to go to Mississippi? Why did SNCC accept his candidacy?*

Further information:

The transcript of an interview with Jan Handke is at the Digital Archives of the University of Southern Mississippi, anna.lib.usm.edu/%7Espcol/crda/oh/ ohmarsfb.htm

Ms. Handke was a white volunteer during Freedom Summer and talks about the summer and the effect on her life.

Recommended Film:

Murder in Mississippi *(Docu-Drama; 95 min, 1989; directed by Roger Young). The story of the murder of the three civil rights workers, Chaney, Goodman and Schwerner.*

SENDING FOR VOLUNTEERS: THE APPLICANTS

Once the decision had been made to recruit volunteers, "Friends of SNCC" became an active network on college campuses across the country. In the spring of 1964, *The Student Voice* announced a "Peace Corps type of operation for Mississippi." A SNCC news release announced that recruiting was being done at selected "Freedom Centers" at colleges both in the North and the South. Getting out the news was difficult. During SNCC's initiatives up to and including the Mississippi Summer Project, the staff of *The Student Voice* frequently found itself at odds with the mainstream press. They knew they needed the media and the movement was dependent upon them. Julian Bond and Mary King continually contacted the press even though King described the experience as "contesting skyscrapers filled with editors sporting green eyeshades."[42] Movement activists and native Mississippians traveled from campus to campus, offering information about the Summer Project. One summer volunteer recalls being moved to go to Mississippi by a speech given by a Delta farmer. "He really got to me," recalled the student, "standing there and asking us so politely to come down for the summer, as though we were future guests of his. He offered to put all of us up, even if he and his neighbors slept in the woods. . . . 'You can live with us and give us some of your strength, and maybe then the white people of Mississippi will stop and take a look and remember that the colored people aren't alone anymore.'"[43]

SNCC raised money and awareness by articles in major publications such as *The Saturday Evening Post, Look, Newsweek,* and *The Nation.* Reprints of the articles were mailed, accompanied by lists of assaults on local residents and SNCC workers. Field staff began interviewing applicants. They were given guidelines for interviewing in an April 14 memo. Interviewers were advised to use the experience gained in the 1963 Freedom Vote. In 1963, "The great majority of students came down with the attitude—'I know I am only going to be here for a very [short] period of time, but I am willing to help in whatever way you think I can.'" There were other students, however, who came to Mississippi with fixed ideas about what they wanted to do and what they hoped to achieve. The case study of an "extremely argumentative" student volunteer who had disrupted the Freedom Vote by his stubborn insistence on working in a "hard-core town where civil rights workers had been driven out." This student's refusal to abide by the "decisions of the local staff head" proved problematic for the staff. "Since no one could reason with him, it was decided that he should remain in Jackson until it was time for him to leave the state." The report continued, "This case study should give the interviewer a general idea of one criterion, perhaps the most important one, for evaluating applicants. If the problem presented by the above student were multiplied enough times (there will be almost a thousand volunteers in Mississippi this summer), the whole program could be jeopardized and lives could even be lost."[44]

> The lack of experience in civil rights activity or in the South need not (and should not) be considered grounds for disqualifying an applicant. . . . But it is essential that an applicant possess a learning attitude toward work in Mississippi. This is not to discourage ingenuity or creativity; it means that an applicant must have some understanding that his role will only be a stop-gap one: that the movement will have to continue after he leaves and that

his role will be to work with local leadership, not to overwhelm it. He can only do this if he shows some respect for what has gone before him and an understanding of what must continue after he leaves. He must be capable of understanding that the success of the Mississippi movement depends on the development of those who live and will remain in the state. A student who seems determined to carve his own niche, win publicity and glory when he returns home can only have harmful effects on the Mississippi program.[45]

Interviewers were advised to look for: "experience in teaching or community work," "Special skills. . .in the arts, in health care, in communication," "A basic sense that the Civil Rights movement (not just abstract justice) is a good thing," "a willingness to admit doubts and fears about going to Mississippi," "an understanding of the risks involved—jailings, possible beatings, etc. . . . Some understanding of the living conditions they will have to work under in Mississippi. . .that they will be living in homes and sharing food with people who are extremely poor." Interviewers tested candidates with a hypothetical situation in which an elderly black woman expected to be called by her first name by white student volunteers. Would the student comply with this expectation?

Question based on Document 7.3 below: When it was impossible to interview an applicant, the decision was made on the basis of a written application. Which questions make the application form below fairly typical? Which questions make the application atypical?

Document 7.3   Mississippi Summer Project Application Form[46]
JUNE 7, 1964–AUGUST 25, 1964
    Please do not use abbreviations—PLEASE PRINT
    Name _____ Age _____ Date of Birth _____
    School Address _____
    Home Address _____
    Telephone Number _____ Race _____
    Mother's Name _____ Her Address _____
    Father's Name _____ His Address _____
    List the schools, their locations, your graduation year: _____

College major: _____

List your major high school and college activities:

List your last three jobs and the years you held them:

List skills and experiences you have for work on the programs you checked: _____

Additional special skills (i.e. photography, journalism) not included in list of programs: _____

_____

The following information is extremely important. It will be used only in case of emergency and will be kept confidential.

List the names of people to contact for bond: _____

(Name) _____ (Address) _____

(Telephone) _____

List of your arrests: give place, time, date, charge, status of case.

_____

_____

Describe briefly your qualifications (training and/or experience) for your first choice. _____

Check the skills you have:

☐ Journalism   ☐ Music   ☐ Library Science

☐ Art   ☐ Photography   ☐ Nursing

☐ Dramatics   ☐ Research   ☐ Recreation

Check the subjects you could teach:

☐ Literacy   ☐ Literature

☐ Remedial reading and writing   ☐ Hygiene

☐ English   ☐ Home Economics

☐ Math   ☐ Federal Programs

☐ Political Science   ☐ Auto Mechanics

☐ Negro History   ☐ Typing

☐ Foreign Language   ☐ Shorthand

(Write "yes" or "no"):

I can _____ drive a car.

_____ Type _____ words a minute.

_____ Work office machinery.

I have a driver's license from the State of _____

_____membership cards in _____

Do you have a car you could use during your time in Mississippi?

I will be able to work in Mississippi from _____ until _____

I will be able to be self-supporting (roughly $150 per two-month period). _____

List your high school, College, College Area, Home Town and City newspapers: _____
(name) _____ (address) _____ (frequency-daily, etc.)

List the social, fraternal, political, community, and other organizations you belong to: give names, addresses, presiding officers:
(name) _____ (officer) _____ (address)
_____

List your Congressman and Senators: _____

List at least 10 people who besides your parents would be interested in receiving information about your activities: _____
_____

Place (1) and (2) in order of preference next to the programs you are interested in working with:

I.   Voter Registration

II. Community Centers

III. Freedom Schools

IV. Special Projects

    A. Research

    B. Law Students

    C. White Community

List two references, one of whom should be persons who have been in a position to observe your work (employers, teachers, etc.) _____
_____

Check (not for purposes of selection)

I ___ have $150 to help finance the summer project

I ___ can raise $150 to help finance the summer project

I ___ will be able to be self-supporting (roughly $15 per week)

I ___ will be able to work for SNCC from _____until _____
Explain below why you would like to work in Mississippi.

INTERVIEWING THE APPLICANTS

Some applicants were rejected for perceived personality problems or philo-sophical differences with SNCC. "I think she's arrogant," commented one interviewer about a rejected candidate. "I explained about running Mrs. Hamer [for office] and that many people would raise eyebrows because she is an ex-sharecropper. She said, 'Well, why are you running her?' Later she asked why we were running a *woman* for office. . . . She also said she wouldn't want to participate in anything to which she was opposed. . . . When I asked her why she had taken part in any of the civil rights activities here, she said she was writing her term thesis. . . . She said that a reporter from *Life* had approached her about doing a picture story during the summer —All-American Girl Mississippi Freedom School sort of thing." Another candidate was rejected for his reservations about nonviolence. "Would like to have athletic programs in which would be incorporated boxing, judo, and other forms of self-defense. If a time came when he felt violence was the way and SNCC maintained its nonviolent policy he would leave SNCC." A member of the Socialist Workers party, the candidate was "about to be investigated by the FBI. I am more disturbed by his apparent pride in this than his actually having belonged." "He is a really dry type of intellectual fellow. He speaks in an ultra-educated way, is rather withdrawn, lacks warmth, spirit, feeling. . . . I think he will have grave difficulty commu-nicating with staff members and others, particularly those who are not educated."[47] "Just spoke with Bob Moses," wrote one interviewer, "and he told me to pick the willing ones (i.e., willing to do anything) and the *non*-rugged individualists."[48]

Most applicants were college age or slightly older, but the Summer Project also received applications from retired persons in their sixties, ex-Marines, housewives, and secretaries. One sixty-seven-year-old former chemistry teacher wrote on her application, "Active since 1923—in all Civil Rights causes." Another retired teacher was described as "a dynamic, vital person with a great deal of teaching experience. She is aware of all the problems that might arise because of her age: e.g., taking orders from 19 year olds, the rigors of living in rural Mississippi, etc. . . . I hope that there is some way that she can be used."[49]

Many applicants reported experience in service organizations outside of the South. They had volunteered at Church, picketed Woolworth's, tutored, protested, and joined sit-ins. But most knew of Mississippi only what they had read. A word frequently used by interviewers was "naive." "Doesn't have much fear," wrote one interviewer, "but recognizes she may not know enough to get frightened." How would the candidate react if attacked? If she got no response from students in Freedom Schools? If he were to meet with hostility from Mississippi blacks? "Said she might feel hurt but would want person to judge her ideas, not her skin color. Rather naive about this and couldn't really imagine it happening (ho ho)." Other assets were considered: "Has car. Also has guitar."[50]

Questions based upon the document below:
  1. *What can you infer about each applicant as an individual?*

  2. *Did you respond with emotion to any of the applications? Why? How do the applicants seem to perceive themselves and their capacity to change the world around them? How do they perceive the people of Mississippi? How does this compare to the way you feel about your capacity to change the world around you?*

Document 7.4   Answers Written By Volunteer Applicants
[The following are answers written by applicants to questions # 1 on the Volunteer application form: "Explain why you want to work in Mississippi?"[51]]

As Peter Countryman said at the Conference on Racial Equality held at Pomona in February: "The only thing necessary for the triumph of evil is for the good men to do nothing.". . . I cannot sit by idly, knowing that there is discrimination and injustice, knowing that there is terror and fear, while I do nothing. I want to work in Mississippi this summer because . . . I feel that I must help. . . .

. . . Today, the Negroes of Mississippi . . . are impatient and will act.

Now I, too, am impatient and will act, because for too many years I have been passively waiting. In endless discussion I have philosophized about the essence of man, and attempted to establish fundamental principles of moral action. With the untroubled detachment of a self-proclaimed liberal, I patiently suffered the rebukes of James Baldwin and the laments of Pete

Seeger. Next year in the insulation of a graduate school, I begin the lengthy study of medicine, dedicated to the alleviation of human suffering.

Such ethical and intellectual dedication, without any bodily commitment, rings hollow, however, and is surely of no avail in the struggle against intransigent injustice in Mississippi. The time for empathy without action is long past. I am impatient and will act now. . . .

[I consider] the Civil Rights Revolution to be one of the most important events in this country since the American Revolution nearly two centuries ago. . . . This movement is like a thunderstorm in the midst of a partched (sic) and arid wasteland. My generation has a responsibility to insure that this "thunderstorm" does not end but remains a lasting "shower" to keep this country "green" for all Americans.

[John F. Kennedy challenged us] to "ask not what your country can do for you, but what you can do for your country." Surely, no challenge looms larger than eradicating racial discrimination in this country. It will not be easy. But SNCC's program would make a sizeable dent in the problem. I want to do my part. There is a moral wave building among today's youth and I intend to catch it.

My teaching experience has given me insights into the actual limitations of students who have emerged from inadequate cultural backgrounds or have not had sufficient training for college; this experience has, however, revealed both the need and possibilities for guidance and remedial work. Moreover, I have become more and more aware and disturbed by the inability of students to think critically or even differently about the world around them. Thus, within the context of the Mississippi project, I would hope to be able to narrow the educational and cultural gaps, as well as to encourage responsible action and critical thinking among the residents of Mississippi. . . .

Because my family is in the upper middle-income bracket, I have never faced any of the oppression which the poorer and less educationally "blessed" Negro must face. No one has ever called me "Boy" or told me to sit "in the back of the bus" because I have never had to ride the bus. I have never regarded the Caucasian as my superior, because my world has been separate from his world and from that of the average Southern Negro. And yet I have always been a Negro. Every time I see a "White Only" sign; every time I pass a motel when I'm sleepy and want to stop; every time I read about the concert "they" are having over in "their" section of town; every time J. Strom Thurmond opens his mouth; every time someone looks at me as though I'm a freak because I have a Yale jacket on; and every morning when I wake up, something reminds me that I'm a Negro. For me, this has been a badge of courage and pride; for some other Negroes it has become a reason to be ashamed. This is what we must eliminate.

Applicants who were accepted received the following memos:

Document 7.5   Memo to Accepted Applicants[52]
To: Mississippi Summer Project Workers
From: Mississippi Summer Project Committee

1.   We hope you are making preparations to have bond money ready in the event of your arrest. Bond money for a single arrest usually runs around $500. . . .

2.   There will be a series of orientation periods starting in mid-June and running until the beginning of July at Berea College. People will be staggered over three sessions, each lasting about four days.

3.   . . . We expect all summer workers to go through some orientation period before going into the field.

4.   A conference was held the weekend of March 21–22 at which various civil rights people and educators gathered in New York to work out a detailed curriculum for the Freedom Schools. The conference broke into small working groups which discussed the various Freedom School programs—remedial instruction, leadership training, cultural activities, etc. At present various people are pulling together the results of their sessions and sending reports to the Jackson office. By the end of April we hope to be able to put together a comprehensive and detailed curriculum with working suggestions which will be circulated to all those who are being assigned to work in Freedom Schools this summer.

5. We are presently in a very critical financial condition. . . . We are running three congressional campaigns as well as a senatorial campaign and conducting a Freedom Registration program—in which we hope to register 400,000 Negroes on our own registration books—and building a grass-roots foundation for our delegation to the Democratic National Convention to challenge the regular all-white party delegation. . . . We need money for office rent, phone, office supplies, transportation, etc. We . . . hope that you could raise some money however small, to help finance our current programs.

6. Of course, we will also be needing a huge amount of funds for this summer. . . . If there is a Freedom Center in your area, this could probably best be done by working along with the people active in the center. Though, in the final analysis, you would be best judge of what approach would produce the best results.

7. We would appreciate two more photos of yourself as soon as possible. These will be needed for publicity and other purposes.

8. . . . the Mississippi leadership must reserve the right to "deselect" any summer worker. . . .

We will try to communicate with you periodically from now until the time you come to Mississippi . . . we will shortly be sending all Freedom School teachers curriculum material as indicated above. In addition, we will be sending out lists of materials which it would be helpful if you could help gather and send to us or bring with you. . . . If you own a car and are planning to bring it to Mississippi this summer there will be some specific information that we will need to know.

Keep in touch with us if you have any suggestions, require any information, etc.

Yours in Freedom,
Bob Moses
COFO Program Director

Document 7.6   Memo to Accepted Applicants (#2)
To: Mississippi Summer Project Workers
From: Mississippi Summer Project Committee

Here is some additional information which we have thought of since the first memo was written:

1. **Money:** The best arrangement for money is probably for you to bring $60.00 expense money with you (above transportation costs) and arrange to have $10.00 to $15.00 living costs sent you weekly.

2. **Arrests:** We must re-emphasize that <u>all</u> workers during the summer are liable to arrest, although Freedom School teachers, white community project workers and researchers will be less likely to be arrested than others. All workers, however, should have bond ready.

3. **Transportation to orientation site:** Everyone who is near a Freedom Center (list sent earlier) should contact the center. . .we will try to help you.

4. **Cars:** Everyone who possibly can should bring a car this summer. The car you bring should be insured. The legal situation on cars in the state is this:

—Anyone who is in the state 60 days must secure a Mississippi driver's license. If you have a license from another state you only have to take a written test, but if you plan to be in the state over 60 days you should get your license before the local authorities know who you are. License costs $2.50

—Any car which is in the state 60 days must have Mississippi license plates. Tags are expensive (about 4% the value of the car). You can plan to purchase the tags. We advise that you plan to take the car out of the state periodically so you can claim that you are only visiting the state and have only been in the state x days. . . . We are asking *all accepted applicants* to fill out the slip below, tear it off, and send it to the COFO office. You should also let the Freedom Center know if you will be driving down, so they can coordinate transportation.

CAR INFORMATION
COFO
1017 Lynch Street, Jackson
Name _____
Present (school) _____
☐   I will be bringing a car to Mississippi.
☐   I will <u>not</u> be bringing a car to Mississippi.

ANDREW GOODMAN

"The road to freedom must be uphill, even if it is arduous and frustrating. A people must have dignity and identity. If they can't do it peacefully, they will do it defensively."[53]

Activism had always been part of the white, privileged yet socially conscious environment in which Andrew Goodman had been raised on New York's Upper West Side. Goodman had attended The Walden School, a progressive private school on the Upper West Side whose curriculum was founded on the "apparently unlimited desire and interest of children to know and to do and to be."[54] While a high school student, Goodman had traveled to Appalachia during his Spring break with a classmate to see first-hand the poverty of the region. They spent their days talking to local people, learning about their economic struggles, and touring an impoverished town with a retired leader of the United Mine Workers. Goodman's friend recalled, "Andy was one of those individuals who was not satisfied with the wisdom and privileges he inherited. He had to struggle to achieve for himself. His decision to go to Mississippi was the result of a simple ability to perceive and feel social evil."[55] During his sophomore year, he had traveled to Washington to attend a "Youth March for Integrated Schools"; at sixteen, he had picketed Woolworth's in New York in support of the Southern sit-ins.

Like many of the summer volunteers, Goodman had inherited a legacy of social activism from his parents. In this, he was typical of many of the white students who volunteered for the Mississippi Summer Project. The majority of applicants credited "their parents with being the models for their actions. . . . Far from using Freedom Summer as a vehicle for rebellion against parents, the applicants simply seem to be acting in accord with values learned at home."[56] Although his parents offered to provide the required $150 fee and the suggested $500 bail money, Andy earned the money himself, taking a job with United Parcel. "Whatever he could do for Mississippi," his father recalled, "he wanted to do on his own."[57]

Goodman had learned about the Summer Project, during "Freedom Week" at Queens College, where he had heard Aaron Henry say, "The thundering silence of the good people is disturbing. This is a family problem, and there are no outsiders."[58] SNCC worker Jim Monsonis commented on his interview with Andrew Goodman, whom he met on April 15: "I've talked with him here and feel he ought to be accepted. He is a white student with some political sophistication and knowledge about the state, is particularly interested in voter registration work and the political campaigns."[59]

The news reporters who covered the training at Oxford, Ohio, captured many images of Andrew Goodman on film. Clad in a dark t-shirt, he listened intently to lecturers who warned the summer volunteers of the dangers of the situation they were entering. Although Goodman was originally assigned to Canton, he met Schwerner and Chaney at Oxford and listened to their experiences in Neshoba County. Deciding that he wanted to work "where he was most needed,"[60] as his mother recalled, Goodman requested, and received, a change of assignment. He made the long drive to Mississippi in the blue CORE station wagon with Schwerner and Chaney. Goodman spent the night in the sleeping bag he had brought with him on the floor of the Community Center at Meridian. He had been in Mississippi less than one day when he was arrested with Schwerner and Chaney and murdered.

At his memorial service, Goodman was remembered by his rabbi: "Certainly neither Andy nor James nor Michael would have us in resentment or vindictiveness add to the store of hatred in the world. They pledged themselves in the way of nonviolence. They learned how to receive blows, not how to inflict them. . . . Theirs is the way of love and constructive service."[61]

See Activity 7.2   Borrowing Power: Does it Work? in the Appendix

Document 7.7   Western Union Telegrams[62]

[Telegrams from Senator Keating to Mr. and Mrs. Schneider (pseudonym) concerning their daughter Sarah, a SNCC volunteer working in the Pine Bluff, Arkansas project. Miss Schneider transferred to the Summer Project in Mississippi.]

THAT YOUR DAUGHTER IS WELL AND HAS NOT BEEN IN ANY WAY MISTREATED. IF I AM ABLE TO SPEAK WITH HER. I WILL CALL YOU. I WANT YOU TO KNOW THAT I HAVE BEEN IN TOUCH WITH THE FBI AND AM FOLLOWING DEVELOPMENTS IN MISSISSIPPI VERY CLOSELY AND DOING ALL IN MY POWER TO SECURE ADEQUATE PROTECTION FOR ALL THE YOUNGSTERS DOWN THERE

= KENNETH B KEATING US SENATE =

MR AND MRS SCHNEIDER =

ALDERTON ST REGO PARK LONG ISLAND NEW YORK=

YOUR TELEGRAM OF JULY 20TH ADDRESSED TO HONORABLE JAMES J.
DELANEY HAS BEEN REFERRED TO ME TODAY DUE TO FACT YOU RESIDE
IN MY CONGRESSIONAL DISTRICT. CONTACTED DEPARTMENT OF JUSTICE
ABOUT YOUR DAUGHTER'S ARREST IN MISSISSIPPI AND URGED THAT EVERY-
THING POSSIBLE BE DONE FOR PROTECTION OF CIVIL RIGHTS WORKERS.
UNDERSTAND THAT 98 DEMONSTRATORS WERE FREED ON BOND TODAY
FOLLOWING REMOVAL OF THEIR CASES FROM STATE TO FEDERAL COURT.
TRUST YOUR DAUGHTER WAS AMONG THOSE FREED. IF NOT, LET ME KNOW
AND FURNISH ME WITH INFORMATION AS TO HER NAME AND CURRENT
ADDRESS IN MISSISSIPPI SO THAT I CAN THEN CONTACT JUSTICE DEPART-
MENT AGAIN IN HER BEHALF

= CONGRESSMAN BEN ROSENTHAL =

Document 7.8   Papers of the Parents Mississippi Emergency Committee[63]
PARENTS MISSISSIPPI EMERGENCY COMMITTEE
604 G Street, SE Washington, D.C.
202 547-8522 or 547-8524
Dear Parents:

We who send you this letter, like you, are parents of young people participating in COFO's Mississippi Summer Project [we are concerned about
their welfare]. . . [these are] our activities up to date.

1. We are enclosing a copy of our press release and a letter from Boston
    legal authorities, presented at a press conference in Washington on
    June 24, for which we received national TV, radio and newspaper
    coverage. . . . We have been assured that groups of parents will have
    no difficulty in arranging local press conferences. If you need guid-
    ance, contact your local Civil Rights organizations. . . .

2. Since we have been in Washington this week (we are parents from
    New York, New Jersey, Maryland, Massachusetts and Washington,
    D.C.) We have been successful in arranging Interviews with [rep-
    resentatives and administration officials] IT IS MOST URGENT THAT
    CONGRESSMEN RECEIVE DELEGATIONS FROM THEIR CONSTITUENTS,
    as well as concerned citizens who feel that all Congressmen represent

all the people of the United States. NOTE: In the event that your son or daughter is arrested, notify your Senator and Congressman immediately and ask them to telephone the jail. We have been advised on Capitol Hill that such a phone call from Washington is effective.

3. Fortunately, the NAACP National Convention is now in progress in Washington. . .many telegrams have gone to the President asking for Federal Marshals to be sent to Mississippi.

4. By means of this letter, we are contacting parents nationally. Enclosed is a list of participants in your state. Will you take the responsibility of contacting other parents immediately to organize group action?. . .It is most urgent that parents and friends from every state converge on Washington to lobby for all available protection immediately.

We are certain that your emphasis, as is ours, will be that the Federal Government can and must assume responsibility for the protection of its citizens any place in the Union. We have asked for Federal Marshals to be sent to Mississippi. If you have any additional ideas or suggestions, please let us know.

Yours in freedom
Parents Mississippi Emergency Committee

. . .

[Personally delivered to the White House on June 9, 1964]
Mr. President:

You are undoubtedly aware that this summer almost 1,000 Americans are traveling to Mississippi under the auspices of the Council of Federated Organizations in that state. The purpose of their trip will be to carry on educational activities, community center programs, and voter registration work, in order to insure equal opportunity for all. Among these volunteer workers will be forty-five students from Harvard, Brandies, Radcliffe, and Boston Universities, whose names are appended to this appeal.

As you know, the record of the past several years indicates that the liberties, and the lives of these people will be in jeopardy this summer. That record is full of intimidations, arrests, beatings, shootings and even murder, inflicted upon Negro and white citizens. It is clear beyond doubt that they cannot depend upon the State of Mississippi for protection.

The Constitution of the United States vests responsibility in you, Mr. President, to enforce the laws of the nation. . . . We ask that you station in Mississippi, in advance of trouble, Federal Marshals sufficient to deter, prevent, or immediately suppress actions which would deprive Americans of their constitutional rights.

The eyes of the nation, and of the world, will be on Mississippi this summer. Let them see right and justice prevail in that State through the authority and dignity of the Executive of our nation.

[47 signatories follow]

cc: Attorney General Robert Kennedy

[List of 45 students attached]

. . .

FOR IMMEDIATE RELEASE

June 25, 1964

As a group of parents representing the mothers and fathers of nearly 1000 young people now actively engaged in the Mississippi Summer Project we wish to express our deepest gratitude to President Lyndon B. Johnson for his thorough and untiring efforts in behalf of James Chaney, Andrew Goodman and Michael Schwerner immediately following their tragic disappearance in Philadelphia, Mississippi. . . . We were shocked by the statement made yesterday by Attorney General Robert Kennedy, as reported in *The New York Times,* that the federal government could not take preventive police action. The hesitant position of the Justice Department is directly challenged by some of the most eminent legal and historical authorities in the country. . . . We concur with the position of these authorities and it is our firm opinion that more than sufficiently strong powers rest within the government to enable it to provide exactly the protection for which we ask. The attached letter to the President, outlining this position, was personally delivered to the White House on June ninth, and copy sent to Mr. Kennedy.

We have come to Washington to plead for the oppressed people of Mississippi and for our sons and daughters. . . . We trust that it will not be necessary for us to go to Mississippi to defend the ideals of our Republic.

EIGHT

Preparations For Freedom Summer

THE ORGANIZERS OF FREEDOM SUMMER were well aware that they needed to prepare not only the project itself, but also prepare Mississippi for the project. The volunteers who participated in Freedom Summer went to Mississippi to face certain resistance from native Mississippians. The characterization of the summer volunteers as an "invasion" of Yankees reawakened the South's traditional image of itself as a noble but defeated province. Added to these existing images were images of communist infiltration and of compulsory "race mixing." The state of Mississippi felt itself singled out as a scapegoat for racial conflicts, which were in fact national problems. A Jackson newspaper columnist wrote of the Yankee invaders:

> Quite a few of the student invaders have preconceived notions about Mississippi . . . almost everybody illiterate, ragged, backward, living in hovels, eating sowbelly and cornpone three times daily. . .toting shotguns and plotting secession. . . .
>
> In turn, Mississippians have preconceived notions about the invading students—smug, shrill, know-it-all extroverts with a savior complex. . . .

It is no preconception but established fact that many of the invading students are coming here from places where racial segregation is the custom, where human life is unsafe on the streets even in broad daylight, and where the local crime rate is among the nation's highest.

Mississippi, in case they don't know it, has had the nation's third lowest rate of major crime . . . according to official FBI figures.

Our parks and streets are generally safe for peaceful, law-abiding people. One can patronize our pubic transportation facilities without being razored or raped by rat packs like those found in New York, Los Angeles, Chicago and other crime jungles which are furnishing volunteers for this 'Project Mississippi' intrusion.

While professing to believe in 'equality,' these self-appointed reformers evidently regard themselves as mentally and morally superior to Mississippians.

What the students think of us is not very important . . . because the invaders couldn't possibly think less of us than the majority here thinks of them and their sponsors. . . . [1]

Following the principles established by Gandhi in his efforts to decolonize India and by CORE in its early demonstrations, COFO workers made an effort to present their position to white Mississippians and to establish cooperation. These efforts took the form of letters explaining COFO's programs to local whites.

Document 8.1: Letter Describing Mississippi Summer Project Sent to Whites in Mississippi by COFO[2] (excerpts)
Council of Federated Organizations
1017 Lynch Street P.O. Box 2896
Jackson, Mississippi 39205

Dear Friend:

The purpose of this letter is to tell you a little about the Mississippi Freedom Summer Project which the Council of Federated Organizations is sponsoring this summer. We have learned that this project is causing fear and hostility in the white community, because it has been characterized as an "invasion" of "several thousand" college students intent on "agitating" and causing "violence." We believe that this hostility is based upon a misunderstanding of the program, and that an explanation of the project's intent and scope is needed to allay the fears of the white people of Mississippi.

The Mississippi Freedom Summer project has come about because the people of COFO have reached this conclusion: The struggle for freedom in Mississippi cannot be won without the substantial aid of the country as a whole, backed by the federal government. . . . Therefore, we have committed our resources to a program where large numbers of Americans can come to Mississippi for two reasons: firstly, to dramatize the need for change in Mississippi. The second purpose is even more simple: they want to participate in the long, laborious process of bringing social services and social justice to a portion of the population which has been denied them throughout American history. . .to Negro Mississippians. . . .

The project itself will bring 800–1000 people to Mississippi. . . . They will be self-supporting and most of them will work in Mississippi for six to eight weeks, concentrating in three major programs, and several other, smaller programs which have been planned in advance by the staff of COFO.

1. **Freedom Schools.** . . . The course of study will concentrate on intensive remedial work in reading, writing, math and science, on a critical study of political and social issues, and on Negro history— because we feel that those are the areas where the public education which the state offers them has been most seriously neglected. To balance the program, there will also be cultural and recreational activities ranging from painting and creative writing to baseball and hiking. This program will use approximately 300 teachers and administrators.

2. **Community Centers.** . . .

3. **Voter Registration.** . . .

4. **Other projects.** There will be a few smaller projects, devoted primarily to research and specialized service in the white and Negro communities.

As you can see from this outline, the project gives no basis for the accusations which have been made incorrectly concerning the summer activity. There is no "invasion"; participants will be spread very thinly across the state in teams of four or five. . . . Estimates of up to 30,000 "invaders" are

similarly exaggerated; the approximately maximum figure of 1,000 represents our most realistic estimate of what we could recruit and administer
efficiently. We feel that this program offers much to Mississippians, both
Negro and white. The program, and the staff, will be concerned with constructive educational and political activities, not with bringing violence
and chaos to the state. . . .

We will welcome further inquiries about the program, addressed to
COFO at the above address. Thank you.

Yours for Freedom Now,
Summer Project Staff
Council of Federated Organizations

THE "WHITE FOLKS PROJECT"

Although the focus was on registering black voters, Freedom Summer and
the Mississippi Freedom Democratic Party were integrated. The people at
COFO knew that poor blacks and poor whites had the same issues and
concerns: jobs, schools, medical treatment and so on. A letter asking for
support was headlined: "We must be allies ... Race has led us both to Poverty." During Freedom Summer, 25 white volunteers became part of the
"White Folks Project." Eighteen went to Biloxi, a Gulf coast town, and in
integrated or all-white teams they canvassed in poor white neighborhoods.
It was slow going, but after three weeks, they had twenty signatures on
the Freedom Registration forms, which increased the number of whites
openly supporting the MFDP from two (Rev. Ed King and his wife) to
twenty-two.[3]

LAWYERS AND FREEDOM SUMMER

The organizers of Freedom Summer recognized the need for increased legal
protection. In the early sixties, there were only three African American
lawyers practicing in the state of Mississippi: Jack Young, R. Jess Brown,
and Carsie Hall. Although barred from Mississippi's law schools, Jack
Young had supported himself and his family as a mailman while studying law at night by correspondence. In 1960, Young began handling civil
rights cases in Mississippi for the NAACP. Young had filed the petition
that contained the names of the Evers children, among others, in a suit to
desegregate the Mississippi public schools. William Higgs, a white lawyer

who accepted civil rights cases, had lost his practice and been driven from the state in 1963.

The Lawyers Constitutional Defense Committee (LCDC), the National Lawyers Guild, and the Law Students Civil Rights Research Council provided legal assistance for those arrested during Freedom Summer. The LCDC was composed of the NAACP Legal Defense Fund, the American Jewish Committee, CORE, the American Civil Liberties Union, the American Jewish Congress, and "The President's Committee," a group of lawyers formed from a White House conference called by John F. Kennedy in the summer of 1963.

The National Lawyers Guild had offered its services to SNCC in 1962 and solicited its membership to volunteer for the Mississippi Summer Project. Under the direction of Detroit attorney George Crockett, the Lawyers Guild briefed the volunteer attorneys in Mississippi law during a weekend session and, in the spring of 1964, opened an office in Jackson. Lawyers contributed "lawyer weeks," weeks spent in Mississippi at their own expense working on civil rights cases. George Crockett met the arriving volunteers each week at the Jackson airport. "We'd tell them the ropes as we understood them: that it's their primary responsibility to get people out of jail and not to get themselves into jail."[4]

Tension between the Ink Fund's Jack Greenberg (NAACP) and SNCC staff existed for two reasons: the NAACP's strategy of working through test cases conflicted with the mass arrests prompted by demonstrations; and the NAACP objected to the involvement of the National Lawyers Guild, which had been labeled a Communist-front organization. SNCC staffers defended their right to accept help from anyone who offered.

Despite political differences, the LCDC and the Lawyers Guild provided similar services during Freedom Summer. Both groups had a bail fund to provide immediate cash for local Mississippians unable to post bail and for volunteers who might have to send home for the five hundred dollar bail fund, which had been a condition of their acceptance as volunteers. Both groups filed petitions to have civil rights cases removed from state courts and transferred to federal courts, on grounds that their clients could not receive a fair trial in Mississippi. Volunteer law students gathered data on arrests and discrimination in voting practices, collected affidavits, and otherwise assisted lawyers in their efforts. During the summer, more than one thousand arrests were made on charges such as disturbing the peace, disorderly conduct, resisting arrest, and violating traffic laws.

1964 Freedom School Curriculum Link:
Case Study on the Civil Rights Bill
   www.educationanddemocracy.org/FSCfiles/C_CC7d_CivilRightsBill.htm

8.A   Hollis Watkins: The Orientation for the Volunteers

Questions to help you adopt a critical stance while reading the section below:
   1. *What are the examples of disconnect between blacks and white volunteers? What could explain it? How would you address those issues and resolve misunderstandings?*
   2. *How does Moses' letter to the President compare to Gandhi's Letter to Lord Irwin (see chapter 1)?*
   3. *What points were the speakers at the Oxford orientation trying to make with the volunteers?*
   4. *Why is training for nonviolence important?*

Further information:
   The transcript of an interview with Hollis Watkins is at the Digital Archives of the University of Southern Mississippi, www.lib.usm.edu/%7Espcol/crda/oh/watkinstrans.htm
   Mr. Watkins also talks about the early work of SNCC in Mississippi and about the conflict between direct action and voter registration.

HOLLIS WATKINS

"I always had questions about the system, and I always wondered how it could be changed. . . . And it was when I saw the Freedom Riders on TV and people sitting in at the lunch counters, and something clicked in my head, and I said hey, if you join up with these guys, this is a way you can help to bring about change that needed to be brought about. I didn't know all what they were, but I knew something needed to be done, had to be done."[5]

Hollis Watkins was nineteen, taking a year between high school and college, and visiting relatives in California. After seeing the Freedom Riders on television and hearing their intention to come to Mississippi, he decided to return home and try to join the Freedom Riders.

> And that's where I found SNCC, and found out about what they were doing. And they invited me to become a part of it. And we began to work in voter registration, trying to get people to register to vote. And shortly thereafter, Marion Barry came down and introduced direct action. . .but it was the students who decided what to do and what to call it. It was run by the students. The whole thing about Montgomery and what the students were doing and how they were adopting the nonviolence grew out of the Gandhian movement in India, and that was my first introduction to the concept and the philosophy.[6]

From the SNCC workers, local teenagers learned methods and tactics used in Nashville and elsewhere in the South. Watkins found that the role playing "helped a great deal. It kind of put you in the frame of mind where you could visualize and have some minute idea how the people might respond. And it also gave you a little practice as to how you might respond, or react to their response."[7] The students also learned how to prepare for direct action, first making a list of all the local places—lunch counters, libraries, bus stations—that were segregated.

> Our initial intention was to have a demonstration that included eighteen to twenty people. But as it turned out, on the day we were supposed to have the demonstration, for various reasons, the others couldn't go. And we decided to go to the library and unfortunately, we had not done thorough investigation, and the library was closed that day. And since the library was closed, we decided that we would not be outdone, that since we could not sit in at the library, we would come back to some of the other places.[8]

Watkins considers the sit-in "the first Mississippi Project-initiated direct action. . . because the Freedom Riders had come into Mississippi."[9] During voter registration work in Greenwood, Watkins was arrested for

> disturbing the peace. They would arrest us for things like refusing to move on. We were told by an officer a lot of times, an officer would come and tell

you to leave, and we would say, "We got a right to be here," so we'd stay. And they would place you under arrest for refusing to obey an officer. . . . We were arrested in Greenwood and sent to the county farm. We were constantly threatened with being killed with shotguns. People riding behind us. They carried us to work and we were working on the roads, cutting grass and weeds and that kind of thing. As we went out to do that work, white people would be riding behind the truck, with guns pointing at us, passing by and pointing guns, saying, "That's the niggers. We're gonna kill the niggers. . . . So after they did that for a few days, we decided we wouldn't go to work. We went on a hunger strike. We were not going back to work and we weren't going to eat any more until we got out of the county farm. So they transferred us from the county farm to Parchman."[10]

Watkins and other SNCC workers were invited into Holmes County by residents like Hartman Turnbow and Ozelle Mitchell, who provided housing and support for the voter registration workers.

That became a must. You had to merge with the people in the community and work with them and live off of what the people in the community were providing for you. . . . Because at that time most of us were not like a lot of the students who came down for the '64 Summer Project, who, when they came down, came down with money to sustain them during the period of time that they were here, but, during this time, we had to live with the people and survive with the people off of whatever the people were giving us.[11]

Shortly after the arrival of the SNCC workers, Hartman Turnbow's home was firebombed and Mr. Turnbow was arrested. Watkins reported the incident both to SNCC Headquarters in Greenwood and to the head of the Justice Department in Mississippi. "I told him what had happened, and I told him that I was expected to be arrested and he suggested that I leave Holmes County, because if I came back I would be arrested. And I told him, "Well, I got to do my job and you got to do yours."[12]

THE ORIENTATION

Hollis Watkins was one of the SNCC workers who organized the orientation for Freedom Summer and taught the volunteers. The first group of summer volunteers settled into the dormitories at Western Women's College in Oxford, Ohio, on June 14, 1964, while the second group arrived on June 22. During their one-week orientation, the volunteers would hear stories of those who had been working in Mississippi for months, take an abbreviated course in nonviolent resistance, and face their own perhaps not-yet-articulated anxieties. The volunteers were also prepared for being teachers in the Freedom Schools.

The first speaker on Monday morning was the Reverend Ed King, who informed the volunteers of the police-state tactics used in Mississippi to maintain the status quo. King told the group that national news reports could be interrupted with a disclaimer stating, "The following is an example of biased untrue Yankee reporting."[13] James Lawson spoke on the need for "moral confrontation" with one's enemies, and charged the students with meeting their enemies with love. "Violence always brings more harm to the people who use it," advised Lawson.[14] Movement veteran Bayard Rustin also spoke of loving the enemy. "All mankind is my community," he said. "When I say I love Eastland, it sounds preposterous—a man who brutalizes people. But you love him or you wouldn't be here. You're going to Mississippi to create social change—and you love Eastland in your desire to create conditions which will redeem his children. Loving your enemy is manifest in putting your arms not around the man but around the social situation, to take power from those who misuse it—at which point they become human too."[15]

Hollis Watkins spoke for the movement veterans who had been laboring without publicity and protection in Mississippi.

> I insisted that we, the SNCC folks, put this out to people and let them know. . . . You're coming to Mississippi, you need to be prepared to do three things—to be beaten, to go to jail and to be killed. If you're not prepared to do all three, you should reconsider your position in coming.
>
> I would give them. . .a little bit about how the black community in many cases would respond to them. At that time. . .anything that white people were going to say, most black people were going to agree with, because you dare not challenge a white person in Mississippi.[16]

Watkins advised the volunteers "to use some creativity and work with the people and get some idea from them what to do. Because you may be right and you may be wrong, but in most cases, whether you're right or wrong, if you put it out there. . .the people are going to agree with you."[17]

There was the whole thing around security. People from the North were used to being able to go to the police and be rescued. That was part of the whole security thing, because we talked about, you know, you don't go to the local police. You don't go to the local sheriff, unless you had someone that was with you, that was very visible, because, in many cases, the sheriff was a part of the Klan. And the police too. So, it was kind of hard to get them to see that. . . . We also explained to them that most of them would be seen as a traitor, and in many cases, the authorities would be even more brutal towards them than they would with others, or equally as brutal. It was hard for them to see that our Federal Government was not what we had it all built up to be, which I thought was good for them to get a taste of the realization of what the Federal Government was.[18]

"You are not going to Mississippi to try to be heroes, you are heroes enough just going into the state," Bob Moses told the volunteers. "This is not a Freedom Ride. The point is to stay out of jail if you possibly can, and don't put yourself in any unnecessarily dangerous situation. You have a job to do. If each of you can leave behind you three people who are stronger than before, this will be almost 3,000 more people we will have to work with next year. This is your job."[19]

Fannie Lou Hamer conveyed to the volunteers the spirit and resilience of the men and women who would be their companions and hosts for the next few weeks. Mrs. Hamer spoke to them of the importance of religion to the people of the Delta. "Our religion is very important to us—you'll have to understand that."[20] To Mrs. Hamer, it was the white man who knew the greatest fear in Mississippi. "The white man is the scaredest person on earth. Out in daylight he don't do nothin'. But at night he'll toss a bomb or pay someone to kill. The white man's afraid he'll be treated like he's been treating the Negroes, but I couldn't carry that much hate. It wouldn't solve any problems for me to hate whites because they hate me. Oh, there's so much hate! Only God has kept the Negro sane."[21]

As Sally Belfrage recalled, "Here was someone with force enough for all of them, who knew the meaning of "Oh, Freedom" and "We Shall Not Be Moved" in her flesh and spirit as they never would. They lost their shyness and began to sing the choruses with abandon, though their voices all together dimmed beside hers."[22] The students sang and clapped and Mrs. Hamer improvised,

Who's that yonder dressed in red?
Let my people go.
Looks like the children Bob Moses led
Let my people go.[23]

Several incidents during the orientation made it clear that the volunteers were entering a world far different from the one they were leaving. One volunteer wrote that they had seen a film in which "a big, fat, really fat and ugly white county registrar prevents Negroes from voting." The film further displayed

> the stupid, really completely irrational and dishonest views of some white Southerners and so on. Six of the staff members got up and walked out of the movie because it was so real to them while we laughed because it was so completely foreign to us*—if anyone had said what they did in the movie, we in the North would lock them up or dismiss them completely, but this is the way many Southerners think.[24]

The volunteers also quickly picked up on the ambivalence that some of the SNCC staffers had toward their participation.**

The organizers of Freedom Summer early on attempted to involve the federal government and to receive its protection. On the first day of the orientation, Bob Moses sent a letter to President Lyndon Johnson informing him of the project and requesting Federal response.

Document 8.2   Bob Moses' Letter to President Johnson[25]

Dear Mr. President,

We are having an orientation session at Western College for Women at Oxford, Ohio. We expect to send the first group of summer volunteers to Mississippi next weekend, June 22.

We are requesting that the Negroes of Mississippi and the summer volunteers receive Federal protection. This may require the stationing of members of the Department of Justice in Mississippi for the summer,

---

* One might consider when and why this happens in classrooms today when students view movies about the Civil Rights Movement.

** See *Letters from Mississippi,* Elizabeth Sutherland Martinez, ed., (Brookline, MA: Zephyr Press, 2002.)

sending special teams of F.B.I. members into the state, stationing Federal Marshals in key areas of the state, or even, in the event of a complete breakdown of law, sending in Federal troops. Whatever the case, we are asking you to give protection for the Negroes in Mississippi and the Civil Rights workers in the state.

. . . In the Delta of Mississippi, there has been talk of lists of leaders who must be wiped out. The killing of Medgar Evers and the shooting of Jimmy Travis demonstrate that this is no empty threat. But surely the number of persons who would sit down, plan, and execute this kind of act of terror are relatively few in number and can be singled out and, if nothing else, kept track of. The story of the Birmingham bombers as told in the *Saturday Evening Post* tells us that it is possible for the F.B.I. to maintain constant watch on those people who are capable of planning and executing such acts. We are asking that the Federal Government move before the fact this summer.

I hope that this is not asking too much of our country.

Sincerely,

Bob Moses

c.c. The Attorney General, Mr. Burke Marshall, Mr. John Doar

PRESIDENT JOHNSON'S RESPONSE

John Doar of the Justice Department came to the orientation in Oxford and explained to the volunteers the Federal Government's role in their protection. Their safety, he explained, was in the hands of the local authorities, the very authorities who had in their brief orientation been presented to them as the enemy. "This is a serious operation you are involved in," he stated. "I wish the world were different. I don't like it any better than you do."

"How is it that the government can protect the Vietnamese from the Viet Cong and the same government will not accept the moral responsibility of protecting the people in Mississippi?" demanded one volunteer.

"Maintaining law and order is a state responsibility," said Doar.

Doar was reminded that in a crisis, the President did have the authority to send federal troops into a state. How could the government not meet their "moral responsibility?"

"I believe we are a government of law," Doar said. "I have taken a vow to uphold the law. I just try to do the best I can under law. I have no trouble living with myself. The people I know in the federal government and administration are fine people, and they have no trouble living with themselves either."[26]

As it had been used in the North by CORE chapters, in Nashville, and in Montgomery, and in Mississippi, role-playing was used in Oxford to prepare the volunteers for the resistance they would certainly encounter in Mississippi. Such techniques had been advocated in Richard Gregg's *The Power of Nonviolence*, originally published in 1935, a book circulated widely in the movement.

Document 8.3   Possible Role Playing Situations[27]

I. Reporter

    1. What would you say if a reporter asked you about staff problems?

    2. What would you say if a reporter asked you about COFO politics?

    3. What would you do if a reporter asked you what do you expect out of the summer project?

    4. Do you think the summer project was a good idea?

    5. Do you like working with Negroes?

    6. Have you found that most Negroes are dirty?

    7. Are Negroes staying with white boys and girls?

II. Police

    1. If a policeman stopped you and asked you to get into his car, what would you do?

    2. If a cop told you, you are under arrest, what would you do or say?

    3. If you are taken to jail, what would you say? What questions would you answer?

4. If you saw another person arrested, what would you do?

5. If you were allowed a phone call, who would you call and what would you say?

6. If you saw a person being beaten, what would you do? By police? By an outsider?

III. Nonviolence

1. How would you react to: teargas, firehoses, dogs, picket line, march to courthouse, verbal intimidations, cattle prod, etc.

IV. Canvassing

1. How would you approach a person in a community you had never seen before?

2. How could you make a person understand what voting is by relating things to everyday life?

3. How would you talk to a real religious person?

4. How would you talk to a community leader?

V. White Local Citizens

1. How would you approach a white local citizen?

2. How would you react if approached by a white local citizen?

See Activity 8.1: Role Play within a Role Play in the Appendix

8.B James Chaney: Facing the Reality of Violence and Jail

Questions to help you adopt a critical stance while reading the section below:

1. Why was it hard for the volunteers to "get a taste of the realization of what the federal government was?" What "was" the federal government?

2. How does John Doar's presentation at the orientation support Jimmy Travis' portrayal of law and order in Mississippi?

3. Why was Moses relieved when a few of the volunteers left the meeting after his announcement that Goodman, Schwerner and Chaney were probably dead?

JAMES CHANEY

"When he came home, he told me how he worked and lived those few weeks he was there; he said, 'Mother, one half the time, I was out behind houses or churches, waiting to get the opportunity to talk to people about what they needed and what they ought to do.' He said, 'Sometime they shunned me off and some would say, 'I want you all to stay away from here and leave me alone.' But he would pick his chance and go back again."[28]

—Fannie Lee Chaney

A resident of Meridian, Mississippi, James Chaney had lost interest in high school after a conflict with the principal of T.J. Harris Senior High School. When Chaney and two friends wore homemade paper NAACP buttons to school to commemorate the 1954 U. S. Supreme Court *Brown vs. Board* decision, the principal ordered the buttons removed. The three refused and were sent home. They continued to wear the buttons for a week despite the principal's order. Early in 1963, at age 20, James Chaney became interested in the Freedom Rides, which he watched on television with his family. According to his brother Ben, ten at the time of Chaney's death,

> By him talking to me and my family, that's when I got an idea what the movement was about. To be a Freedom Rider meant sitting in the front of the bus. But it didn't only mean riding on the bus. Bucking the system, not getting off the sidewalk when white people walked by, not saying 'mister'. Anything that would be a sign of rebellion, rebelling against the system, rebelling against the status quo, rebelling against segregation."[29]

The movement provided Chaney with a vehicle for his political activism and an alternative to the limited opportunities offered him in Mississippi. At 21 years old, Chaney volunteered his services at the CORE office, where he met Michael and Rita Schwerner. The Schwerners requested that Chaney, who had worked tirelessly in supporting the efforts of the office, be offered a small salary. "Since the office was established here, long before any of the three of us arrived in town," wrote the Schwerners and Lenora Thurmond, "he has been working full time, doing whatever work was necessary. When he started to get the community center in order, James worked with Mick building shelves, loading books, painting. He has canvassed, set up meetings, gone out into some of the rough rural counties to make contacts for us. Tonight he is running a mass meeting here in Meridian."³⁰ The Schwerners pointed out that Chaney had helped to organize the Freedom Days in Canton and Greenwood and had done extensive canvassing for voter registration. "James has never so much as asked us to buy him a cup of coffee, even though he has no means of support."³¹

James Chaney's knowledge of the local people and of the highways and back roads of Mississippi made him an invaluable advisor in the work of the out-of-town CORE staff. His upbringing had made him fully aware of the risks he was taking in working for CORE. "On one occasion," recalled Rita Schwerner,

> the two men, James and Michael, were planning to drive to Philadelphia during the day to see some people. As I had met several of the Neshoba County contacts in Meridian, and I had information to relate to them about community center programs which I believed would benefit them, I requested permission of the two men to accompany them. At first they both refused, but when I persisted, Michael finally agreed. . . . James, however, . . . was able to rationally say that if I went, he would not, as he said that if he was seen in Neshoba County with a white women we would all be killed. His sound advice was heeded, and I did not enter Neshoba County on that day.³²

A visitor who accompanied Chaney on one of his "practice runs" to find out if the Mount Zion Church congregation had agreed to allow Schwerner to speak to them about the Freedom School, remembered

> We left Meridian about dusk, so it was dark when we reached the Neshoba County line. Chaney turned off the main road and began speeding along narrow, red-clay, back-country roads. He seemed to know the terrain like the back of his hand. And, man, he flew! . . . Sometimes he'd cut down to his parking lights like I've seen in war pictures, with guys speeding through blackouts. . . . I'll never forget our visit to that house. . . . When Chaney pulled in there I thought the place was deserted. But he cut the engine and we got out. He whistled two or three times and I saw a crack of light. Honest, it was just like war! . . . When I gave the woman a handful of leaflets about voter instruction, you'd have thought she was handling TNT. . . . We left

that house like the Israelites spying out Canaan. Chaney drove even faster, with less light, and I thought every curve might be our last one.[33]

While assisting with the training of volunteers at Oxford, Ohio, Chaney and the Schwerners received word of the burning of the Mount Zion Methodist Church. Having been instrumental in convincing the congregation of the Mount Zion Baptist Church in Neshoba County to house a Freedom School, Chaney was eager to return to Mississippi with Schwerner and Goodman. At Chaney's suggestion they left at three in the morning so that the entire drive through Mississippi would be conducted in daylight. Nevertheless, they disappeared that night and were later found murdered.

Ben Chaney, who had himself been arrested several times while picketing and had been alternately gotten from jail by his brother and Michael Schwerner, spoke at the funeral. He ended his eulogy by saying, "And I want us all to stand up here together and say just one thing. I want the sheriff to hear this good. We ain't scared no more of Sheriff Rainey!"[34] Lawrence Rainey, sheriff of Neshoba County, was later convicted of charges of conspiring to deprive James Chaney, Andrew Goodman, and Michael Schwerner of their civil rights.

FACING THE REALITY OF VIOLENCE AND JAIL

Shortly after the second orientation began, the possibility of death became a reality for all present when word arrived that Chaney, Schwerner and Goodman had not reported back after investigating the burning of the church in Philadelphia, Mississippi. Bob Moses announced the disappearance to the assembled volunteers.

> We heard that they had been arrested by the sheriff in Neshoba County and then we heard that they had been taken out of the jail. I remember Rita Schwerner, who was Mickey's wife, was still at the orientation session and spoke to the volunteers about that incident. And then she left and she was very emotional. And she was asking for students to help put pressure on the Justice Department and so forth. I spoke after her. I waited until she left, because we had to tell the students what we thought was going on. If, in fact, anyone is arrested and then taken out of the jail, then the chances that they are alive were just about zero. We had to confront the students with

that before they went down, because now the ball game had changed. We talked to them about the fact that as far as we could see, all three of them were dead. And that they had to make the decision now as to whether they really wanted to carry through on this and go down. We sang a couple of songs, and for a while I was worried because no one was leaving. But finally a few of them did leave, so I did think that the message had gotten through. You couldn't think that all of those who came to that orientation session were prepared to face the actual murder of their fellow students.[35]

Jimmy Travis, shot during his voter registration work in Mississippi, spoke passionately at one evening's session shortly after the three workers disappeared:

It's hell in Mississippi! And you've got to realize that nobody *cares*. We care. We've got to change the *system*. It's hard. It's just like one person beating his head against this building to tear it down. It's impossible, but we have got to *do* it. They say that democracy exists in America. But it's an idea. It doesn't function. You have got to make it function in Mississippi so that it can function in the rest of the country and in the world.

The three people. I don't know. I hurt. These people are lost. I don't know where they are. What can we do? The *system!* The system is the reason these people are missing. It's easier to know that someone is in jail, even that someone is dead, than to wait and wonder what happened.

This cat is from Birmingham, Alabama. This cat knows what's going on. I'm black. You're white. If you're going down there, you're going to be treated worse than black. Because you're supposed to be free. But I say that no one is free until everyone is. And until we can show the people of Mississippi that we are willing to make the extreme sacrifice, we can't change the world.

It's hard. So hard. But all we have is each other. When something happens to you, we care. We really *care*.[36]

Exhausted, Travis slumped and disappeared through a door in the room. When the white volunteers applauded, one of the SNCC workers from Mississippi gently admonished them. "You've got to understand Jimmy," she explained. "He was nearly killed. It was something he had to say. You shouldn't applaud."[37]

After the announcement of the disappearance, Staughton Lynd, political activist and professor of history at Spelman College, and later statewide direct of the Freedom Schools, spent part of the evening counseling teachers who were reconsidering their decision to go to Mississippi. Much of the time at the orientation was spent to prepare the students for violence and jail and to ensure that the students were aware of the risks. Kirsty Powell, one of the volunteers, wrote after the summer was over, that

> The main effect of Oxford (was it the main design?) was to bring each of us to the point of asking: "Do I really believe in this enough to go? Ought I go? Do I want to go?" This was as it should have been, I think.[38]

Question based on Documents 8.4 and 8.5:

   What events can you imagine inspired the creation of the "Security Handbook" and the requirements of the "Security Check-Out Form"? If a volunteer followed the advise of the Handbook do you think the chances of him or her having a violent experience would be lessened?

Document 8.4   Security Handbook[39]

   1.   Communication personnel will act as security officers.

   2.   Travel

      a.   When persons leave their project, they <u>must</u> call their project person for <u>themselves</u> on arrival at destination point. Should they be missing, project personnel will notify the Jackson office. WATS line operators will call each project every day at dinnertime or thereabouts, and should be notified of changes in personnel, transfers, etc. (If trips are planned in advance, this information can go to Jackson by mail. Phone should be used only where there is no time. Care should be taken at all times to avoid, if possible, full names of persons traveling.) Checklists should be used in local projects for personnel to check in and out.

      b.   Doors of cars should be locked at all times. At night, windows should be rolled up as much as possible. Gas tanks must have locks and be kept locked. Hoods should also be locked.

c.   No one should go <u>anywhere</u> alone, but certainly not in an auto-mobile, and certainly not at night.

d.   Travel at night should be avoided unless absolutely necessary.

e.   Remove all unnecessary objects from your car which could be construed as weapons. (Hammers, files, iron rules, etc.) Absolutely no liquor bottles, beer cans, etc. should be inside your car. Do not travel with names and addresses of local contacts.

f.   Know all roads in and out of town. Study the county map.

g.   Know locations of sanctuaries and safe homes in the county.

h.   When getting out of a car at night, make sure the car's inside light is out.

i.   Be conscious of cars which circle offices or Freedom Houses. Take license numbers of all suspicious cars. Note make, model and year. Cars without license plates should immediately be reported to the project office.

3.   Living at Home or in Freedom Houses

a.   If it can be avoided, try not to sleep near open windows. Try to sleep at the back of the house, i.e., the part farthest from a road or street.

b.   Do not stand in doorways at night with the light at your back.

c.   At night, people should not sit in their rooms without drawn shades.

d.   Do not congregate in front of the house at night.

e.   Make sure doors to Freedom Houses have locks, and are locked.

f.   Keep records of suspicious events, i.e., the same car circling around the house or office several times during the day or week. Take license numbers, makes, years and models of cars. Keep records of the times these cars appear.

g. If an "incident" occurs, or is about to occur, call the project, and then notify local FBI and police.

h. Depending on project needs and circumstances, it may be advisable for new personnel to make deliberate attempts to introduce themselves immediately to local police and tell them their reason for being in the area.

i. A phone should be installed in each Freedom House, if there isn't one already. If a private phone is used, please put a lock on it. Otherwise, install a pay phone, this will avoid immediate pick-ups on suspicion.

4. Personal Actions

a. Carry identification at all times. Men should carry draft cards.

b. All drivers should have in their possession drivers licenses, registration papers, and bills of sale. The information should also be on record with the project director. If you are carrying supplies, it might be well to have a letter authorizing the supplies from a particular individual to avoid charges of carrying stolen goods.

c. Mississippi is a dry state and though liquor is ostensibly outlawed, it is available everywhere. You must not drink in offices for Freedom Houses. This is especially important for persons under 21.

d. Try to avoid bizarre or provocative clothing, and beards. Be neat.

e. Make sure that prescribed medicines are clearly marked, with your name, the doctor's name, etc.

5. Relations with the Press

a. Refer questions about SNCC's perspective or policies to the Project Director.

b. Do not argue with the press. Do not exaggerate. Give the facts only.

   c.   The Project Director and communications person will ask for credentials of press. If you do not know the reporter, check with one of them or ask to see the reporter's credentials.

   d.   Try to relate your activities to the lives of the local residents. This will not be hard to do, or unnatural, if you remember your role in the state.

Document 8.5   Security Check-Out Form[40]

Date: _____

1.   List driver and all passengers: _____

2.   Describe the car: Make: _____ Model _____ Color: _____
Year: _____ License No.: _____ State: _____
Registered in name of: _____

3.   Destination: _____ and phone no.
of contact if not regular office.) Time leaving: _____
Estimated time arriving: _____ Route:_____

_____

(Do not write below this line.)
Checked in by: _____ Time: _____

See Activity 8.2: To Go or Not to Go to Jail? *in the Appendix*

8.C   Michael Schwerner: "Mississippi Burning"

Question to help you adopt a critical stance while reading the section below:
   How did Schwerner's definition of his role as social worker provide an indication of his future life choices?

Further information:
   The transcript of an interview with Florence Mars is at the Digital Archives of the University of Southern Mississippi, anna.lib.usm.edu/%7Espcol/crda/oh/ohmarsfb.htm
   Florence Mars is a white inhabitant of Philadelphia and the author of "Witness in Philadelphia," a book about the murder of the three Civil Rights workers.

The interview gives good insight to the thinking and reaction of the white community.

MICHAEL SCHWERNER

"The vocation for the rest of my life is and will be to work for an integrated society. . . . I want to know and work with the people, not just read about situations or take someone else's subjective view. I want to be there firsthand."[41]

When he was eighteen years old, Michael Schwerner purchased a Volkswagen, a questionable choice, his mother thought, for a Jewish boy's first car. Schwerner saw the decision as an act of faith in the human capacity to triumph over Auschwitz and other horrors inspired by bigotry. As a student at Cornell University, Schwerner majored in rural sociology, hoping for a career in social work. While in college, Schwerner conducted a successful campaign to admit the first black student to his fraternity. In 1962, Schwerner applied for his first job at Hamilton-Madison House, a community center in a housing project in Lower Manhattan. Here Schwerner sometimes differed with co-workers about the job of social worker. A friend recalled, "Mickey insisted that many social workers believe that they know what is best for the people they try to help, and they fail because they try to make people do as the social worker says."[42]

Schwerner also joined CORE during this period, rising at 6 A.M. to volunteer at the CORE office before his job began. During CORE demonstrations, he was arrested twice. On July 4, 1963, he and his wife Rita joined one hundred other demonstrators at a sit-in in Maryland. Later that year, he was arrested during a CORE demonstration at a building site in protest of racist practices within labor unions. Soon, however, he decided that he wanted a greater challenge and was drawn to Mississippi. "This man was free of hate," recalled a coworker. "He didn't hate any Ku Klux Klansman in Alabama, Mississippi, or anywhere. What he recognized was that the *hardest core problem* existed in that area."[43] So he and Rita Schwerner applied for the positions of CORE field secretaries in Mississippi.

Driving Michael's second car, also a Volkswagen, the Schwerners left for Mississippi in January of 1964, leaving behind with regret their cocker spaniel, Gandhi. The couple's task was to create a Community Center in Meridian, an important central location in Civil Rights activities in Mississippi. For a community center, they found a crumbling five-room building sublet to them by a local NAACP member who rented it from a white woman. Housing for the Schwerners, however, was a problem. Local people, both black and white, were reluctant to rent an apartment to them fearing retaliation. A few black families offered them accommodations in their homes, but soon found themselves the target of threats and harassment. Frequently the Schwerners slept on the floor in the Community Center. In a CORE memo, Schwerner expressed his determination: "The Meridian Community Center of Lauderdale County, Mississippi, *must* succeed. . . . Sure, the task looks hopelessly large, but we must not fail if the South is to take its rightful place in American society. . . ."[44] In the same memo, Schwerner detailed the tasks he and his wife had undertaken. They had started a story hour to attract young children to the center and were start-ing a tutoring program for bright high school students to assist youngsters with reading and math. Each day, they canvassed door-to-door to encour-age voter registration, and twice a week were holding evening classes for prospective voters.

Although they were not arrested during their first months in Meridian, the telephone was proving a constant problem. Calls were frequent, and ranged from the menacing to the obscene. Mickey Schwerner urged his wife to ignore the callers and, if she could, understand them. "You want to kill those people [who made the calls]?" he asked. "Do you kill a par-rot for repeating words he has been taught? Those people are reacting as they have been taught to react. You change them by changing what they are taught."[45]

From his arrival in Mississippi, he was earmarked by the locals as a par-ticular threat. They nicknamed him "Goatee" and considered his "beatnik" beard symbolic of his other forms of challenging Southern conventions. Careless of his appearance, Mickey Schwerner wore blue jeans, sweat shirts, and sneakers and allowed local student barbers to cut his hair for practice. When local whites insisted that he address them as "Mister" and taunted him with names like "Jew-boy," he genially suggested that they call him "Mr. Jew-boy." After his efforts to organize pickets to prompt downtown store owners to hire black clerks, his local enemies moved from surveillance and name-calling to more direct harassment.

With the assistance of James Chaney, Schwerner organized "the kids," about fifty high school students into a team wearing t-shirts reading

"Freedom Now." They held CORE-style training sessions at the Community Center, and on Saturday, April 25, the group picketed a local dime store. The young trainees withstood taunts from the crowd calmly, and there were no arrests and no violence. On Monday, however, Michael Schwerner was arrested for blocking a cross walk. His request to be jailed in the segregated black section of the jail was ignored.

On May 31, Schwerner and Chaney spoke to members of the congregation of the Mount Zion Methodist Church to encourage them to allow the Church to be used for a Freedom School.

> Former Governor Ross Barnett says that now is the time for white men to stand up like men and say to you 'Never!' I say that now is the time for Negroes in Mississippi to stand up like men and say to Barnett 'Now!'. . . Let us hold a Freedom School in this church. Meet us here, and we'll train you so you can qualify to vote. Then you can march into Philadelphia and the sheriff and all the Ku Klux can't keep you from walking into the courthouse and writing your name on the poll list. Because the Government of the United States must be walking right there beside you.[46]

At the beginning of June, a group of local activists were arrested while picketing a downtown store, and Mickey Schwerner went to the police station to learn the charges against them. At this time, he was directly threatened by the desk sergeant. "From what Michael told me," recalled Rita Schwerner, "his words were something like this: 'If you get any more of these damn kids arrested, Schwerner, I'm going to get you and that's a promise.'"[47]

"MISSISSIPPI BURNING:"
THE MURDER OF SCHWERNER, CHANEY AND GOODMAN

Shortly after the members of the Mount Zion Methodist Church of Neshoba County in Philadelphia agreed to allow the church to be used as the site of a Freedom School, the congregation found one of its evening meetings surrounded by armed white men, "most of them masked," according to the New Orleans *Times Picayune*. "Three Negroes attending a church board meeting were beaten and chased away. A short time later the church went up in flames."[48] News of the church burning and the beatings reached

Michael Schwerner and James Chaney in Oxford, Ohio, where they were assisting in the training of summer volunteers. As it had been Schwerner and Chaney who had persuaded the church members to house the school, the two were eager to offer their support. They drove down to Philadelphia, accompanied by volunteer Andrew Goodman, visited the site of the burned church, and talked with members of the congregation.

On their way back to Meridian, they were arrested by local deputy Cecil Price. Neshoba County Sheriff Lawrence Rainey claimed later that the three men had been held briefly and released at approximately ten P.M. on June 21. However, the three men failed to return as expected, and shortly after their disappearance, the blue station wagon in which the three had been riding was found burned in the Bogue Chitto swamp.

To charges that the civil rights workers had met with violence, many white Mississippians responded that the disappearance was a hoax, designed further to discredit Mississippi and to justify increased Federal surveillance. Governor Paul Johnson implied it was a hoax.[49] An organization calling itself "Americans for the Preservation of the White Race" published circulars that charged that the hoax was a familiar enemy tactic:

> The new technique is the well known persecution hoax. That is, to kill one of their own members, bomb one of their own installations, or arrange a 'disappearance' of some of their own agitators. This is now becoming a familiar pattern.
>
> 1. The Communists killed their own pet, Kennedy, in Dallas, hoping to blame it on the south. The only trouble was, Oswald got caught. No serious National Police Investigation. Whitewash by Communist Earl Warren.
>
> 2. Greenwood has had numerous shootings and bombings, no serious damage, much propaganda, much harassment of local citizens by National Police. No evidence. No arrests. No prosecution. . . .
>
> 3. Civil rights Agitators 'disappear' in Philadelphia. Cheap car burned. No evidence of foul play. Massive propaganda campaign. Lyndon sends Commie spy-master, Dulles, to confer with Paul. Intensive harassment by local citizens by National Police.[50]

Ku Klux Klan leader Sam Bowers publicly claimed, "We were NOT involved, and there was NO DISAPPEARANCE."

Document 8.6   THE KLAN LEDGER[51]

An Official Publication of the White Knights of the Ku Klux Klan of Mississippi (July, 1964)

Shaw, July 19

. . . The arch-traitor and long-time betrayer of patriots the world over, Dulles, has used his lying tongue to try and convince the American public that this organization was involved in the so-called "disappearance." We were NOT involved, and there was NO DISAPPEARANCE. Anyone who is so simple that he cannot recognize a communist hoax which is as plain as the one they pulled on Kennedy in Dallas (and which Earl Warren is working so hard to cover-up), had better do a little reading in J. Edgar Hoover's primer on communism, "MASTERS OF DECEIT". . .

There is no racial problem here in this state. Our system of strict segregation permits the two races to live in close proximity and harmony with each other and eliminates any racial problem. . . . Bi-racial groups are the greatest danger we face in this State today. . . .

We are not going to recognize the authority of any bi-racial group, NOR THE AUTHORITY OF ANY PUBLIC OFFICIAL WHO ENTERS INTO ANY AGREEMENT WITH ANY SUCH SOVIET ORGANIZATION. We Knights are working day and night to preserve Law and Order here in Mississippi, in the only way that it can be preserved; by strict segregation of the races, and the control of the social structure in the hands of the Christian, Anglo-Saxon White men, the only race on earth that can build and maintain just and stable governments. We are deadly serious about this business. We have taken no action as yet against the enemies of our State, our Nation and our Civilization, but we are not going to sit back and permit our rights and the rights of our posterity to be negotiated away by a group composed of atheistic priests, brainwashed black savages, and mongrelized money-worshipers, meeting with some stupid or cowardly politician. Take heed, atheists and mongrels, we will not travel your path to Leninist Hell, but we will buy YOU a ticket to the Eternal if you insist. Take your choice, SEGREGATION, TRANQUILITY AND JUSTICE, OR BI-RACISM, CHAOS AND DEATH. . . .

OTHER VICTIMS

A massive search, overseen by the federal government, for Goodman, Schwerner, and Chaney uncovered other victims of the White Knights. Among the bodies discovered during the search for the three civil rights workers were those of Eddie Charles Moore and Henry Dee. Moore, twenty, and Dee, nineteen, had been singled out for execution as part of the campaign to rid the state of invaders and racial dissidents. In a signed confession, two members of the White Knights admitted that they had abducted the two young men and taken them to the Homochitto National Forest, where they had beaten them unconscious. Dee and Moore were then taken to the Mississippi River, where their bodies were tied with heavy weights and thrown into the water. The two Klansmen testified that Moore was singled out because he had participated in a student demonstration at Southern University in Baton Rouge; Dee, because he had once lived in Chicago. For these reasons, the Knights believed them to be part of a suspected uprising of Black Muslims in the area. Rumors of a Muslim plot in Mississippi later proved to be completely unfounded.

Claims that the disappearance of Chaney, Schwerner and Goodman were a hoax ended in early August, when the bodies of the three Civil Rights workers were found buried in an earthen dam on the farm of local Klansman Olen Burrage. Michael Schwerner had died of a single bullet wound through the heart, as had Andrew Goodman. James Chaney had been shot and savagely beaten.

Sometimes discouraged, Michael Schwerner had retained his essential faith that human beings were capable of progress. According to an FBI informant, Schwerner's last words to his murderer were, "Sir, I know just how you feel."*

---

* Only in the fall of 1964, Klansmen James Jordan and Delmar Dennis broke rank and informed the FBI of the events surrounding the deaths of Goodman, Schwerner, and Chaney. As a result, the charge of "conspiracy" was brought against nineteen defendants on December 4, 1964. On December 10, the charges against the nineteen were dismissed when Esther Carter, US Commissioner for the Southern District of Mississippi, refused to admit the signed confession of Horace Doyle Barnette as evidence. On February 28, 1967, the defendants were reindicted. This time, the list of those charged with "conspiracy" was slightly different. The group was tried before a jury in proceedings beginning October 7, 1967. The following were found guilty of conspiracy: Cecil Price, Bernard Akin, Jimmy Arledge, Sam Bowers, Wayne Roberts, Jimmie Knowden, Billy Wayne Posey, and Horace Doyle Barnette. No Verdict: Edgar Ray Killen, Jerry McGrew Sharpe, and "Hop" Barnette. Acquitted: Lawrence Rainey, Olen Burrage, and Frank Herndon. The convictions represented the first successful jury conviction of white officials and Klansmen against blacks and civil rights workers. Price and Roberts were released on five thousand dollars' bail. Roberts and Bowers were sentenced to ten years apiece; Posey and Price received six; Barnette, Snowden, and Arledge received three.

The murder of the three civil rights workers focused the attention of the nation on Mississippi and became famous as "Mississippi Burning" (*MIBURN* was the FBI file name; see foia.fbi.gov/foiaindex/miburn.htm). COFO kept a detailed report of the developments under the name of "The Philadelphia, Mississippi, Case."

Question based on Document 8.7 below:
  What indication does this evidence give of an FBI reluctant to intervene? What are the possible reasons for delays?

Document 8.7   COFO Report: The Philadelphia, Mississippi, Case[52] (excerpts)
Chronology of Contacts with Agents of the Federal Government (All times are Central Standard Time except where otherwise noted.)
Sunday June 21
10 PM   H.F. Helgesen, Jackson FBI agent, was contacted by law student Sherwin Kaplan. Helgesen was informed that [Goodman, Schwerner and Chaney were] missing. . . . An investigation was asked for; Helgesen said something like, "Keep me informed of what happens."
10:30 PM   A Mr. Schwelb, a Justice Department lawyer, . . was informed of the disappearance of the party.
11:00 PM   . . . Schwelb [called] but he gave no indication of having taken any action.
12 PM   . . . requested an investigation. Schwelb stated that the FBI was not a police force and that he was not yet sure whether any federal offense had occurred; so he could not act. He was informed of the provision in the US code providing for FBI arrests; he still insisted that he did not have authority.
12 PM   . . . Helgesen took [license plate numbers] curtly and did not allow a chance for further conversation. . . . also called the Mississippi Highway Patrol, with similar results.

Monday, June 22
1 AM (EST)   . . . SNCC offices called John Doar of the Justice Department in Washington, D. C., and informed him of the case. He said he was concerned, and asked to be kept informed. He said he would look into the case. He suggested that the Mississippi State Highway Patrol be alerted.

3–4 AM   John Doar was called again. . . .

6 AM   On being called again, Doar replied that "I have invested the FBI with the power to look into this matter."

7:30 AM   Information concerning the arrest on traffic charges of the three which had been gathered from the Philadelphia jailer's wife was phoned in to the Jackson FBI office. The agent said he would give the information to FBI agent Helgesen, whom we had contacted the night before.

8:30 AM   New information from the jailer's wife, Mrs. Herring, to the effect that the three had been released at 6 PM, plus the results of phone calls to various neighboring jails were called in to Agent Helgesen. Helgesen said he could do nothing until called by the New Orleans FBI office.

9 AM   . . . called the Highway Patrol. Though they had been called at least four times during the night, they did not seem to know about the case.

9:15 AM   Attorney Doar was called again at 9:15 from Atlanta and apprised of new developments.

11 AM   Helgesen was called and given new information reported by some white contacts in Philadelphia to the effect that the three were still in jail at 9 PM and appeared to have been beaten, though not seriously. Helgesen said he would "take the necessary action." He said that the alleged beating threw new light on the FBI's role in the case. He said he would call our source.

12 PM   Helgesen was called again. He said that he had only called New Orleans and had not received instructions to investigate.

12:15 PM   Atlanta SNCC called Jackson and said they had spoken to Agent Mayner in New Orleans, who had said he had received no orders from Washington.

1 PM   . . . CORE had contacted FBI Agent Delloch, second in command of the FBI, as well as Lee White, Presidential Assistant and Burke Marshall, head of the Civil Rights Division of the Justice Department. [CORE] said that if they got no action from the FBI, they would call the President. . . . Farmer in Washington had called the FBI in New Orleans. . . . Robert Kennedy had been contacted.

1:40 PM   Meridian reported that attempts had been made to call local air force bases to institute an air search, but were unsuccessful. Atlanta

SNCC called John Doar; he was speaking on another line. They left word for him to call back.

2:10 PM   Our source with the white contacts in Philadelphia reported that as of that hour the FBI had not yet called him, as Helgesen had promised he would two hours earlier. Meridian reported that Marvin Rich was calling the Defense Department to try to institute an air search [prevented by stormy weather].

2:45 PM   Atlanta informed us that calls were made to Burke Marshall and John Doar at 2:30 and 2:45 respectively. Word was left, as the two men could not be reached by phone.

2:55 PM   It was reported that reporters had been permitted to go through the Philadelphia jail and were satisfied that the three were not there.

3:30 PM   As of this time neither the Atlanta nor the Jackson offices had received any return phone calls from Doar or Marshall, nor did the FBI office in Jackson have any word from them.

5 PM   Doar called Atlanta. He informed them that the Mississippi Highway Patrol had put out an ALL POINTS ALERT bulletin and that both the sheriff of Neshoba County and the FBI were searching. The sheriff claimed that the trio were last seen heading South on Route 19 toward Meridian.

8 PM   Bill Light in Jackson called Agent Helgesen. He was asked five times if the FBI was investigating the case. Five times Helgesen answered, "all inquiries are to be directed to the Justice Department in Washington."

8:45 PM   Meridian reported that they called Doar in Washington. Doar was busy. A collect call was placed to John Doar at his home in Washington, from Meridian. He would not accept the call.

9:30 PM   Reporters called from Philadelphia that four FBI agents from the New Orleans office were in Philadelphia. No men from the Justice Department were reported. The FBI agents reportedly were talking to people and were planning to launch a road search and investigation in the morning.

10 PM   UPI reported that Edwin Guthman of the Justice Department in Washington had announced that the FBI was ordered into the case to determine whether the trio were being held against their will or whether there was a violation of Civil Rights involved.

Tuesday, June 23

8:45 AM   Meridian called to say that Marvin Rich had informed them that the Air Force might come by. As of this time, nothing had been heard from them.

10:10 AM   . . . FBI agents, were in the Meridian office. They were investigating, asking questions, and getting photographs of Schwerner. We were told that Nathan Schwerner (Mickey's father) has an appointment with Lee White, Presidential Assist.

1 PM   Meridian called to tell us that Marvin Rich had made contact with the White House (Lee White). He was told that the Naval Air Station near Meridian was available to the FBI for an air search. . . .

2:10 PM   The Naval Air Station near Meridian was called. They said that as far as they knew, no search was being conducted. There were only student flights taking place in the area.

2:50 PM   . . . Attorney General Robert Kennedy. Kennedy assured [the Goodmans and Mr. Schwerner] that all authorities were working on the case and that Navy helicopters were searching the area. . . . there was hope that President Johnson would make a statement to the nation.

3:55 PM   Meridian heard that local radio station WMOX broadcasted that the FBI had found the car, charred and burned and cold. There was no trace of the missing persons.

5:15 PM   Attorney Wolf informed us that Mr. and Mrs. Goodman, Mr. Schwerner, and two congressmen saw President Johnson for about 21 minutes this afternoon. . . .

5:25 PM   Attorney Larry Warren heard a confirming report on local radio that the Navy Helicopter was being used in the search. . . . FBI had been working on the [burned church] case since Friday, June 19.

6 PM   . . . Gov. Johnson had not called President Johnson or the Justice Department, but he was working with the FBI.

7:30 PM   [meeting between Robert Kennedy et al. and the Goodmans et al.] The FBI, according to Mr. Kennedy, was acting on the assumption that this was a kidnapping; it was on this assumption that they are assuming jurisdiction on the case. The parent's group made it clear that the Federal Government must make every effort to: (1) find the boys, and (2) protect the rest of the workers in the state. They made a special point that what was needed was not just investigation, but protection. . . .

[Kennedy agreed] . . . . The group then went to the White House. They met the Presidential assistants. . .were told there was a possibility that military personnel might be used in the search. . . . Then the President himself saw them and said he was using every available force. . . .

8 PM   The President called Goodman at his home in New York. He told him that there was no evidence that bodies had been found, but that tracks had been found leading away from the car. He said he had ordered more FBI and Defense Department personnel to "comb the countryside."

Wednesday, June 24
8:30 AM   Allen Dulles, ex-chief of the CIA, President Johnson's personal investigator, arrived.

1 PM   Meridian informed us that a young boy from Meridian who is often around the office had seen Mickey and Andy. . .and remembered what they were wearing. . . . This information was phoned to the FBI in Jackson, as the FBI in Meridian could not be reached.

Thursday, June 25
3 PM   Allen Dulles and Tom Finney, representatives of the President, met with leaders of the groups working in Mississippi. Dulles stated his mission was a fact-finding one. The leaders expressed the sense of frustration and isolation felt by Negroes because of police and civilian brutality of the state and the seeming unwillingness of the Federal Government to do anything about it. Dulles said he had been under the impression that the situation was improving in Mississippi, especially in the area of education. The leaders told him all visitors were given that sort of brainwashing. They related to Dulles and Finney examples of incidents where police were involved with local citizens in committing atrocities. Mr. Dulles was also told of the dangerous situations in various parts of the state, and was told what the leaders were demanding of the Federal Government:

A.   The president should meet with local leaders, as he has already been requested several times to do.

B.   That the Civil Rights Commission should immediately hold full hearings in the state of Mississippi.

C. That the President should see to it that new Federal Judgeships were filled by men of integrity and fairness.

D. Government officials should not publicly state that they cannot protect people.

E. There should be Marshals and FBI mobilized in all potentially dangerous areas.

See Activity 8.3 "Mississippi Burning" or "The Philadelphia, Mississippi Case" *in the Appendix*

NINE

Freedom Summer: Freedom Schools and the Arts

THE MISSISSIPPI FREEDOM SCHOOLS arose from the same impulses that led Miles Horton to establish Highlander and for Horton to join with Esau Jenkins and Septima Clark to start the Johns Island Citizenship School (see Chapter 4). Charlie Cobb envisioned the goal of such schools in Mississippi as developing democratic leadership within local communities so that ordinary people would be able to affect social change. As part of Mississippi Freedom Summer, the Freedom Schools were also an outgrowth of the literacy workshops that Cobb and other SNCC workers were conducting in order to successfully register increasing numbers of black voters. The written curriculum that was distributed to many of the teachers (but not all and not all in one piece) reflected these two impulses as it was divided into the Academic Curriculum and the Citizenship Curriculum. But it was the vision or the goal of the Freedom School Curriculum, rather than its specific written components, that guided the volunteer teachers and students during each of the two three-week summer sessions.

One of the most central and radical aspects of both the Freedom Schools and the movement, of which the schools were an integral part, was the role of the arts. In Freedom Schools, as in the movement, individuals were not passive spectators; they were active creators. The arts placed the individual in the stream of history, a stream in which he or she was both inheritor and creator. The stage provided a transition from the class to the street, preparing activists for the confrontations that were the inevitable result of political action. Drama woke the heroes of the past and fought the battles of the present. Modern-day recollections of the movement are filled with stories of singing, of the making of music that was deeply rooted in African American tradition and yet paradoxically freed the singers from the barriers of race. Volunteer musicians visited Freedom Schools performing for and giving workshops with the students and voter registration workers. The music not only "settled the terror" but also "directed it." In the Freedom Schools, writing became a form of testimony, a telling of truth, which required courage and vision. It gave voice to the silenced and freed the human personality imprisoned by racism and poverty. The Free Southern Theater performed throughout Mississippi during the summer of 1964 in order to "stimulate the growth and self-knowledge of a Negro audience" and develop "patterns of reflective and creative thought" which "are restricted by Mississippi's closed educational system and controlled mass media."[1]

9.A   Charles Cobb: The Freedom Schools

Questions to help you adopt a critical stance while reading the section below:
1. *Why is "the asking of questions" what the Freedom Schools were all about?*
2. *Why are "questions" so subversive?*
3. *What is the importance of being able to see patterns?*
4. *In what ways does the traditional curriculum inhibit the asking of questions?*
5. *How does a curriculum driven by standardized tests inhibit the asking of questions? Is such a curriculum inherently conservative?*

Further information:
The transcript of an interview with Sandra Adickes is at the Digital Archives of the University of Southern Mississippi, www.lib.usm.edu/%7Espcol/crda/oh/adickestrans.htm. Dr. Adickes is a teacher from New York and taught at the Freedom School in Hattiesburg.

An Oral History with Charles Cobb, where he describes the life of a SNCC field secretary, can be found at the Digital Archives of the University of Southern Mississippi, www.lib.usm.edu/~spcol/crda/oh/cobbtrans.htm

CHARLES COBB

Charlie Cobb was in his last year in high school when the sit-ins started and SNCC was founded, and Cobb participated in picketing Woolworth's in support of the Southern students. The following year, in 1961, he enrolled at Howard University, a black college in Washington, D.C. and directly became involved in nonviolent protest. In the summer of '62, he received a grant from CORE to participate in a workshop in Houston. On his way to Texas he traveled through Mississippi, and met the SNCC staff in Jackson—and stayed, to become a SNCC field secretary in Sunflower County in the Mississippi Delta. Cobb joined the voter registration drives, daily going from door to door to talk to the locals to explain why voting was important and going with those that agreed to the courthouse to support them in the face of violence and intimidation. Since voter registration laws in Mississippi required the interpretation of a section of the Mississippi Constitution, Cobb and others in SNCC became involved in adult education, teaching the Mississippi Delta sharecroppers to read and write.[2]

Although Cobb was skeptical about the idea of bringing hundreds of white Northerners to the South for the Summer Project, he thought that the volunteers could be used to help teach, and in December of '63, before the decision for the Summer Project had been taken, he wrote a proposal for the Freedom Schools. Cobb understood that, in Mississippi, "schools as institutions were part of the apparatus of oppression."[3] Every aspect of traditional Mississippi schools conveyed the state's message of racial inferiority and of the need for black children to adjust to their "place." In the cotton lands of the Delta, schools were closed during picking season. Libraries with books discarded from the white schools and science labs without equipment were the rule. In order to keep their jobs, African American public school teachers were often silent on political issues. In "Notes on Teaching in Mississippi," Cobb stated:

> Here, an idea of your own is a subversion that must be squelched. . . . Learning here means learning to stay in your place. Your place is to be satisfied—

a "good nigger." They have learned the learning necessary for immediate survival: that silence is safest, so volunteer nothing; that the teacher is the state, and tell them only what they want to hear; that the law and learning are white man's law and learning.[4]

The Freedom School concept proposed by Cobb added the school to the institutions that SNCC had set out to challenge, to transform or, if necessary, to replace. In addition to opening the minds of the students to questioning, the schools would be an effective tool for political organizing; in the classroom, students would be trained to become local Civil Rights workers. "The overall theme of the school," Cobb wrote, "would be the student as a force for social change in Mississippi."[5]

What if we showed what was possible in education? We had already been approaching this through 'literacy workshops' within the context of organizing for voter registration. And SNCC itself had created a 'nonviolent high school' during the 1961 protests in McComb. . . . But we hadn't really tackled education as an approach to community organizing in and of itself.

Significantly, the model for how to do this emerged from a specific political organization that also grew out of grassroots organizing: the Mississippi Freedom Democratic Party.[6]

1964 Freedom School Curriculum Link:
Prospectus for a Freedom School
   www.educationanddemocracy.org/FSCfiles/B_05_ProspForFSchools.htm
For more information on the Freedom Schools, go to "Introduction" and "Supplemental Documents"
   www.educationanddemocracy.org/FSCfiles/A_03_Index.htm

THE FREEDOM SCHOOLS
In the Freedom Schools, as they had in the Freedom Vote and the Mississippi Democratic Party, COFO and the SNCC workers set about creating an alternative. Ed King saw the Mississippi Freedom Democratic Party and the Freedom Schools as allies in the process of social change. "Our assumption was that the parents of the Freedom School children, when we met them at night, that the Freedom Democratic Party would be the PTA. . . .

We were going deliberately to reach the parents through the children. At the same time, we felt that we were liberating the children." In both situations, the goal was the sharing of power.

> The teacher has something to share, but the teacher would believe that the students have something, that each student has something, more than the teacher has and that, in the dynamic between teacher and student, there is something greater than either. . . . What we were doing with Freedom Schools, or with adult literacy classes, was helping people understand themselves, respect themselves, understand their world, and therefore seize power. . . . Education is sharing, and then enabling, and then letting go.[7]

The first step in creating the Freedom Schools was the planning of curriculum. In the spring of 1964, the National Council of Churches sponsored a conference in New York to plan for the Freedom Schools. The sessions were attended by, among others, the SCLC's Septima Clark; Highlander's Myles Horton; Noel Day, a junior-high school teacher who had organized a one-day program during the 1963 Boston school boycott; Norma Becker, New York teacher and activist member of the United Federation of Teachers; and Staughton Lynd, later state-wide director of the Freedom Schools. At the center of the curriculum was education's most powerful tool: the question. The curriculum was to focus on the students' experience; to encourage questioning, discussion, and action; and to offer remediation in both skills and content. In addition to African American history and political organizing, the students would study math, science, reading, art, and music. The curriculum written during the conference was reproduced by Staughton and Alice Lynd on a mimeograph machine in their Atlanta apartment and brought to Ohio for the orientation session in the trunk of their car.

The teaching staff was to consist of Mississippi Summer Project volunteers. In the two orientation sessions held in June at Western College for Women in Oxford, Ohio, the volunteers, few of whom were professional teachers, received an orientation in the political and economic conditions of Mississippi, in the type of education their students would have received in the state's segregated schools, and in techniques that might help open the minds of their students to new ideas and possibilities. Historian Howard Zinn described the advice the teachers were given at Oxford:

You'll arrive in Ruleville, in the Delta. It will be 100 degrees, and you'll be sweaty and dirty. You won't be able to bathe often or sleep well or eat good food. The first day of school, there may be four teachers and three students. And the local Negro minister will phone to say you can't use his church basement after all, because his life has been threatened. And the curriculum we've drawn up—Negro history and American government—may be something you know only a little about yourself. Well, you'll knock on doors all day in the hot sun to find students. You'll meet on someone's lawn under a tree. You'll tear up the curriculum and teach what you know.[8]

The dangers the teachers might face were communicated to them dramatically when the disappearance of CORE workers Chaney and Schwerner, and summer volunteer Andrew Goodman was announced during the second week of the orientation. The church burning that the Civil Rights workers were investigating had occurred after the members had voted to house a Freedom School. After the announcement, Staughton Lynd spent part of the evening counseling teachers who were reconsidering their decision to go to Mississippi.

The first Freedom School teachers arrived in Mississippi in late June, planning to open twenty schools with approximately one thousand students. Like SNCC field secretaries and other summer volunteers, the teachers stayed in the homes of local people. Classrooms were found anywhere the black community was willing to house them—in churches, in basements, on porches, under trees. All together, there were forty-one Freedom Schools. Attendance was entirely voluntary; part of a teacher's task was to canvass for students. Like voter registration workers, teachers knocked on doors, explained their purpose, and encouraged participation. Often, to establish their link with the community, they were accompanied by local teenagers who had showed up at the COFO office.

Word of the schools spread from one student to another, and gradually the classes began to fill. The anticipated enrollment of one thousand grew, day by day, student by student, to two thousand. Classes were attended not only by the teenagers for whom they were planned but by younger children and adults.

Document 9.1   Kirsty Powell: A Report, Mainly on Ruleville Freedom School[9]
See entire document at www.educationanddemocracy.org/FSCfiles/B_15_Report Ruleville.htm

First Week in Ruleville. We arrived on the Sunday—slight chill at our first view of police truck and dog—but for those of us working at the center, the fear went when we got on the job, and found Ruleville quiet. The center was at the back of an old house which contained two other occupied dwellings. It consisted of a yard, with trees for sitting under; porch, with bathroom at one end; a wide hallway which was to become office; an incredible attic—beams reasonably sturdy, but floor/ceiling of cardboard—where we later stored unwanted books; and two small rooms about 12 x 12 which were to be library and everything else. The first job was to sort 7000 books and cull a library of about 4000, shelve it, and store the rest. We were lucky to have somewhere to store it! This was all we did thru' Thursday, apart from volunteers' meetings to plan school and center programmes. One night at the mass meeting we were asked when school would begin. We decided we'd never be "ready," so we said we'd open for registration Friday, and for a brief introductory session. Regular school was in session in the mornings, so we decided to have adults, with baby minding in the mornings, kids in the afternoons, and leave the evenings clear for individual tuition or special classes if called for.

Writing. As with Citizenship and Health all the adults remained in one class for writing. Usually, this was about 12 to 15 students, numbers fluctuated somewhat between six and 30. The method used was to have three to six teachers on hand circulating while the writing was being done, to help and to answer questions and to correct. The topic usually arose out of the preceding citizenship session. Very little was done to structure it, the idea being simply to encourage them to put thoughts on paper as freely as possible. I think this unstructured approach was good and perhaps liberating in a way. Certainly it produced some very interesting, albeit weirdly punctuated and spelled genuine writing, most revealing of thoughts, feelings and experience.

Later in the summer, we did attempt to teach certain structures: form filling, the sentence and with it the period and the capital letter; personal letter; business letter; report of a meeting.

I think we were wise to leave this till the end of the summer. Though there is a great eagerness to learn the proper forms, I think that to have begun this way might have been rather inhibiting.

A few of the people who came were near illiterates and were in need of straight out handwriting practice. Even these, I think, benefited from the fairly free approach, provided they continued to come. I think we should probably have had a special class for them, and perhaps we'd have attracted more and held them.

At least the team teaching approach guaranteed fairly individual teaching of each person.

Reading. Practically all the adults were given an individual textbook test (sometimes called "informal reading inventory") using a set of basal school readers. This test is familiar to all teachers of reading. The purpose of the test was to discover the *instructional reading level* of each student; i.e., the level at which, over 100 running words, he makes 2% – 5% errors in word recognition. On the basis of this testing we divided the students into 3 reading groups.

1. **All below 3rd Grade** went into a literacy class. These worked on the Gattengo "Words in Color" system. . . . The success of the method depends on faithful attendance and a pretty high degree of concentration on the part of the student, and, with the exception of the one woman mentioned, the less literate students attended least faithfully. My own feeling was that the method postponed actual reading for such a long time that it tended to be a bit discouraging . . .

2. **3rd and 4th Grade** . . . used an easy reading newspaper (not Junior Scholastic, but something similar) which people seemed to enjoy reading. Only trouble was that the paper was rather expensive.

3. **5th Grade and above** . . . were, in fact, the largest group. We read materials on Negro history, most of them written by us especially for the purpose, because most available materials were too difficult even for this group. We began with the Ebony Emancipation issue, in which we found plenty of good material written in impossibly difficult and high flown language. We began with the "Ten Dramatic Moments" which when rewritten, proved excellent. We read also parts of the Sarah Patton Boyle and Frederick Douglass articles, the M.L.K. "I Have a Dream" speech, several issues of. . ."Freedom Fighter," the mimeod [sic] newspaper produced by the Center. In the last few weeks, we read materials written by all the teachers, following the last Citizenship syllabus. . . .

On two occasions we read poems. . . . If a teacher likes poetry, and has a few simple clues about how to present it, I think it is often very much appreciated. . . .

Baby Minding . . . I think what made the task hard was that all of us, those involved, and those not involved, tended to underrate its importance. It was important not just because it made the attendance of mother possible, but for its own sake, and because it paved the way for the permanent kindergarten that now exists. . . .

At the end of the 3rd week, we lost 3 teachers . . . as they went to Indianola to set up a Freedom School there. The three different schedules which we worked to during the summer reflect the staff changes.

Schedule I

- 1st Hour: in Age Groups for Citizenship, Reading, Writing.

- 2nd Hour: Electives – most met 2 days a week, some 1 day only

- Typing   Reading   Art

- French   African Culture   Biology

- Music   Health

The electives were taught not only by Freedom School teachers but by Community Center people also.

- 3rd Hour: Principally Recreation

Also some electives
Also canvassing—when needed.

One feature of this schedule was that we never met as a whole school together in a general session. I think this was a weakness. We did have one general session in the last week, when we sang a few freedom songs and then heard a talk about M.F.D.P., and then broke into age groups to discuss it. The kids liked this. . . .

Schedule II

- 1st Hour: Mass Meeting [songs, speakers, general announcements]

- 2nd Hour: Expression Groups—Art, Role Playing, Writing

- 3rd Hour: Electives (same) and Recreation, and Canvassing

Schedule III

- 2nd Hour: Age Groups . . . 13 – 14's—my class. I took Negro History as a core, following roughly the adult course (p.2), but leaving out the more sociological topics (like the Negro in the North etc.) My method was to introduce a topic, like Harriet Tubman, for instance, by telling the story, talking about it, looking at pictures, reading about it. This generally took one day. Then for the next two or three days, the kids followed up on this topic in their own way. I brought all the books, magazines, mimeoed material, pictures, etc. I could find to class, and got kids to choose what they wanted to do, and use the resource materials to help them. Some did historical, some creative writing, some drew pictures, or copied poems, or copied historical documents like runaway slave notices, etc. At the end of the summer, we displayed the work on all the units, arranged chronologically, to present a kind of perspective on Negro history. . . .

Highlights of the School Program

1. **Caravan of Music.** We had about 6 visits from folk singers . . .

2. **The Visit of 13 of the Women from National Women's Organizations** gave us all a boost. . . . Mrs. Hamer, Mrs. MacDonald, Mrs. Johnson, and Mrs. Tucker told the story of the Movement in Ruleville, after which followed some very good discussion . . .

3. **Meridian Freedom School Convention.** Three kids went from Ruleville. . . . Ruleville made a good contribution to the Convention. The story of the school protest and the motion of Bobbie Cannon inspired plans for the state-wide boycott. [two of the students] were impressed by how hard work it was. As Eddie said in his report, "It wasn't fun!" Actually I think that next year the program might include a bit more fun—a dance [or other forms of recreation]. . .

4. **In White America.** This was a great success. It was done on the back porch. . . .

1964 Freedom School Curriculum Links:

Liz Fusco: Freedom Schools in Mississippi, 1964

www.educationanddemocracy.org/FSCfiles/B_16_FSchoolsInMSFusco.htm

Examples of Student Work
   www.educationanddemocracy.org/FSCfiles/B_18_ExcerptsOfStudentWork.htm

9.B   Staughton Lynd: The Freedom School Convention

Staughton Lynd had been an activist all of his life. He was the son of Robert and Helen Lynd, whose book "Middletown" was a pioneering work in sociology. During the Korean war he was granted non-combatant status in the U.S. Army as a conscientious objector. After his discharge, he and his wife Alice lived in a cooperative community in Georgia for three years.

Lynd had graduated from Harvard and earned a Ph.D. in History at Columbia, and in the early 1960s went to teach at Spelman, a black college for women. Lynd became active in the southern Civil Rights Movement, and was invited to come to the conference that planned the curriculum for the Freedom Schools. He became the statewide coordinator of the Freedom Schools, before he started teaching history at Yale in the fall.[10]

When Freedom Summer volunteer Tom Wahman agreed to take care of the administrative work at the office in Jackson, Lynd was free to visit many of the Freedom Schools, and to plan and be actively involved in the Freedom School Convention. In an article he wrote for *Freedomways* in 1965, Staughton Lynd proposed "If I were to start a Freedom School now (and we are about to start one in New Haven), I would suggest: Begin with a Freedom School Convention and let that provide your curriculum." He began to come to this conclusion on August 7, the second day of the Freedom School Convention during which the students had begun to reject the advice of the adults. They had discovered that they could do everything themselves. What came out of this convention was a political program. Lynd believed at that time that "it would have been better if the schools had begun with such a convention, and if the statewide program brought back to each school by its delegates had then become the curriculum for the summer." Lynd worried that the Civil Rights Movement was being "strangely neglectful of program." The Freedom School Convention delegates, on the other hand, were not being so neglectful. Lynd anticipated that the Freedom Schools could provide future political candidates who would be able "to declare themselves intelligently on a variety of issues" if the Freedom School Platform became the new curriculum of the Freedom Schools.

1964 Freedom School Curriculum Link:
Staughton Lynd: Freedom Schools, Concept and Organization
   www.educationanddemocracy.org/FSCfiles/B_19_MSFSchoolsLynd.htm

THE FREEDOM SCHOOL CONVENTION

Throughout Freedom Summer, Freedom School students had been educated for political empowerment. While the voting-age adults attended the MFDP state convention in Jackson, the students held their own convention in Meridian on August 6–8 and addressed many of the same issues. The students held a parallel convention, rather than leaving politics to their elders. Just as the students were asked to do voter registration work, they participated in the convention process as well. Edwin King described the MFDP as the PTA of the Freedom Schools. The Freedom Schools and the MFDP were, in many ways, the same organization.

The convention was held at the Baptist Seminary Meridian, close to Philadelphia, where Michael Schwerner, James Chaney and Andrew Goodman had been murdered when they had attempted to start a Freedom School there. Coincidentally, the convention started at the end of the week when the bodies of the three had been found buried in an earthen dam, and the students arrived in time for the first memorial service on Friday night.

Each Freedom School sent three representatives and a coordinator, so that there were 120 people at the convention. They brought to the conference lists of grievances and suggestions, and during the next two days discussed these in eight committees on different areas of legislation. Plenary sessions included talks by A. Philip Randolph of the Brotherhood of Sleeping Car Porters and Jim Forman, SNCC's Executive Secretary. Bob Moses asked questions, helping the students to articulate what they wanted for the future. There was also lots of song, the Holly Springs Freedom School presented "Seeds of Freedom," a play based on the life of Medgar Evers, and the Free Southern Theater presented Martin Duberman's play *In White America*. On Sunday afternoon, the Platform was adopted in plenary session, and the delegates voted to send copies to the United Nations and to the Library of Congress for its permanent records.[11]

Freedom Schools—Final Report, 1964, suggested that the best way to evaluate the effectiveness of the Freedom Schools was to read the Platform of the Freedom School Convention in Meridian. The *Report* wanted the reader to "Note particularly the proposal for a state-wide school boycott.

School boycotts are already in progress in Shaw and Harmony. A boycott is about to begin in Indianola. There will be many such boycotts during the winter . . . ." Implicit in this statement is that if the primary purpose of the Freedom Schools was to empower students to take direct action, the existence of school boycotts was evidence of the success of the curriculum.

Questions based on Document 9.2 below:

  1. *If the Freedom School Platform was the "final exam" of the Citizenship Curriculum, what grade would you give the exam and why?*

  2. *Would you want the Platform to be the only document used to evaluate whether the Freedom School Curriculum was a success? Why or why not?*

  3. *Can the Platform function as a final exam? If yes, why don't your courses at your school today have final exams like this? If no, what kind of final exam would you create for the Citizenship Curriculum? Is it appropriate, relevant, or useful to think in terms of "exams" in connection to the Citizenship Curriculum? Is such a curriculum only conceivable during revolutionary moments in history? Do "exams" function to maintain the status quo (things as they are)?*

  4. *Does it make sense to you that the Platform could be the curriculum of a school? Why or why not?*

Document 9.2   1964 Platform of the Mississippi Freedom School Convention[12]
AUGUST 6TH, 7TH, 8TH, MERIDIAN, MISSISSIPPI

PUBLIC ACCOMMODATIONS

  1. We resolve that the Public Accommodations and Public Facilities sections of the Civil Rights Act of 1964 be enforced.

  2. We demand new and better recreation facilities for all.

  3. We support the right of the Negro people and their white supporters to test the Civil Rights Act via demonstrations such as sit-ins. We are not urging a blood-bath through this means; we are simply demanding our Constitutional right to public assembly and seeking to test the Federal government's position.

  4. Conversion of public accommodations into private clubs should be treated as a violation of the Civil Rights Act of 1964.

HOUSING

The home, being the center of a child's life as well as the center of a family's, must have certain facilities in order for it to be a home and not just a building in which one eats, sleeps, and prepares to leave for the rest of the day. Therefore, be it resolved:

1.   That there be an equal-opportunity-to-buy-law which permits all persons to purchase a home in any section of town in which he can afford to live.

2.   That a rent control law be passed and that one should pay according to the condition of the house.

3.   That a building code for home construction be established which includes the following minimum housing requirements:

    a.   A complete bathroom unit

    b.   A kitchen sink

    c.   A central heating system

    d.   Insulated walls and ceiling

    e.   A laundry room and pantry space

    f.   An adequate wiring system providing for at least three electrical outlets in the living room and kitchen, and at least two such outlets in the bedroom and bath

    g.   At least a quarter of an acre of land per building lot

    h.   A basement and attic

4.   That zoning regulations be enacted and enforced to keep undesirable and unsightly industries and commercial operations away from residential neighborhoods.

5.   That slums be cleared, and a low cost federal housing project be established to house these people.

6.   That federal aid be given for the improvement of houses, with long term low interest loans.

7.   That the federal government provide money for new housing developments in the state. Anyone could buy these houses with a down

payment and low monthly rate. There must be absolutely no discrimination. The federal government should take action if this law is not complied with.

8. That a federal law make sure that the projects are integrated and that they are run fairly.

9. That there be lower taxes on improvements in the houses so that more people will fix up their house.

10. That the federal government buy and sell land at low rates to people who want to build there.

EDUCATION

In an age where machines are rapidly replacing manual labor, job opportunities and economic security increasingly require higher levels of education. We therefore demand:

1. Better facilities in all schools. These would include textbooks, laboratories, air conditioning, heating, recreation, and lunch rooms.

2. A broader curriculum including vocational subjects and foreign languages.

3. Low fee adult classes for better jobs.

4. That the school year consist of nine (9) consecutive months.

5. Exchange programs and public kindergarten.

6. Better qualified teachers with salaries according to qualification.

7. Forced retirement (women 62, men 65).

8. Special schools for mentally retarded and treatment and care of cerebral palsy victims.

9. That taxpayers' money not be used to provide private schools.

10. That all schools be integrated and equal throughout the country.

11. Academic freedom for teachers and students.

12. That teachers be able to join any political organization to fight for Civil Rights without fear of being fired.

13. That teacher brutality be eliminated.

HEALTH

1. Each school should have fully developed health, first aid, and physical education programs. These programs should be assisted by at least one registered nurse.

2. Mobile units, chest x-rays semi-annually and a check-up at least once a year by licensed doctors, the local health department or a clinic should be provided by the local or state government.

3. All medical facilities should have both integrated staff and integrated facilities for all patients.

4. Mental health facilities should be integrated and better staffed.

5. Homes for the aged should be created.

6. Free medical care should be provided for all those who are not able to pay the cost of hospital bills.

7. We demand state and local government inspection of all health facilities.

8. All doctors should be paid by skill, not by race.

9. Titles should be given to the staff.

10. The federal government should help the organization pay the salaries of workers.

11. All patients should be addressed properly.

12. We actively seek the abolition of any sterilization act which serves as punishment, voluntary or involuntary, for any offense.

13. In a reasonable time we seek the establishment of a center for the treatment and care of cerebral palsy victims.

FOREIGN AFFAIRS

1. The United States should stop supporting dictatorships in other countries and should support that government which the majority of the people want.

2. Whereas the policy of apartheid in the Republic of South Africa is detrimental to all the people of that country and against the concepts

of equality and justice, we ask that the United States impose economic sanctions in order to end this policy.

3. We ask that there be an equitable balance between the domestic and foreign economic and social support provided by our country.

FEDERAL AID

1. We demand that a Public Works Program be set up by the federal government to create jobs for the unemployed.

2. Because of discrimination in the past, we demand preferential treatment for the Negro in the granting of federal aid in education and training programs until integration is accomplished.

3. To help fight unemployment, we demand that federal funds be lent communities to set up industries and whole towns which shall be publicly owned by the communities, for example: textile and paper mills, stores, schools, job relocation programs for those put out of work by automation, job retraining, recreational facilities, banks, hospitals.

4. We demand that social security benefits should be given according to need, and not according to how much one earned previously. In addition, we demand guaranteed income of at least $3,000.00 annually for every citizen.

5. The federal government should give aid to students who wish to study for the professions and who do not have the necessary funds.

6. We feel that federal aid in Mississippi is not being distributed equally among the people. Therefore we adopt Title VI of the Civil Rights Law which deals with federal aid. We demand federal agents appointed to Mississippi expressly for this purpose. We demand that action be taken against the state of Mississippi so that this aid may be distributed fairly.

7. We demand that the federal government divert part of the funds now used for defense into additional federal aid appropriations.

8. We demand that the federal government refuse to contract with corporations that employ non-union labor, engage in unfair labor practices, or practice racial discrimination.

JOB DISCRIMINATION

1. We demand that the federal government immediately open to Negroes all employment opportunities and recruitment programs under their auspices, such as in post offices, Veterans Hospitals, and defense bases.

2. The fair employment section (Title VII) of the 1964 Civil Rights law be immediately and fully enforced.

3. The guarantee of fair employment be extended fully to all aspects of labor, particularly training programs.

4. We encourage the establishment of more unions in Mississippi, to attract more industry to the state.

5. We will encourage and support more strikes for better jobs and adequate pay. During the strikes the employers should be enjoined from having others replace the striking workers.

6. Vocational institutions must be established for high school graduates and dropouts.

7. The federal Minimum Wage law be extended to include all workers especially agriculture and domestic workers.

8. Cotton planting allotments to be made on the basis of family size.

9. We want an extension of the Manpower Retraining Program.

10. Whenever a factory is automated, management must find new jobs for the workers.

11. Workers should be paid in accordance with their qualifications and the type of work done.

THE PLANTATION SYSTEM

1. The federal government should force plantation owners to build and maintain fair tenant housing.

2. In cases where the plantation farmers are not being adequately paid according to the Minimum Wage Law, the government should

intervene on behalf of the farmers in suit against the plantation owner.

CIVIL LIBERTIES

1. Citizens of Mississippi should be entitled to employ out-of-state lawyers.

2. Section Two of the Fourteenth Amendment should be enforced, specifically in Mississippi and other Southern States, until the voter registration practices are changed.

3. The citizens should have the privilege of exercising their Constitutional rights

    a. to assemble,

    b. to petition,

    c. to freedom of the press,

    d. to freedom of speech, in such ways as picketing, passing out leaflets and demonstrations. We oppose all laws that deprive citizens of the above rights.

4. We want the abolition of the House Un-American Activities Committee because it deprives citizens of their Constitutional rights.

5. We resolve that the Freedom Movement should accept people regardless of religion, race, political views or national origin if they comply with the rules of the movement.

LAW ENFORCEMENT

1. We want qualified Negroes appointed to the police force in large numbers. We want them to be able to arrest anyone breaking the law, regardless of race, creed or color.

2. All police must possess warrants when they demand to enter a house and search the premises. In the absence of a search warrant, the police must give a reasonable explanation of what they are looking for. In any case, with or without a warrant, no damage should be

done unnecessarily to property, and if damage is done, it should be paid for.

3. A national committee should be set up to check police procedures, to insure the safety of people in jail: their food, sleeping and health facilities; to protect them from mobs, and to see that no violence is done to them.

4. All cases against law enforcement agencies or involving Civil Rights should be tried in federal courts.

5. Law enforcement officers should provide protection against such hate groups as the KKK. Police and public officials should not belong to any group that encourages or practices violence.

CITY MAINTENANCE

1. The city should finance paving and widening of the streets and installing of drain systems in them.

2. Sidewalks must be placed along all streets.

3. A better system of garbage disposal, including more frequent pick-ups, must be devised.

4. Streets should be adequately lighted.

5. We oppose nuclear testing in residential areas.

VOTING

1. The poll tax must be eliminated.

2. Writing and interpreting of the Constitution is to be eliminated.

3. We demand further that registration procedures be administered without discrimination, and that all intimidation of prospective voters be ended through federal supervision and investigation by the FBI and Justice Department.

4. We want guards posted at ballot boxes during counting of votes.

5. The minimum age for voting should be lowered to 18 years.

6. We seek for legislation to require the county registrar or one of his deputies to keep the voter registration books open five days a week except during holidays, and open noon hours and early evening so that they would be accessible to day workers. Registrars should be required by law to treat all people seeking to register equally.

DIRECT ACTION

1. To support Ruleville, we call for a state-wide school demonstration, urging teachers to vote, and asking for better, integrated schools.

2. We support nonviolence, picketing and demonstrations.

See Activity 9.1   Writing a Political Platform in the Appendix

9.C   Bernice Johnson Reagon: The Music of Freedom Summer

Why did "We Shall Overcome" become the "Marseillaise" of the Freedom Movement?

Further information:

Bernice Johnson Reagon has compiled a collection of recordings of singing at mass meetings and of the different Ensembles. The 2 CD set also includes an introductory booklet by Reagon with explanations and analysis of the songs and their history. Smithsonian Collection of Recordings: "Voices of the Civil Rights Movement, Black American Freedom Songs, 1960–1966;" CD SF 40084.

Recommended Film:

We Shall Overcome (Documentary; 58 min, 1990; produced and directed by Jim Brown). By tracing the sources of the song, this film uncovers the diverse strands of social history which flowed together to form the Freedom Movement.

MUSIC

"Black music is also social and political . . . Through song, a new political consciousness is continuously created, one antithetical to the laws of white society."[13]

The songs of the Civil Rights Movement were part of the African American musical heritage begun by the songs of the slaves and the spirituals.

The spirituals were frequently not the creation of a single composer but represented a collective creation. In many churches, the congregation responded to the sermon, affirming the preacher's words or the words of the Scriptures with a fervent "Amen." This response could also be sung. "From somewhere in the bowed gathering another voice improvised a response. . .then other voices joined the answer, shaping it into a musical phrase. . .from this molten metal of music a new song was smithed out, composed then and there by no one in particular and by everyone in general."[14] The spirituals transformed their listeners and suggested the possibility of transforming their lives as well. James Cone comments that "the theme of heaven in the spirituals and in black religion generally contained double meanings. 'Steal Away' referred not only to an eschatological realm, but it was also used by Harriet Tubman as a signal of freedom for slaves who intended to run away with her to the north, or to Canada."[15] The camp meeting and the revival brought the practice of improvisation into the period of Reconstruction. "The texts of the composed songs were not lyric poems. . .but a stringing together of isolated lines from prayers, the Scriptures, and orthodox hymns (with) the addition of choruses and. . .refrains between verses. . . . Spontaneous songs were composed on the spot."[16] The spirituals and the songs of the Civil Rights Movement were part of the same African American tradition. They were often collectively and spontaneously composed or adapted, they linked present struggles to Biblical or historical themes, they had veiled or direct political content. And they created unity and purpose in the listeners.

In *The Power of Nonviolence,* Richard Gregg suggests that music can create a sense of unity in a political movement. In his suggestions for training nonviolent resisters, Gregg says, "Get unity by singing together. . . . Music stirs our emotions deeply, gives form to our feelings, helps us to understand the life of feeling, educates our feelings, stimulates our imagination, helps to solve inner conflicts, enriches our consciousness, brings about subtle and profound inner integration of character, and expresses feelings and sympathies which cannot be put into words or even into acts. . . ."[17] Music contributed to the creation of group solidarity in the Labor movement. Such solidarity was what gave people the courage to face resistance and even violence. In 1931, Florence Reese, wife of labor leader Sam Jackson, wrote "Which Side are You On?" a labor song that was to be adapted to the Mississippi movement.

They say in Harlan County
There are no neutrals there
You'll either be a union man
Or a thug for J.H. Nair

Like many other protest songs, this song was adapted to the struggle in Mississippi:

They say down in Hinds County
No neutrals can be met,
You'll be a Freedom Rider,
Or a thug for Ross Barnett

As activists had for generations, workers in Mississippi remembered their heroes in ballads. Herbert Lee was the subject of the song "We'll Never Turn Back," an anthem of the Mississippi movement, written by Bertha Gober.[18] Lee had been shot by State Representative E.H. Hurst outside of the cotton gin in Liberty.

We've been 'buked and we've been scorned.
We've been talked about sure's you're born.
But we never will turn back,
No, we'll never turn back
Until we've all been freed.
And we have equality.

We have walked through the shadows of death.
We've had to walk all by ourselves.
We have hung our head and cried
For those like Lee who died,
Died for you and died for me
Died for the cause of equality.

Hartman Turnbow was a Mississippi farmer who had invited SNCC workers into Holmes County. A proud and independent man known for his private arsenal of guns, Turnbow was one of the "First Fourteen," a group of Mississippi farmers who appeared at the county courthouse in

Lexington to register to vote in 1963. The group was met outside of the courthouse by the Deputy Sheriff and thirty members of the local auxiliary police force. The Deputy Sheriff shouted at the group, "All right now, who will be first? Who will be first?" Turnbow stepped forward. "I, Hartman Turnbow, will be first," he replied. Turnbow and another were allowed to fill out the forms and the other twelve returned the next day to do so as well. They were, however, all declared "illiterate" and denied the right to register.[19]

Turnbow was committed to the vote but not to non-violence. "He'd rather it be known that he was not nonviolent and that wherever he went, he'd carry his gun," recalled Hollis Watkins. "He'd go to the meetings, and. . .he'd unzip his briefcase, and the first thing that would come out would be his pistol, and then he'd take the papers that he needed out, and kind of put the pistol way back up in there."[20] In retaliation for his voter registration efforts, Turnbow's house was firebombed. When investigators arrived at the scene, Turnbow was arrested for setting his own house on fire. Undeterred, Turnbow served as a delegate for the Mississippi Freedom Democratic Party in Atlantic City. He was honored in a song by Mike Kellin of Santa Monica, California: "Hartman Turnbow."

> Chorus:
> *My name is Hartman Turnbow and I belong to ME,*
> *I live in Mississippi, down in Holmes County;*
> *There's bullet-holes in my front door,*
> *They've set my house on fire*
> *But I'm gonna vote this fall because*
> *It's Freedom I desire.*
>
> Refrain:
> *Last spring I went to Register, to cast my "One Man" vote*
> *They called me "Boy," said "tip your hat," but they didn't get my goat.*
> *But come the very next morning, when the clock was striking three*
> *I heard this noise, and I saw this fire, and I knew they'd come for me.*
>
> *My name is Hartman Turnbow . . .*

Now, down in Delta country, we got no running water
So my missus drew some buckets, and she passed 'em to my daughter
While I greeted my guests with buckshots, till the 4 of 'em drove away
Then I went to see the sheriff, as soon as it was day.

I told him what had happened, he said, "Boy, yer a liar"
He said, I, Hartman Turnbow had set my own house on fire
He threw me in the jailhouse, but he had to set me free
'cause there's law in this here country, and law means liberty.

My name is Hartman Turnbow . . .

I still won't bow and shuffle when I come into town
My mind is set on voting—they ain't gonna scare me down
I been to Atlantic City, as a Freedom-Democrat
And they tip their hat to me, why, then I'll tip my hat

My name is Hartman Turnbow . . .[21]

WE SHALL OVERCOME

"The path from traditional to political usage was in many instances simple and uncomplicated," writes Bernice Johnson Reagon. "Songs like 'Oh Freedom,' 'We Shall not be Moved,' and 'We Shall Overcome'. . .were used repeatedly in social and political crises involving large groups of Blacks."[22] "We Shall Overcome" can trace its ancestry to "I'll Be All Right," a traditional song of the black church, which some Southerners recall being performed as a "shout." The "ring shout" is a form of worship, which is a survival of African ritual dance. In 1941, "I Will Overcome" was brought to the picket line by black members of the Food, Tobacco, and Agricultural Workers Union in Charleston, South Carolina. In 1947, some of the white union members attended a workshop at the Highlander Folk School and were asked by Zilphia Horton if they knew any new songs. "Well, they said that there was a song some of the Black people sang around and kind of changed up and made it kind of a union song. They sat down and worked on it and that night they came in with their version of 'We Shall

Overcome. . .," said Myles Horton. In 1947, Pete Seeger visited Highlander and learned the song from Zilphia Horton. Seeger changed the "will" to "shall" and recalled adding the verses "The whole wide world around" and "We'll walk hand in hand." "An individual writes a song, and pretty soon there's ten variations of it being sung in different places."[23]

In 1957, after the death of Zilphia Horton, white folk singer Guy Carawan came to Highlander as Musical Director. By the late 1950s, Highlander had shifted the focus of its workshops from union to Civil Rights and was conducting workshops for college students engaged in Civil Rights work. Carawan taught the song to Nashville students who attended a Highlander workshop in early April of 1960 and those same students invited him to attend SNCC's founding conference in Raleigh, North Carolina, that same month. According to Bernice Reagon, "Guy started to sing 'We Shall Overcome.' And I was told that everybody in the room stood, and joined hands, and sang the song in a way it had never been sung before. When people who were present talk about WSO, they say it is that singing and that moment that WSO became the Freedom song of the movement."[24]

Memories of Mississippi in 1964 include the singing of "We Shall Overcome," mostly at the conclusion of meetings, with the participants standing, linking arms and forming a wide, yet tight, circle. It was sung at Oxford and vividly remembered by the volunteers. It was sung at the funeral of James Chaney in August. Those who remember the movement recall that the songs, more than any other experience, created the world the singers could only imagine, the world beyond the barriers of race, even beyond time and place. As the Reverend Edwin King remembered,

> We used to say, 'This song came from Albany. Here's what happened there' . . . They would tell the story. The songs would mention names, like Herbert Lee. We later changed a verse there. Sometimes we would say, 'Like Goodman, Schwerner, Chaney.' We were being united with people in other places . . . . Once, we transcend the immediate geographic boundaries, we are also saying, yesterday, last year, in another place, in another time, the people and what I'm saying without really preaching is 'We are one.' [The singers became a] part of the entire past, the whole history of people struggling for freedom, and we were linked though the movement with the future, even if the practical linkage was saying this song started in Georgia,

and a little bit of a story, a story about yesterday and another place and our songs would link us with them, even if we died. There was a place beyond the horror we were in, and we were one. Life and death and geography did not define that unity.[25]

BERNICE JOHNSON REAGON

"The voice I have now I got the first time I sang in a movement meeting after I got out of jail. I did the song 'Over My Head I See Freedom in the Air,' but I had never heard that voice before. I had never been that me before. And once I became that me, I have never let that me go. A transformation took place inside of the people. The singing was just the echo of that."[26]

A veteran of the student movement in Albany, Georgia, Bernice Johnson Reagon was one of the first group of Freedom Singers, singer/activists who traveled across the country, bringing with them the story of the demonstrations in the South. The idea of the Freedom Singers originated with Pete Seeger. "In 1962, I stopped in at the office of SNCC in Atlanta and told Jim Forman you've got some great singers down there," said Seeger. "You ought to be booking them around the country. You could raise money for SNCC and spread the word."[27] Within a year, the original Freedom Singers—Charles Neblett, Cordell Reagon, Rutha Harris, and Bernice Johnson—were performing on college campuses before audiences who knew little about the movement in the South. In nine months, the first group traveled 50,000 miles through 48 states. A second group of all male singers (Charles Neblett, Cordell Reagon, James Peacock, Mathew Jones and Marshall Jones) was formed in 1964. Cordell Reagon and James Peacock briefly left to form the Freedom Voices, while others joined the Freedom Singers. The SNCC Freedom Singers were not the only Civil Rights music ensemble during those years, there were other ensembles like the CORE Freedom Singers and the Alabama Christian Movement Choir, but the SNCC Freedom Singers traveled more widely and spread the news around the country, while being a very successful fundraising tool for SNCC.[28]

The Freedom Singers "were not just singers, all of us were organizers," said Cordell Reagon. "We were out there in the backwoods of Mississippi and in Rutha and Bernice's home town of Albany, Georgia, desegregating the bus station."[29] The Freedom Singers were instrumental in bringing students to Mississippi for Freedom Summer. "We took the message of what was going on in the South to people in the North," explained Charles Neblett. "Many times when people came to a Freedom Singers concert, by coming, they were witnessing and becoming active," said Bernice Reagon. "So this was an initiating experience for many people. It was the first time they got an intimate chance to talk with people who actually had a day to day experience."[30]

During demonstrations, singing created solidarity and intimidated law enforcement officers. "They could not stop our sound," recalled Ms. Reagon. "They would have to kill us to stop us from singing. Sometimes the police would plead and say, 'Please stop singing.' And you would just know your word was being heard, and you felt joy. There is a way in which those songs kept us from being touched by people who would want us not to be who we were becoming."[31]

Reagon compared the work of a political organizer to that of a song leader. Both issue a call, which contains risk and the possibility of new creation; it is up to the listener to respond.

> In congregational singing, you don't sing a song, you raise it. By offering the first line, the song leader just offers the possibility, and it is up to you, individually, whether you pick it up or not. . . . It is a big personal risk because you will put everything into the song. It is like stepping off into space. A mini-revolution takes place inside of you. . . . This transformation inside yourself that you create is exactly what happens when you join a movement. You are taking a risk—you are committing yourself and there is no turning back. . . . When you get together at a mass meeting you sing the songs that symbolize transformation, which make that revolution of courage inside of you. . . . You raise a freedom song.[32]

See Activity 9.2   Call and Response in the Appendix

9.D   Pete Seeger: The Mississippi Caravan of Music

Questions to help you adopt a critical stance while reading the section below:

1. *Are songs integrated into the curriculum of your school or community-based institutions? If so, what role do they play? If not, why aren't they?*

2. *What institutions use songs? Are church services the only place where songs are sung? What are the implications of your answers?*

3. *Do you sing? How do you feel when you sing? What is the difference between reciting a poem and singing it?*

MISSISSIPPI CARAVAN OF MUSIC

In the summer of 1964, the Mississippi Caravan of Music, coordinated by Bob and Susan Cohen, brought to Mississippi performers like Bob Dylan, Pete Seeger, Cordell Reagon, Phil Ochs, Judy Collins, Tom Paxton, Len Chandler, Barbara Dane, Alix Dobkin, Carolyn Hester, Julius Lester, Theodore Bikel, and others. Volunteer musicians arrived in Jackson and were given a brief orientation in Mississippi politics by Bob and Susan Cohen before being booked on a tour. Traveling in groups, the performers visited more than thirty sites during the Summer Project. In the afternoons, often the performers held workshops for Freedom School students and voter registration workers. "These 'workshops'—a better name for it would have been 'playshops,'" recalled Len Holt, "generally wound up with what the singers or children were most interested in: anything from folk dancing and African rounds to English ballads and learning the banjo chords to 'Skip to My Lou.' After time out for supper, there was a mass meeting with singing or perhaps a 'hootenanny,' where the adult population of the community attended with the younger people, who were at the Freedom Schools during the day. It was not uncommon for these evening sessions to go on for more than three hours."[33]

In an article for *Broadside* magazine, Bob Cohen described the Caravan's visits to the Freedom Schools.

> A typical Caravan day would begin with the singers participating in a class on Negro history at the freedom school. They showed that freedom songs were sung back in the days of slavery—and how some songs even blueprinted the way to freedom on the underground railroad. The singers demonstrated the important contribution of Negro music in every aspect of American musical and cultural history. For children who have been educated—or rather brainwashed—by the public school system to accept the myth of their own inferiority, this was an exhilarating revelation.[34]

Like the summer volunteers, the performers were regarded as invaders and subject to the same reprisals. Ochs captured the apprehension of the summer workers as well as his own fear in the song, "I'm Going Down to Mississippi."

> I'm going down to Mississippi
> I'm going down a southern road
> And if you never ever see me again
> Remember I had to go

> It's a long road down to Mississippi
> It's a short road back the other way
> If the cops pull you over to the side of the road
> You won't have nothing to say
> No, you won't have nothing to say[35]

Judy Collins, a performer in the Caravan of Music, recalled her feelings as she drove to a performance near Ruleville, home of Senator James Eastland and Mrs. Fannie Lou Hamer. "I had seen enough," she recalled, "to suffer from total fear. I knew I was going to be shot at or beaten. My hands as we rode trembled so much I made myself change the guitar strings to keep them occupied." She and her companions began to sing "Ain't Gonna Let Nobody Turn Me Around." "It was then that I found out just a little of what freedom music can really mean. The music was the only way to settle the terror—to direct it."[36]

The Rev. Ed King described a concert in which Theodore Bikel performed in a cotton field as local whites circled in cars. "Bikel sang, and he sang folk songs from his youth in Vienna, and he talked about being Jewish and about Nazis. We're out in a cotton field. . .and he was at that time performing with Mary Martin in *The Sound of Music*. But here he was. He could have been killed. The riders are coming by, but the art was universal."[37]

PETE SEEGER

"There is a big, beautiful world that could be destroyed by selfishness and foolishness. We musicians have it within our power to help save it. In a small way, every single one of us counts."[38]

After leaving college, Seeger, along with Alan Lomax and Woodie Guthrie, compiled a collection of union and protest songs called *Hardhitting Songs for Hardhit People* during the early '40s. "I'm a New England radical. . . . But during the '30s, I was marching in May Day parades along with Woody Guthrie and Lee Hayes and others. During the '40s, I was involved in trying to build a singing labor movement."[39] Seeger recalls that the transition from labor activism to Civil Rights work was not entirely smooth.

> You have to understand that until the 1930's, the labor movement of the U.S.A. was largely white and frankly racist. . . . But in the 1930's, came a new kind of radical, especially when the CIO came through, black workers joined the unions and built them in the South, as well as the North, bringing with them their wonderful African tradition of singing. No matter what you do, you sing; whether you're washing dishes or hoeing corn or worshipping the Lord, you sang. So the unions, which had sung at times—the old 'wobblies,' I.W.W. (Industrial Workers of the World) used to sing—the black workers really made them singing unions in the 1930's. It was this tradition that Woody Guthrie and Lee Hayes and I were trying to build on in the 1940's.[40]

In the forties and fifties, Seeger was a member of both the Almanac Singers and the Weavers, folk singers whose uncompromising political views prompted accusations of Communist affiliation. Guthrie left the Almanac Singers to join the merchant marine, and the remaining Weavers were blacklisted during the McCarthy era. Seeger's music served to link the tradition of the American folk song with the African American music that formed the center of the music sung during the demonstrations of the early 1960s. Songs like "We Shall Overcome," according to Seeger, bear out "what I've long been convinced of, that it's a very fruitful interchange between white and black that has produced some of the best things in America."[41]

Although at first worried about being "just one more Yankee to Mississippi in 1964," Seeger participated in the Caravan of Music, and came twice during Freedom Summer. During his second, week-long visit, the bodies of Chaney, Goodman and Schwerner were discovered, and Seeger remembers announcing it during his concert.[42] Seeger saw connections between Freedom Summer and the work of the labor unions in the 1930s.

> Namely, a small group of very brave people sticking their neck out and trying to swing a larger group behind them. . . . There were times when a union organizer had to be very careful where he went to make sure he didn't

end up getting dumped in a ditch. . . . I've never taken dangers particularly myself, but I really admire the people who have—the way Bob Moses and his friends did in 1964. . . . For two hundred years at least, we've had one example after another of a small group of people sticking their necks out. Often their leaders get put in jail. At first it looks like they've lost. . . . But these small struggles which look like they lose they eventually win, but somebody has to stick his neck or her neck first, in order to force the issue.[43]

See Activity 9.3   My Music in the Appendix

9.E   John O'Neal: The Free Southern Theater

Questions to help you adopt a critical stance while reading the section below:
   1. *Is live music or theater important? Have you been to live theater? Who usually goes to theaters, and why? Should theater be more available? Is live theater more "subversive" than movies?*

   2. *Do you perform school or community plays? Which plays? Who decides which plays are performed?*

Question regarding Role Playing:
   Both the Freedom School Curriculum and the Civil Rights Movement frequently employed drama and role playing. Drawing from the models below, are there important distinctions between role-playing and dramatic acting? What is its effect on the actor for each? The audience?

JOHN O'NEAL AND THE FREE SOUTHERN THEATER

After graduating from Southern Illinois University, John O'Neal became a SNCC field secretary, working in Mississippi. In 1963, he worked full time on voter registration work in Hattiesburg. During the winter of that year, John O'Neal and the artists and activists Gil Moses and Doris Derby met in Jackson, Mississippi. Like O'Neal, Derby was a field secretary for SNCC and Moses was a reporter for the *Mississippi Free Press*. All three had backgrounds in the theater. Their vision of theater grew from their involvement in the movement. "We wanted to open Jackson up," wrote Moses, "to bring people there who normally were outside of state control and police authority. We wanted freedom: for thought, and involvement, and the celebration of our own culture."[44] Together, the three wrote "A General Prospectus for the Establishment of a Free Southern Theater," a document that was both an indictment of the institutions of the state of Mississippi and a statement of their vision of a theater grounded in African American experience.

Document 9.3 A General Prospectus for the Establishment of a Free Southern Theater[45] (excerpts)

1. The development of patterns of reflective and creative thought have been restricted.

   A. Education: The segregated Mississippi public school system restricts the learning process rather than nourishes it. School textbooks are controlled, discussion of controversial topics is forbidden, teachers have no choice in school programming and are under constant supervision and pressure. It is apparent that competent teachers and honest education will not be the concern of a school system fundamentally built to keep Negroes out of white schools. Since the majority of the schoolteachers are products of the same system, the students' legacy is inadequate training and an unclear understanding of the world in which they live.

   B. Mass Media: The newspapers in Mississippi are not a source of information concerning the activities of the community or of the state. The distortions of these newspapers are twofold: (1) What is not printed—any valid information about Mississippi's economics and politics; (2) what is printed—highly distorted and biased articles supporting the Mississippi "way of life." . . .

      i. Television: Controlled and almost never admits controversial topics.

      ii. Radio: Jackson, Mississippi, has one Negro radio station which is dedicated to rock and roll.

      Conclusion: The Civil Rights movement has greatly affected the vacuum in which the Mississippi Negro lives. Yet, it is still probable that the Negro is the last to be informed of a situation which directly concerns him . . .

2. The Negro Community and its Cultural Resources: Although Jackson is the largest urban area in Mississippi with a population of approximately 200,000, its 75,000 Negroes are without cultural resources other than one recreation center controlled by the state, one movie theater, two inadequate Y's each with 1,000 members, quite a few juke joints, and bout 175 churches. The municipal auditorium is closed to Negroes . . .

   Conclusion: Mississippi's closed system effectively refuses the Negro knowledge of himself, and has stunted the mental growth of the majority of Mississippi Negroes . . .

3. It is necessary that an education program coincide with and augment the program of the Freedom Movement.

4. There will be opposition from the present power structure to the theater program.

While it is true that the theater which we proposed would by no means be a solution to the tremendous problems faced by the people who suffer the oppressive system in the South, we feel that the theater will add a necessary dimension to the current Civil Rights movement through its unique value as a means of education.

A FREE SOUTHERN THEATER

The founders of the Free Southern Theater (FST) believed that, especially for disempowered people, theater was not a luxury but a necessity. "What precisely is this need? It relates to the need to articulate an experience. There is something in the human spirit that is reflective, that asks for someone to 'tell it like it is.'"[46] The FST began as a series of workshops at the Tougaloo College Playhouse. With the cooperation of Bill Hutchington, professor of Speech and English at Tougaloo, Moses, O'Neal and Derby formed a group composed of students from Tougaloo and Jackson State. Initially, the group performed for audiences of twenty-five, who "responded enthusiastically."[47] Moses, Derby, and O'Neal hoped soon to reach people "who were not the sole property of the academic community."[48] They explored various avenues of fund-raising, including negotiations with the Fuller Products Company for door-to-door sales. Moses made a trip to New York in March of 1964, hoping to acquire technical equipment, new scripts, and sponsors. "It will be a very difficult trip," he wrote. "I see a picture of myself prancing around New York, talking about the theater in Mississippi. . . . I feel like a vaudeville barker. Exhorting spectators to pay their dues. Step right up and see the fire next time in Mississippi. Like the rest of America is about to pay their way to see a bullfight, to see the lions clawing at the Christians."[49]

Document 9.4   Free Southern Theater Workshop, Tougaloo College, Mississippi[50] *(excerpt)*
[Note the unusual question regarding bail money in the following application.]
Name _____

   Mailing address
   Present occupation _____
   Do you plan a career in the theater? _____

   Name, address and phone number of person(s) to be contacted in the event of your arrest _____

   If necessary, will these persons be able to provide as much as $500.00 for bail bonds and fines on short notice? _____

   The Free Southern Theater is to be a network of repertory and stock companies throughout the South. We invite your participation in this pilot venture.

   The Actors: Negro students from the South and, with the cooperation of appropriate performers' unions, a selected number of professionals desiring to participate in the program.

   The Stage: Community centers, schools, churches, fields of rural Mississippi and other parts of the South. In Jackson, the company will perform in an auditorium which is being converted for the purposes of theater by the installation of lights and of a portable stage.

   A summer stock company based in Jackson will run a ten week playing season, the first production opening in Jackson on June 13–14. In ten weeks, five separate bills will be presented using materials selected from scripts submitted by Langston Hughes, James Baldwin, John O. Killens, Ossie Davis and a number of playwrights, Negro and white.

ON TOUR

In the summer of 1964, the Free Southern Theater toured Mississippi, presenting two plays: Martin Duberman's *In White America,* a dramatization of major events in African American history based on documents, and Samuel Beckett's *Waiting for Godot*. Their first tour included Pike, Holmes, Sunflower, Bolivar, and Lowndes Counties; frequently, their audiences, which often included Freedom School students and their families, had never before seen live theatre. The actors, who, like SNCC workers received subsistence wages, stayed afterward to discuss the plays with their audiences. In Ruleville, Mississippi, Fannie Lou Hamer commented on *Waiting for Godot*, "We been waitin' and waiting.' "[51] Their first brochures promised that their stage would be "community centers, churches, fields, of rural Mississippi and other parts of the South."[52] The performances were often the subject of scrutiny, threats and violence by the local white population. Actress Denise Nicholas recalled,

> In McComb, a bomb was thrown near the stage. People scattered but came back when the smoke settled. No one was hurt so we continued the performance. Had I taken leave of my senses? I was afraid but so was everyone. In Indianola, the White Citizens Council came out to 'see' our show. People were hanging from the rafters of the building. We gave them a performance they'll never forget.[53]

A native Mississippian, who had never before seen a play, responded, "I sat there on the edge of my seat, with one hand holding me to it, to keep from jumping up and screaming through the veil of Heaven, 'Yes, tell it!' . . . I was born in Mississippi. And by the act of God or a cracker sheriff I'll probably die here. They were telling my story on that stage."[54] Another audience member recalled, "They were only seven players, but a thousand could not have done a better job. . . . We listened to the slaves themselves. . . . As I sat there with one hand clutching the bench and the other wiping my face, trying to hold back the tears, I could not stop my heart from crying, for I am the grandson of a slave."[55] "It's pretty strong stuff," commented a Freedom School teacher who took her class to a performance, "what the slaves ships were like, what being a slave was like, the lynchings, Father Divine in the '30s, Little Rock, and an added scene: a speech by Rita Schwerner. . . . This was the first theater most of these people had ever seen. . . . They shouted, 'Sho nuff' and 'You said it' when they agreed with something and joined in the singing of songs. One of the actresses said, 'You can't imagine what it was like under slavery' and a 15-year-old girl next to me said, 'Oh, yes, I can.' "[56]

1964 Freedom School Curriculum Link:

In White America by Martin Duberman

    www.educationanddemocracy.org/FSCfiles/C_CC3b_InWhiteAmericaExpt.htm

See Activity 9.4 Constructing a Play from Documents *in the Appendix*

TEN

Freedom Summer:
Mississippi Freedom Democratic Party

Questions to help you adopt a critical stance while reading the section below:

 1. *Why was the strategy of creating an alternative political system chosen for Mississippi?*

 2. *What was the purpose of such a strategy (what was the theory from which it came)?*

For more information and analysis see essay by Otis Pease[1] for an analysis of party politics in the South from 1900–1964.

Recommended Film:

Freedom on my Mind *(Documentary; 110 min, 1994; produced and directed by Connie Field and Marilyn Mulford). The story of the Mississippi Freedom Move-ment in the early 1960s, from voter registration efforts to Freedom Summer and the formation of the Mississippi Freedom Democratic Party.*

EVERYTHING THAT HAPPENED during Freedom Summer was geared towards one goal—breaking the white monopoly of Mississippi politics and power. The means by which to achieve this goal was the creation of the Mississippi Freedom Democratic Party (MFDP), a party in which both blacks and whites could be represented, as opposed to the regular, white only, Mississippi Democratic Party. The MDP was kept white through systematic exclusion of black voters. The main goal of Freedom Summer was, thus, to help local blacks register to vote. As the Freedom School Curriculum explained:

> Rather than subject people to certain violence for the sake of a lunch counter, COFO asks people to go to the registrar office and try to become registered voters. This is hard enough. This is direct action as far as Mississippi is concerned. . .and, if you get the vote, you have gotten something much more powerful than a lunch counter seat in the long run.[2]

The activities of Freedom Summer were meant to empower African Americans in their political rights, be it through education, through arts and music, or direct and political action. The Freedom Schools provided, among many other things help in citizen education, since a requirement for registration to vote was the ability to read and write and to explain a section of the Mississippi Constitution.

As the regular Democratic Party continued to block African American participation, SNCC joined forces with CORE, NAACP and SCLC, and under the umbrella group COFO all worked to create a new party—one open to both black and white voters—the Mississippi Freedom Democratic Party. The first step was to send African American representatives to the delegate-selection meetings held by the Mississippi Democratic Party throughout the state. These representatives were rejected, which allowed the MFDP to argue that they, not the regulars, upheld the principles of the Democratic Party. Following carefully the guidelines of the Democratic Party, the MFDP held a primary in which African Americans could register, vote, and send a delegation to the Democratic Convention in 1964. There, they would challenge the presence of an all-white Mississippi delegation. Their argument was direct: the all-white Democratic Party ticket was not legitimate, as it had used violence and intimidation to control voting. As such methods were illegal, the delegates elected by these methods were also deemed not to hold their positions legally. The MFDP delegates, elected without coercion and loyal to the procedures, candidates, and platform of the National Democratic Party should, therefore, be seated.

THE FOUNDING OF THE MFDP

On April 26, 1964, the Mississippi Freedom Democratic Party was officially formed at the Masonic Temple in Jackson, Mississippi.[3] SNCC Field

Secretary Lawrence Guyot was elected Chairman. Ella Baker, in the keynote address, reminded her audience that, "At no point were the Southern states denied their representation on the basis of the fact that they had denied other people the right to participate in the election of those who govern them."[4] The work of educating potential voters and registering them for the MFDP election had now begun. Literature that clearly explained the process of government was distributed by COFO to encourage voter registration.

1964 Freedom School Curriculum Link:
COFO Flyer: MFDP
> *www.educationanddemocracy.org/FSCfiles/B_03_FlyerMFDP.html*

The MFDP entered four write-in candidates in the June 2 Democratic primary. Mrs. Victoria Gray opposed Senator John Stennis; Mrs. Fannie Lou Hamer opposed Rep. Jamie Whitten; Rev. John Cameron opposed Representative William M. Colmer, and Mr. James Houston opposed Representative John Bell Williams. The candidates traveled the state, making speeches and raising awareness about the need for stronger voting-rights legislation.

See Activity 10.1   Understanding Your Local School Board *in the Appendix*

1964 Freedom School Curriculum Links:
Unit V: The poor Negro, poor White and their Fears
> *www.educationanddemocracy.org/FSCfiles/C_CCI_Units1to6.htm#Unit5*
Unit VI: Material Things and Soul Things
> */www.educationanddemocracy.org/FSCfiles/C_CCI_Units1to6.htm#Unit6*
Nazi Germany
> *www.educationanddemocracy.org/FSCfiles/C_CC4c_NaziGermany.htm*

10.A   Edwin King: Freedom Registration and Candidates

Questions to help you adopt a critical stance while reading the section below:
> *1. What was the purpose of Freedom Registration—why not simply continue with the regular voter registration? Was it different from the Freedom Vote of 1963? If so, how?*

2. *Do you think the Freedom Registration was a good strategy? What would you
    have done differently? How would you do voter registration today?*

EDWIN KING

*"The cause of the Movement was to live the kind of life we wanted for the
world in the midst of the struggle to change the world."*[5]

Raised in Vicksburg, Mississippi, Edwin King first became aware of the
devastating poverty of his region when he assisted with the clean-up after
a tornado. Seeing the devastation done by the storm to an impoverished
black neighborhood, King recalled, "Several blocks of houses had been completely burned out. I was not the only white student to realize that this was
partially the result of segregation, that there was no such thing as 'separate
but equal.' Before that, I had been blind."[6] Influenced by the liberal social
gospel of the national Methodist church, King attended Millsaps College
in Jackson and began participating in the Intercollegiate Fellowship, an
interracial alliance that included Ole Miss, Jackson State, Tougaloo, and
Millsaps, led by activist and Tougaloo professor Aaron Borinski.

As a white minister, Ed King hoped to serve as a liaison between blacks
and whites working for change. As part of an interracial group attempting to have lunch together at the black-owned Regal Cafe in Montgomery,
Alabama, he was arrested for disorderly conduct;* shortly afterward, he
was arrested with a fellow Methodist minister when the two attempted to
have lunch together at the downtown Jefferson Davis Hotel. King served
four days on a chain gang for this offense. While in prison, King told an
Alabama reporter that he "refused to put a pinch of incense on the altar
of segregation."[7] Because he was a white minister and because his politics
were unknown to the guards, King was able to visit the Freedom Riders
jailed in Parchman. King entered the prison

> wearing my clerical collar and taking in stacks of Billy Graham books and
> *Sinner, Have You Repented?* In a very un-Gandhi-style—Gandhi would have
> been totally honest—I wrapped copies of Gandhi's biography and Martin

---

* Segregation *laws* did not always cover every instance in which blacks and whites might
interact in public. Segregated custom was often enforced by vigilantes, like the Klan, who
would beat up whites who crossed the color line or call the police who would use existing
laws to punish those, like Ed King, who crossed the color line.

Luther King works in Billy Graham covers, smuggled them into Parchman Penitentiary and was able to get information from Parchman out and messages from parents to bewildered prisoners who had no idea who I was but would come with the police who thought I was on their side.[8]

Because of his arrest record, King found securing a position with a white church impossible. He returned to Mississippi where he was given the opportunity to become the chaplain at Tougaloo, a black college in Jackson, Mississippi. King's politics still caused conflict with the white Methodist establishment. When he visited Northern clergymen in jail after a sit-in and gave them communion with a jail biscuit, he was criticized by the white Methodist establishment in Mississippi. "But wouldn't Jesus have visited the jails?" King asked. "Not for common criminals," the minister replied.[9]

King's activism at times placed him at odds with conservative forces at Tougaloo. On the night that Jimmy Travis was shot, Bob Moses was scheduled to speak at Tougaloo College, and Ed King observed the anxiety of the school's administration. "Many of the black faculty members just wanted to be known as teachers at the best (for Negroes) private college in Mississippi. It must have been a matter of embarrassment to them to have their school mentioned so frequently as a place of agitation. There was no status or security in that."[10] When King's activism became more public, Tougaloo students took turns guarding his house during the night.

King at first expressed reservations about accepting the nomination for Lieutenant Governor on the MFDP ticket, as he was still recovering from jaw and facial injuries received after another car forced his car into a head-on collision. The attack was believed to be retaliation for King's involvement in the Jackson movement. King was active in the controversial kneel-ins, efforts of integrated groups to worship at white churches. King felt that the Church demonstrations were, to the white power structure, the most threatening of the Jackson demonstrations. "The last demonstration Medgar led, before his murder," explained King, "was the church demonstration. . . . And I think that was one of the reasons he was murdered. And Mickey Schwerner and some blacks and whites in Meridian were over here in Jackson talking to us about what we had done, and they had visited churches there." The church "was the place where the contradiction was the greatest. And where whites <u>had</u> to start looking at themselves. And individual whites had to say, 'Do we have any responsibility in this?' And that's why we were doing it."[11]

Like many others who were there, Ed King saw the movement in Mississippi as a "fullness of time. Politically, sociologically, a million things came together at the right point." It would be, he felt, difficult for those who were not there "to understand dreams and things this deep."[12]

FREEDOM REGISTRATION AND FREEDOM CANDIDATES

In July 1964, Bob Moses issued an "Emergency Memorandum" to all SNCC workers that the Mississippi Challenge (i.e., attempting to seat MFDP delegates in Atlantic City) would replace the regular voting registration work. "We cannot do everything at one time, and the challenge, which we have committed ourselves to, is by itself an overwhelming task for our limited staff. If it is done correctly, there will be no time to do regular voter registration work."[13] SNCC's strategy was now officially committed to supporting the MFDP. Moses urged the staff not to be discouraged if turnout for FDP precinct meetings was small. "Round up a few people for a meeting," he advised. "Even if it means that all the people at the meeting come as delegates."[14] The goal of the Challenge was to enroll 200,000 members by the time of the Democratic Convention in Atlantic City.

MFDP Freedom Registrars were set up throughout the state, using a simplified version of voter registration forms used in other states. Registration would be held within the African American community, so eligible voters could register without the threats or intimidation involved in attempting to register at the courthouse. Freedom Days, which had relied on the protection of a mass action to encourage African Americans to attempt to register to vote, were replaced with "Freedom Registration Days." Registration was held in beauty parlors, gas stations, barber shops, and churches.

SNCC workers and summer volunteers sought prospective voters by canvassing the fields, the churches, and the stores on Saturday, when farmers came into town to shop. "Volunteers had to take their clipboards out at three A.M. to catch the plantation buses and sign up riders. The buses, hideous ramshackle affairs, started their rounds at 3:30 or 4:00 in the morning collecting the cotton-choppers from various pickup points around the town; the workers had fifty cents deducted from their wage for this transportation. If the volunteers could find a bus on one of its first stops, the Negro driver would let them stay on as it filled and get off just before it left for the fields."[15] Churches were again a focus of the movement. Foregoing their SNCC overalls for Sunday clothes, SNCC workers attended services and made their appeals during the time allotted for announcements. "When the congregation emerged at the end, we'd be waiting with our forms."[16]

Canvassing downtown on shopping days exposed the voter registration workers to retaliation. They were threatened with arrest for blocking the sidewalk and on some occasions attacked. African Americans who cooperated with the voter registration process were also the victims of attack; a minister and barbershop owner who had allowed his shop to be used as a polling place found bricks thrown through his window and was soon evicted. One volunteer described a precinct meeting:

> Fear reigned at first—but soon people were excited about the prospects of the party and neighbors were talking to neighbors about this 'New Thing.' Block parties and mass meetings were being held many times a week in various parts of town. Spirit grew. Hundreds of people risked their lives and jobs to come. Representatives were elected after the election of a permanent chairman and secretary. Resolutions were introduced, minutes were kept. . . . The precinct meeting was one of the most exciting events of my life.[17]

Question based on Documents 10.1 and 10.2 below:
> *What kind of inferences can you draw from comparing the two different registration forms (e.g., where and why is the MFDP form significantly different from the official state form)?*

Document 10.1   Mississippi Voter Registration Form[18]
[Reproduced below is a facsimile of the form currently in use for registration: 7/23/64]

SWORN WRITTEN APPLICATION FOR REGISTRATION

(by reason of the prospectus of Section 244 of the Constitution of Mississippi and House Bill No. 95, approved March 24, 1955, the applicant is required to fill in this form in his own handwriting in the presence of the registrar and without assistance or suggestion of any other person or memorandum.)

1. Write the date of this application _____

2. What is your full name? _____

3. State your age and date of birth: _____

4. What is your occupation? _____

5. Where is your business carried on? _____

6. By whom are you employed? _____

7. Are you a citizen of the United States and inhabitant of Mississippi? _____

8. For how long have you resided in Mississippi? _____

9. Where is your place of residence in the District? _____

10. Specify the date when such residence began: _____

11. State your prior place of residence, if any: _____

12. Check which oath you desire to take:

    1. General _____

    2. Minister's _____

    3. Minister's Wife _____

    4. If under 21 years at present, but 21 years by date of general election _____

13. If there is more than one person of your same name in the precinct, by what name do you wish to be called _____

14. Have you ever been convicted of any of the following: bribery, theft, arson, obtaining money or goods under false pretenses, perjury, forgery, embezzlement, or bigamy? _____

15. If your answer to Question 14 is "Yes", name the crime or crimes of which you have been convicted, and the date and place of such convictions: _____

16. Are you a minister of the gospel in charge of an organization, church, or the wife of such a minister? _____

17. If your answer to Question 16 is "Yes", state the length of your residence in the election district: _____

18. Write and copy in the space below: Section _____ of the Constitution of Mississippi: (Instruction to Registrar: You will designate the section of the Constitution and point out same to applicant.)

19. Write in the space below a reasonable interpretation (the meaning) of the section of the Constitution of Mississippi which you have just copied:

20. Write in the space below a statement setting forth your understanding of the duties and obligations of citizenship under a constitutional form of government:

21. Sign and attach hereto the oath or affirmation named in Question 12.

_____

The applicant will sign his name here.

STATE OF MISSISSIPPI COUNTY OF_____
Sworn to and subscribed before me by the within named_____
_____ on this the ____day of _____ 19_____

_____

COUNTY REGISTRAR

Document 10.2   MFDP Voter Registration Form[19]

1. Write today's date _____

2. Write your full name _____

3. How old are you today? _____

4. Are you a United States citizen? _____

5. How long have you lived in Mississippi? _____

6. What county do you live in? _____

7. How long have you lived in that county? _____

8. What is your address now? _____

9. Are you a minister or the wife of a minister? _____

All of the statements above are true

_____

(signature of applicant)

Do not write below this line

_____

State of Mississippi, County of _____
Sworn to and subscribed before me by the above named _____
on this, the _____ day of _____, 196_.

. . .

At the age of forty-six, Mrs. Hamer, who had managed despite repeated opposition to register to vote (and was a candidate as well), voted for the first time in this election. "I cast my first vote for myself," she stated.[20]

1964 Freedom School Curriculum Link:
COFO Flyer: Freedom Registration
www.educationanddemocracy.org/FSCfiles/B_04_FlyerFreedomRegstrn.html

See Activity 10.2   Voter Registration Drive *in the Appendix*

10.B   Unita Blackwell: The MFDP Convention
Questions to help you adopt a critical stance while reading the section below:
1. *Why did Unita Blackwell and Fannie Lou Hamer become SNCC field secretaries?*

2. *Why did SNCC invite people to join who were not students, maybe even hardly literate? Do you think it is important that local people control a movement?*

3. *Bob Moses' concept of organizing was to let people decide for themselves what the issues are. Does that make sense? What would be the advantage in that strategy? Who decides what the issues are in your community or town?*

Further information:
The transcript of an interview with Unita Blackwell is at the Digital Archives of the University of Southern Mississippi, www.lib.usm.edu/%7Espcol/crda/oh/ blackwelltrans.htm

Amongst others, Mrs. Blackwell talks about her work with SNCC, Freedom Summer and the Convention in Atlantic City

Recommended Film:

Standing on my Sisters Shoulders *(Documentary; 60 min, 2002; directed by Joan and Robert Sadoff, and Laura Lipson). The documentary describes the Civil Rights movement in Mississippi in the 1950s and '60s from the point of view of the courageous women who lived it and emerged as its grassroots leaders. With original interviews of twelve women from Mississippi.*

THE MFDP CONVENTION

The MFDP's strategy was to demonstrate its legitimacy by carefully following the procedures outlined by the Democratic Party itself. They would then present themselves to the convention in Atlantic City, in August, as the legal representatives of the Democratic Party in Mississippi. On August 6, 1964, the MFDP held its own state convention at the Masonic Temple in Jackson to select sixty-eight delegates to the Democratic National Convention. Eighty thousand eligible black voters had registered, and the campaign was beginning to attract publicity. Party members were optimistic and the Temple was filled to capacity. Ella Baker, in a forceful address, commented on the deaths of Chaney, Schwerner, and Goodman, whose bodies had finally been discovered just days before, on August 4. "The symbol of politics in Mississippi lies in those three bodies that were dug from the earth this week."[21] She deplored the fact that the search for the three missing Civil Rights workers had uncovered the bodies of young black men, victims of crimes ignored by the national media. "Until the killing of black mothers' sons becomes as important to the rest of the country as the killing of white mothers' sons," she declared, "we who believe in freedom cannot rest."[22] Baker saw the party as a public declaration of the desire of blacks to participate in the political process. "It is important that you go to the convention whether you are seated or not. It is even more important that you develop a political machinery in this state. The Mississippi Freedom Democratic Party will not end at the convention. This is only the beginning. You are waging a war against the closed society of Mississippi. You have not let physical fear immobilize you."[23] A volunteer wrote:

Right after Miss Baker's speech, there was a march of all the delegates around the convention hall—singing freedom songs, waving American flags, banners, and county signs. This was probably the most soul-felt march ever to occur in a political convention. I felt, as we marched with a mixture of sadness and joy—of humility and pride—of fear and courage, singing "Go Tell it on the Mountain," "Ain't Gonna Let Nobody Turn Me 'Round," and "This Little Light of Mine."[24]

The convention selected forty-six delegates and twenty-two alternates, and care was taken that the delegation reflect the people who had chosen them. The delegation included SNCC workers Charles McLauren, Jimmy Travis, and Lawrence Guyot: sharecroppers Fannie Lou Hamer, Unita Blackwell, Hartman Turnbow; independent businesswoman Victoria Gray, minister Ed King, and pharmacist Aaron Henry. Although Guyot was elected FDP chair, he was unable to attend the convention, as he was jailed on questionable charges following an arrest in Hattiesburg. Mrs. Gray recalled the mood of the delegation. "We can't get past these people at the state level, because they've locked us out, but we just know that once we get to the national level, with all of the proof that we had been locked out and the fact that we've had the courage to go ahead and create our own party, then we feel like we were going to get that representation that we'd been denied for so long."[25]

The MFDP delegates were introduced in a primer distributed to the delegates of the National Democratic Convention in Atlanta.

Question based on Documents 10.3 and 6.4:

> *How does the "Manual for Southerners" (see Chapter 6) compare with the "MFDP Primer for Delegates" below? How is the language different, and why? What is the audience for the primer? What does the primer say about the candidates, what type of people were they?*

Document 10.3   Primer for Delegates[26]

... We think that [the delegates of the Mississippi Democratic Party] do not deserve their seats, and that the [National] Democratic Party should tell them so. And we have come here to challenge [them], and those like [them] who endorse state party platforms which call for separation of the races ...

And who are we?

We are FREEDOM Democrats

Our state party is integrated, and some of our members have lost their jobs, been beaten, spent days in jail, been shot at and had their homes fire-bombed and dynamited, all because we want to participate as voters in the democratic process.

It is up to you to decide which group should be seated. . . . We would like you to know something about us, AND SOMETHING ABOUT THEM:

Mrs. **Fannie Lou Hamer** is 46. She is married and has two children. She has lived all of her life in Mississippi. It is not unusual, among those Negroes for whom she is a representative, that she has only eight years of schooling. . . . [pamphlet gives a short biography] In Ruleville, where Fannie Lou Hamer lives, people crowd around her house. That's because she is a leader even though her house doesn't look like much. She is an ample woman. Ample means BIG. She is big in girth, and big in spirit. And when she sings she can make a church tremble. She is big in love, too, and when she smiles, her smile embraces you in warmth. As if by a miracle, she hasn't as yet learned to hate, and that makes her strong and vital. . . .

She was blackjacked in jail in Winona, Mississippi after she told people there about voting. And she finally got registered and ran for the U.S. Congress against Jamie Whitten. Whitten is noted for having killed a program to train tractor drivers because it included Negroes. Jamie Whitten won. Not enough of Mrs. Hamer's friends could vote for her. Many of them had tried and for their concern were beaten, shot at, jailed, and run off the land. Some were murdered. [examples given] Well, that is how Mississippi congressmen get elected. It's how sheriffs are elected. And presidents, too. Mrs. Hamer doesn't think it is right. . . .

Aaron Henry is a delegate . . . His people call him "Doc" because to them anyone who dispenses medicine is a doctor. It doesn't matter that he doesn't have an M.D. He sells the right kinds of medicine to people who can't afford a doctor and who come and stand at his counter and tell him what is wrong with them, or with their children. "Doc" is a pharmacist, and he sees a lot of people. When the country was young, people like "Doc" used to get elected to office. When you see a lot of people, and you talk a lot, and they get to know that you believe in things that are right and good for everybody, then you ought to have the chance to get elected to office. . . . "Doc" has served on a chain gang. He was with a group of people who picketed some churches in a community to remind the Christians that they weren't doing their duty by fellow Americans and fellow human beings. . . .

A.D. Beittel is a real doctor. He has a Ph.D., and he is president of Tougaloo Southern Christian College. Anybody can go to school there: white or black.

He is secretary of the Mississippi Advisory Committee of the U.S. Commission on Civil Rights. That is the long name for a group that is supposed to see that ALL Americans are treated alike. The group must do that because some white people in places like Mississippi don't believe Americans are the same. No matter what the Constitution says. He is a member of the Mississippi Council on Human Relations. Somebody has to belong to groups like this because human relations aren't good these days. Dr. Beittel is the kind of man that people think will help make things better for everybody. . . .

Mrs. Victoria Gray is from Hattiesburg, Mississippi. She is married and has three children. She was one of the first Negroes registered in Forrest County. That doesn't mean that she is an old woman. It just means that they haven't been letting Negroes get registered there for long. Mrs. Gray is just 37. Her husband was fired from his job because Mrs. Gray tried to get other people registered. She is a coordinator of the voter registration drive in her hometown, and she is a supervisor of citizenship education classes for the Southern Christian Leadership Conference. . . .

Hartman Turnbow is from Tchula, Mississippi. He only has six years of school. At the courthouse where he went to register to vote, his way was blocked with a gun. He hasn't stopped going back. After the first time, somebody tried to burn his house down. . . .

All of our delegates are people like these. They believe in the same things that you do. . . . It is hard for them to understand why you let people who don't believe what YOU believe sit down with you and call themselves members of the Democratic Party.

If you want to talk with them, they are at the Gem Hotel, 505 Pacific Avenue. If you want to find out what they believe, and whether or not they will vote for the man you think should be president, just come by and talk to them at the Gem Hotel.

Then you can ask the Regular Democrats what they believe, and who they will vote for, and see who deserves to be here. If you are a thoughtful Democrat you will do that.

See Activity 10.3   Creating a Pamphlet in the Appendix

UNITA BLACKWELL

"SNCC went where nobody went. They was about the nuttiest ones they was. Ended up in some of the most isolated places and drug people out of there to vote. . . . Mrs. Fannie Lou Hamer said to me, 'Girl, these here young people know something, don't they?' And I said, 'Yeah, they sure do.'"[27]

Like many other black Mississippians, Mrs. Blackwell felt rooted to the Delta and saw, in its rich natural landscape, the place it could be if freed from its legacy of violence. "People like myself was born on this river," she explained. "I love the land. It's the Delta. . . It's everything to what black people is all about. We came up out of slavery. This is where we acted it out, I suppose. All that work. All that hard work. We put in our blood, sweat, and tears. And we love the land. This is Mississippi."[28] Mrs. Blackwell was a resident of Sunflower County and first saw SNCC workers speak at a local church. Through the efforts of SNCC staffers, she became aware of her right to vote and the deficiencies in education offered to blacks in Mississippi. At the time of SNCC's arrival, her children were attending school only two to three months a year. Mrs. Blackwell assisted with the food distribution in Leflore County.

The example created by SNCC workers' challenge to local authority was transformative for Mrs. Blackwell. She recalled, "Bob Moses was a little bitty fella. And he stood up to this sheriff and Bob said, 'I'm from SNCC.' I had never saw that happen before. From that day on, I said, 'Well, I can stand myself.'"[29] Mrs. Blackwell believed that women's role in the church showed the way for their involvement in politics.

> Who's the people that really keeps things going? It's women. The women is the ones that supports the deacon board. They holler the Amen. The women is the ones that support the preacher. . . . Without women in these churches and whatever in the United States, you wouldn't have so many people there. . . . So in the black community the movement, quite naturally I suppose, emerged out of all the women that carried out these roles. We didn't know we was leaders. You knew you did things, but you never saw it as a high political leadership role.[30]

Mrs. Blackwell was a member of the MFDP delegation to the Democratic National Convention and, with Mrs. Hamer, she was uncompromising in her belief that the MFDP should be seated.[31]

1964 Freedom School Curriculum Link:
Unit VII, Part 2: COFO's Political Program
www.educationanddemocracy.org/FSCfiles/C_CC7_UnitVII.htm#Part2

10.C   Fannie Lou Hamer:
The Challenge at the Democratic National Convention

Questions to help you adopt a critical stance while reading the section below:

1. *Why was Mrs. Hamer, a sharecropper without any political experience and who cast the first vote in her life for herself, chosen to run for Congress? What is she representing? Was she first a community leader, and then a politician?*

2. *What should a representative in Congress represent? What and who do you feel your congressman/woman represents?*

3. *Was the "compromise" at Atlanta really a compromise? If so, how? Why did the MFDP delegates lose the support of their allies? Would you also have rejected the compromise?*

4. *Should the MFDP delegates have used a different strategy? Which? What did they gain by their course of action?*

Further information:

The transcript of an interview with Fannie Lou Hamer is at the Digital Archives of the University of Southern Mississippi, www.lib.usm.edu/%7Espcol/crda/oh/hamertrans.htm

FANNIE LOU HAMER

"When they asked for those to raise their hands who'd go down to the court-house the next day, I raised mine. Had it up as high as I could get it. I guess if I'd a had any sense, I'd a-been a little scared, but what was the point of being scared? The only thing they could do to me was kill me and it seemed like they'd been trying to do that a little bit at a time ever since I could remember."[32]

Fannie Lou Hamer was the kind of local leader that SNCC organizers hoped to recruit and support. A lifelong resident of Ruleville, Mississippi, Mrs. Hamer was a forty-six-year-old sharecropper when she became involved in the voter registration drive sponsored by SNCC. At an evening meeting, she heard James Forman of SNCC speak on the possibility of voting brutal local sheriffs out of office. "It made so much sense to me because right then, you see, the man that was our night policeman here in Ruleville was a brother to J.W. Milam, which was one of the guys helped to lynch this kid Emmett Till."[33] When the SNCC staff asked for volunteers to attempt to register, Mrs. Hamer raised her hand.

On her way back to Ruleville from a voter registration attempt, Hamer was one of eighteen prospective voters riding on a bus that local authorities cited for being too "yellow" and therefore too closely resembling a school bus. As the passengers on the bus waited nervously as the driver of the bus was taken away, Mrs. Hamer emerged as a strong voice. According to SNCC worker Charles McLauren,

> While the driver of the bus was away, the people on the bus became restless and afraid. They didn't know what was going on. They began to talk about their fear, to worry. Such things as, 'I sure hope I don't get put in jail.' 'I gotta go home. My family will be coming in from the field.' Or 'I gotta cook dinner.' In the midst of all this grumbling about the problems, a voice, a song, a church song, just kind of smoothly came out of the group. 'Down by the Riverside.' Or 'Ain't Gonna Let Nobody Turn Me Around' or 'This Little Light of Mine.' . . . So Fannie Lou Hamer was on that bus. And as a result of her songs, came forward.[34]

For her activism, she was evicted from the land she and her husband had worked for seventeen years. She recalled a confrontation with the land's owner. "Marlowe came to the house. . . . I could hear him telling my husband what he was going to do to me if I did not withdraw. . . . So I went to the door. . . . Marlowe asked me why I went to register. I told him that I did it for myself not for him. He told me to get off the plantation and don't be seen near it again."[35] Even after her eviction, she was harassed by local authorities. On one occasion, she was presented with a nine-thousand dollar water bill when the house to which she and her husband had moved had no running water. Mrs. Hamer persisted in her voter registration work during the most discouraging times.

Andrew Young recalled Mrs. Hamer's presence at a Citizenship Education Program workshop. "She immediately took over a leadership role." Not only was Mrs. Hamer "very open" about sharing her experiences, she had an extraordinary singing voice. During any lull in the discussion, "she would just start up one of those good ol' hymns, so there was no question about her leadership ability." Mrs. Cotton recalled,

> She became the dynamic personality in the Mississippi group. We would ask them to describe the work they were doing in their hometowns, and she would shine her light in these workshops. This was a folk workshop, so even if we were talking about the Constitution, we started our sessions singing, and she was a powerhouse. I would stress her determination, no matter what she was talking about, and people caught this spirit.[36]

On their way back to Ruleville, Mrs. Hamer and the others traveling with her attempted to desegregate the facilities at the bus station in Winona, Mississippi. They were arrested and brutally beaten in the jail. Mrs. Hamer's arrest and the beating she received during her imprisonment was the subject of her testimony at the Democratic Nominating Convention in Atlantic City in 1964.

Mrs. Hamer became a registered voter early in 1963, and continued her work to register others. An unwavering supporter of and worker for voter registration in Mississippi, Mrs. Hamer had the ability to articulate the experiences of Mississippi sharecroppers. Many had suffered in silence, and Mrs. Hamer could give their suffering a voice. As Attorney Eleanor Holmes Norton stated,

> Her speeches had themes. They had lessons. They had principles. And then when you'd heard all that said with such extraordinary brilliance—like WOW, that's what it is. She has put her finger on something truly important that all of us had felt but she had said. . . . What really gets you is that person somehow concretizes an idea that you had never been able to fully form. And she did that in this extraordinary singing style and then ended up singing 'This Little Light of Mine.'[37]

Mrs. Hamer's power as a singer matched her power as a speaker. Bob Cohen, Director of the Mississippi Caravan of Music, recalled,

> When Mrs. Hamer finishes singing a few freedom songs one is aware that he has truly heard a fine political speech, stripped of the usual rhetoric and

filled with the anger and determination of the Civil Rights movement. And on the other hand in her speeches there is the constant thunder and drive of music. . . . When she was running for the U.S. Congress earlier in the year one of the verses of one of her campaign songs went:

> *If you miss me in the Missus' kitchen,*
> *And you can't find me nowhere,*
> *Come on over to Washington,*
> *I'll be Congresswoman there.*
> (To the tune of 'Oh, Mary')[38]

Mrs. Hamer felt that SNCC's presence in Mississippi transformed her life. "If SNCC hadn't of come into Mississippi, there wouldn't have been a Fannie Lou Hamer," she later said. "They treated me like a human being, whether the kids was white or black. I was respected with the kids, and they never told nobody what to say, nobody. . . . They brought every hope into the state of Mississippi."[39]

1964 Freedom School Curriculum Link:
Campaign Literature on Mrs. Hamer
> *www.educationanddemocracy.org/FSCfiles/C_CC7f_COFOMaterialOnFS.htm*

THE CHALLENGE AT THE DEMOCRATIC
NATIONAL CONVENTION IN ATLANTIC CITY

The MFDP's challenge at the Democratic National Convention was based on the charge that the Mississippi Democratic Party (MDP) was not genuinely affiliated with the National Democratic Party. The MDP had stated publicly that it did not endorse the National Democratic Party's platform or support its candidates. Moreover, in 1964, the Mississippi Democrats reaffirmed their commitment to segregation; at their convention on July 28, the party resolved, "that the Southern white man is the truest friend the Negro ever had; we believe in separation of the races in all phases of life."[40]

Questions based on Document 10.4 below:
> 1. *What is the operating definition of "individual freedom" in the platform of the State Democratic Party?*

2. *What do people mean when they talk about "States Rights?" Rights to do what?
   Should the States be allowed to have different laws than the federal laws?*

3. *What does "eleven and eight" mean?*

*Document 10.4   The Platform and Principles of the Mississippi State Democratic
Party*[41] *adopted June 30, 1960. (excerpts)*

We are opposed to strong centralized government, national or state.

We believe in States' Rights and local self-government, and are unalterably opposed to any encroachment upon the rights of the states by the federal government. . . .

We are opposed to. . .[the] Fair Employment Practices Committee.

We are opposed to the enactment by the Congress of the United States of the so-called anti-poll tax measure as being in violation of the rights of the states to fix the qualifications of electors and in violation of the provisions of the Constitution of the United States.

We believe in the time-honored and cherished traditions of the South. . . .

We oppose the ratification by the United States of the Genocide Convention of the United Nations, the proposed Human Rights Convention and the Civil Rights Convention, the so-called World Government, World Court, or any other proposal of the United Nations. . . .

We believe in the segregation of the races and are unalterably opposed to the repeal or modification of the segregation laws of the State. . . .

We believe in the statements and principles of the Southern Manifesto. . . .

We believe in the separation of the races. . .in all spheres of activity where experience has shown that it is for the best interest of both races that such separation be observed.

Under God, the Author of Liberty, we stand for individual freedom and personal dignity of the American citizen.

"ELEVEN AND EIGHT"

The Mississippi Freedom Democratic Party hoped to bring their challenge to the convention floor for a debate and a roll call vote. Joseph Rauh, legal counsel for the United Auto Workers, had outlined the MFDP's strategy for gaining seating at the convention. If ten percent of the credentials committee—eleven members—expressed support for the MFDP and filed a minority report, then the case would be brought to the convention floor. The claims of the MFDP would then be debated before the entire convention. If eight states then requested a roll call vote, then every state delegation would have to make its stance on the MFDP public. Mrs. Hamer translated these rules into the slogan, "Eleven and eight," and led the delegates in a spirited chant. Even before the dramatic testimony at the credentials hearing on August 22, Rauh was convinced that the MFDP easily had their "eleven and eight."

The MFDP delegation had traveled by Greyhound bus from Mississippi, dining on the familiar SNCC workers' diet of crackers and soda. "The bus ride to Atlantic City was full of enthusiasm," Mrs. Hamer recalled.

> We had done this. We had had our own elections. We had our delegates. And we were going to challenge the regular party. I remember one man, he was supposed to have been nonviolent, but he was sitting there with an old rusty gun and he said, 'Well, if the Klans come at us, I think that's when I'm going to have to take care of business this time.'[42]

After arriving in Atlantic City and checking into the segregated Gem Motel, they immediately began the work of lobbying for their cause, convinced that they would get their "eleven and eight."

> So sixty-eight delegates from Mississippi—black, white, maids, ministers, carpenters, farmers, painters, mechanics, school teachers, the young, the old—they were ordinary people but each had an extra-ordinary story to tell. And they could tell the story! The Saturday before the convention began, they presented their case to the Credentials Committee, and through television to the nation and to the world. . . . Many tears fell. Our position was valid and our cause was just.[43]

The delegation had prepared "information worksheets" on the delegates from each state, highlighting those whose support they could expect. Positioning themselves in a walkway, they argued their position to passing delegates by passing out their "Primer to Delegates" (see Document 10.3).

On August 22, 1964, both the Freedom Democratic Party and the Mississippi regulars presented their cases to the Convention's Credentials Committee, a group of one hundred and eight Democrats containing many staunch supporters of Lyndon Johnson. E. K. Collins of Laurel, Mississippi, made a case for the regulars. Collins cited Mississippi's traditional support for Democratic candidates, and denied that African Americans had any difficulty voting in Mississippi. Throughout the testimony, the regulars argued that the MFDP was a "rump" group operating outside of the legitimate democratic processes, consisting of non-residents and dissidents, some of whom were thought to be communists. According to their logic, Mrs. Hamer's participation in the June 2nd primary showed that she had not been hampered in her efforts to become part of the Democratic Party. As she had received only six hundred votes from black voters in Mississippi, she could not be said to represent even the black electorate. The white Mississippi Democrats concluded, "that there can be no surer way of forever killing the Democratic Party in the state of Mississippi than to seat this rump group who represent practically no one."[44]

The MFDP representatives presented a very different case. Aaron Henry testified that the delegation would face arrest upon their return to Mississippi, as the state attorney general had charged that they were illegally using the name "Democratic." "But, sir, if jail is the price that we must pay for our efforts to be of benefit to America, to the national Democratic Party, and to Mississippi, then nothing could be more redemptive."[45] Ed King pointed to the "over one hundred ministers and college teachers" who had been "forced to leave the state" because they had supported the formation of the MFDP. In spite of such a violent campaign, four white delegates were among the freedom delegation. King explained:

> We were not able to hold a county convention in Neshoba County or precinct meetings in Philadelphia because the church we wanted to meet in was burned to the ground. Three of our workers were murdered in Philadelphia. We do not apologize to you for not being able to hold a county convention in Neshoba County, Mississippi.[46]

When Fannie Lou Hamer attempted to testify before television cameras about her brutal beating in the Winona, Mississippi jail, Johnson interrupted Mrs. Hamer's testimony with a speech, but the networks ran her deleted testimony on the evening news. Rita Schwerner testified about her efforts to speak to Governor Paul Johnson after her husband's disappearance. Governor Johnson, as Aaron Henry had just testified, had referred to the missing Civil Rights workers as "first generation aliens."[47] Martin Luther King pleaded with the Credential Committee to seat the MFDP representatives, which would have given the delegation the right to vote for the Democratic Presidential nominee.

> Can we preach freedom and democracy in Asia, Africa and Latin America if we refuse to give voice and vote to the only democratically constituted delegation from Mississippi? The extension and preservation of freedom around the world depends on its unequivocal presence within our borders. . . . [48]

During the course of the next days, the MFDP and the Democratic Party attempted to negotiate a solution, and a series of plans and offers were discussed. On August 22, the *New York Times* endorsed a proposal that would allow both delegations to be seated. "The seating of both delegations, each with a half vote" the *Times* argued, "would seem a sensible middle ground. Until the president works out a comparable settlement, he will stand open to the charge that he chose silence in order to compete more effectively with his Republican opponent for Southern white racist votes." [49]

After the Credentials Committee hearings, the White House made an offer. The Mississippi regulars would be required to pledge their support to the Democratic ticket. The MFDP would be allowed seating on the convention floor, but not allowed to vote. The Administration promised to investigate the problem of segregated delegations.

The MFDP rejected this offer, but negotiations continued, and the MFDP was offered a second compromise: the delegation would continue as guests of the convention, and any state delegation that discriminated against blacks would be barred from the 1968 convention—the next presidential campaign convention. Congressman Al Ullman proposed that the delegates be offered two seats at the convention in addition to guest status for the rest.

For the MFDP, Rauh proposed a solution, which had originated with Congresswoman Edith Green of Oregon. Every member of both delegations who signed the loyalty pledge would be seated. The state's voting power would then the divided proportionately among seated delegates. Rauh and his staff discovered that precedent for the Green Proposal had been created by FDR at the 1944 Convention, when two Texas delegations had presented themselves to be seated. Roosevelt had allowed the seating of both. Further, Lyndon Johnson himself had been a member of the dissident delegation. Rauh believed that, if both delegations were seated, the regulars would refuse to take a loyalty oath and would refuse to stay, whereas the MFDP was willing to take the loyalty oath and eager to participate in the convention.[50]

In support of the MFDP challenge, CORE and SNCC began a silent vigil on the boardwalk at Atlantic City from August 24 to August 27. They held large placards bearing portraits of James Chaney, Andrew Goodman, and Michael Schwerner. The CORE-LATOR reported,

> The number of vigilers reached a peak of over 1500 during the second evening when the vigil's silence was broken for a rally at which members of the Freedom delegation, including Aaron Henry and Rev. Edwin King spoke. Mrs. Fannie Lou Hamer, a member of the Freedom delegation, led a spirited session of freedom songs. There were other brief periods of speeches and songs. During a heavy thunder shower, a session of freedom songs started. Having decided against taking shelter, the group decided to sing until the rain stopped. The vigilers alternately stood and sat on the boardwalk throughout the day and nights of the convention in view of thousands of boardwalk strollers. Many eastern CORE groups dispatched buses and cars of participants to Atlantic City. Throughout the demonstration, the CORE-SNCC sponsoring committee was in consultation with the Freedom delegation and followed their advice as to tactics.[51]

On August 25, 1964, the Johnson administration made its final offer, which became known as the Compromise. First, the Mississippi Freedom Democratic Party would be offered two at-large seats, which would be occupied by Aaron Henry and Ed King. Second, the sixty-six remaining MFDP delegates would be treated as guests of the convention. Third, only the Mississippi Democratic party regular who took a loyalty oath would be seated and, finally, a committee would be appointed to ensure that all future delegations to the Democratic National Convention were chosen without regard to race, religion, or national origin.[52] Labor leader Walter Reuther, Joseph Rauh later recalled, urged him and the MFDP to accept the offer. "This is the decision. They are going to exclude the Mississippi people unless they take an oath, which they said they won't take. So they're being excluded. They're going to give you two delegates, so you've won that. They're going to give you a pledge that they'll never seat lily-white delegates again. So you've won that. This is a tremendous victory, and I want you to take it."[53]

The MFDP, however, wanted to reject this compromise offer. Those who argued for acceptance of Johnson's proposal claimed it would be a "moral victory." But Mrs. Hamer explained how pointless such a "victory" was given the realities of life in Mississippi.

> What do you mean, moral victory? We ain't getting nothing. What kind of moral victory was that, that we'd done sit up there, that they'd seen us on television. We come on back home and go right on up the first tree that we get to because, you know, that's what they were going to do to us. What had we gained?[54]

It was clear to the majority of the MFDP delegates that they needed real power, which was to have their votes for the next Democratic Presidential candidate be real, not honorary votes. Anything less than a legitimate seat at the table was a defeat.

While the Credentials Committee continued their official meeting, the MFDP met with Johnson's representative, Hubert Humphrey, as well as Martin Luther King, Andrew Young, Bayard Rustin, and Walter Reuther. Their negotiations were interrupted with the news that Walter Mondale had just announced that the Credentials Committee had voted unanimously for the Compromise. Moses was furious. Joseph Rauh later reported, "It was like hitting him with a whip, like a white man hitting him with a whip."[55] A television was wheeled into the meeting, and the group watched Walter Mondale announce that the Mississippi Freedom Democratic Party had accepted the Compromise. "You cheated!" cried Moses.[56] Humphrey had managed to keep the MFDP delegates and allies distracted while Mondale twisted the arms of the members of the Credentials Committee.

The Mississippi State Democratic Party was just as angry as the MFDP delegates about the Compromise. All but three of the Mississippi regulars walked out of the Convention, leaving their seats on the Convention floor vacant. Mississippi governor Paul Johnson announced, "Mississippi's debt to the national Democratic Party is now paid in full, and we stand tonight—

as a state, as a people, and as a member of an organized political group—absolutely free of all obligations, all old ties, and all debts."[57]

The MFDP, however, did not give up the fight. On the night of the Convention's official opening, refusing the Compromise, the MFDP tried direct action. Joining their supporters who had kept vigils on the Boardwalk, delegates marched toward the convention hall and at first were refused admission. Friendly delegates from other states passed on credentials to members of the FDP delegation, and they gained access to the convention floor. Members of the FDP attempted to occupy the seats vacated by the regulars. When asked by a television reporter about the Compromise, Moses replied, "What is the compromise? We are here for the people. . . . They don't want symbolic votes. They want to vote for themselves."[58] Convention officials tried unsuccessfully to evict them, as a few supporters began shouting, "Freedom now!" Reporters rushed to the scene. Aware of the potential damage to be done by the sight of uniformed guards struggling with the MFDP delegates, Johnson and his supporters allowed them to remain in the seats abandoned by the Mississippi regulars. "We didn't come all this way for no two seats, for all of us is tired," explained Mrs. Hamer.[59]

"The political leaders of the nation had met that greatest of all dangers to the professional politician—the people," wrote Jack Minnis, Director of SNCC's Research Department. "The political elite of the nation had had to face and deal with, not the manipulators and sycophants with whom they are accustomed to dealing, but with a delegation that was representative, in the truest sense, of a large proportion of the people of the United States. The confrontation frightened them."[60] By this point, the mainstream press had begun challenging the MFDP. "Do you think by sitting here in this manner you will be dramatizing your case?" one reporter asked a delegate who had joined the sit-in.

On August 26, the Mississippi Freedom Democratic Party met and was told by Joseph Rauh how their apparently solid support had been eroded by pressure tactics from the Johnson administration. Bob Moses had been convinced to surrender the MFDP's list of potential supporters to a black congressman, who had apparently given the list to the Johnson camp. "Every person on that list, every member of that credentials committee who was going to vote for the minority, got a call. They said, 'Your husband is up for a judgeship, and if you don't shape up, he won't get it.'"[61]

During the meetings held that day, many liberal and black leaders spoke to the MFDP and urged them to accept the Compromise. Bayard Rustin, ever the builder of coalitions, urged that the MFDP make concessions. He told the delegates that they were now engaged in "politics," which, unlike protest, required compromise. Rustin reminded the delegates that a rejection of Johnson's final offer would be interpreted by "our friends in labor, Walter Reuther and the others" as a rejection of their support. This message would endanger future support by the leadership of the AFL-CIO.* While he was speaking to the group, SNCC's Mendy Samstein shouted angrily, "You're a traitor, Bayard, a traitor! Sit down!"[62] Martin Luther King, Jr. spoke of "the need for pragmatism even in the most idealistic of situations."[63] King believed that the Compromise would lead the Southern segregationists to leave the Democratic Party for the Republican Party, thereby strengthening the coalition of labor, white liberals, and blacks within the Democratic Party. From this coalition could come federal protection and federal programs that could improve the economic status of blacks throughout the country. Forman recalled King's remarks:

> This is your decision. But I want you to know that I have talked to Hubert Humphrey. He promised me there would be a new day in Mississippi if you accept this proposal.
>
> He promised me he would get the Civil Rights Commission to hold a hearing in Mississippi, something we have been wanting for many years.
>
> He promised me they were going to make sure that segregation would leave the Democratic Party.
>
> He promised me there would be seats on the convention floor for the entire delegation.
>
> And finally, my friends, I have been assured by Hubert Humphrey that the meeting you have been seeking with the President of the United States can be and will be obtained.[64]

Finally, on television that evening, Joseph Rauh announced that, although the MFDP continued to reject the Compromise, he and other liberals who

---

* See Bayard Rustin's "From Protest to Politics: The Future of the Civil Rights Movement." *The Eyes on the Prize Civil Rights Reader.* Carson, Clayborne, et al., editors. (New York: Penguin Books, 1991). 201–203.

had previously supported the Freedom Democrats were now supporting the Johnson Administration.

Faced with the breaking away of their allies, but unimpressed with the arguments presented, Mrs. Hamer expressed her disappointment. "I don't understand that—I really don't to save my life. Them folks will sell you—they will sell your mama, their mama, anybody else for a dollar."[65] Bob Moses "tore up" King's "wishy washy speech" arguing that "We're not here to put politics into our morality but to bring morality into our politics."[66] James Forman argued that the delegates had to reject the offer of two honorary, at large, seats at the Convention because of what the friends, family and fellow workers back in Mississippi would think about such a compromise. What was important was to return to the Convention in 1968 to continue to challenge "the racism in the Democratic Party, the party of Lyndon B. Johnson."[67]

Mrs. Blackwell explained the resolve of the MFDP. "When we left Jackson, Mississippi, to pick up people and head toward Atlantic City, we went saying we were coming at all of the seats or half. . .nothing less. And we kept to that."*[69]

Although Aaron Henry considered the compromise acceptable at the time, he later explained, "Lyndon made the typical white man's mistake. Not only did he say, 'You've got two votes,' which was too little, but he told us to whom the two votes would go. . . . He didn't realize that sixty-four of us came up from Mississippi on a Greyhound bus, eating cheese and crackers and bologna all the way there. . . . Ed and Aaron can get in but the other sixty-two can't. This is typical white folks picking black folks' leaders, and that day is gone."[68]

Later, in New York, Moses explained his frustration:

They say we can't be seated for legal reasons. I mean legally we can't be seated. . . . That's exactly how to miss the whole issue. . . . You say we're

---

* Furthermore, Mrs. Blackwell objected to the middle-class consciousness among black delegates to the Convention. "And them people had not been even talking to us poor folks. They had a certain clique that they would talk to. The big niggers talked to the big niggers, and the little folk, they couldn't talk to nobody except themselves, you know. . . . They had decided they was going to take that compromise, you know. But the little folks told them no, they wasn't going to take it and they meant business." (from Kay Mills, *This Little Light of Mine*, 129).

not legal because we don't abide by Mississippi's laws, but the laws of Mississippi are illegal. . . . They don't abide by the laws of the U.S.[69]

The delegates of the MFDP eventually rejected the Compromise, persuaded by many of the arguments above, and returned home to Mississippi to continue the struggle. That fall, the Klan continued to bomb the homes of blacks in Mississippi who asserted their political rights under SNCC leadership. The escalation of violence marked white supremacist attempts to reverse the gains made by the MFDP during the summer of 1964. But this white-initiated violence was now national news and began to affect the pockets of local white business owners as white customers were afraid to shop downtown. These two factors led southern white moderates to begin to break the code of silence and work with agents of the federal government to negotiate an end to violent reprisals against blacks. Such tactics succeeded in driving a wedge between SNCC and the NAACP. SNCC organizers and their local following wanted both economic and political rights, while the NAACP was willing to settle for an end to Jim Crow segregation laws.

The peaceful desegregation of a handful of elementary schools in the late fall of 1964 represented the end of control of the state government by the White Citizens' Council, since they were now "discredited for its failure to prevent the desegregation of schools and lunch counters."[70] Freedom Summer marked a watershed moment. Jim Crow and Klan violence was giving way to the cooptation of moderate blacks into the establishment fold. This had not been anticipated by SNCC leaders, and besides, they were exhausted and white liberal funding of their organization was drying up. Moderate, middle class black leaders were able to build up political power in Mississippi as long as they stayed within the confines that white leaders created for them.

See Activity 10.4 Re-enacting the Democratic National Convention *in the Appendix*

ELEVEN

Beyond Freedom Summer

Questions to help you adopt a critical stance while reading the section below:

1. *Do you think the Freedom Summer achieved its goals? Was it worth the lives of those who died?*

2. *What is a race-blind society? Do you think we have one now?*

3. *What role or function does "diversity" play in various institutions today?*

4. *Which organization or institution do you know that is diverse? What is, then, your definition of diversity? Is there a difference between tolerating and celebrating diversity? What are the obstacles to obtaining diversity? Is diversity an important goal or a means to a goal?*

5. *What is the role of affirmative action? Should we still use it, do we still need it? Should we use a quota system?*

6. *Should the government be allowed to require registration of male immigrants from certain, mostly Muslim, countries?*

Recommended Film:
> Mississippi, America *(Documentary; 60 min, 1995; produced by Judith McCray). The film concentrates on the legal struggle to ensure voting rights in Mississippi during and after Freedom Summer.*

THE DISILLUSIONMENT of Atlantic City deeply affected the Civil Rights Movement. The political institutions of the United States had been tested and found lacking, and many who had appealed to them turned away. Cleveland Sellers, a SNCC organizer during Freedom Summer, explained:

> Never again were we lulled into believing that our task was exposing injustices so that the 'good' people of American could eliminate them. We left Atlantic City with the knowledge that the movement had turned into something else. After Atlantic City, our struggle was not for Civil Rights, but for liberation.[1]

The bitterness of defeat at the Democratic National Convention, however, was only the bitterness of losing a battle and not the war. Challenging the MDP in Atlantic City was one of the goals of Freedom Summer. A sea change in consciousness was the another. And there was a great deal of evidence that such a change had occurred. One Mississippian activist has assessed the impact of the Freedom Movement in this way:

> Economically, I think things are worse [today] in many ways. I can take you places where people still live under very oppressive poverty . . . . But the most significant thing that the Movement gave to us was it removed people from fear. The freedom from fear of being dragged out of your house in the middle of the night for daring to want to be part of the mainstream, of daring to dream or want to participate, to want to have equal justice, that equal pay for equal work that my father used to talk about. The generations since the movement have not been taught to stay in their place or to understand that there's a certain way to walk and stand and look at and relate to white people. For white and blacks, I think that is the most significant contribution [the Freedom Movement] made to people in [Mississippi].[2]

11.A   Mississippi Beyond Freedom Summer

Further information:

> In their respective interviews at the USM Digital Archives, Fannie Lou Hamer and Aaron Henry talk about the next years of the MFDP and the Democratic convention of 1968. www.lib.usm.edu/~spcol/crda/oh/hamer.htm. anna.lib.usm.edu/%7Espcol/crda/oh/ohhenryap.html

Recommended Film:

A Southern Town *(Documentary; 55 min, 2003; produced by Mark Mori, directed by Peter Gilbert). The film explores, through the prism of what happened in Jackson, race relations forty years ago and today and what has changed and what hasn't. Includes interviews with Rev. Edwin King, Bob Moses, Hollis Watkins and others.*

After the summer, many remained committed to continuing to work hard to change things in Mississippi. Freedom Schools continued to operate in the fall of 1964. The Mississippi Freedom Labor Union was organized in January of 1965 at a Freedom School discussion. In the spring of 1965, a group of summer volunteers began to set up the Child Development Group of Mississippi, which they called "Freedom Schools at the nursery level." The MFDP continued to register voters.

Once the summer ended, most volunteers returned to their homes but some stayed. Liz Fusco, who had been the head of the Indianola Freedom School, became coordinator for the fall program. In a report entitled "Freedom Centers—What's Happening," dated September, 1964, Liz Fusco described some progress and some failures. Some Freedom Schools suspended daytime classes and held adult classes in the evening to support voter registration; other schools continued with daytime classes for children whose regular public school classes had been suspended for cotton picking. Many places maintained community centers that housed libraries and sponsored after-school tutoring. The Mississippi Student Union (MSU), an organization of teenagers, offered support for the continuing Freedom Schools. In Ruleville, Fuzco noted that there was

> kindergarten in the daytime, high school and adults in the evenings. Extensive use of library. . . . The adults meet two nights a week for reading and discussion. The MSU kids hold Sunday-afternoon meetings instead of Saturday-night dances, then refreshments. [In Cleveland, the] MSU is active in school, refusing by letter to raise money by the campus queen drive. Talking about eating in public places and boycotting stores. [In Tchula, Fuzco noted:] In process of building new community center. Freedom School staff mostly in jail.

Charles Cobb wrote that the Freedom School program, like the Movement, was "a victim of its success." Freedom Summer had focused the attention of the country on Mississippi, and some change followed. "We had in one sense accomplished what we set out to do: a public accommodations law had been passed; a voting rights law seemed certain. Mississippi was now prominently on the political map. New organizations, like the Mississippi Child Development Group, with deeper financial pockets, were establishing themselves."[3]

The Child Development Group of Mississippi (CDGM) was started with a grant of over a million dollars from the newly created U.S. Office of Economic Opportunity. Former Freedom Summer volunteers and their allies went about setting up over 60 day-care centers in the spring of 1965. The hope was to create a nucleus of parents and volunteers who would build an integrated pre-school, medical and community action program. It was to be a school system that would build "iron egos needed by children growing up to be future leaders of social change in a semi-feudal state."[4]

At the five day teacher orientation in July, much of hallmarks of Freedom Summer were evident. Northern summer volunteers had been recruited to produce a "blending of Southern Negro talents and needs with those of college students and professionals."[5] There was much singing and the leaders only asked questions. CDGM was firmly committed to integration. Expecting the same kinds of trouble that was experienced by the teachers of Freedom Schools the year before, the teachers were trained in the making of security plans.

The principle guiding the organization of the schools during the summer of 1965 was the need to start with parent and community involvement and then "work toward quality in the classroom." There was "no point" for children to attend "ideal classrooms if they returned home to parents not actively involved in decision making."[6] The main thrust of the organization was to involve the parents in the development of the curriculum:

> The poor may not be 'qualified' to design and staff a school system, but then, of course, the middle class isn't qualified either . . . [the only qualification the middle class have is that] they will use their judgement in hiring people who will look out for their interests and promote their values; they will see to it that no great changes occur which might seriously jeopardized their childrens' future . . . status level; and they will move slowly and cautiously . . .[7]

The curriculum that emerged from many meetings between staff workers and local parents and community members was one in which

- Children were encouraged "to talk. . . instead of sitting quietly in their places."
- Lesson plans included "moving activities instead of paper and pencil activities."
- There was much "practising remembering, offering ideas."
- Teachers were encouraged to be "physically active instead of gazing over the children's heads from behind a desk."
- The school day was "filled . . . instead of waiting for it to evaporate."[8]

From May through August, 1100 teachers and 5 psychologists worked with 6400 students in 84 centers. By mid-July, however, the success of the program was brought to the attention of the U.S. Senator from Mississippi, John Stennis. Stennis was head of the Appropriations Committee from which the Office of Economic Opportunity, and thus CDGM, received its funding. Stennis' influence was immediately felt when OEO representatives met with the CDGM staff and ordered them to move their headquarters 200 miles away to an isolated corner of the state within 6 days or lose their funding. In August, the local and national media began to print reports of the program's financial mismanagement. Stennis ordered his committee's chief investigator to audit CDGM shortly after the newspaper reports emerged. The CDGM staff and board of directors was thrown into turmoil. The result of this turmoil was the replacement of the director and the withholding of funding.

Somehow, the program was able to survive in skeleton form through the winter of 1965–66 and fought successfully for a renewal of money from OEO. The constant demands for "fiscal accountability" by OEO higher ups resulted in much energy diverted from community and curriculum development.

At the opening of 1968 CDGM found itself mobilizing to fight for a fourth grant. Only by then the fire had gone out of it. What could it do? The Green Amendment gave Head Start to Community Action Programs and the governor's control. President Johnson had cut 25 million dollars out of the

Head Start budget nationally, so he could put more money into Northern ghettos before voting time. Seven million dollars was cut from Head Start in Mississippi alone. . . . The creativity had somewhere, slowly, seeped out of CDMG. The many experimental elements had become as many mere routines . . . [Nevertheless, OEO] couldn't stifle CDGM's afterlife in the minds of men all over the country who had learned many things from the grand experiment, and in the hearts of poor people in Mississippi.[8]

In spite of, or maybe because of the tremendous gains made during Freedom Summer, the strains that had always existed within COFO (the alliance of SNCC, NAACP, SCLC and CORE in Mississippi from 1962–65) began to pull the organization apart after the Atlantic City Convention. SNCC organizers had been the backbone of the Summer Project and had gained national prominence as a result of the successes of Mississippi Freedom Summer. SCLC and NAACP leaders, perhaps because they felt threatened by SNCC's success, began to attack SNCC for its focus on relying on poor people to become leaders of their own movement. For example, at a coalition meeting in New York, three weeks after the Atlantic City Convention, Allard Lowenstein argued against the process by which the MFDP was created. He insisted that the movement now needed "structured democracy, not amorphous democracy."[9] After the November elections of 1964, the Mississippi state NAACP voted to withdraw from COFO.

The demonstrations and violence surrounding the voting rights struggle in Alabama in the spring of 1965 drove a lasting wedge between SNCC and SCLC. Many SNCC organizers were appalled at SCLC's inability to understand that, at times, one had to be prepared to shoot back when being shot at. The pressures on the COFO alliance also undermined attempts by SNCC leaders to figure out what their own organization's overall structure and purpose should be after August 1964. Many of the SNCC organizers were exhausted by the effort they exerted during the summer and left the movement. The MFDP leaders, perhaps having learned their lessons all too well, wished to determine their own course of action regardless of whether SNCC leaders approved or not. For example, over SNCC objections, MFDP leaders endorsed Lyndon Johnson for President. Throughout 1965, Freedom Schools and Community Centers closed due to lack of personnel and funds, the MFDP pursued inclusion within the Democratic Party, and federal poverty programs began to successfully co-opt locally run organizations. Federal oversight meant that decisions on how the programs would be run and for what purposes were made by bureaucrats and political appointees in Washington, not by the people who worked in the programs or by those for whom the programs were ostensibly there to help. The successful cooptation of the these programs completely undermined SNCC's purpose of developing local or "group-centered" leadership. In November of 1965, SNCC decided to disband COFO.[10]

Polly Greenberg argues that the MFDP during the summer of 1965 was "falling apart"—"it was weakly staffed, underfunded" and "sporadic."[11] In spite of this, however, voter registration workers seemed to have enough leverage with the 1965 Civil Rights Act to increase black registration from 6.7 percent of those registered in 1965 to 59.8 percent in 1967.[12] In the 1968 Democratic Convention, the Mississippi delegation had three black delegates.[13] As of April 1973, Mississippi had 152 black elected officials.[14] The MFDP demands in Atlantic City led to a Democratic Party "pledge to prevent racial discrimination in the selection of future delegations," which, in turn, led to an increase in black delegates to the national nominating conventions: 2 percent in 1964; 5 percent in 1968 and 15 percent in 1972.[15]

Did the political gains translate into social and economic gains? Howard Zinn observed:

> Those blacks in the South who could afford to go to downtown restaurants and hotels were no longer barred because of their race. More blacks could go to colleges and universities, to law schools and medical schools. Northern cities were busing children back and forth in an attempt to create racially mixed schools, despite the racial segregation in housing. None of this, however, was halting what Frances Piven and Richard Cloward called "the destruction of the black lower class"—the unemployment, the deterioration of the ghetto, the rising crime, drug addiction, violence.[16]

James Q. Wilson wrote in 1966:

> Negro political activity must be judged as a strategy of limited objectives. Where Negroes can and do vote, they have it in their power to end the indifference or hostility of their elected representatives, but these representatives do not have it in their power to alter fundamentally the lot of the Negro: the vote. . .can force. . .the removal from office of race-baiters and avowed

segregationists. [But] it can only marginally affect the income, housing, occupation, or life chances of Negro electorates.[17]

Freedom Summer had many ripple effects because it had been about more than just getting the vote. This is why, during a discussion at a Freedom School in January 1965, a group decided to form a union for sharecroppers, maids, tractor drivers and anyone else they could manage to unionize. In March, about 90 people in Shaw, Mississippi canvassed workers to strike for higher wages. By April, the group was calling itself the Mississippi Freedom Labor Union. It established its headquarters in Shaw, held workshops and sponsored strikes throughout the Delta ("100 people in Rosedale, 68 in Glenallen and 135 in Shaw").[18] One MFLU memo reported that

> On April 14th and 15th people from 8 counties picketed the Motor Inn Hotel in Greenville. They were having a U.S. Department of Labor meeting. We were trying to get them to let us in and meet our demands. The second day they let us come in and listen to speeches. Mr. Hawkins a Shaw union member asked a question about wages for farm work. Mrs. Hamer spoke inside the meeting the first day and she read the union forms her and 6 more people sent in. . . . One plantation 37 people in Issaquena county went on strike for $.50 an hour and they were successful on Monday they will strike for $1.00 an hour. . . . [T]ractor drivers. . .on a place in Shaw. . .struck for more money.[19]

When the plantation workers of Greenville, Mississippi, went on strike in the spring of 1965, the owners evicted seventy workers and their families from their homes. On January 31, 1966, forty black farmers and ten Civil Rights workers occupied several of the buildings of the abandoned U.S Air Force Base just outside of town. The base commander demanded that they leave. The protesters told him they would if their list of demands for food, land, jobs and job training were met. Sixty more joined the "squatters" the next day. Federal police forcibly removed the protesters. Attorney General Katzenbach advised President Johnson that there had to be more to the federal response than removal of bodies from the base. If the federal government didn't institute some form of poverty program, Katzenbach warned then "there is a real possibility that Mississippi will be the Selma, Alabama of 1966."[20] The homeless strikers called a press conference on February 1, 1966 to announce their intention to set up a new city and government in Tribbett, Mississippi. Those who spoke on behalf of the strikers were Isaac Foster, a strike leader; Unita Blackwell, member of the executive committee of the MFDP; Ida Mae Lawrence, chair of the Mississippi Freedom Labor Union and the Rev. Arthur Thomas, a founding member of the Mississippi Child Development Group and director of the Delta Ministry of the National Council of Churches. Mrs. Lawrence ended the press conference by stating:

> You know, we ain't dumb, even if we are poor. We need jobs. We need food. We need houses. But even with the poverty program we ain't got nothin but needs. That's why we was pulled off that building that wasn't being used for anything. We is ignored by the government. The thing about property upset them, but the things about poor people don't. So there's no way out but to begin your own beginning, whatever way you can. So far as I'm concerned, that's all I got to say about the past. We're beginning a new future.[21]

The federal government promised food, housing and job training, but reneged on these promises once the crisis had passed.[22]

11.B   Beyond Mississippi

Question to help you adopt a critical stance while reading the section below:
Some of the founders of the first women's rights and suffrage movement came out of the abolitionist movement (like Lucretia Mott and Elisabeth Cady-Stanton) and many of the women active in the Civil Rights Movement in the '60s became active in the women's rights/liberation movement (see SNCC's position paper on Women in the Movement at www.assumption.edu/dept/history/Hil13net/ SNCC%20Position%20Paper%20%20Women%20in%20t). Why do you think that is? Does reading about Freedom Summer make you question the status of you own civil rights? Or the rights of others?

Recommended Film:
Walkout (Docu-Drama; 110 min, 2006; directed by Edward James Olmos)
Walkout is the stirring true story of the Chicano students of East LA who, in 1968, staged several dramatic walkouts in their high schools to protest academic prejudice and dire school conditions.

The debates within SNCC over its goals and organizational structure were articulated in a series of working papers during its November 1964 retreat in Waveland, Mississippi. These working papers did not lead to any consensus but did provide a road map articulating the nature of the issues that would be explored during the next decade of social protest—gender, separatism, and participatory democracy being chief among those issues. The strategic value of nonviolence in the Civil Rights Movement began to be questioned as violence erupted in the form of inner city riots (e.g., Harlem 1964 and Watts in 1965), in assassinations (Malcolm X and Jimmie Lee Jackson in 1965, Sammy Younge in 1966 and King in 1968) and in response to peaceful protests (Bloody Sunday in Selma in 1965). The failure of white liberals to support the MFDP and the decision of 70 white summer volunteers to stay on in Mississippi led many SNCC leaders to believe that the presence of whites inhibited the development of black leadership and power. In December of 1966, SNCC voted to exclude whites from membership.

Freedom Summer ended the isolation of Mississippi from the rest of the nation, and was the point of no return for legal segregation in the country. But 1964 was a turning point of another kind as well. When Lyndon Johnson routed Barry Goldwater in the November Presidential election, conservatives decided then and there to begin the long process of building an infrastructure of foundations and think-tanks. It was this movement that would eventually propel Ronald Reagan into the White House and once again demonstrate the ability of the power structures of this country to adapt to its challenges. It remains for the participants of the next social justice movement to move the country to the next stage of freedom.

These obstacles did not deter Freedom Summer volunteers and organizers from continuing to work for social justice. Bob Moses spent the summer of 1965 speaking to students across the country to get political involved. Moses was representing an organization called the Committee of Unrepresented People. From 1969 to 1975, he lived in Tanzania and taught math. In 1976, he returned to the United States to earn a doctorate in philosophy from Harvard University. With a McArthur Fellowship, Moses worked as a teacher in a Cambridge elementary school from 1982–87. During that period, he developed the concept of the Algebra Project,[23] which he explains in his book, *Radical Equations* (2001) and promotes in school districts across the country today.

Aaron Henry helped to form a "loyalist" Democratic Party in Mississippi in 1965. In 1976, Henry served as co-chair of the Democratic Party. From 1979–96, he was a representative in the Mississippi House.

Fannie Lou Hamer was a delegate to the 1968 Democratic Convention as a member of the Mississippi Loyalist Democratic Party. In Mississippi, Hamer continued work on behalf of the poor, of which she herself was still one. From 1968 until she died of cancer in 1977, Hamer raised money for low-income housing, started a day-care center, and was instrumental in establishing the Freedom Farm Cooperative. Hamer raised enough funds from speaking tours to buy 680 acres on which 5,000 people were able to support themselves.[24]

Dick Gregory continued to develop and use his celebrity status. For example, Gregory joined Al Sharpton and Martin Luther King III, in a meeting with the U.S. Attorney General on August 25, 2000, to urge President Clinton to actually do something with the data on racial profiling that the Federal Government had collected during the previous year.[25]

Bernice Johnson Reagon became Curator at the Smithsonian Institution, National Museum of American History, and was Distinguished Professor of History at American University. In 1973, Reagon founded *Sweet Honey In The Rock*. This group of African American women have an annual international concert tour. Along with concerts, the group offers workshops designed to develop the skills and knowledge of the role that African and African American music has played and continues to play in people's lives.

Most Freedom volunteers returned after that summer to the various communities from which they came. They had learned a great deal about organizing in Mississippi and they would use their knowledge and skills throughout the next decade around housing, living wages, voter registration, women's rights, free speech and the anti-war movement. For example, Chude Allen, a Freedom School teacher moved to New York and helped start the modern woman's movement. Staughton Lynd became heavily involved in the anti-Vietnam War movement and labor struggles. Mario Savio returned to Berkeley and helped organize the Free Speech Movement. Mike Miller, a SNCC organizer went to Kansas City and worked with Saul Alinsky on a variety of urban reform issues. John Salter had been an advisor to the NAACP youth group involved in the Jackson Movement and participated in the sit-ins. He took back his Indian name, Hunter Bear, and helped organize the Native American Community Organizational Training Center in the north end of Chicago in 1973. (You can access more biographical information about veterans of Freedom Summer and other Southern Freedom Movement veterans at crmvet.org or at usm.edu/oralhistory.)

Freedom Summer volunteer Mario Savio, provides a good example of the impact organizing in Mississippi had. He left Mississippi determined to apply its lessons by founding the Free Speech Movement at the University of California at Berkeley. Hollis Watkins recalled Savio as "real dedicated and committed. When he left, he said, 'Hollis, I'm going to go back and I'm going to give 'em hell.'"[26] Edwin King also recalled Savio's promise not to forget Mississippi. "I don't know what the struggle's going to be, but it will never be the same. And when we get home, home will never be the same."[27] That fall at Berkeley, Savio and a group of other students were arrested for "politics on campus." Their activities had included disrupting local businesses with Civil Rights protests and picketing the Republican convention and its 1964 Presidential nominee, the conservative Barry Goldwater. In "An End to History" (document below), Savio compared the Berkeley activities with those of the Mississippi Summer Project. Savio died of a heart attack in 1996.

Document 11.1   An End to History[28]

Last summer I went to Mississippi to join the struggle there. . . . This fall I am engaged in another phase of the same struggle, this time in Berkeley. The two battlefields may seem quite different to some observers, but this is not the case. The same rights are at stake in both places—the right to participate as citizens in democratic society and the right to due process of law. Further, it is a struggle against the same enemy. In Mississippi an autocratic and powerful minority rules, through organized violence, to suppress the vast, virtually powerless, majority. In California, the privileged minority manipulates the University bureaucracy to suppress the students' political expression. That "respectable" bureaucracy masks the financial plutocrats; that impersonal bureaucracy is the efficient enemy in a "Brave New World."

In our free speech fight at the University of California, we have come up against what may emerge as the greatest problem of our nation—depersonalized, unresponsive bureaucracy . . .

As bureaucrat, an administrator believes that nothing new happens. [To protest against] arbitrary edicts suppressing student political expression. . .we held a sit-in on the campus. We sat around a police car and kept it immobilized for over thirty-two hours. . . . Most people who will be put out of jobs by machines will not accept an end to events, this historical plateau, as the point beyond which no change occurs. Negroes will not accept an end to history here. . . .

This free speech fight points up a fascinating aspect of contemporary campus life. Students are permitted to talk all they want so long as their speech has no consequences.

. . . [T]he university . . . stands to serve the need of American industry; it is a factory that turns out a certain product needed by industry or government. Because speech does often have consequences which might alter this perversion of higher education, the university must put itself in a position of censorship. . . .

Many students . . . find at one point or other that for them to become part of society, to become lawyers, ministers, businessmen, people in government, that very often they must compromise those principles which were most dear to them. They must suppress the most creative impulses that they have; this is a prior condition for being part of the system. . .and looking toward a very bleak existence afterward in a game in which all of the rules have been made up, which one cannot really amend.

See Activity 11.1   Summer Project in the Appendix

11.C   Lessons: Freedom Is a Constant Struggle

In the documentary film, *Freedom on My Mind*, Bob Moses provides a bitter assessment of Freedom Summer from the perspective of 1994:

> What happened in 1964 symbolized the situation that we are in now. The National Democratic Party and the political leadership of that party at the time, said, "okay, there's room for these kind of people." And it was the professional people within our group who were asked to become part and did become part of the Democratic Party. On the other hand they said, "there isn't room for these people"—grassroots people, the sharecroppers,

the common workers, the day workers. There's room for them as recipients of largesse—poverty programs and the like. There isn't room for them as participants in power-sharing. A different scenario that could have worked its way out could have been for empowering the MFDP. There would have been a struggle, a vicious struggle but not an armed struggle and rioting and shooting and calling in the National Guard. Then you got into a polarization which we are not out of yet. It's one of the great tragedies of this country.

That President Lyndon Johnson used all the leverage he had in order to prevent the MFDP from taking its rightful place in the Convention indicates the degree to which the MFDP delegates represented a radically different vision of society from the system Johnson was defending and that continues to exist today. Johnson opposed the seating of the MFDP possibly because, by doing otherwise, he would have opened a door towards real power sharing with the "have nots" in this country. Both liberal elites and conservatives have a longstanding agreement that such a door should never be open in case the "grassroots people, the sharecroppers, the common workers, the day workers" might actually walk through and demand a seat at the table. If that were to happen, then a fairly radical reordering of society would necessarily have to take place. And it is this reordering that the elites of this country desperately oppose and have been able to stop from happening through an alliance with the middle class. Such an alliance, however, is not unassailable.

Each major social movement in U.S. history (c. 1840s; c. 1880s; c. 1930s; c. 1960s) has challenged the fundamental structures and ideologies that, together, have been and continue to be used to exploit the many for the benefit of the few. During each social movement, some freedom and dignity has been wrung from the system. It remains to be seen what the next fundamental social movement will look like, where it will come from and what freedoms it can force the power structure to concede. We believe that much will depend on the degree to which people today are "getting ready, to be ready."

In this book, we have attempted, as did the Freedom School teachers, to encourage the "asking of questions so society can be improved." We hope that the story of Freedom Summer in its historical context can provoke questions leading to a closer examination of the structures and ideologies of today. We believe that if everyday, ordinary people ask each other and attempt to answer such questions, then they can better understand how they can contribute to bringing about the next social movement or sustaining the existing momentum for social justice. It is in this spirit that we offer some examples of relevant lessons that can be drawn from the past.

One legacy of Freedom Summer is the effective organizing principles of SNCC. If we want "grassroots people" to be part of the decision-making process in this country, then it behooves current organizers to

- absorb the wisdom of indigenous leaders,

- build respectfully on pre-existing strengths within communities,

- and provide what is missing from their analysis and organization.[29]

It would also seem wise for organizers to better understand the necessity of coalitions but also the problems inherent in such alliances. The strategic decision to bring white northern volunteers down to Mississippi was necessitated by the successful use of violence and murder against freedom fighters before 1964. But SNCC organizers were adamant that the presence of white volunteers inhibited the development of local leadership. It was the alliance of the rank and file of the four major Civil Rights organizations—NAACP, CORE, SCLC, SNCC—that contributed to the success of Freedom Summer. Yet, with the successful creation and mobilization of the MFDP, disputes over goals, tactics, decision-making processes and organizational structure created divisiveness and competition among and within each of the groups. The success and defeat of the summer removed the "prize" that everyone had kept their eyes upon. Once that ideal, that guide to action was achieved and abandoned, other, more parochial incentives emerged such as the NAACP leaders' desires to maintain the preeminent status of their organization. Such narrowing of goals made it much more difficult to maintain unity and momentum as the historical forces shifted, putting different and tougher pressures on those fighting for freedom.

The growing U.S. military involvement in Vietnam and President Johnson's War on Poverty Programs represented fundamental shifts in the historical landscape, shifting the ground seemingly faster than the freedom fighters could handle. This suggests another lesson from Freedom Summer—social movements emerge not just when everyday, ordinary people act collectively, but when they act at a right historical moment.

World War II and the beginning of the Cold War created conditions that laid the groundwork for Freedom Summer. Black World War II veterans returned to the South no longer willing to submit to the humiliations and fear of segregation. Veterans like Amzie Moore created the networks and developed the political capital that was a precondition for SNCC workers to be able to begin organizing. A grassroots mass movement emerged in Mississippi in 1964 out of many years of dangerous, arduous and tedious organizing. When one is in between major social movements, it is perhaps helpful for organizers to understand this and share their understanding with their community.

Another lesson from Freedom Summer is suggested by the role that the Highlander Folk School played in training Civil Rights workers as well as offering a model for the SCLC Citizenship Schools and the Mississippi Freedom Schools. Freedom fighters, regardless of their level of involvement in a movement, are more effective if they understand their own motivations, their own prejudices, their own histories. They can increase their effectiveness if they have the opportunity to study key concepts of nonviolent direct action, principles of community organizing, the relationship of arts to social protest, and how the power structures of the moment function. Highlander has provided the space and opportunity for this kind of education to take place. A few people are born organizers, but many can learn. There is a role for Freedom Schools *in between* as well as *during* social movements.

One topic that might be useful for modern day Freedom Schools to address would be the apparent success of nonprofits in co-opting organizing capacity today. In describing and explaining why SNCC lost its ability to maintain the momentum of Freedom Summer past 1965, Clayborne Carson pointed to the more daunting objective SNCC had after its success in ending Mississippi's political isolation. In 1965, SNCC's "objective now was to challenge liberal power rather than prod that power into action on behalf of Southern blacks."[30] But an interesting thing happened when SNCC proceeded to lay out, in its working papers, the broad outlines of such a challenge. By the end of 1965, SNCC "no longer received substantial contributions from churches, unions and foundations. . . . By December, SNCC had to take out a $10,000 loan to keep its operations going."[31] Such circumstances raise the question as to whether or not liberal churches, unions and foundations are willing to fund organizers, in a sustainable way, who help "grassroots people, the sharecroppers, the common workers, the day workers" to gain a seat at the decision-making table.

There are many examples throughout U.S. history where grassroots impulses have taken hold due to infusions of money and resources from established institutions such as corporate foundations, unions and organized religion. And when these grassroots movements have threatened to alter the political landscape, the funding and resources were withdrawn with predictable withering effects. Most foundations will not fund organizations beyond three years regardless of whether they have achieved success or not. Today, more so than in the past, nonprofits depend upon corporate, government and family foundations who attach limitations to their largesse. This is a central conundrum of organizers—can you depend upon funding from the institutions who have a vested interest in maintaining the status quo? Is the next major social movement being delayed (indefinitely?) because the potential organizers of that movement are being kept busy writing endless grant proposals for programs that do not challenge the fundamental premises upon which "grassroots people" are denied a place at the table?

There are many lessons to be learned and many questions that arise from studying how the rank and file of four Civil Rights organizations came together in Mississippi during the summer of 1964 to "prod liberal power" into helping local leaders dismantle segregation and liberate communities from fear. We have tried to raise some of those questions and propose some possible lessons to be learned. We are hoping that this book contributes to a desire to study history in a deep and detailed way to gain perspective on today's struggles, perhaps even to avoid the mistakes of the past and build upon its successes.

Further Research, Debate and Activities

Below are questions, debate topics and activities grouped according to chapters and vary widely in the degree of time and extra resources needed to find them useful. They are not intended to be comprehensive but provocative. We hope that the questions and activities inspire you to create space and time for *collective* study that informs action in the service of social justice.

Chapter 1 Abolitionists and the Nonviolent Tradition

Further Research:

1. Did white abolitionists get more media coverage than black abolitionists? Did this allow white abolitionists to set the agenda for reform? Does that make black abolitionists dependent on whites and is such a dependence the basis of a workable alliance? Eric Foner has suggested that David Walker (with his 1829 "Appeal"), not William Lloyd Garrison, should get the credit for launching the Abolitionist Crusade. Is this an important debate?

2. Read Howard Zinn's discussion of "extremism" in his article, "Abolitionists, Freedom Riders and the Tactics of Agitation," (this article can be found in *The Zinn Reader*, Seven Stories Press, 1997). How does Zinn argue that Garrison's words are "mild"? Can you find references in news reports today in which groups or actions are characterized as "extremist"? Can you apply Zinn's analysis to those references?

3. Compare several standard United States history textbooks, which can be found in local libraries. How many black abolitionists are named and how many white abolitinists are named? What role does the text ascribe to the white abolitionists? to the black abolitionists? Does such an analysis prove the relevance of the argument made by Douglass in his 1847 editorial (see Document 1.2)?

Chapter 2   National Association for the Advancement of Colored People (NAACP)

Debate Resolution:

Laws serve only to catalogue existing abuses and are never effective solutions.

Further Research:

1. What are the current issues of the NAACP? (You can find this out on their website.) How do the present day battles that the NAACP chooses to fight compare to those in the past?

2. Compare the American Civil Liberties Union (ACLU) and the Lambda Legal Defence Fund to the NAACP Legal Defence Fund.

3. How effective have legal remedies been today in solving the problem of unequal education? (Pay particular attention to attempts by state courts to mandate equal spending among school districts.) What parallels can you draw between the *Brown* strategy and state courts' mandates to equalize spending today?

4. Read Walter White's *Rope and Faggot*. Then answer the following questions: How does White's approach to the issue of lynchings

differ from Ida B. Wells'? Is he more "extreme"? Less extreme? (see question #2 in Chapter 1 section above). Do both Wells and White seem open to the possibilities of black/white alliances? Is there any evidence in their positions, as they express them, that they might find such an alliance problematic?

5. Can the killing of Mathew Sheppard in Wyoming be called a lynching? Does your state have legislation against "hate crimes?" Which groups are covered by that legislation?

6. Compare Booker T. Washington's "Atlanta Compromise Speech" (at historymatters.gmu.edu/d/39/) and W.E.B. DuBois' "Of Mr. Booker T. Washington and Others" (at historymatters.gmu.edu/d/40/). What were the issues? Who do you agree with? Why do you think that all black students in Mississippi were taught who Booker T. Washington was, but hardly anyone knew about W.E.B. DuBois? If you were a leader of emancipated slaves after emancipation, how would you go about educating an illiterate population? What problems would you face? What would come first? Given limited resources would you try to prepare everyone with a college education? Would you teach them all Greek and Latin? Does every one have to learn Algebra now? How would Civil Rights veteran Bob Moses answer that question? (Information on his Algebra project at www.learntoquestion.com/seevak/groups/2001/sites/moses/ap/crossover-page1.htm.)

7. In his song on the murder of Medgar Evers, "Only a Pawn in the Game," how does Bob Dylan characterize the role uneducated whites play in the power structure in Mississippi? Do you agree with his view of De LaBeckwith? How, according to Dylan, are white Mississippians educated? Is there a popular singer today whose lyrics offer a similar critical analysis of an urgent social or economic problem? How do they compare to Dylan?

8. Are the arguments about lynching made by Ida B. Wells and the song *Strange Fruit* the same? Are their audiences the same?

Activity 2.1   Emphasis and Omission

What are the ways in which "emphasis and omission" (Dubois quotation at beginning of his "profile"—section 2.B) operates today? One way to examine this is to analyse comparable programs on each of the four major commercial TV networks—FOX, ABC, CBS and NBC. One can look at the evening news, prime time sitcoms and prime time docu-dramas. A group can be divided up into six sub-groups, each assigned to a network and TV category. Each sub-group, for a week, counts how many and the number of times (or minutes) Afro-Americans (Asian Americans and/or Latinos, etc.) appear versus the number of times whites appear within its assigned category—including commercials. Then identify the quality of the appearances (e.g., what kind of characters do the actors play?). You might want to create a chart (example below) with which to record the data from each show. You might also just want to do a demographic analysis of the movie advertisements over a month or so that appear in your daily newspaper.

ABC Monday	white characters	black characters	male	female
PM	show				
7:00					
7:30					

Activity 2.2   Facts and Theory

Mary White Ovington, Ida B. Wells, and W.E.B. Dubois believed that investigation of the facts was crucial for an accurate understanding of how a system worked. The course of action one took to try to change a system depended on one's understanding or theory. Only good theory is based on a thorough and systematic gathering of facts led to effective action. Good theory is one that can predict what will happen.

A. Evaluate the statement above by following the steps below for each person (Ida B. Wells, W.E.B. Dubois, Medgar Evers, Booker T. Washington). You can use information from this text only, or supplement that knowledge with other sources.

  1. What was his or her theory?

  2. What was the process by which the theory was arrived at or what facts were used or to what degree do the facts support the theory?

3.   What plan of action or strategy arose out of the theory?

4.   What evidence exists that the plan of action was successful?

5.   What alterations would you make in the theory and thus in the strategy based upon the evidence in (4)?

B.   Give an example of how you do use or might use such an analytical framework (defined above) in your life. In other words, when you act in response to a problem, how do you think about it? Do you think about it? Do you ever consider the possibility of collective or direct action or only individual action in response to a problem you face at work or at home? Why or why not? How often do you share your problems with a group (fellow workers, neighbors, church members, fellow students)? What happens when you begin to share your personal problems with others? When does that sharing lead to thinking about the problem as political rather than personal?

C.   Project: Choose a local organization in your town or city that is committed to social justice reform (e.g., affordable housing, educational equity, public health, immigration rights, or anti-violence work). Ask to interview a staff organizer or veteran leader in or associated with the organization. Some questions you can ask: What is their theory of change? What is the goal of the organization? How do recent actions or events put on by the organization illustrate the strengths and weaknesses of their theory, or how did these events advance their goals? Write up the results of your interview (or share it orally with a group) ending with a summary in which you decide the degree to which the organization has a clear theory of change and to what extent they actually have one?

Chapter 3   Congress of Racial Equality (CORE)

Further Research:

1.   What are the current issues of CORE (CORE website: www.core-online.org/). What conclusions or inferences can be made by comparing past and present issues?

2. What is the biggest reason for jail terms now? What effect does that have on our society as a whole, or for certain groups? What is the purpose of prison? Are prisons effective?

3. Has accusing someone of being a homosexual ("outing them") been comparable to red-baiting, the charge of communist influence (look specifically at the history of this during the 1920s and 1950s)? What other divide-and-conquer techniques have been or are often successful? Have you experienced divide-and-conquer tactics?

4. Would charges of homosexuality or of being a communist destroy a career today? Should gays be allowed to work in any position? In teaching, or the military? What were the arguments behind Clinton's policy of "Don't Ask, Don't Tell?" How many countries in the world allow gays and lesbians to openly serve in their nation's military? To be married?

5. Research A. Philip Randolph and the Brotherhood of Sleeping Car Porters, including the planned March on Washington. Write a profile of Randolph and the Brotherhood. If possible, include the film, "10,000 Black Men Named George" in your research. During the last two centuries, how did labor unions (for example, Knights of Labor, AFL, IWW, CIO) deal with the race issue? How did their approaches change over time?

Activity 3.1   CORE Budgets

As a field secretary in Mississippi for CORE in the spring of 1964 and having $2,000 to spend in the next three months, how would you spend it and why, given the following requests:

1. More staff for Community Centers ($100 per person per month).

2. Bail money ($200 per jailed Freedom Rider).

3. Advertisements in northern newspapers for volunteers and donations ($10 per newspaper per week).

Defend your budget to the "CORE staff"—other members of your class or study group.

Chapter 4   Southern Christian Leadership Conference (SCLC)

Further Research:

1. Is your church or the churches in your neighborhood active in Civil Rights struggles today? What politics are they supporting? Do they have a voice and influence in your city? Should they?

2. What are the current issues of the SCLC (see their website)?

3. What is liberation theology and what effect did it have on the societies in South America, and on the church itself?

4. What might explain black churches' support of Gandhian inspired leaders but not of Marxist inspired leaders?

5. The Montgomery Bus Boycott was not the first of its kind. Where else did boycotts happen during the 1950s in the South? Why is the Montgomery Boycott the most famous?

6. To what degree does the media today present individual behavior as disconnected from social, economic and political contexts (see Activity 2.1)? What effect does such reporting have on people's understanding or theory and thus on their own decision to act or not act (see Activity 2.2)?

7. Are you aware of any current consumer boycotts? Are you participating in any? Do you think it is fair to boycott products or services? What makes them work (for example the boycott of South Africa during the Apartheid regime). Have there been any recent boycotts that have been successful?

8. How are Crispus Attucks and Sojourner Truth portrayed in a standard United States history text? Compare these portrayals with those in SCLC's Citizenship Curriculum (CEP). Does such a comparison provide insight to the issue of "brainwashing"? What other black historical figures are included in the standard history text? Why did the CEP curriculum writers choose the figures that they did? Does it matter how the material is taught?

9. Read Chapter 10, "Charisma," in Myles Horton's autobiography, *The Long Haul*. What evidence do you see in the history of the

Civil Rights Movement (e.g., the story told in this book or others) that supports Horton's criticism of charismatic leaders like Martin Luther King, Jr.?

10. Find out what adult education courses are offered in your town or city. Examine the curriculum of these courses. How do they compare to the CEP curriculum? How do they compare to the requirements to pass a U.S. citizenship exam? (Do they have the same goals? Similar kinds of content? Does a different historical context affect how and what people learn?)

11. How important is it today to have a high school diploma? Defenders of high school exit exams, like Education Trust, argue that high school diplomas are worthless? Are they?

12. Reverend Martin Luther King, Jr. wrote:

> The experience in Montgomery did more to clarify my thinking on the question of nonviolence than all of the books that I had read. As the days unfolded I became more and more convinced of the power of nonviolence. Living through the actual experiences of the protest, nonviolence became more than a method to which I gave intellectual assent; it became a commitment to a new way of life.[1]

Research the details of the Montgomery Bus Boycott. What are the details of the Boycott that you believe affected King to the extent he describes in the above quotation? What is the relative value of experience to book learning for you? In what ways is book learning given value or prestige over experience in our society? Does the devaluing of experience over books have political implications?

13. Compare the SCLC Citizenship Curriculum with the 1964 Mississippi Freedom School Curriculum (educationanddemocracy.org). What explains the differences and similarities in the two curricula?

Activity 4.1   The Montgomery Bus Boycott:

Use the documents below (they can all be found in Clayborne Carson's *The Eyes On The Prize Civil Rights Reader,* Penguin Books, NY, 1991) in order to answer these questions:

- The roles of Martin Luther King and Rosa Parks are familiar. What other individuals or groups contributed to the success of the Boycott?

- How might the story of the Boycott been different without the contributions of these groups?

- What further conclusions can you draw about the factors contributing to the success of a political action?

Write a dialogue between two veterans of the Boycott reminiscing many years after the Boycott occurred to illustrate the answer to your questions. Perform the dialogue for your class.

- "A Letter from the Women's Political Council to the Mayor of Montgomery, Alabama"—page 44

- Interview with Rosa Parks—page 45

- "The Movement Gathers Momentum," by Martin Luther King, Jr.—page 47

- Speech by Martin Luther King, Jr., at the Holt Street Baptist Church—page 48

- "At the Holt Street Baptist Church," by Joe Azbell—page 51

- Resolution of the Citizens' Mass Meeting, December 5, 1955—page 54

- "The Violence of Desperate Men" by Martin Luther King, Jr.—page 56

- "Desegregation at Last" by Martin Luther King, Jr.—page 57 (contains the complete "Integrated Bus Suggestions" mentioned at the end of the Montgomery Bus Boycott section in this chapter)

Activity 4.2   Heroes of the Past

We have only included excerpts of the written SCLC Citizenship Curriculum in this book. The Citizenship Curriculum also included biographies of Benjamin Banneker, Harriet Tubman and Mary Bethune followed by "Things to Do" and "Questions to Discuss." Research and write biographies of these people or others you think should have been included, and attach "Things to Do" and "Questions to Discuss." Then try it out on some volunteer "students." How do they like it? Would you want to change any of the questions or activities based on the volunteers responses?

Recommended reading for this activity:

- Chapter Seven, "Great Men and Women" in Kozol, J. (1986). *The Night is Dark and I am Far from Home*. (Third ed.). New York: Continuum.

- Chapter One, "Handicapped by History: The Process of Hero-making" in Loewen, J. (1995). *Lies My Teacher Told Me*. New York: The New Press.

- Chapter One, "Columbus, Indians and Human Progress" (especially pp. 7–11) in Zinn, H. (1980). *A People's History of the United States*. New York: Harper & Row.

Activity 4.3   The Role of Teachers

1. Compare Highlander School and the SCLC Citizen Education Program. (See our bibliography for more information.) What was the role of the teacher in each school, how was it defined? Why was it crucial to the success of the Citizenship Curriculum that the teacher's role be so defined?

2. Each person in your class or study group goes out and interviews a teacher to find out what she believes her responsibilities are as a teacher (tape it). Questions should be generated in advance, preferably in group discussion with other interviewers. Some ideas for questions:

   - How do you define your role in the classroom?

   - Is teaching citizenship part of your responsibility?

   - How do you *define* citizenship?

   - Do you *teach* citizenship, if so how and when?

   If you have time, type up the transcript of the tape (try to borrow or rent a transcriber machine). Write an analysis of the interview(s). (Typing up the transcript and then writing an analysis forces one to pay more attention to what was really said by the teachers.) What are the commonalities? the differences? Did it matter what the demographics of the students were that the teacher worked with? The school? The subject matter? Compare (differences and similarities) the information from the interviews with that of the Citizenship Education Program. *Evaluate* the results of the comparison, i.e., what is good and bad about what you found out. Then define your own ideal of what a teacher's role should be. Compare the teachers interviewed and the CEP teachers with your ideal.

Chapter 5   Student Nonviolent Coordinating Committee (SNCC)

Debate Resolutions:

1. The Civil Rights movement was a young people's movement.

2. Non-violence is a way of life not merely a political strategy.

Further Research:

1. SNCC is the only organization involved in Freedom Summer that does not exist anymore. When did it dissolve and why?

2. Compare SNCC and the Ruckus Society.

3. Is "student power" the solution to the problem of attacking a power structure whose "power to starve" seems unassailable? [Refer to Robert Moses' "Those Who Want to Be Free" in Herbert Aptheker, *A Documentary History of the Negro People in the United States,* vol. 1–7 (New York: Citadel Press, 1993), p. 190, Document # 44 p. 190. Also see "The Economy of Ruleville, Mississippi" document.]

4. What percentage of eligible voters vote in elections (local, state, federal)? How does that compare to other countries. What factors might explain the difference in voting patterns?

5. What is "proportional representation" as opposed to the "winner-takes-all-system"? How does that affect a multi-party system. What system do other democracies use? What are the advantages/disadvantages?

6. Does every vote count? Who supervises elections (local, county, state, federal)? Are there differences in methods between states or counties? Do your relatives vote? Others in your community? Is it different from other communities? Do more people of one community vote than people of another? Is there a difference in race? In class?

7. Would nonviolence work in current conflicts with a long history of violence, like Northern Ireland or the Israeli-Palestinian conflict?

8. What are examples of non-violent direct action in recent history (e.g., the Orange, Cedar and Rose Revolutions)? Were they effective? Did they turn into violence?

9. Can you find other examples of similar relationships during the Civil Rights Movement that supports your answer to the following question: What general principle(s) of movement creation can one establish with the evidence of Bob Moses' relationships with Henry, Moore and Evers?

10. Who has economic power in your community, your town? How is it being used? Does your community have power? What would have to happen for your community to have power, or to exert power?

11. What are the connections between economic power and political power? For example, in regards to campaign contributions and lobbying?

12. Compare food commodities to food stamps. Who controls food stamps? Do food stamps "encourage dependency"? Should the government provide food for those in need? What are the alternatives to food stamps (what needs to happen to eliminate the need for food stamps)? Can you find other examples of similar relationships during the Civil Rights Movement that supports your answer?

13. Research based on Document 5.2—*Testimony before the U.S. Commission on Civil Rights, 1965.* Interview the city or county registrar where you live. What kind of information does he or she know about the voting population of the district? Compare with Hood's professed knowledge. Re-enact the interview with the city/county registrar with your class or study group.

Activity 5.1   Convene a Student Conference

[NOTE: While we use the SNCC founding conference as a model for the activity below, we don't expect a full fledged social movement to arise out of such an exercise, or that only students can benefit from such an exercise. But you never know. One of the five legal cases that led to the historic Supreme Court decision *Brown vs. Board* was started by a school strike for a new school led by a 16 year old student, Barbara Johns. The 1968 walkouts by Chicano students in Los Angeles started with a student designed survey. Even if no "movement" emerges from doing the activity below, important skills will be developed and some consciousness may be raised. Any activity that allows people to come together to share their stories around a specific problem and includes an analysis of those experiences is empowering.]

1. Identify a problem that your class, study group or organizing committee feels passionate about and believes is of concern to other people in your community (e.g., dirty bathrooms, boring and irrelevant curriculum, leaky ceilings, vermin infested walls, too many standardized tests, lack of free speech, no recycling, environmental racism, homophobia, loss of jobs or too many low-paying jobs for the local community, the U. S. military-industrial complex, etc.). You might want to read some recent newspapers looking for stories of activism or call local activists to find out what they know of recent social protests. Pick an issue because that is what people are upset about, not because it is a small or big issue.

2. Arrange with the administration of a school, community center, labor hall or church for time and space to hold a one day conference.

3. Compose a letter addressed to similar groups to yours calling for a conference "To help chart future goals for effective action."

4. A week before the conference, send a letter to those who have decided to attend. The letter should identify the agenda of the conference, which will include a session where conference participants "share their stories." Include in the letter a list of questions that will guide the composing process of such "stories." The questions will have to be as specific and as relevant to the issue of the conference as were Ella Baker's questions to the participants of Shaw University.

5.   Hold the conference, the outcome of which should be some consensus as to what the next *concrete* steps will be. Then see if there
is any traction or follow up.

Activity 5.2   Registering to Vote (Role Play)

Choose a partner, one of you decides to be the county registrar and one
decides to be an applicant to register to vote (During Freedom Summer).
Act out a historically accurate but fictional scenario that would illustrate
each of the following (exchange roles with each scenario):

a.   the process by which a white attempted to register to vote and
passed;

b.   the process by which a black attempted to register to vote and
was failed;

c.   the process by which a black attempted to register to vote and
passed.

Activity 5.3   Nonviolence and/or Self-defence

Read the following documents:

- A.J. Muste's essay "Rifle Squad or the Beloved Community" in
the Freedom School Curriculum (www.educationanddemocracy.
org/FSCfiles/C_CC7b_RifleSquadsBelComm.htm), or his essay
"Nonviolence and Mississippi" at www.mkgandhi.org/g_relevance/
chap17.htm

- Debate between Robert F. Williams and Martin Luther King Jr., 1959,
in Carson's *Eyes on the Prize Civil Rights Reader*, pp. 110–114.

- Readings in Nonviolence from the Freedom School Curriculum
(www.educationanddemocracy.org/FSCfiles/C_CC6a_Statements
Discipline.htm

Watch the film *Deacons for Defense*. Directed by Bill Duke. 99 minutes. Showtime 2003. Then discuss, drawing on the material and your
own experience:

a.   What are the differences between violence and self-defence?

b.   What are the limitations of non-violence and self-defence? Are
they mutually exclusive or can they be co-existing strategies?

Do a role play re-enacting the last scene of the film *Deacons For Defense*. What would have happened if the sheriff, the leader of the Ku Klux Klan and the leader of the Deacons had acted differently? Act out different scenarios.

Activity 5.4 Connecting Parental Income and High School Test Scores

Educational equity has long been a goal of civil rights activists. But defining what is educational equity is very difficult. Today, most state legislatures have mandated standardized test scores as the single indicator of whether schools are successfully educating their students or not. Some policy experts and legislators define equal education as equal test scores. For some leaders, integration and equal spending are no longer important as long as schools have equal test scores. As a result, much of the focus of current high-stakes testing policy is on the "achievement gap"—the difference between what white middle class students score and all other groups. And teachers are being held responsible solely for the test results of their students, thereby limiting even more their range of responses to the demands, interests and needs of their students.

But what do standardized tests really measure? What is their purpose? Below are selections from Harold Berlak and James Popham, both experts in how the tests are designed, or the technology of the tests. Berlak argues that the tests, because they are based on 19th century assumptions, are inherently racist. Popham explains that the tests, because their purpose is to sort, are intentionally designed to correlate highly with socio-economic status. Read the selections below before pursuing the activities.

The following activities are suggestions. Perhaps you can think of more interesting activities that explore the degree to which standardized test scores perform a gate-keeping function—e.g., how they discourage poor and minority students from going on to college while disproportionately enhancing the educational opportunities of white middle class students.

1. Draw three outline maps of your school district (your district may have maps on its website). On one map, identify all the high schools, on another the middle schools and on the third map, identify all the elementary schools. Then go to your state department of education's website and find out what the state test scores (or their translated indicators) are for each of the schools in your district and add those scores to the maps (see www.educationanddemocracy.org/SF/

StateOFSFUSD.html to access examples of how one can do this). What patterns emerge? Are there parts of the city or town that have a disproportionate number of schools that score at a similar level? What is the ethnic and economic make-up of these sections of town? (U.S. census website can tell you the median income of individual census tracts.) Do the patterns support James Popham's contention that the tests have a strong correlation to socio-economic status?

2. Read newspaper articles that report on local and national test scores. Do any of them give any indication of the problems pointed out by James Popham or Harold Berlak in their writings below? Write a letter to the reporter of one of these articles and ask him or her why they report the scores the way they do given what we know about the limitations of the tests. What kind of response do you get from the reporter? You can launch a letter writing campaign if you don't get any response at all.

3. Interview students, parents, teachers or other local community members. What do they think standardized tests measure and why do they think this way? What effect have standardized tests had on their lives? Do you see any correlation between the response to your questions by those interviewed and their economic or racial identify? Using the information gathered from your interviews and the information in the readings below, write an opinion piece for your local newspaper's opposite-editorial page section.

4. Get into groups of 3 or 4. Each group write a multiple choice test based on the information in this chapter. Exchange the test with another group. Evaluate the test from the other group: Is it a good test? What are the writers of the test assuming when writing the test? What are the criteria for a good multiple choice test? Does the test that your group designed meet the criteria for a good test? What are other ways of "testing" or assessing students? What kind of assessment was used by the 1964 Freedom Schools? Is there a relationship between the goals of schools and the method by which those schools are assessed?

Readings: The excerpts below are to help you understand how the articles are relevant to this activity and not meant to discourage you from reading the full articles on the web.

High stakes testing serves as a form of institutional racism. The racial and cultural bias is not primarily lodged in the content of test items. What makes standardized tests racist is:

- Disproportionate (from 30% to 70+%) test failure rates for persons of color and English language learners as compared to white native English speakers.

- The technology of standardized tests creates and inflates differences that have little or no educational significance. The actual 'race gap' in scores is about 10% (range of 8–15% regardless of the test.) On a 50 item multiple choice test this represents a difference of 2–4 test items.

- The tests encourage holding students back a grade, which disproportionately affects African-Americans and Latinos. Retention contributes to academic failure rather then to success in school. A single grade retention increases the chances that a student will drop out by 50%. A second retention increases the risk by 90%.

- Since there is no demonstrable connection between performance on a standardized test and a person's actual academic achievement, to deny a person access to educational opportunities on the basis of test scores alone is to institutionalize racism.

Paraphrased from Harold Berlak, *In Brief:* www.educationanddemocracy .org/Resources/InBriefCA_fededregs.htm
www.educationanddemocracy.org/testing_facts.pdf

Virtually absent in discussions of educational excellence by mainstream press and political leaders is the pervasiveness of institutional racism, and of the enormous inequities in human and material resources, between the richest and poorest schools

It is of vital importance that the accountability system specifically address the legacy of white supremacy and institutionalized racism legitimated by standardized testing, a legacy that lives on in the present. Institutional racism is manifest not only in disproportionate outcomes, but is built into the instruments and the assessment technology itself. Racism, of course, is also about who has power and who doesn't when basic decisions are made about allocation of resources, curriculum content and teaching methods, eligibility for programs, grade advancement, and the awarding of educational credentials. And most important, who sets the rules, names the 'stakeholders' and makes the final decisions.

The accountability system to be fair and effective must make affirmative efforts to counter the institutional racism currently built into the technology of the instruments of assessment. Procedural and structural protections against institutionalized racism depend on proportionate distribution of decision-making power with a significant degree of cultural control vested at the school and community levels.

From Harold Berlak, *Race, Academic Achievement, and School Reform*
www.rethinkingschools.org/archive/15_04/Race154.shtml

The fundamental purpose of [nationally standardized achievement tests] is to compare a student's score with the scores earned by a previous group of test takers (known as the "norm group"). It can then be determined if Johnny scored at the 95th percentile on a given test (attaboy!) or at the 10th percentile (son, we have a problem).

Because of the need for nationally standardized achievement tests to provide fine-grained, percentile-by-percentile comparisons, it is imperative that these tests produce a considerable degree of score-spread—in other words, plenty of differences among test takers' scores. So producing score-spread often preoccupies those who construct standardized achievement tests.

Statistically, a question that creates the most score-spread on standardized achievement tests is one that only about half the students answer correctly. Over the years, developers of standardized achievement tests have learned that if they can link students' success on a question to students' socioeconomic status (SES), then that item is usually answered correctly by about half of the test takers. If an item is answered correctly more often by students at the upper end of the socioeconomic scale than by lower-SES kids, that question will provide plenty of score-spread. After all, SES is a delightfully spread-out variable and one that isn't quickly altered. As a result, in today's nationally standardized achievement tests, there are many SES-linked items.

From James Popham, *F for Assessment* www.edutopia.org/magazine/
ed1article.php?id=art_1267&issue=apr_05

Chapter 6   The Challenge of Mississippi

Further Research:

1. What are red-lining and Restrictive Covenants? Are they still being used? Do you know of examples of housing discrimination in your neighborhood? What relationship does it have to the racial make-up your schools? Do ethnic groups choose to live in segregated neighborhoods or are there external factors at play? An excellent article on the historical roots of red-lining is in Hays, S. P. (1983). "The Politics of Reform in Municipal Government in the Progressive Era." In L. Dinnerstein & K. T. Jackson (Eds.), *American Vistas* (4th ed., Vol. 2, pp. 102–129). New York: Oxford University Press.

2. What is the program, the purpose of business organizations and citizen's groups in your city? Who holds the power in your city?

3. How segregated is your school (what kind of tracking exists?), your neighborhood? Make an ethnic/racial statistical breakdown of the students of your school and compare it to other schools (your school district's website might have this information, or interview district personnel).

4. How long does it take for the police to come to your house when you call 911? Is that different in other neighborhoods? How are there differences, and why? Does your city, county, state have a policy on racial profiling?

Debate Resolution:

"The debates preceding the submission of the 14th Amendment clearly show that there was no intent that it should affect the systems of education maintained by the States." (From *The Southern Manifesto*.)

Debates and Role Plays based on Documents 6.1 and 6.2 (Bilbo Hearings)

1. Debate Resolution: The reaction of Senator Ellender of the Senate Committee to the investigators' report was reasonable.

2. Role Play: "Talking Heads" or "pundits" discussion about Bilbo's appearance on Meet the Press (such as one might see on national news programs like PBS's Washington Week in Review). Discussion

after role play: Do "national" news programs have a northern bias? Would such a bias feed reactionary fears among southerners?

3. Role Play: Conversation between Bilbo and Steele in a restaurant the night before they are both to testify before the Senate Committee.

Activity 6.1   The Movies

1. Watch the films, *Birth of a Nation, Gone with the Wind,* or another film that recreates the pre-Civil War South. Identify the elements of the Plantation Myth in the films.

2. Watch a film currently playing in the movie theaters or on DVD (e.g., *Song of the South*). Examine it for the myths it contains. Are there African American characters in the film? Describe them. Be as specific as you can, quoting dialogue and describing specific visual images in detail. Do these films contain elements of the Plantation Myth or other myths cited in the Freedom School curriculum? Remember that social mythology is capable of retaining its essential beliefs while altering surface details. Does the film reinforce the myths? Challenge the myths? Point to a reality which might exist beyond the myths?

Activity 6.2   Race Mixing and Communism

Watch the movie *The Cradle Will Rock* (1999). Compare how the accusations of "race mixing" and communism (and why they are associated with one another) was used to undermine the Federal Theater Project and how they were used by the white power structure in Mississippi. Research: Examine the historical sources to assess the validity of the depiction of the role of red-baiting in the controversy surrounding the demise of the Federal Theater Project.

Activity 6.3   Lynchings Today?

Research the murders of James Byrd in Texas (1998) and Matthew Shepard in Wyoming (1999).

1. What are the similarities, what are the differences?

2. Compare the cases (including the court proceedings and verdicts) to the Emmett Till case. Can the murders be called lynchings?

3. What are Hate-Crime Bills? Does your state have one?

4. Which groups became active or vocal in connection with the murders? What was their background and their message regarding the murders? Examples: the Ku Klux Klan; the Black Panther (start with www.posse-comitatus.org/kuklux.htm,); Fred Phelps' Westoboro Baptist Church; and the Gay and Lesbian Alliance.

Activity 6.4   Segregation Under Attack
Based on Documents 6.7 to 6.9 and 8.7
Role Play: Part I
Participants:

- Robert Patterson (White Citizens Council)

- H.F. Helgesen (FBI agent)

- The sheriffs from the following towns: McComb; Ruleville; Jackson; Hattiesburg; Greenwood; Holly Springs; and Philadelphia

- Two members of the KKK (e.g., Bowers)

- Two members of the Mississippi State Legislature.

The participants listed above have decided to meet during the summer of 1955 to discuss the implications of the 1954 *Brown vs. Board of Education* Supreme Court decision as well as possible strategies that could be used to prevent desegregation. Someone must volunteer to act as moderator of the discussion. The participants wish to address the following two questions in detail:

a. What changes to the Southern Way of Life would result if schools and other public institutions were to be integrated?

b. What can the participants do (individually and politically) to prevent the enforcement of such a decision?

After the discussion, various follow up activities could be employed to encourage reflection: a letter written by the participant to friends informing them of his experiences in the meeting and how he felt the meeting had gone; write the report that FBI agent Helgesen might have written to his superior in FBI Headquarters in Washington; or write a critique of the conclusions drawn by the participants at this meeting.

Role Play—Part II
June 24, 1964 (the day before Dulles meets with black leaders regarding the missing trio). The people identified by the list in Part I have been called to have individual discussions with Allan Dulles during his fact finding tour through Mississippi on June 24, 1964. (Dulles is not aware of the membership status in the Klan of Bob Rainey and Jim Connor although it is possible that his aides may be aware.)

A. Dulles works with three aides preparing questions for each witness. (The aides may wish to interview witnesses in advance of the actual hearing.)

B. Each witness prepares an opening statement that addresses the witness' understanding of the status of black/white relations as of June 24, 1964, the reasons for that status, and what the best role of the federal government could play in the future given the present conditions.

During the hearing, Dulles calls upon each witness and asks his questions.

Follow up activity: As a newspaper reporter (choose your bias before writing—communist; Klan; liberal; north or south and so forth), you have to write a story for your paper, giving an update on conditions in Mississippi and include an interview with Dulles on June 25, 1963.

Activity 6.5   Role Play: What Really Happened

Role Play (in groups of two): One person is a SNCC or COFO field worker. The other person is a Mississippi sheriff. Have a conversation based on the following conditions: Several civil rights workers have claimed to have been assaulted by several attackers. Both of you—field worker and sheriff—have arrived on the scene the day after the incident. You are trying to convince the other of what you think actually happened. After 5–6 minutes, switch roles and replay the conversation. Perhaps a few of the pairs can volunteer to replay the conversations in front of the entire study group or class.

Discussion: What are the assumptions that allow for very different interpretations of the same facts?

Chapter 7   Toward Freedom Summer

Further Research:

1. Which civil rights or grassroots organizations exist in your city? Do they cooperate on any projects or campaigns?

2. Has your voting district changed recently? How has that affected your ability to vote? What effect does redistricting have on representation of your community? What effect has the increasing popularity of absentee ballots had on elections? What is the controversy over electronic voting (by computer)?

3. FOR YOUTH: How is your "generation" defined in popular media? Bring to class a news article, an advertisement, a video which reflects the dominant media view of youth now. Do you recognize yourself in this characterization? Do you agree with it? Why or why not? What is missing? What is distorted? What is accurate? What factors shape the experience of young people in your neighborhood?

4. Many summer volunteers learned to be socially active from their parents. What have you learned about how the present political, social and economic system works (and your role in it) from you own parents? from school? from other sources?

Activity 7.1   Taking Action: A Hypothetical Case

Research and Role Play: Below is an exercise based upon the history and documents of four major organizations of the Southern Freedom movement—SCLC, CORE, SNCC and the NAACP. The purpose of the exercise is to help one learn the principles that guided each of the four groups and how their strategies followed from those principles. Another purpose is to gain insight into the degree to which these organizations and their tactics were historically determined. How well can the tactics of the Civil Rights Movement be applied to a major issue today? Proceed through each step below one at a time. Use the information found in this textbook as well as original documents from other sources. The bibliography of this book can be a starting place for further research about the programs and principles of each of the four organizations represented.

1. Divide up your group into four sub-groups: SCLC, CORE, SNCC, and NAACP.

2. Each sub-group represents the executive committee of each of the four organizations. As a committee, and being as historically accurate as possible:

    a. Decide the internal structure of your group (e.g., do you need to elect an executive director? secretary? What is the decision making process?).

    b. Write a position statement that includes the principal goals of your organization, the range of acceptable strategies and tactics in your arsenal of action and your theory of how those strategies and tactics will allow your organization to achieve its goals.

3. The time period is the present. You have just received a letter from the community leaders of a major U.S. city (see letter below). They need your help in combating a serious and urgent problem. Decide what you can do that is consistent with what you have written in your position statement.

    a. If you decide that you can't help them, write a letter back to them to explain why.

    b. If you decide that you can help them, then decide what form such help will take:

        •   write an immediate reply.

        •   develop a plan of action that includes both short-term and long-term goals. What is the nature (legal, economic, activist, militant, etc.) and scope (local, national, international?) of the response? What kind of structure (new organizations? coalitions? hierarchical? grassroots? elite/vanguard?) will the response take? What is your time frame (when will you accomplish what)?

        •   write a reply that describes your plan of action.

        •   Debrief with entire class the results of steps 1–3.

THE LETTER

Dear Sirs and Madams,

Our communities are under attack. The most difficult task facing us right now is loss of jobs. Already, we have 30% unemployment in our city (50% among our youth 18–25 years old). Those of us who do have jobs suffer from low pay, so that even if every member of the household is lucky enough to have a job, we still can't make ends meet. We are writing to you now because the two largest employers of our community (pharmaceutical and auto parts factory) have just announced that they will close in 12 months and move their operations out of the United States. We need your help in attempting to avoid this catastrophe.

We have made repeated appeals to the city government to help keep these manufacturers here. But the city government has responded with the promise of more jobs being created by the recent ground breaking of a new state prison and a WalMart. We have tried for years to unseat the mayor and her city council with little effect. Only 60% of the city's eligible voters are registered. But even more frustrating is the fact that only 40% of those registered vote in local elections. Most of those who vote are the white middle class who live on the hill and the government continually gives priority to their concerns. Our communities do not vote often or regularly enough. When we try to get them to, they say that there is no point, "All politicians are the same" or they are afraid of having their legal status questioned (they fear arrest and deportation). Some among us have tried to unionize the work force, but every attempt has been met with either the firing of the organizers or court decisions in favor of the company. As leaders of our communities we have been struggling to maintain the social and cultural fabric of our neighborhoods. Most adults, if not working, sit behind closed windows and watch TV, while the unemployed youth join gangs. Nevertheless, there has been more angry talk lately in the streets. People seem to want to do something. But, we are at a loss as to how to begin to tap into these rumblings. We know you have had much success and a great deal of experience in inspiring and organizing. Can you help us?

Sincerely,

People's Coalition for Community Rights (PCCR)

Keisha Washington, President, African American Center for Self-Help (AACSH)

Juan Lopez, Chicanos Fighting for Justice (CCFJ)

My-Kyung Kim, Coalition of Pacific Rim Peoples against Racism (CPRPR)

Abdul Muhammed, Arab/Palestinian Coalition for Jobs (APCJ)

Activity 7.2   Borrowing Power: Does it Work?

"Concept: That there are many kinds of power we could use to build a better society. What is power? (Power is the ability to move things.) What kinds of power are there?"

— from Unit VI of the 1964 Freedom School Curriculum

Review: Documents 7.1 and 7.2

Read:

- Documents 7.7 and 7.8

- Excerpts from "That Long Walk to the Courthouse" from Elizabeth Sutherland, ed., *Letters from Mississippi* (New York: McGraw-Hill Book Company, 1965), 83–150.

- Fannie Lou Hamer, "To Praise Our Bridges" in Carson, Clayborne, et al., eds. *The Eyes on the Prize Civil Rights Reader.* New York: Penguin Books, 1991.

Role Play:

1. Each participant is randomly assigned to one of two groups with the instruction that each participant is to develop his or her own individual personality within the parameters of the group's general position:

   > Group A is made up of white student volunteers from various universities in the Boston area at the end of a week long training session at Western College.

   > Group B is made up of SNCC staff members (half assigned and half volunteered) having just finished a week long training session with the above group of white students.

2. Each of the two groups must discuss the following questions, recording the major discussion points. The participant assigned to do the recording should be different for each question. REMEMBER, group

members are not to answer all the questions the same—differences of opinion within each group are expected (read documents carefully to pick up on the differences within Groups A and B). Such differences or disagreements are to be noted in recording the major discussion points.

  a. What was your original reason for coming to this week long orientation?

  b. What was your initial impression of the other group upon arriving at Western College?

  c. Did this initial impression change at all? If so, at what point and for what reason did this first impression begin to change? If not, how did your experiences with the members of the other group confirm your initial impressions?

  d. Have your reasons for participating in the summer project in Mississippi changed from those that led you to volunteer for the training? Can you cite a specific experience or a person who either confirmed or changed your reasons?

  e. What are the doubts you have had or continue to have about the people and goals of the summer project?

  f. Do you think you participation during this week has been a waste of time, might contribute to the success of the goals of SNCC (explain qualifications) or will be crucial to the success of the summer projects?

3. Each group now must divide itself into six SUB-GROUPS and assign one of the questions above to each group. Each sub-group needs to prepare a dramatized answer of its assigned question to perform before everyone. The discussions do not have to be extensive.

4. After each of the twelve groups have presented their role-play, everyone can now depart from their originally assigned roles and analyze the presentations. One might consider any of the questions below when critically evaluating the exercise.

  a. Was the training session at Western College productive?

b. How might such an alliance formed by the dynamic of such a training session backfire? In other words, could such experiences lead to greater divisions than already existed between whites and blacks? Were there expectations created by the training session that could not be fulfilled? What happens when expectations go unfulfilled?

c. Was it realistic to expect white middle class northern liberals to unlearn their prejudices and misconceptions in a week?

d. Why might it be more difficult for blacks to 'fight' northern liberal prejudice than southern conservative prejudice?

e. Were there only two positions at Western College—white and black? Did gender complicate the dialogue between white and black?

f. How might the experience of role-playing the Western College training session have changed the way you interpret contemporary, daily events in your life? For example, you walk into the lunchroom or lounge in your school or workplace. People are sitting together seemingly according to their ethnicity (whites with whites, Asians with Asians, Latinos with Latinos, and Afro-Americans with Afro-Americans, etc.). You overhear two whites, one says to the other "I don't understand why those blacks over there [pointing to a table of black people talking and laughing among themselves] always keep to themselves. They're the ones rejecting us. Then they have the balls to say we reject them." What might you now say to those whites that you might have not said before this experience?

g. Can the seeds of the future Black Power movement be seen in the issues raised by such discussions?

h. What resources did each group bring to the movement?

i. How would you compare the level of commitment of each group?

j. Look at previous alliances between *haves* and the *have nots*, for example, during the Abolitionist Movement or within the NAACP, or the Labor movement? Why are such alliances formed? Do they work? Why or why not? What are some of the inherent problems?

Chapter 8   Preparations for Freedom Summer

Activity 8.1   Role Play Within a Role Play

Based on Document 8.3—*Possible Role Playing Situations*:

1. Large group divides into five sub-groups—one group per category of role play (Reporter, Police, Non-violence, Canvassing, White Local Citizens).

2. Each sub-group develops a mini-skit for one or more of the questions in its category. One person in a mini-skit needs to be a SNCC staffer who is coaching the rest of the members of the sub-group who are playing "volunteers." The skit should be constructed so as to demonstrate how the role play helped the volunteers learn what to expect in Mississippi.

3. Each group presents its skits to the large group as a whole.

4. Debrief: Why were role plays an effective training technique? What did they add to the speeches and videos to which the volunteers were exposed.

Activity 8.2   To Go or Not to Go to Jail?

Role Play: The local university has sponsored a weekend conference on "Apathetic Voters: How to Motivate Them." The conference organizers are hopeful that the weekend strategy session will be particularly effective since the opening workshop features the following panelists: Martin Luther King, Bob Moses, James Foreman, Robert Zellner, Lawrence Guyot, Brenda Lewis and two white college student members of SNCC. (These people exist today as they recently have fallen through an anomaly in the space-time continuum.) The *panelists* are all eager to join the conference as keynote speakers. Each one has expressed hope that they could provide some insight into the causes and solutions of present day voter "apathy."

Present day conference *participants* represent local activist groups such as the following:

- Act-up (direct action AIDS advocacy group)

- Food Not Bombs (direct action homeless advocacy group)

- UAW (United Automobile Workers; AFL-CIO affiliated)

- UFW (United Farm Workers)

- AFT (American Federation of Teachers) or UFT (United Federation of Teachers)

- National Coalition Against Sexual Assault

- Animal Rights Direct Action Coalition

- Earth First!

- Greenpeace

- Habitat for Humanity (a person needs a home as a plant needs soil)

- WHAM (Women's Health Action and Mobilization)

- National Coalition for the Homeless

- Peace Action Outreach of Greater Los Angeles

- Lesbian Avengers

PRE-WORKSHOP PREPARATION

Research (some suggestions):

- "Letter from the Birmingham Jail," Martin Luther King, Jr. in Clayborne Carson et al., eds., *The Eyes on the Prize Civil Rights Reader* (New York: Penguin Books, 1991), 153–158. You can find a copy of this letter and other original documents with lesson plans on the King Institute's website: www.stanford.edu/group/King/liberation_curriculum/

- "Revolution in Mississippi," 1962, Tom Hayden in *Birth of a Movement*, 303–308.

- "Inside Agitator," Lawrence Guyot, in *My Soul is Rested* by Howell Raines, 238–243.

- "Some Random Notes from the Leflore County Jail," James Forman in *Birth of a Movement*, 329–335.

- *Letters from Mississippi*, Elizabeth Sutherland, ed., (Brookline, MA: Zephyr Press, 2002), Chapter 3, "That Long Walk to the Courthouse."

1. The conference *participants* need to do research on the group to which they belong. Most of the above groups have websites but their activities will also have been reported in newspapers and magazines such as *The New York Times, The Washington Post, The Los Angeles Times, The Chicago Tribune, Time, Newsweek, The Nation, Dollars and Sense,* and many more. The workshop participants will need to:

   a. Research the goals, strategies and tactics of the group to which they belong. Do the members of the organization have a theory of how change occurs?

   b. Prepare questions for the panelists that elicit from them ideas and suggestions as to how to better achieve their group's goals. (When asking questions, remember that the panelists know nothing of the present so you will have to give them some background information so they can understand your questions.)

   c. Write an action plan incorporating insights gained from the discussion.

2. Each of the *panelists* must research original source material (see suggestions for reading and edited document below) and answer (in writing) as many of the following questions as he or she can:

   a. What is the history of political imprisonment as a means of protesting injustice?

   b. What was the history of African Americans and the jails of the South?

   c. What relationship existed between jails and lynching?

   d. What dangers did civil rights workers face when they exposed themselves to arrest? What dangers did local people face when

they exposed themselves to arrest? Where did the various civil
rights groups stand on jailing and arrest?

    e.   How is this stand reflective of their policies and strategy?

    f.   What was the purpose of the "jail no bail" tactic?

Upon completion of the pre-activity preparation, the workshop can
begin.

WORKSHOP *(one person acts as panel moderator)*

1.   Each of the panelists introduces him or herself briefly, thanks the
conference organizers for the opportunity to attend the weekend
conference and expresses his or her hopes for what the weekend
can accomplish.

2.   After the brief introductions, each of the panelists makes a statement
concerning the importance of voting, the effectiveness of going to
jail as a tactic to achieve voting and the obstacles they confronted (in
their time of origin) during the implementation of such a tactic.

3.   Question and Answer period: Members of the various groups ask
questions (and follow-up questions) of the panelists. These questions
should be aimed at creating a dialogue among the workshop participants in order to understand if the theory, strategies and tactics
of going to jail and or voting can be applied to achieving the goals
of each of the groups.

Activity 8.3   "Mississippi Burning" or "The Philadelphia, Mississippi Case"

Watch the film *Mississippi Burning*, Directed by Alan Parker and written
by Chris Gerolmo, 1988. Review Document 8.9, "The Philadelphia, Mississippi, Case."

Some Questions:

1.   How are the civil rights workers portrayed, the Klan, the FBI, the
local people, the Sheriff?

2.   How are the local African Americans portrayed?

3. How is it different from the profiles of Chaney, Goodman and Schwerner in this book?

4. How does the film compare to the COFO report of the incident?

5. How do reviews of the film when it came out compare with your assessment of the film after answering the questions above?

Further information about the incident and the court case, including some documents, newspaper articles, and the FBI "Missing" poster, are on www.law.umkc.edu/faculty/projects/ftrials/price&bowers/price&bowers. htm

Chapter 9   Freedom Summer: Schools and the Arts

Debate Resolution:

Commercially popular songs are politically conservative.

Further Research:

1. Compare Spirituals, the Blues, Rap, Hip-Hop and Civil Rights songs. What is/has been the purpose or function of these songs? Are the differences in the kind of music produced dependent on whether the purpose is commercial or socio-political? How do you account for the differences in musical form (tone, rhythm, arrangement) and content (lyrics) among these four types of music?

2. What function or role has music played both in the Labor movement and the Civil Rights Movement?

3. Do present day political movements use songs? (Attend a rally or demonstration and report on the use and effect of music.)

4. Which musicians have been or are currently banned/boycotted, and why (for example The Weavers, Dixie Chicks)? What are current day explanations for the popularity of some music over others?

5. How have artists used their clout to be/become activists, or become politicians (for example Robbins, Sarandon, Glover, Belafonte, Penn, Reagon, Heston, Schwarzenegger)? Have they been equally effective?

6. What plays have been banned in U.S. History? Are the dynamics surrounding current bans on plays the same as those in the past? For example, "Grease" and "The Crucible" have been banned in Fulton, MO (see Schemo, *NY Times*, February 11, 2006).

7. Compare the Free Southern Theater to the Federal Theater Project During the 1930s (see Activity 6.2 and the film, *The Cradle Will Rock*).

8. Can live theater performances achieve the same effects as role-playing or extemporaneous dramatic acting? Can TV programs? Under what conditions? Why or why not? Answer these questions for each of the following types of role play:

    a. the use of role playing advocated by Richard Gregg in *The Power of Nonviolence*.

    b. the use of role playing by James Lawson in his training of the students in the Nashville movement (see *A Force More Powerful* by Peter Ackerman and Jack Duvall which has a DVD version). John Lewis recalled switching traditional roles to offer new perspectives. "Blacks played white roles in our training socio-dramas, and whites played black. It was strange—unsettling but effective, and very eye-opening as well—to see a black student pushing a white off a chair, screaming in his or her face, "Coon!" and "Ape!" and "Nigger!" or to see a white student shoving a black, yanking his or her hair, yelling "White trash!" and "Nigger lover!" (John Lewis and Michael D'Orso, *Walking with the Wind: A Memoir of the Movement*, Durham: Duke University Press, 1998. p. 99).

    c. the use of role playing at the training sessions in Oxford, Ohio.

    d. the use of role playing in the Freedom School classrooms. Consider Noel Day's advice:

        Using Drama: Probably the best way of using the dramatic method is the extemporaneous approach. In this approach, learning lines in a formal way is avoided. A story is told, or a "Let us suppose that" or a "Pretend that . . ." situation is structured, and then parts assigned. The actors are encouraged to use their own language to interpret the story or situation and some participants are assigned to act the part of non-human objects as well (e.g., trees, a table, a mirror, the wind, the sun, etc.). Each actor is asked to demonstrate how he thinks the character he is portraying looks, what expression, what kind of voice, how he walks, what body posture, etc. As soon as each actor has determined the characteristics of his part, the story outlined is reviewed again, and then dramatized. This method can permit the expression of a wide range of feelings by the students, involve their total selves, stimulate creativity, provide the teacher with insights about the students, and, at the same time, get across the content material (www.educationanddemocracy.org/FSCfiles/B_10_NotesOnTeachingInMS.htm).

Activity 9.1   Writing a Political Platform

Based on Document 9.2

1. Divide everyone into seven sub-groups.

2. Each sub-group is responsible for one of the following topic headings from the Freedom School Convention Platform:

   • Public Accommodations

   • the Plantation System

   • Housing

   • Education

   • Health

   • Foreign Affairs

   • Federal Aid

   • Job Discrimination

3. Each group rewrites its section of the Platform so it reads as a description of the reality of people's lives today.

   For example—Housing: Many homes are built with bathrooms that either lack a sink, toilet or bathtub. There are houses built without kitchen sinks and central heating. Walls and ceilings are built without proper insulation. Houses are built without any space to store food or do laundry, often there is no basement or attic. Rooms are built with only one outlet or even none at all. Some neighborhoods have houses without front and back yards.

4. The sub-groups reconvene and each group explains its platform to everyone else, answering any questions that arise. Option: groups rewrite their platforms, based on questions and comments during their initial presentation, for a second round of presentations to the entire body.

Debriefing Discussion: What was the purpose of having the Freedom School students create a "Party Platform"? Do the categories of the 1964 Platform cover all the issues that confront students' lives today? Should the categories be different today? Do the differences between the 1964 Platform and the current platform reveal more about the differences between the socio-economic status of the past and present students or does it reveal more about the historical changes that have occurred since 1964? (This last question could generate hypotheses for future research assignments.)

Activity 9.2 Call and Response

Many songs followed a "Call and Response" pattern. For example the gospel song "Have you been to the River," changed to "Have you been to the Jail?"

> Call: *Have you been to the jail?*
> Response: *Certainly, Lord.*
> Call: *Have you been to the jail?*
> Response: *Certainly, Lord.*
> Call: *Have you been to the jail?*
> Response: *Certainly, certainly, certainly, Lord.*

Listen to several examples, which can be found on the Smithsonian Collection of Recordings: Voices of the Civil Rights Movement, Black American freedom Songs 1960–1966; CD SF 40084.

1. Divide into two groups. One group uses some form of "Freedom" the other group responds with a version of "Now" until you have a rhythmical/melodic pattern.

2. Divide up into pairs: Make up your own call and response based on issues that are important to you. Teach your song to the rest of the class.

Discussion: What do you think about the effectiveness of the "call and response" in a political sense? How did it make you feel? What effect might it have had on the participants of mass meetings? Do any modern songs or performers use a form of "call and response" today? At what point and why do they use it (or what effect does it have)?

Activity 9.3   My Music

Share your favorite music with your class or study group:

1. What is the content of the lyrics, what does it promote?

2. Why do you like it, what does it represent to you? What statement are you making with your music?

3. What role do songs play in your life? How does that compare to the role songs played in the lives of those who fought for civil rights in the South during Freedom Summer?

Activity 9.4   Constructing a Play from Documents

The play, *In White America,* was entirely constructed from documents. Read the excerpts of the play at www.educationanddemocracy.org/ FSCfiles/C_CC3b_InWhiteAmericaExpt.htm.

A. ACT OUT A MONOLOGUE:

From this book or the Freedom School Curriculum (www.educatio-nanddemocracy.org), choose a document from which you can extract a speech or monologue. Choose one that particularly moves you or one about which you have questions. Before you read the monologue to an audience, consider the circumstances. Who is the speaker? To whom is he or she speaking? Why? What events immediately preceded the mono-logue? As an actor, try to reenter the history and use the monologue as a way of bringing the speaker into the classroom so that he or she can be experienced as a living presence. The actor might remain in character and respond to questions from members of the audience.

B. DEVELOP AND ACT OUT A DIALOGUE:

Work in pairs to create dialogues in any of the following ways:

1. Read one of the hearings out loud. You might select the Bilbo hearings, the Voting Rights Hearings of 1965, or the Credentials Committee Hearing in Atlantic City in 1964. To expand one of these hearings into a dialogue, use your knowledge of the place and time to write or complete a dialogue for either speaker.

2. Allow your character to address another character. Using your knowledge of any of the historical figures mentioned in the book, allow that figure to address another figure. You might try to recreate one of the confrontations mentioned in the book—Mrs. Hamer's confrontation with her landlord, for example.

3. Create a dialogue from any of the role plays suggested for the volunteers at the Oxford workshop, at the Montgomery bus boycott, or the Nashville sit-ins.

C. CREATING A PLAY:

Consider the documents of any historical period as material that might be dramatized. If your group is especially interested in a particular period, you might consider creating a play by combining the dialogue created in your improvisations with historical documents—newspaper accounts, speeches, and songs of the period. You might: Assemble all of the documents you find interesting. Include with each document your notes on the background of the document. Identify the speaker or writer and the circumstances under which the document was produced. Arrange the documents in a logical order. Usually, it's easiest to follow chronological order, but you might choose to group together documents that show how a single theme appears in various times and place. Don't worry about documents contradicting each other. Conflict is an essential part of drama. To create your final script, combine narration and documents to produce a unified effect. Use the notes from your research to provide background that the audience needs in order to understand the document. You might also want to include any scenes that worked particularly well in your improvisations. Be sure to include in your final script any cues for music or dance.

Chapter 10   Freedom Summer: Mississippi Freedom Democratic Party

Further Research:

1. Analyze the voting patterns in Southern states from Reconstruction to today. Was there, and is there a connection between ethnic groups and party affiliation or voting pattern? How did the Democratic and the Republican Party develop regarding their position on racial equality. Look specifically at Johnson's claim that the Democratic Party would lose the South over Civil Rights and Nixon's "Southern Strategy."

2. What do you think was behind the Presidential candidate Howard Dean's remark during the campaign for the Democratic primaries (on October 31, 2003) that he wants to be the candidate "for guys with Confederate flags in their pickup trucks." What was behind the furor about it?

Activity 10.1 Understanding Your Local School Board

Note: You can easily substitute city government for school board.

1. Participants can choose one of the questions below to answer (make sure that every question has at least one person doing research on it). Some methods of gaining information are: attend school board meetings; interview school board members; interview reporters who have reported on school board issues/members; interview principals and teachers in your school district; interview PTA members or leaders of community-based organizations who work on education issues; and go to the library and ask the librarian for help— particularly in finding back issues of the local newspaper that have articles about school board activities.

    a. What is the process by which one gets elected to the school board?

    b.   What powers does the school board have?

    c.   What have been the major decisions made by the board in the last year?

    d.   How is the school board agenda determined?

    e.   What is the make-up of the present school board? Write a biography of each member. How do these biographies compare with the biographies in the *Primer For Delegates to the Democratic National Convention*?

    f.   Identify an issue brought to the school board's attention by a parent or community group. Write a history of the process by which the issue emerged and what happened to it. Does any part of the history of the issue under study share any resemblances to the history of the MFDP's attempts to replace the MDP at the convention in Atlantic City in 1964? What are the differences? the similarities?

    g.   What is the process by which people register to vote in your town/city/county? What is the socio-economic and ethnic make-up of the school district? What percentage of eligible voters are registered in your town/city/county at this moment? What percentage of registered voters voted in the last school board election? Are there any newspaper articles that report on why people didn't vote in the last school board election? If so, what information was used and how was it gathered (interview reporter/reporters)?

2.   After each person or sub-group has reported the results of their research, everyone can then addresses the following question as a whole group: How representative is the school board of its constituency/constituencies? What changes in the decision making processes might make the school board more responsive to or representative of its constituency?

Activity 10.2   Voter Registration Drive

1.   Assemble data on voter registration in your town, including but not limited to these questions:

- What is the percentage of registered voters?
- How high is the voter turn out?
- How do people register in your town?

2. Divide into groups and contact different political parties and citizen groups in your town to inquire about their voter registration drives. When do they do it, who do they target, by what method? How much time and money do they spend? Participate in one of their voter registration drives, or in a "get out the vote campaign."

3. Meet again in class and compare experiences.

Activity 10.3 Creating a Pamphlet

Review *Primer For Delegates* (Document 10.3) and the COFO pamphlets, copies of which can be found at www.educationanddemocracy.org/FSCfiles/A_03_Index.htm

These documents show how MFDP strategists made contact with the poor people who were the focus of their work.

1. Investigate present day political organizations (e.g., Planned Parenthood). Examine the literature that they distribute to potential supporters, people who have native intelligence but who may not have officially sanctioned education or access to existing power structures. How are the complex ideas explained in these pamphlets?

2. Using (as your models) the pamphlets examined for question 1 as well as the COFO brochures reproduced in this chapter, construct similar brochures for a project of your choice. Use this skill also in the planning of the Summer Project activity (Activity 11.1).

Activity 10.4 Re-enacting the Democratic National Convention

Divide your study group or class into four sub-groups. Each sub-group will be responsible for writing one act of a play dramatizing the events leading up to the Democratic National Convention in Atlantic City in 1964. Each group will be responsible for one of the Acts below (except for Act V, which the entire class will write after the presentation of the first four acts are made).

Act I: Precinct meetings of the Mississippi Freedom Democratic Party.

Act II: MFDP lobbying of Atlanta Delegates.

Act III: Hearing of the Credential Committee on August 22.

Act IV: Negotiations of the various compromise proposals among the authors of those proposals and the MFDP representatives.

Act V: —?— (e.g., setting: County Courthouse in Mississippi, 1965)

Before writing the dialogue and blocking for your Act, decide on the following:

    a. Who the main characters will be.

    b. Outline the plot.

    c. Will you subdivide the plot into separate "scenes"?

After each group has completed writing their Act, the groups will reconvene as a whole and proceed with the following activities:

    a. Combine the Acts so the play has integrity—it flows.

    b. Assign parts and perform the play.

    c. Discuss play.

        • What were the play's strongest moments and why?

        • What were its weakest moments and why?

        • Does the play work dramatically? historically?

    d. Does the play need an Act V? If so, what would the outline be for it?

Chapter 11   Beyond Freedom Summer

Debate Resolutions:

    1. Understanding, and participating in the fight against discrimination against others empowers you to face the discrimination in your own life.

    2. The biggest obstacle to social change today is people's fear of social ostracization.

Further Research:

Investigate what the following people (feel free to add to the list) have been doing since Freedom Summer: Ella Baker, Ed King, Hollis Watkins, John Doar, Annelle Ponder, Septima Clark, and David Dennis.

Activity 11.1   Summer Project

Design a project that requires that two groups be brought together in order to achieve a goal. The experience (whether goal or process) needs to be beneficial to both groups. Outline the project (3–4 months in length) including the goal, the groups, the source(s) of funding, what kind of training or orientation program will be needed, the obstacles expected to be encountered during the implementation of the project and the advantages for each group.

Step One: Identify an issue, preferably one from personal experience. For example, are you upset that the city is going to build an incinerator in your neighborhood or is there a planned closing of a hospital or grocery store that will deprive a neighborhood of access to medical care or dietary needs (like fresh vegetables at an affordable price)?

Step Two: Identify the goal. For example, to shut down the incinerator or bring national media attention to bear upon strip mining practices on Indian Reservations.

Step Three: Identify the groups you wish to form an alliance. The selection of the groups needs to logically come out of the goal. Perhaps one group being personally or politically involved in the issue for quite some time and another group capable of bringing in needed resources in terms of access to funding or organizational skills and knowledge. For example, if the issue is strip mining on Navajo-Hopi reservations then perhaps Greenpeace and a local Navajo organization are two groups whose alliance may serve to accomplish the summer goal. *To make this more than just an intellectual exercise,* the summer project would originate from one of the groups. This would mean that you as a student/activist would offer to a group your services. Perhaps the elimination of standardized testing in your and other schools would be a goal worth researching and generating support for.

Step Four: Identify your sources of funding. This might involve some research on how groups raise money and choosing among the various strategies those that suit your particular groups and goals. [Discussion: Is organizing capacity drained by the existence of tax exempt nonprofits?

In other words, do the strings attached to funding, especially from corporate foundations, inherently limit the kinds of organizing that would
necessarily lead to radical, fundamental reform?]

Step Five: Training and orientation. Your tactics will depend on your
goals and theory. Will you want to employ direct action? mass meetings?
workshops (schools?) create new organizations? You strategy for the summer project will consist of an array of tactics chosen to produce expected
results. Obstacles must be anticipated. How will you train or prepare the
summer team (volunteers?) for the summer project?

Step Six: Write a position paper explaining how each of the participating groups will benefit from the experience of participating in the summer
project. Or, if you implement a real summer project, write a paper explaining how you think the groups did or did not benefit from the experience.

For more references on the history of the Civil Rights Movements see:
http://www.crmvet.org/biblio.htm

Adams, Frank, and Myles Horton. *Unearthing the Seeds of Fire: The Idea of Highlander.* Winston-Salem, South Carolina: John F. Blair, 1992.

Adickes, Sandra. *Legacy of a Freedom School.* New York: Palgrave MacMillan, 2005.

Allen, Gay Wilson. *Waldo Emerson.* New York: Viking Press, 1981.

Anderson, Jervis. *Bayard Rustin: Troubles I've Seen.* Berkeley: University of California Press, 1998.

Aptheker, Herbert. *A Documentary History of the Negro People in the United States.* Vol. 1–7. New York: Citadel Press, 1993.

Baldwin, Lewis. *Toward the Beloved Community.* Cleveland, Ohio: The Pilgrim Press, 1995.

Belfrage, Sally. *Freedom Summer.* Charlottesville: University Press of Virginia, 1990.

Blanding, Thomas. "Music of the Higher Spheres." In *Program for the Weekend Festival Exploring Transcendentalism and Music*, edited by Joseph Horowitz. Brooklyn, New York: Brooklyn Academy of Music, 1994.

Blaustein, Albert P., and Robert L. Zamgrando, eds. *Civil Rights and African Americans.* Evanston, Illinois: Northwestern University Press, 1991.

Blumberg, Rhoda Lois. *Civil Rights: The 1960s Freedom Struggle.* Boston: G. K. Hall and Company, 1984.

Bode, Carl, and Malcolm Cowley, eds. *The Portable Emerson.* New York: Penguin Books, 1984.

Bond, Horace Julian. "The Southern Youth Movement: Readers Forum." *Freedomways*, Summer 1962, 309–310.

Branch, Taylor. *Parting the Waters: America in the King Years, 1954–1963*. New York: Simon & Schuster, 1988.

Branch, Taylor. *Pillar of Fire: America in the King Years, 1963–65*. New York: Simon & Schuster, 1998.

Branch, Taylor. *At Canaan's Edge: America in the King Years, 1965–68*. New York: Simon & Schuster, 2006.

Brown, Cynthia Stokes. *Like it Was: A Complete Guide to Writing Oral History*. New York: Teachers and Writers Collaborative, 1988.

Bullard, Sara, ed. *Free at Last: A History of the Civil Rights Movement and Those Who Died in the Struggle*. Montgomery, Alabama: The Civil Rights Education Project, The Southern Poverty Law Center.

Burner, Eric. *And Gently He Shall Lead Them: Robert Parris Moses and Civil Rights in America*. New York: New York University Press, 1994.

Cagin, Seth, and Philip Dray. *We Are Not Afraid: The Story of Goodman, Schwerner, and Chaney and the Civil Rights Campaign for Mississippi*. New York: Macmillan, 1988.

Carson, Clayborne. *In Struggle: SNCC and the Black Awakening of the 1960s*. Cambridge: Harvard University Press, 1981.

Carson, Clayborne, et al., eds. *The Eyes on the Prize Civil Rights Reader*. New York: Penguin Books, 1991.

The Citizen: Official Journal of the Citizens' Councils of America. Jackson Mississippi: Senator James Eastland, papers of the Mississippi State Sovereignty Commission, MDAH, Jackson, Mississippi.

Colaiaco, James. *Martin Luther King, Jr: Apostle of Militant Nonviolence*. New York: St. Martin's Press, 1993.

Coles, Robert. *Children of Crisis*. New York: Dell Publishing Company, 1967.

Cone, James. *The Spirituals and the Blues: An Interpretation*. New York: The Seabury Press, 1972.

Congress on Racial Equality. Papers. Martin Luther King Jr. Center for Nonviolent Social Change, Inc. Atlanta, Georgia

Congress on Racial Equality. "What Then Are the Principles of CORE." New York: Congress on Racial Equality (CORE)

Council of Federated Organizations (COFO). Papers. Martin Luther King Jr. Center for Nonviolent Social Change, Inc. Atlanta, Georgia.

Council of Federated Organizations (COFO). *Mississippi Black Paper*. New York: Random House, 1965.

Dallard, Shyrlee. *Ella Baker: A Leader Behind the Scenes.* New York: Silver Burdett Press, 1990.

Dalton, Dennis. *Mahatma Gandhi: Nonviolent Power in Action.* New York: Columbia University Press, 1993.

Davis, Michael, and Hunter R. Clark. *Thurgood Marshall: Warrior at the Bar, Rebel on the Bench.* New York: Citadel Press, 1994.

Davis, Townsend. *Weary Feet, Rested Souls: A Guided History of the Civil Rights Movement.* New York: W. W. Norton & Company, 1998.

Dent, Thomas, R. Schechner, and Gilbert Moses. *Free Southern Theater by the Free Southern Theater.* Indianapolis: Bobbs-Merrill Company, 1969.

Dittmer, John. *Local People: The Struggle for Civil Rights in Mississippi.* Chicago: University of Illinois Press, 1994.

Duberman, Martin. *In White America.*

Dubois, W. E. B. *The Souls of Black Folk.* New York: Fawcett Publications, Inc., 1961.

Dubois, W. E. B. *Darkwater: Voices from Within the Veil.* New York: Schocken Books, 1969.

Dulles, Foster Rhea, and Melvyn Dubofsky. *Labor in America: A History.* Wheeling, Illinois: Harlan Davidson, Inc., 1993.

Dunbar, Anthony P. *Against the Grain: Southern Radicals and Prophets, 1929–1959.* Charlottesville: University Press of Virginia, 1981.

Eagles, Charles W. *The Civil Rights Movement in America.* Jackson: University of Mississippi Press, 1986.

Egerton, John. *Speak Now Against the Day.* New York: Alfred A. Knopf, 1995.

Erenrich, Susie, ed. *Freedom is a Constant Struggle: An Anthology of the Mississippi Civil Rights Movement.* Montgomery, AL: Black Belt Press, 1999.

Evers, Medgar. Program. Aired on WLBT-TV, 8 PM EST, May 20, 1963. Jackson, Mississippi. Available from http://www.effinghman.net/medgar/page3.htm.

Evers, Medgar. "NAACP Appeals to Negro, White Citizens." *Mississippi Free Press*, December 22 or 29, 1962.

Evers, Megar, and Francis H. Mitchell. "Why I Live in Mississippi." *Ebony*, November (1958): 65–70.

Evers, Myrlie, and William Peters. *For Us, the Living.* Garden City, New York: Doubleday, 1967.

Farmer, James. *Lay Bare the Heart: An Autobiography of the Civil Rights Movement.* New York: Arbor House, 1985.

Field, Connie, *Freedom on My Mind,* Producer/Directors Connie Field and Marilyn Mulford, Writer/Editor: Michael Chandler (San Francisco: California Newsreel, 1994)

Fischer, Louis. *Gandhi: His Life and Message for the World.* New York: The New American Library of World Literature, Inc., 1954.

Flexner, Eleanor, and Ellen Fitzpatrick. *Century of Struggle.* Cambridge, Massachusetts: Harvard University Press, 1996.

Flower, Dean, ed. *Henry David Thoreau: Essays, Journals, and Poems.* Greenwich, Connecticutt: Fawcett Crest Books, 1975.

Foner, Philip. *Organized Labor and the Black Worker (1619–1981).* New York: International Publishers, 1982.

Foner, Philip, and Ronald Lewis, eds. *Black Workers, A Documentary History from Colonial Times to the Present.* Philadelphia: Temple University Press, 1989.

Forman, James. *The Making of Black Revolutionaries.* Seattle: University of Washington Press, 1997.

Frazier, E. Franklin. "The Negro Church in America." In *The Black Church Since Frazier,* edited by Eric C. Lincoln. New York: Schoken Books, 1974.

Frazier, Franklin E. *Black Bourgeoisie.* New York: Collier Books, 1962.

Frazier, Franklin E. *The Negro Church in America.* New York: Schocken Books, 1974.

Free Southern Theater. "Announcing a Summer Stock Repertory Theatre in Mississippi, May 30, 1964-August 22, 1964." Free Southern Theater, Drama Department, Tougaloo College, Tougaloo, Mississippi. National Headquarters: Free Southern Theater, c/o Philip Rose Productions, 157 West 57th Street, New York, New York, 10019. Papers of the Free Southern Theater, King Center, Atlanta.

Freedom Summer Applications. Martin Luther King, Jr. Center for Nonviolent Social Change, Inc. Atlanta, Georgia.

Freedom Vote Papers. King Center. Jackson, Mississippi.

Gandhi, Mohandas K. *Autobiography.* New York: Dover Publications, 1983.

Garrow, David J. *Bearing the Cross: Martin Luther King, Jr. and The Southern Christian Leadership Conference.* New York: William Morrow, 1986.

Giddings, Paula. *When and Where I Enter: The Impact of Black Women on Race and Sex in America.* New York: William Morrow, 1984.

Ginzburg, Ralph. 100 *Years of Lynching.* Baltimore: Black Classics Press, 1962.

Gish, Lillian. *The Movies, Mr. Griffith, and Me.* Englewood Cliffs, New Jersey: Prentice-Hall, 1969.

Glen, John M. *Highlander: No Ordinary School.* Knoxville: University of Tennessee Press, 1996.

Goldman, Roger, and David Gallen. *Thurgood Marshall: Justice for All.* New York: Carroll & Graf Publishers, Inc., 1992.

Grant, Joanne. *Black Protest: History, Documents and Analyses, 1619 to Present.* Greenwich, Connecticut: Fawcett Publications, 1968.

Grant, Joanne. *Ella Baker: Freedom Bound.* New York: John Wiley and Sons, 1998.

Greenberg, Iris. Papers. New York: Schomberg Center for Research in Black Culture.

Greenberg, Polly. *The Devil Has Slippery Shoes, A Biased Biography of the Child Development Group of Mississippi.* London: The Macmillan Company, Collier-Macmillan, 1969.

Greenberg, Jack. *Crusaders in the Courts.* New York: Basic Books, 1994.

Gregg, Richard. *The Power of Nonviolence.* Nyack, New York: Fellowship Publications, 1959.

Gregory, Dick. *Nigger.* New York: Pocket Books, 1969.

Halberstam, David. *The Children.* New York: Random House, 1998.

Hampton, Henry, and Steve Fayer. *Voices of Freedom: An Oral History of the Civil Rights Movement from the 1950s through the 1980s.* London: Vintage, 1995.

Harris, Jacqueline L. *History and Achievement of the NAACP.* New York: Franklin Watts, 1992.

Hays, S. P. (1983). "The Politics of Reform in Municipal Government in the Progressive Era." In L. Dinnerstein & K. T. Jackson (Eds.), *American Vistas* (4th ed., Vol. 2, pp. 102–129). New York: Oxford University Press.

Hillegas, Jan. Freedom Information Service (FIS). PO Box 3234, Jackson, Mississippi 39207.

Hodgson, Godfrey. *America in Our Time*. New York: Vintage Books, 1976.

Holt, Len. *The Summer that Didn't End: The Story of the Mississippi Civil Rights Project 1964, and its Challenges to America*. London: Heinemann, 1966.

Honey, Michael. *Southern Labor and Black Civil Righs: Organizing Memphis Workers*. Chicago: University of Illinois Press, 1993.

Hood, Phil. *Artists of American Folk Music*. New York: William Morrow, 1986.

Horton, Myles, and Paulo Freire. *We Make the Road by Walking: Conversations on Education and Social Change*. Edited by Brenda Bell, John Gaventa and John Peters. Philadelphia: Temple University Press, 1990.

Horton, Myles, Judith Kohl, and Herbert Kohl. *The Long Haul: An Autobiography*. New York: Teachers College Press, 1998.

Huie, William Bradford. *Three Lives for Mississippi*. New York: Signet Books, 1968.

Hutchinson, Earl Ofari. *Betrayed: A History of Presidential Failure to Protect Black Lives*. Boulder, Colorado: Westview Press, 1996.

Johnson, Charles. *Growing Up in the Black Belt: Negro Youth in the Rural South*. New York: Schocken Books, 1967.

Johnson, James Weldon. *Along This Way*. New York: Viking Press, 1961.

Johnson, James Weldon, and J. Rosamond Johnson. *The Book of American Negro Spirituals*. New York: DeCapo Press, 1969.

Johnston, Erle. *Mississippi's Defiant Years 1953–1973*. Forest, Mississippi: Lake Harbor Publishers, 1990.

Katz, William Loren. *Eyewitness: A Living Documentary of the African American Contribution to History*. New York: Simon and Schuster, 1995.

Kellin, Mike. "Freedom Song: Hartman Turnbow." *Freedomways* Second Quarter (1965): 292–293.

King, Ed. Interview by Linda Gold. Jackson, Mississippi, 19 August 1998.

King Papers. King Center, Atlanta, Georgia.

King, Mary. *Freedom Song: A Personal Story of the 1960s Civil Rights Movement*. New York: William Morrow, 1987.

Lader, Lawrence. *The Bold Brahmins: New England's War against Slavery, 1831–1863.* Publisher New York: E. P. Dutton, 1961.

LaPrad, Paul. "Nashville: A Community Struggle." In *Sit Ins: The Students Report*, edited by Jim Peck. New York: Congress of Racial Equality, 1960.

Lerner, Gerda. *Black Women in White America: A Documentary History.* New York: William Morrow, 1972.

Levine, Ellen. *Freedom's Children: Young Civil Rights Activists Tell Their Own Stories.* New York: G. P. Putnam and Sons, 1993.

Lewis, David Levering. *W. E. B. DuBois: Biography of a Race.* New York: Henry Holt and Company, 1993.

Lewis, John, and Michael D'Orso. *Walking with the Wind: A Memoir of the Movement.* Durham: Duke University Press, 1998.

Library for Marxist Studies. New York.

Lincoln, Eric C., and Lawrence Mamiya. *The Black Church in the African American Experience.* Durham: Duke University Press, 1990.

Litwack, Leon, and August Meier, eds. *Black Leaders of the Nineteenth Century.* Chicago: University of Illinois Press, 1991.

Madison, Charles. *Critics and Crusaders.* New York: Henry Holt and Sons, 1947.

Mars, Florence. *Witness at Philadelphia.* Baton Rouge: The Louisiana State University Press, 1977.

Marsh, Charles. *God's Long Summer.* Princeton: Princeton University Press, 1997.

Marshall, Thurgood and Bob Carter, "The Meaning and Significance of the Supreme Court Decree," *Journal of Negro Education,* vol. 24 (Summer 1955) in Mark Tushnet, ed., *Thurgood Marshall: His Speeches, Writings, Arguments, Opinions and Reminiscences.* Chicago: Lawrence Hill, 2001. 157–164.

Martin, Waldo E., "Frederick Douglass: Humanist as a Race Leader," in Meier and Litwack, eds. *Black Leaders of the Nineteenth Century* Urbana: University of Illinois Press, 1988. 59–84.

Martinez, Elizabeth (Betita) Sutherland. *Letters from Mississippi.* Brookline, MA: Zephyr Press, 2002.

McAdam, Doug. *Freedom Summer.* New York: Oxford University Press, 1988.

McClymer, John F. *Mississippi Freedom Summer.* Belmont, CA: Thomson/Wadsworth, 2004.

McKissack, Patricia, and Frederick McKissack. *A Long Hard Journey: The Story of the Pullman Porter.* New York: Walker and Company, 1989.

McPherson, James M. *The Abolitionist Legacy: From Reconstruction to the NAACP.* Princeton: Prineton University Press, 1975.

Meier, August, and Elliott Rudwick. *CORE: A Study in the Civil Rights Movement.* Urbana: University of Illinois Press, 1975.

Meltzer, Milton, ed. *The Black Americans: A History in Their Own Words.* New York: Harper & Row, 1984.

Meltzer, Milton, ed. *In Their Own Words: A History of the American Negro.* New York: Thomas Y. Crowell Company, 1965.

Mendelsohn, Jack. *The Martyrs.* New York: Harper & Row, 1966.

Mississippi Freedom Democratic Party. Papers. Martin Luther King Jr. Center for Nonviolent Social Change, Inc. Atlanta, Georgia.

Miller, Michael V., and Susan Gilmore, eds. *Revolution at Berkeley: The Crisis in American Education.* New York: Dell Publishing Company, 1965.

Mills, Kay. *This Little Light of Mine: The Life of Fannie Lou Hamer.* New York: Penguin, 1993.

Mills, Nicolas. *Like a Holy Crusade.* Chicago: Ivan R. Dee, 1992.

Minnis, Jack. "The Mississippi Freedom Democratic Party: A New Declaration of Independence." *Freedomways,* Second Quarter 1965, 271.

Mississippi, America. Produced by Judith McCray, WSIU Carbondale and the Department of Radio-Television at Southern Illinois Unversity at Carbondale. Copyright 1995 by Judith McCray. Distributed by Warner Home Video, a division of Time Warner Entertainment Company, L.P., 4000 Warner Boulevard, Burbank, California 91522.

Mississippi Free Press, Saturday, May l9, 1962, Page 2, Vol. 1, #23.

Mississippi Freedom Democratic Party Papers. King Center, Atlanta.

Mississippi State Sovereignty Commission. Papers. Mississippi Department of Archives and History, Jackson, Mississippi.

Mitchell, Margaret. *Gone with the Wind.* New York: Warner Books, 1994.

Moody, Anne. *Coming of Age in Mississippi.* New York: Dell Publishing Company, 1968.

Morris, Aldon D. *The Origins of the Civil Rights Movement: Black Communities Organizing for Change.* New York: The Free Press, 1984.

Moses, Robert, and Cobb, Charles. *Radical Equations: Math Literacy and Civil Rights.* Boston: Beacon Press, 2001.

Myrdal, Gunnar. *An American Dilemma.* New York: Harper & Row, 1962.

Newsweek, "Shall Now Also Be Equal," July 13, 1964.

Nossiter, Adam. *Of Long Memory: Mississippi and the Murder of Medgar Evers.* New York: Addison-Wesley Publishing Company, 1994.

Oshinsky, David M. *Worse than Slavery: Parchman Farm and the Ordeal of Jim Crow Justice.* New York: Simon and Schuster, 1996.

Ovington, Mary White. *Black and White Sat Down Together: The Reminiscences of an NAACP Founder.* New York: The Feminist Press at the City University of New York, 1995.

Payne, Charles M. *I've Got the Light of Freedom: The Organizing Tradition and the Mississippi Freedom Struggle.* Berkeley: University of California Press, 1995.

Peake, Thomas R. *Keeping the Dream Alive: A History of the Southern Christian Leadership Conference from King to the Nineteen-Eighties.* New York: Peter Lang, 1987.

Phillips, Wendell. *On Civil Rights and Freedoms.* Edited by Louis Filler. New York: Hill and Wang, 1965.

Piven, Frances Fox, and Cloward, Richard A. *Poor People's Movements: Why they Succeed, How They Failed.* New York: Vintage Books, 1979.

Ploski, Harry A., and James Williams. *The Negro Almanac: A Reference Work on the Afro American.* New York: John Wiley & Sons, 1983.

Ponder, Annell. Report, "Citizenship Education in the Heart of the Iceberg," August 2, 1963. Ponder Papers, King Center, Atlanta.

Popham, James. *The Truth about Testing: An Educator's Guide to Action.* Alexandria, Va.: Association for Supervision and Curriculum Development, 2001.

Quarles, Benjamin. *The Negro in the Making of America.* New York: Collier, 1969.

Raines, Howell. *My Soul is Rested.* New York: Penguin Books, 1983.

Ransby, Barbara. *Ella Baker and the Black Freedom Movement.* Chapel Hill: University of North Carolina Press, 2003.

Reagon, Bernice Johnson. "Songs of the Civil Rights Movement, 1955–1965: A Study in Cultural History." Washington: Schomberg Library, 1975.

Rudwick, Elliott. *W. E. B. DuBois: Voice of the Black Protest Movement.* Urbana: University of Illinois Press, 1983.

Savio, Mario. "An End to History." *Humanity,* December, 1964, 239–243. Available at proactivist.com, fsm-a/org.

Seeger, Pete, interview by H. T. Holmes and Bill Hanna, November 2, 1979. Mississippi Department of Archives and History, Jackson, Mississippi. Acquisition Number: OH 80-02, 5.

Seeger, Pete with Bob Reiser. *Everybody Says Freedom: A History of the Civil Rights Movement in Songs and Pictures.* New York: W. W. Norton and Company, 1989.

Sharp, Gene. *The Politics of Nonviolent Action.* Boston: P. Sargent (Extending horizons books), 1973.

Sharp, Gene. *Gandhi as a Political Strategist.* Boston: P. Sargent Publishers, 1979.

Shirer, William. *Gandhi: A Memoir.* New York: Washington Square Press, 1979.

Silver, James W. *Mississippi: The Closed Society.* New York: Harcourt, Brace & World, Inc., 1964.

Silvester, Christopher, ed. *The Norton Book of Interviews.* New York: W. W. Norton & Company, 1993.

Sitkoff, Harvard. *A New Deal for Blacks.* New York: Oxford University Press, 1978.

Slade, Madeleine. *The Spirit's Pilgrimage.* The Norton Book of Interviews: Coward-McCann, Inc., 1960.

Smith, Lillian. *Killers of the Dream.* New York: W. W. Norton & Company, 1961.

Smith, Lillian. "Only the Young the the Brave." In *Sit Ins: The Students Report,* edited by Jim Peck. New York: Congress of Racial Equality, 1960.

Southern Christian Leadership Council. Papers. Martin Luther King Jr. Center for Nonviolent Social Change, Inc. Atlanta, Georgia.

Stampp, Kenneth M. *The Era of Reconstruction, 1865–1877.* New York: Knopf, 1965, t.p. 1978.

Stewart, James B., *William Lloyd Garrison and the Challenges of Emancipation.* Arlington Heights, Ill.: Harlan Davidson, Inc., 1992.

Student Nonviolent Coordinating Committee. Papers. Martin Luther King Jr. Center for Nonviolent Social Change, Inc. Atlanta, Georgia.

Student Nonviolent Coordinating Committee. Papers. Tougaloo College Library, Tougaloo, Mississippi.

Sutherland, Elizabeth, ed. *Letters from Mississippi*. New York: McGraw-Hill Book Company, 1965.

Thoreau, Henry David. *Civil Disobedience and Other Essays*. New York: Dover Publications, Inc., 1993.

Thoreau, Henry David. "A Plea for Captain John Brown." In *Civil Disobedience and Other Essays*, 40. New York: Dover Publications, Inc., 1993.

Thoreau, Henry David. "Slavery in Massachusetts." In *Civil Disobedience and Other Essays*, 23. New York: Dover Publications, Inc., 1993.

Trippett, Frank. "An Account of Some Covenversations on U.S. 45," *Newsweek*, July 13, 1964, 21.

Tushnet, Mark. *The NAACP: Legal Strategy Against Segregated Education, 1925–1950*. Chapel Hill: University of North Carolina Press, 1987.

U.S. Commission on Civil Rights. *Voting: Hearing before the Civil Rights Commission*. Jackson, Mississippi, Vol. 1, February 16–20, 1965.

U. S. Senate Special Committee on Senatorial Campaign Expenditures. *Bilbo Hearings: Before the Special Committee to Investigate Senatorial Campaign Expenditures*. Jackson, Mississippi, October 31–December 16, 1946.

Vicksburg Citizens Appeal, vol. 1, No. 1, August 22, 1964.

Viorst, Milton. *Fire in the Streets: America in the 1960s*. New York: Simon and Schuster, 1979.

Vollers, Maryanne. *Ghosts of Mississippi*. Boston: Back Bay Books, 1995.

Walter, Mildred Pitts. *Mississippi Challenge*. New York: Alladin Paperbacks, 1992.

Washington, Booker T., and W. E. B. DuBois. *The Negro in the South*. New York: Carol Publishing Group, 1970.

Washington, James Melvin, ed. *Testament of Hope. The Essential Writings and Speeches of Martin Luther King, Jr*. San Francisco: HarperSan Franciso, 1986.

Watkins, Hollis. Interviewed by Linda Gold. Jackson, Mississippi, 20 August 1998.

Watters, Pat. *Down to Now: Reflections on the Southern Civil Rights Movement.* New York: Random House, 1971.

We Shall Overcome. Produced by Ginger Group Productions, 1988. Copyright 1990 by PBS Home Video, 50 N. La Cienega Blvd., Beverly Hills, California, 90211.

Wedin, Carolyn. *Inheritors of the Spirit: Mary White Ovington and the Founding of the NAACP.* New York: John Wiley & Sons, 1998.

Weisberger, Bernard. "Here Come the Wobblies" in *American Vistas* (fourth edition) edited by Dinnerstein and Jackson, 1967.

Weisbrodt, Robert. *Freedom Bound.* New York: Penguin Books, 1991.

Wells-Barnett, Ida. *On Lynchings.* New York: Arno Press, 1969.

Wilkins, Roy. *Standing Fast.* New York: Penguin Books, 1984.

Wilkinson, Brenda. *The Civil Rights Movement: An Illustrated History.* New York: Crescent Books, 1997.

Williams, Juan. *Eyes on the Prize: America's Civil Rights Years, 1954–1965.* New York: Viking, 1987.

Williams, Juan. *Thurgood Marshall: American Revolutionary.* New York: Random House, 1998.

"Without These Songs . . ." *Newsweek,* August 31, 1964, 74.

Wolff, Miles. *Lunch at the 5 & 10.* Chicago: Ivan R. Dee, Inc., 1970.

Woloch, Nancy. *Women and the American Experience.* New York: Alfred A. Knopf, 1984.

Wren, Christopher. "An Insider Stays to Fight: A Profile of Edwin King." *Look,* September 8 1964, 27–28.

Wren, Christopher. "Mississippi: The Attack on Bigotry." *Look,* September 8 1964, 20–26.

Young, Andrew. *An Easy Burden: The Civil Rights Movement and the Transformation of America.* New York: HarperCollins, 1996.

Zinn, Howard. *A People's History of the United States.* New York: The New Press, 1997.

Zinn, Howard. *A People's History of the United States.* Volumes I and II, Teaching Edition. New York: The New Press, 2003.

Zinn, Howard. *The Zinn Reader.* New York: Seven Stories Press, 1997.

Foreword

1. Freedom School Curriculum, Unit VII, Part I, (http://www.education
   anddemocracy.org/FSCfiles/C_CC7_UnitVII.htm)
2. Howard Zinn, A People's History of the United States, Volume II: The
   Civil War to the Present. Teaching Edition (New York: The New
   Press, 2003). 343–4.

About Using This Book

1. Freedom School Curriculum, Unit V (http://www.educationanddemoc-
   racy.org/FSCfiles/C_CC1_Units1to6.htm#Unit5)
2. Staughton Lynd, "You Are History" in Freedom, Vol. I, No. 4, April 18,
   1964 (Iris Greenberg Collection, Schomburg Library, New York).

Chapter 1   Abolitionists and the Nonviolent Tradition

1. James Melvin Washington, ed., Testament of Hope. The Essential
   Writings and Speeches of Martin Luther King, Jr. (San Francisco:
   Harper San Franciso, 1986). 164.
2. Russel B. Nye, William Lloyd Garrison and the Humanitarian Reformers. (Boston: Little Brown, 1955). 200.
3. Charles Madison, *Critics and Crusaders*. (New York: Henry Holt and
   Sons, 1947). 16
4. Ibid., 21.

5. James Stewart, *William Lloyd Garrison and the Challenges of Emancipation*. (Arlington Heights, Ill.: Harlan Davidson, Inc, 1992). 52

6. Madison, *Critics and Crusaders*. 24.

7. William Loren Katz, *Eyewitness: A Living Documentary of the African American Contribution to History* (New York: Simon and Schuster, 1995). 165

8. William Lloyd Garrison, "The Governing Passion of My Soul," (1865). (http://afgen.com/garrison.html).

9. *The Liberator*, Vol. I, January 1, 1831.

10. Frederick Douglass, *What to the Slave is the Fourth of July?* (1852), (http://douglassarchives.org/doug_a10.htm)

11. Frederick Douglass, *Narrative of a Life of a* Slave (1845), (http://docsouth.unc.edu/douglass/douglass.html). CSN

12. Waldo E. Martin, "Frederick Douglass: Humanist as a Race Leader," in Meier and Litwack, eds. *Black Leaders of the Nineteenth Century* (Urbana: University of Illinois Press, 1988). 64.

13. Katz, *Eyewitness*. 178.

14. Stewart, . 141–142.

15. Katz, *Eyewitness*.158.

16. Martin, "Frederick Douglass." 69.

17. Ibid., 84.

18. *North Star*, Voluntary. 1, No.1 1847. Reprinted in Herbert Aptheker, *A Documentary History of the Negro People in the United States* (New York: Citadel Press, 1951), 255–56.

19. Nye, *William Lloyd Garrison*. 157.

20. Katz, *Eyewitness*.165.

21. Lawrence Lader, *The Bold Brahmins: New England's War against Slavery, 1831–1863*. (New York: E. P. Dutton, 1961). 212.

22. Joanne Grant, *Black Protest: History, Documents and Analyses, 1619 to Present*. (Greenwich, Connecticut: Fawcett Publications, 1968). 66.

23. Lader, *The Bold Brahmins*. 214.

24. Aptheker, *A Documentary History*. 371.

25. Henry David Thoreau, *On Civil Disobedience* (originally published as *Resistance to Civil Government*), 1849.

26. Carl Bode and Malcolm Cowley, eds., *The Portable Emerson* (New York: Penguin Books, 1984). 575.

27. Thomas Blanding, "Music of the Higher Spheres," in *Program for the Weekend Festival Exploring Transcendentalism and Music*, ed. Joseph Horowitz (Brooklyn, New York: Brooklyn Academy of Music, 1994). 26.
28. Ibid., 26.
29. Ibid., 25.
30. Ibid.
31. Gay Wilson Allen, *Waldo Emerson* (New York: Viking Press, 1981). 591.
32. Henry David Thoreau, "A Plea for Captain John Brown," in *Civil Disobedience and Other Essays* (New York: Dover Publications, Inc., 1993), 40.
33. Ibid., 44.
34. Also in Henry David Thoreau, *Civil Disobedience and Other Essays* (New York: Dover Publications, Inc., 1993). 46.
35. Gandhi on the events of 1906, 1907 in South Africa in Dennis Dalton, *Mahatma Gandhi: Nonviolent Power in Action* (New York: Columbia University Press, 1993). 12.
36. Christopher Silvester, ed., *The Norton Book of Interviews* (New York: W. W. Norton and Company, 1993). 377.
37. Dalton, *Mahatma Gandhi: Nonviolent Power in Action*. 170.
38. Ibid., 96
39. William Shirer, *Gandhi: A Memoir* (New York: Washington Square Press, 1979). 87–89.
40. Madeleine Slade, *The Spirit's Pilgrimage* (The Norton Book of Interviews: Coward-McCann, Inc., 1960). 111.
41. Dalton, *Mahatma Gandhi: Nonviolent Power in Action*. 115.
42. Ibid., 112.
43. Ibid., 130.
44. Ibid., 13.
45. Shirer, *Gandhi: A Memoir*. 92.
46. Ibid., 93–94.
47. Dalton, *Mahatma Gandhi: Nonviolent Power in Action*. 98.
48. Ibid., 118.
49. Ibid., 119.
50. Ibid., 113.
51. Shirer, *Gandhi: A Memoir*. frontpiece.

52. The complete text is at http//:www.mkgandhi.org/nonviolence/faith%20
    in%20nonviolence.htm

Chapter 2   National Association for the Advancement of Colored People (NAACP)

1. William Loren Katz, *Eyewitness: A Living Documentary of the African American Contribution to History* (New York: Simon and Schuster, 1995). 365–367.

2. James Weldon Johnson, Along This Way (New York: Viking Press, 1961). 320.

3. Ibid., 321.

4. Ibid., 321.

5. Jacqueline L. Harris, *History and Achievement of the NAACP* (New York: Franklin Watts, 1992). 35.

6. Johnson, *Along This Way*. 318.

7. Milton Meltzer, *In Their Own Words* (New York: Thomas Y. Crowell Company, 1967). 154.

8. Paula Giddings, *When and Where I Enter: The Impact of Black Women on Race and Sex in America* (New York: William Morrow, 1984). 23.

9. Ibid., 17.

10. Ibid., 19.

11. Ibid., 19.

12. Ibid., 20.

13. Harris, *History and Achievement of the NAACP*. 37.

14. Ibid., 38.

15. Aptheker, *A Documentary History*. 30.

16. Ida Wells-Barnett, *On Lynchings* (New York: Arno Press, 1969). 96–98. written in 1920 from W. E. B. (William Edward Burghardt) Dubois, *Darkwater: Voices from Within the Veil* (New York: Schocken Books, 1969). 31.

17. Written in 1920 from W. E. B. (William Edward Burghardt) Dubois, Darkwater: Voices from Within the Veil (New York: Schocken Books, 1969). 31.

18. Elliott Rudwick, *W. E. B. DuBois: Voice of the Black Protest Movement* (Urbana: University of Illinois Press, 1983). 95.

19. Aptheker, *A Documentary History*. 905.

20. Rudwick, *W. E. B. DuBois.* 108.

21. Ibid., 152.

22. Woodrow Wilson, quoted in D.W. Griffith's *Birth of a Nation*

23. Katz, *Eyewitness.* 365.

24. Lillian Gish, *The Movies, Mr. Griffith, and Me* (Englewood Cliffs, New Jersey: Prentice-Hall, 1969). 154.

25. Carolyn Wedin, *Inheritors of the Spirit: Mary White Ovington and the Founding of the NAACP* (New York: John Wiley & Sons, 1998). 155.

26. Ibid., 154.

27. Michael Davis and Hunter R. Clark, *Thurgood Marshall: Warrior at the Bar, Rebel on the Bench* (New York: Citadel Press, 1994). 113.

28. Supreme Court of the United States, *Smith v. Allwright* (321 U.S. 649) No. 51 Argued: November 10, 12, 1943; Decided: April 3, 1944.

29. Thurgood Marshall and Bob Carter, "The Meaning and Significance of the Supreme Court Decree," Journal of Negro Education, vol. 24 (Summer 1955) in Mark Tushnet, ed., Thurgood Marshall: His Speeches, Writings, Arguments, Opinions and Reminiscences (Chicago: Lawrence Hill, 2001). 164.

30. Juan Williams, Thurgood Marshall: American Revolutionary (New York: Random House, 1998). 35.

31. Ibid., 41–46.

32. Ibid., 49.

33. Ibid., 76–7.

34. Ibid., 82.

35. Ibid., 105.

36. Ibid., 118.

37. Ibid., 128.

38. Ibid., 145–6.

39. Ibid., 150.

40. Ibid., 198–205.

41. Ibid., 247.

42. Ibid., 271.

43. Maryanne Vollers, *Ghosts of Mississippi* (Boston: Back Bay Books, 1995). 108.

44. Megar Evers and Francis H. Mitchell, "Why I Live in Mississippi," *Ebony* , November (1958): 65–70.

45. Ibid.
46. Ibid.
47. Ibid.
48. Adam Nossiter, *Of Long Memory: Mississippi and the Murder of Medgar Evers* (New York: Addison-Wesley Publishing Company, 1994). 39.
49. Evers and Mitchell. 65–70.
50. Michael Davis and Hunter R. Clark, *Thurgood Marshall: Warrior at the Bar, Rebel on the Bench* (New York: Citadel Press, 1994). 201.
51. David J. Garrow, *Bearing the Cross: Martin Luther King, Jr. and The Southern Christian Leadership Conference* (New York: William Morrow, 1986). 91.
52. Evers and Mitchell. 65–70.
53. Charles M. Payne, *I've Got the Light of Freedom: The Organizing Tradition and the Mississippi Freedom Struggle* (Berkeley: University of California Press, 1995). 61.
54. Vollers, *Ghosts of Mississippi*. 114.
55. Medgar Evers, "NAACP Appeals to Negro, White Citizens," *Mississippi Free Press*, December 22 or 29 1962.
56. Vollers, *Ghosts of Mississippi*. 106.
57. Vollers, *Ghosts of Mississippi*. 107; and Charles W. Eagles, *The Civil Rights Movement in America* (Jackson: University of Mississippi Press, 1986). 65.
58. Pete Seeger and Bob Reiser, *Everybody Says Freedom: A History of the Civil Rights Movement in Songs and Pictures* (New York: W. W. Norton and Company, 1989). 143.
59. Seeger and Reiser, *Everybody Says Freedom*. 144.
60. Ibid., 144.
61. Vollers, *Ghosts of Mississippi*. 119.
62. Ibid., 139.

Chapter 3   Congress of Racial Equality (CORE)

1. CORE, "What Then are the Principles of CORE," (New York: Congress on Racial Equality).
2. August Meier and Elliott Rudwick, *CORE: A Study in the Civil Rights Movement* (Urbana: University of Illinois Press, 1975). 10.
3. Ibid., 118.
4. Ibid., 116.

5. Jervis Anderson, Bayard Rustin: *Troubles I've Seen* (Berkeley: University of California Press, 1998). 19.

6. Ibid., 56.

7. Ibid., 60.

8. Ibid.,. 61.

9. Ibid., 98.

10. Ibid., 159.

11. Ibid., 169.

12. Ibid., 223.

13. Ibid., 231.

14. Ibid., 248.

15. Ibid., 263.

16. Meier and Rudwick, *CORE: A Study.*, 36.

17. Ibid., 103.

18. Brenda Wilkinson, *The Civil Rights Movement: An Illustrated History* (New York: Crescent Books, 1997). 116.

19. Henry Hampton and Steve Fayer, *Voices of Freedom: An Oral History of the Civil Rights Movement from the 1950s through the 1980s* (London: Vintage, 1995). 74.

20. Ibid., 76.

21. Meier and Rudwick, *CORE: A Study.* 139

22. Juan Williams, *Eyes on the Prize: America's Civil Rights Years, 1954–1965* (New York: Viking, 1987). 154.

23. James Farmer, *Lay Bare the Heart: An Autobiography of the Civil Rights Movement* (New York: Arbor House, 1985). 2.

24. Hampton and Fayer, *Voices of Freedom.* 93.

25. David M. Oshinsky, *Worse than Slavery: Parchman Farm and the Ordeal of Jim Crow Justice* (New York: Simon and Schuster, 1996). 234.

26. Ibid., 234.

27. Ibid., 235.

28. Ibid., 236.

29. Farmer, *Lay Bare the Heart.* 27.

30. Oshinsky, *Worse than Slavery.* 236.

31. Meier and Rudwick, *CORE: A Study.* 142.

32. Hampton and Fayer, *Voices of Freedom.* 96.

33. John Dittmer, *Local People: The Struggle for Civil Rights in Mississippi* (Chicago: University of Illinois Press, 1994). 170.

34. Meier and Rudwick, *CORE: A Study.* 116.

35. Ibid., 180.

36. Ibid., 178.

37. Ibid., 179.

38. Ibid., 275.

39. Seth Cagin and Philip Dray, *We Are Not Afraid: The Story of Goodman, Schwerner, and Chaney and the Civil Rights Campaign for Mississippi* (New York: Macmillan, 1988). 255.

40. Howell Raines, *My Soul is Rested* (New York: Penguin Books, 1983). 273.

41. Cagin and Dray, *We Are Not Afraid.* 259.

42. William Bradford Huie, *Three Lives for Mississippi* (New York: Signet Books, 1968). 57.

43. COFO, *Mississippi Black Paper* (New York: Random House, 1965). 61.

44. Sally Belfrage, *Freedom Summer* (Charlottesville: University Press of Virginia, 1990). 12.

45. COFO, *Mississippi Black Paper.* 61.

46. COFO, *Mississippi Black Paper.* 63.

47. Jack Mendelsohn, *The Martyrs* (New York: Harper & Row, 1966). 111.

48. CORE Papers, King Center, Atlanta, Georgia.

49. Iris Greenberg Collection (New York: Schomburg Library).

Chapter 4   Southern Christian Leadership Conference (SCLC)

1. Aldon D. Morris, *The Origins of the Civil Rights Movement: Black Communities Organizing for Change* (New York: The Free Press, 1984). 84.

2. Franklin E. Frazier, *Black Bourgeoisie* (New York: Collier Books, 1962). 24.

3. David J. Garrow, *Bearing the Cross: Martin Luther King, Jr. and The Southern Christian Leadership Conference* (New York: William Morrow, 1986). 50.

4. From SCLC Citizenship School Curriculum, SCLC Papers, King Center, Atlanta.

5. Eric C. Lincoln and Lawrence Mamiya, *The Black Church in the African American Experience* (Durham: Duke University Press, 1990). 212.

6. Morris, *The Origins*. 86.

7. Ibid., 112.

8. *Crusade for Citizenship*, pamphlet, SCLC papers, King Center, Atlanta.

9. Thomas R. Peake, *Keeping the Dream Alive: A History of the Southern Christian Leadership Conference from King to the Nineteen-Eighties* (New York: Peter Lang, 1987). 54.

10. Lincoln and Mamiya, *The Black Church*. 115.

11. Ibid., 115.

12. Morris, *The Origins*. 160.

13. Ibid., 98.

14. Ibid., 98.

15. Pat Watters, *Down to Now: Reflections on the Southern Civil Rights Movement* (New York: Random House, 1971). 198–199.

16. Garrow, *Bearing the Cross*. 63.

17. Ibid., 58.

18. Ibid., 81.

19. James Melvin Washington, ed., *Testament of Hope. The Essential Writings and Speeches of Martin Luther King, Jr.* (San Francisco: Harper San Franciso, 1986). 8–9.

20. Lewis Baldwin, *Toward the Beloved Community* (Cleveland, Ohio: The Pilgrim Press, 1995). 2–3.

21. Garrow, *Bearing the Cross*. 16.

22. Ibid., 17.

23. Peake, *Keeping the Dream Alive*. 38.

24. Morris, *The Origins*. 161.

25. Ibid., 161.

26. Garrow, *Bearing the Cross*. 82.

27. Myles Horton, Judith Kohl, and Herbert Kohl, *The Long Haul: An Autobiography* (New York: Teachers College Press, 1998).

28. Ibid., 14.

29. Ibid., 2.

30. Ibid., 16.

31. Ibid., 27

32. Ibid., 31.

33. Seeger and Reiser, *Everybody Says Freedom*. 5.

34. Horton, *The Long Haul*. 44.

35. Morris, *The Origins*. 147.
36. Seeger and Reiser, *Everybody Says Freedom*. 3.
37. Horton, *The Long Haul*. 34.
38. Frank Adams and Myles Horton, *Unearthing the Seeds of Fire: The Idea of Highlander* (Winston-Salem, South Carolina: John F. Blair, 1992). 12.
39. Horton, *The Long Haul*. 49.
40. Adams and Horton, *Unearthing the Seeds*. 20.
41. Ibid., 23.
42. Myles Horton, *The Long Haul*. 53.
43. Ibid., 53.
44. Ibid., 55.
45. Ibid., 62.
46. Brenda Wilkinson, *The Civil Rights Movement: An Illustrated History* (New York: Crescent Books, 1997). 91.
47. John M. Glen, *Highlander: No Ordinary School* (Knoxville: University of Tennessee Press, 1996). 283–4.
48. A Hedy West song? Lyrics can be found both in Woody Guthrie's and Zilphia Horton's archives. You might be able to listen to the song at http://www.wfmu.org/playlists/shows/14364
49. Adams and Horton, *Unearthing the Seeds*. 33.
50. Ibid., 122.
51. Horton, *The Long Haul*. 118.
52. Ibid., 145.
53. "Report of Myle's Trip to the Sea Islands", Highlander papers, King Center, Atlanta.
54. Adams and Horton, *Unearthing the Seeds of Fire*. 120.
55. Morris, *The Origins*. 238.
56. SCLC Papers, King Center, Atlanta.
57. Kay Mills, *This Little Light of Mine: The Life of Fannie Lou Hamer* (New York: Penguin, 1993). 53.
58. Ibid., 54.
59. Payne, *I've Got the Light of Freedom*. 331.
60. Ibid., 75.
61. Seeger and Reiser, *Everybody Says Freedom*. 25.
62. Ibid., 119.
63. Adams and Horton, *Unearthing the Seeds of Fire*. 131–2.

64. Septima Clark papers, SCLC, the King Center, Atlanta.

65. Adams and Horton, *Unearthing the Seeds of Fire.* 144.

66. Letter to Louis Martin, Septima Clark papers, SCLC, King Center, Atlanta.

67. SCLC Papers, King Center, Atlanta

68. Annelle Ponder, *Report*, "Citizenship Education in the Heart of the Iceberg," August 2, 1963. Ponder Papers, King Center, Atlanta. 2.

69. Ibid., 4.

70. Ibid., 4.

71. "Memo to CEP Teachers", April 2, 1964, page 1, Ponder Papers, King Center, Atlanta.

72. June 1 memo, Ponder papers, King Center, Atlanta.

73. Greenwood file, SCLC papers, King Center, Atlanta.

74. Ibid.

75. Excerpts from *Reports from Citizenship School Teachers*, SCLC Papers, Boxes 156–164, King Center, Atlanta.

76. Mills, *This Little Light of Mine.* 64.

77. Ponder, *Report*, 8.

78. Ibid., 11–12.

79. Mills, *This Little Light of Mine,* 58.

80. Ibid., 59.

81. Ibid., 64.

Chapter 5   Student Nonviolent Coordinating Committee (SNCC)

1. Lillian Smith, "Only the Young and the Brave," in *Sit Ins: The Students Report*, ed. Jim Peck (New York: Congress of Racial Equality, 1960).

2. John Lewis and Michael D'Orso, *Walking with the Wind: A Memoir of the Movement* (Durham: Duke University Press, 1998). 95

3. John Lewis and Michael D'Orso, *Walking with the Wind.* 106.

4. Howell Raines, *My Soul is Rested* (New York: Penguin Books, 1983). 99.

5. Paul LaPrad "Nashville: A Community Struggle." In *Sit Ins: The Students Report*, edited by Jim Peck. (New York: Congress of Racial Equality, 1960).

6. Ibid.

7. Ibid.

8. Ibid.

9. Ibid.

10. Lewis and D'Orso, *Walking with the Wind.* 116.

11. Ibid., 117.

12. Ibid.

13. Ella Baker Letter, King Papers in SCLC Collection, King Center, Atlanta.

14. Ibid.

15. SNCC Papers, Box 25, King Center, Atlanta.

16. Ibid.

17. Gerda Lerner, *Black Women in White America: A Documentary History* (New York: William Morrow, 1972). 351.

18. Charles M. Payne, *I've Got the Light of Freedom: The Organizing Tradition and the Mississippi Freedom Struggle* (Berkeley: University of California Press, 1995). 405.

19. Paula Giddings, *When and Where I Enter: The Impact of Black Women on Race and Sex in America* (New York: William Morrow, 1984). 269.

20. Lerner, *Black Women.* 346.

21. Giddings, *When and Where.* 312.

22. Payne, *I've Got the Light.* 67.

23. Joanne Grant, *Ella Baker: Freedom Bound* (New York: John Wiley and Sons, 1998). 164.

24. Ibid., 171.

25. Ibid., 177.

26. Payne, *I've Got the Light.* 375.

27. Clayborne Carson, *In Struggle: SNCC and the Black Awakening of the 1960s* (Cambridge: Harvard University Press, 1981). 20.

28. Lerner, *Black Women.* 350.

29. Clayborne Carson and et. al, eds., *The Eyes on the Prize Civil Rights Reader* (New York: Penguin Books, 1991). 87.

30. Aldon D. Morris, *The Origins of the Civil Rights Movement: Black Communities Organizing for Change* (New York: The Free Press, 1984). 220.

31. Eric Burner, *And Gently He Shall Lead Them: Robert Parris Moses and Civil Rights in America* (New York: New York University Press, 1994). 66.

32. Ibid., 5.
33. Ibid., 83.
34. Ibid., 3.
35. Kay Mills, *This Little Light of Mine: The Life of Fannie Lou Hamer* (New York: Penguin, 1993). 128.
36. James Forman, *The Making of Black Revolutionaries* (Seattle: University of Washington Press, 1997). 286.
37. Civil Rights Act of 1957 in Albert P. Blaustein and Robert L. Zamgrando, eds., *Civil Rights and African Americans* (Evanston, Illinois: Northwestern University Press, 1991). 471–476.
38. Carson et. al,, *The Eyes on the Prize.* 170–171.
39. Forman, *The Making of Black Revolutionaries.* 227.
40. Carson, *The Eyes on the Prize.* 171.
41. Nicolas Mills, *Like a Holy Crusade* (Chicago: Ivan R. Dee, 1992). 49.
42. Carson, *The Eyes on the Prize.* 171–172.
43. Forman, *The Making of Black Revolutionaries.* 362.
44. Ibid., 359.
45. John F. McClymer, *Mississippi Freedom Summer* (Belmont, CA: Thomson/Wadsworth, 2004). 35.
46. Carson, *The Eyes on the Prize.* 131–132.
47. Jack Newfield, "Amite County" in *Freedom is a Constant Struggle*, edited by Susie Erenrich (Montgomery, AL: Black Belt Press, 1999). 91.
48. Bob Zellner, "McComb, Mississippi" in *Freedom is a Constant Struggle*, edited by Susie Erenrich. 14.
49. See Frances Piven and Richard Cloward, "Presidential Efforts to Channel the Black Movement" in *Poor People's Movements: Why they Succeed, How They Failed (*New York:: Vintage Books, 1979). 231–235. Also, see Geoffrey Hodgson, *America in Our Time* (New York: Vintage Books, 1976). 194–199.
50. Carson, *The Eyes on the Prize.* 81.
51. Seth Cagin and Philip Dray, *We Are Not Afraid: The Story of Goodman, Schwerner, and Chaney and the Civil Rights Campaign for Mississippi* (New York: Macmillan, 1988). 145.
52. Forman, *Black Revolutionaries.* 232.
53. John Dittmer, *Local People: The Struggle for Civil Rights in Mississippi* (Chicago: University of Illinois Press, 1994). 113.
54. Cagin and Dray, *We Are Not Afraid.* 159.

55. Raines, *My Soul is Rested.* 236

56. Payne, *I've Got the Light of Freedom.* 31.

57. Raines, *My Soul.* 234.

58. Forman, *The Making of Black Revolutionaries.* 279.

59. Ibid., 279.

60. Ibid., 281.

61. Eric Burner, *And Gently He Shall Lead Them: Robert Parris Moses and Civil Rights in America* (New York: New York University Press, 1994). 28.

62. Raines, *My Soul.* 237.

63. Cagin and Dray, *We Are Not Afraid.* 138.

64. Burner, *And Gently.* 3.

65. Pete Seeger and Bob Reiser, *Everybody Says Freedom: A History of the Civil Rights Movement in Songs and Pictures* (New York: W. W. Norton and Company, 1989). 160.

66. Kay Mills, *This Little Light of Mine.* 49.

67. Dittmer, *Local People.* 131. (Bob Moses)

68. See "A Proposal of the Student Non-Violent Coordinating Committee" in Herbert Aptheker, *A Documentary History of the Negro People in the United States*, vol. 7 (New York: Citadel Press, 1993). 115.

69. Dittmer, *Local People.* 131. (Mike Thelwell)

70. Clayborne Carson, *In Struggle: SNCC and the Black Awakening of the 1960s* (Cambridge: Harvard University Press, 1981). 80.

71. Robert Moses, "Those Who Want to Be Free," Volume 7, Document 44, 191, in Herbert Aptheker, *A Documentary History of the Negro People in the United States*, vol. 1–7 (New York: Citadel Press, 1993).

72. Eric Burner, *And Gently.* 86.

73. Dick Gregory, *Nigger* (New York: Pocket Books, 1969). 157.

74. Ibid., 159–160

Chapter 6   The Challenge of Mississippi

1. James W. Silver, *Mississippi: The Closed Society* (New York: Harcourt, Brace & World, Inc., 1964). 5.

2. Erle Johnston, *Mississippi's Defiant Years 1953–1973* (Forest, Mississippi: Lake Harbor Publishers, 1990). xv.

3. U. S. Senate Special Committee on Senatorial Campaign Expenditures, *Bilbo Hearings: before the Special Committee To Investigate Senatorial Campaign Expenditures* (Jackson, Mississippi, October 31-December 16, 1946).

4. Johnston, *Mississippi's Defiant Years.* xiv.

5. Florence Mars, *Witness at Philadelphia* (Baton Rouge: The Louisiana State University Press, 1977). 52. Also in Kay Mills, *This Little Light of Mine: The Life of Fannie Lou Hamer* (New York: Penguin, 1993). 49.

6. Johnston, *Mississippi's Defiant Years.* 17.

7. Ibid., 44.

8. Maryanne Vollers, *Ghosts of Mississippi* (Boston: Back Bay Books, 1995). 84.

9. Ibid., 85.

10. Ibid., 86.

11. *The Citizen: Official Journal of the Citizens' Councils of America* (Vol. 9, No. 5, February,1965). 29.

12. Joanne Grant, *Black Protest: History, Documents and Analyses, 1619 to Present* (Greenwich, Connecticut: Fawcett Publications, 1968). 268–271. (Quoted from the *U.S. Congressional Record*, 84th Cong., 2nd Sess., 1956, 4515-16.)

13. Mars, *Witness at Philadelphia.* 57.

14. Clayborne Carson and et. al, eds., *The Eyes on the Prize Civil Rights Reader* (New York: Penguin Books, 1991). Gold Cover, 62.

15. Mars, *Witness.* 56.

16. *The Citizen* (Vol. 9, No. 5, February, 1965).

17. Mars, *Witness at Philadelphia.* 54.

18. Ibid., 55.

19. *The Citizen* (Vol. 1., No. 59, June, 1956).

20. Ibid., (Vol. 2., No. 5, February, 1957). 1.

21. Anne Moody, *Coming of Age in Mississippi* (New York: Dell Publishing Company, 1968). 126.

22. Mars, *Witness at Philadelphia.* 67.

23. John Dittmer, *Local People: The Struggle for Civil Rights in Mississippi* (Chicago: University of Illinois Press, 1994). 57.

24. Mars, *Witness at Philadelphia.* 68.

25. Dittmer, *Local People*. 57.
26. Mars, *Witness at Philadelphia*. 68.
27. David Levering Lewis, *W. E. B. DuBois: Biography of a Race* (New York: Henry Holt and Company, 1993). 57.
28. Charles M. Payne, *I've Got the Light of Freedom: The Organizing Tradition and the Mississippi Freedom Struggle* (Berkeley: University of California Press, 1995). 54.
29. Moody, *Coming of Age in Mississippi*. 126.
30. Lewis, *W. E. B. DuBois*. 57.
31. Johnston, *Mississippi's Defiant Years*. 36.
32. NAACP pamphlet. Library for Marxist Studies, New York City.
33. Trippett, Frank. "An Account of Some Conversations on U.S. 45" (*Newsweek*, July 13, 1964). 21.
34. Margaret *Mitchell, Gone with the Wind* (New York: Warner Books, 1994). 639.
35. Ibid., 676.
36. Charles Marsh, *God's Long Summer* (Princeton: Princeton University Press, 1997). 56.
37. Mars, *Witness in Philadelphia*. 82.
38. Marsh, *God's Long Summer*. 50.
39. Ibid., 64–66.
40. Nicolas Mills, *Like a Holy Crusade* (Chicago: Ivan R. Dee, 1992).. 143–144.
41. Johnston, *Mississippi's Defiant Years*. 84.
42. John Lewis and Michael D'Orso, *Walking with the Wind: A Memoir of the Movement* (Durham: Duke University Press, 1998). 183.
43. Johnston, *Mississippi's Defiant Years*. 153.
44. Ibid., 153.
45. Seth Cagin and Philip Dray, We Are Not Afraid: The Story of Goodman, Schwerner, and Chaney and the Civil Rights Campaign for Mississippi (New York: Macmillan, 1988). 204.
46. Johnston, *Mississippi's Defiant Years*. 234.
47. *Newsweek*, July 13, 1964. "Shall Now Also Be Equal." 17.
48. Ibid.
49. Ibid., 18.
50. U.S. Commission on Civil Rights, *Voting Rights Hearing* (Jackson, Mississippi.)February 16, 1965.

51. Ibid.

52. Johnston, *Mississippi's Defiant Years.* xvi.

53. Robert Moses, Hollis Watkins, Samuel Block, Papers of the Mississippi State Sovereignty Commission, MDAH, Jackson, Mississippi.

54. Sara Bullard, ed., *Free at Last: A History of the Civil Rights Movement and Those Who Died in the Struggle.* (Montgomery, Alabama: The Civil Rights Education Project, The Southern Poverty Law Center). 36.

55. Ibid., 36.

56. Jack Mendelsohn, *The Martyrs* (New York: Harper & Row, 1966). 7.

57. Aldon D. Morris, *The Origins of the Civil Rights Movement: Black Communities Organizing for Change* (New York: The Free Press, 1984). 105.

58. Mendelsohn, *The Martyrs.* 11.

59. Ibid., 12.

60. Ibid., 13.

61. Iris Greenberg Collection (New York: Schomberg Library).

62. Ibid.

Chapter 7   Toward Freedom Summer

1. Hodgson, *American in Our Time.* 196.

2. Elisabeth Sutherland (Betita) Martinez, *Letters from Mississippi* (New York: McGraw-Hill, 1965). 42.

3. Ibid.

4. U. S. Commission on Civil Rights, *Voting Rights Hearings.* 157.

5. Seth Cagin and Philip Dray, *We Are Not Afraid: The Story of Goodman, Schwerner, and Chaney and the Civil Rights Campaign for Mississippi* (New York: Macmillan, 1988). 214.

6. John Dittmer, *Local People: The Struggle for Civil Rights in Mississippi* (Chicago: University of Illinois Press, 1994). 121.

7. Ibid., 121.

8. Ibid., 122.

9. Ibid., 204.

10. Carson, *In Struggle.* 97.

11. Ibid.

12. Mills, *This Little Light of Mine.*79.

13. Forman, *Black Revolutionaries.* 354.

14. Dittmer, *Local People.* 202.

15. "Mississippi Freedom Vote Campaign," (Atlanta: King Center). King papers.

16. "Memo to District Managers and Field Workers from State Office in Jackson concerning Election Procedures" (Atlanta: King Center). Papers of the MFDP, October 25, 1963.

17. Forman, *Black Revolutionaries.* 356.

18. Carson, *In Struggle.* 98.

19. 403   , "Aaron Henry for Governor" (Jackson, MI: Martin Luther King Center). Freedom Vote papers, Press Release, November 5, 1963.

20. "Summary of Events" (Jackson, MI:Martin Luther King Center). Freedom Vote papers ,October 22–28, 1963. VIII:2.

21. "To the President of the United States" and "The Attorney General of the United States, (Atlanta: King Center). Telegram, Freedom Vote papers.

22. Dittmer, *Local People.* 17.

23. King, *Freedom Song.* 335.

24. Dittmer, *Local People.* 220.

25. John Lewis and Michael D'Orso, *Walking with the Wind: A Memoir of the Movement* (Durham: Duke University Press, 1998). 243.

26. Hollis Watkins, interview by Linda Gold, Jackson, Mississippi, 20 August 1998.

27. Dittmer, *Local People.* 210.

28. Carson, *In Struggle.* 99.

29. Carson, *In Struggle.* 98.

30. Burner, *And Gently.* 129.

31. Ibid., 207.

32. Burner, *And Gently.* 125–126.

33. Ibid.

34. Iris Greenberg Collection (New York: Schomberg Library).

35. John Lewis, "SNCC Shifts National Headquarters" (Atlanta: King Center). Papers of the Student Nonviolent Coordinating Committee, June 12, 1964

36. Papers of the Student Nonviolent Coordinating Committee, Tougaloo College Library, Tougaloo, Mississippi.

37. Forman, *The Making of Black Revolutionaries*. 106.

38. Ibid., 30.

39. Ibid., 278.

40. Ibid., 236–237.

41. Payne, *I've Got the Light*. 331.

42. Mary King, *Freedom Song: A Personal Story of the 1960s Civil Rights Movement* (New York: William Morrow, 1987). 231.

43. Robert Coles, *Children of Crisis* (New York: Dell Publishing Company, 1967). 190–191.

44. COFO papers, "Memorandum from Mississippi Summer Project Committee to interviewers for the Mississippi Summer Project" (Atlanta: King Center.) April 14, 1964.

45. Seth Cagin and Philip Dray, *We Are Not Afraid: The Story of Goodman, Schwerner, and Chaney and the Civil Rights Campaign for Mississippi* (New York: Macmillan, 1988). pp. 229–30.

46. courtesy of Jan Hillegas (Jackson, MI: Freedom Information Service).

47. Freedom Summer Applications (Atlanta: King Center). Box 31

48. Burner, *And Gently*. p. 153.

49. Freedom Summer Applications (Atlanta: King Center). Box 31

50. Ibid.

51. Ibid.

52. Iris Greenberg Collection. (New York: Schomberg Library)

53. Cagin and Dray, *We Are Not Afraid*. 241.

54. Ibid., 53.

55. Jack Mendelsohn, *The Martyrs* (New York: Harper & Row, 1966). p. 120.

56. Don McAdam, *Freedom Summer* (New York: Oxford University Press, 1988). p. 49.

57. Mendelsohn, *The Martyrs*. 118.

58. Cagin and Dray, *We Are Not Afraid*. p. 47.

59. Ibid., 235.

60. Mendelsohn, *The Martyrs*. p. 123.

61. Cagin and Dray, *We Are Not Afraid*. 411.

62. Iris Greenberg Collection (New York: Schomberg Library).

63. McAdam, *Freedom Summer*. Appendix E, 263.

Chapter 8   Preparations For Freedom Summer

1. William Bradford Huie, *Three Lives for Mississippi* (New York: Signet Books, 1968). 93.

2. COFO papers, Martin Luther King Center, Atlanta, Georgia.

3. Len Holt, *The Summer that Didn't End: The Story of the Mississippi Civil Rights Project 1964, and its Challenges to America* (London: Heinemann, 1966). 129–149.

4. Ibid, 92.

5. Hollis Watkins, interview by Linda Gold, Jackson, Mississippi, 20 August 1998.

6. Ibid.

7. Ibid.

8. Ibid.

9. Ibid.

10. Ibid.

11. Ibid.

12. Ibid.

13. Elizabeth Sutherland, ed., *Letters from Mississippi* (New York: McGraw-Hill Book Company, 1965).10.

14. Ibid., 29.

15. Sally Belfrage, *Freedom Summer* (Charlottesville: University Press of Virginia, 1990). 20.

16. Hollis Watkins, interviewed by Linda Gold, Jackson, Mississippi, 20 August 1998.

17. Ibid.

18. Ibid.

19. Kay Mills, *This Little Light of Mine: The Life of Fannie Lou Hamer* (New York: Penguin, 1993). p. 97.

20. Kay Mills, *This Little Light*. p. 97.

21. Ibid.,97.

22. Ibid. 97.

23. Ibid. 97.

24. Elizabeth Sutherland, ed., *Letters*. .5.

25. SNCC Papers, King Center.

26. Sally Belfrage, *Freedom Summer* (Charlottesville: University Press of Virginia, 1990). 23.

27. COFO Papers, King Center, Atlanta.

28. Herbert Aptheker, *A Documentary History of the Negro People in the United States*, vol. 1–7 (New York: Citadel Press, 1993). 326.

29. Ellen Levine, *Freedom's Children: Young Civil Rights Activists Tell Their Own Stories* (New York: G. P. Putnam and Sons, 1993). 101.

30. William Bradford Huie, *Three Lives for Mississippi* (New York: Signet Books, 1968). 58

31. Ibid., 59

32. COFO, *Mississippi Black Paper* (New York: Random, 1965). 62.

33. William Bradford Huie, *Three Lives*. 77.

34. Ellen Levine, *Freedom's Children*. 104.

35. Henry Hampton and Steve Fayer, *Voices of Freedom: An Oral History of the Civil Rights Movement from the 1950s through the 1980s* (London: Vintage, 1995). 82.

36. Sally Belfrage, *Freedom Summer*. p. 14.

37. Ibid., p.14.

38. *A Report, Mainly on Ruleville Freedom School, Summer Project, 1964* by Kirsty Powell

39. Courtesy of Jan Hillegas, Freedom Information Services

40. Len Holt, *The Summer that Didn't End: The Story of the Mississippi Civil Rights Project 1964, and its Challenges to America* (London: Heinemann, 1966). 331

41. Howell Raines, *My Soul is Rested*, (New York: Penguin Books, 1983). 259.

42. William Bradford Huie, *Three Lives for Mississippi* (New York: Signet Books, 1968). 35.

43. Ibid., 36.

44. Ibid., 49.

45. Ibid., 51.

46. Ibid., 77.

47. COFO, *Mississippi Black Paper* (New York: Random House, 1965). 59.

48. Florence Mars, Witness. 84.

49. Nicolas Mills, Like a Holy Crusade (Chicago: Ivan R. Dee, 1992). 141.

50. Florence Mars, Witness. 91.

51. Elizabeth Sutherland, ed., Letters from Mississippi (New York: McGraw-Hill Book Company, 1965). 118–9.

52. Iris Greenberg Collection (New York: Schomburg Library).

Chapter 9   Freedom Summer: Freedom Schools and the Arts

1. "Announcing a Summer Stock Repertory Theatre in Mississippi, May 30, 1964-August 22, 1964." Papers of the Free Southern Theater, King Center, Atlanta.
2. Charles Cobb Oral history, HTTP://WWW.EDUCATIONANDDEMOCRACY. ORG/FSCFILES/B _ 05_ProspForFSchools.HTM
3. Cobb, "Organizing Freedom Schools," in Erenrich, ed., *Freedom is a Constant Struggle.* 136
4. Len Holt, 105–106
5. Cobb, SNCC papers, Reel 27, quoted by Chilcoat and Ligon, "Developing Democratic Citizens: The Mississippi Freedom Schools," in Erenrich, ed., *Freedom is a Constant Struggle.* 110
6. Cobb, "Organizing" in *Freedom is a Constant Struggle*, 136
7. Ed King. Interview by Linda Gold. Jackson, Mississippi, 19 August 1998.
8. Howard Zinn, "Freedom Schools," *The Zinn Reader*, p. 531
9. From the Freedom School papers, Boxes 15–17, King Center, Atlanta, Georgia.
10. Dan O'Brien, *For Staughton Lynd the Fight Never Ends.* http://karws. gso.uri.edu/JFK/The_critics/Lynd/Fight_never_ends.html
11. Staughton Lynd, "The Freedom Schools: Concept and Organization," *Freedomways*, Second Quarter, 1965. Also available at http://www. educationanddemocracy.org/FSCfiles/B_19_MSFSchoolsLynd.htm
12. Iris Greenberg Collection (New York: Schomberg Library).
13. James Cone, *The Spirituals and the Blues: An Interpretation* (New York: The Seabury Press, 1972). 6.
14. Eric C. Lincoln and Lawrence Mamiya, *The Black Church in the African American Experience* (Durham: Duke University Press, 1990). 349.
15. James Cone, quoted in Eric C. Lincoln and Lawrence Mamiya, *The Black Church.* 352.
16. Eric C. Lincoln and Lawrence Mamiya, *The Black Church.* 350
17. Richard Gregg, *The Power of Nonviolence* (Nyack, New York: Fellowship Publications, 1959). 161..
18. John Dittmer, *Local People: The Struggle for Civil Rights in Mississippi* (Chicago: University of Illinois Press, 1994). 131, 242.

19. Ibid., 192..

20. Hollis Watkins, interviewed by Linda Gold.

21. Mike Kellin, "Freedom Song: Hartman Turnbow," *Freedomways* (Second Quarter, 1965): 292–293

22. Bernice Johnson Reagon, "Songs of the Civil Rights Movement, 1955–1965: A Study in Cultural History," (Washington: Schomberg Library, 1975). 6.

23. Pete Seeger, interview by H. T. Holmes and Bill Hanna, November 2, 1979, Mississippi Department of Archives and History, Jackson, Mississippi, acquisition number: OH 80–02, 5.

24. *We Shall Overcome*, produced by Ginger Group Productions, PBS Home Video, 1990.

25. Ed King, interviewed by Linda Gold.

26. Juan Williams, *Eyes on the Prize: America's Civil Rights Years, 1954–1965* (New York: Viking, 1987). 176.

27. *We Shall Overcome*, produced by Ginger Group Productions, PBS Home Video, 1990.

28. Bernice Johnson Reagon, Introduction to *Voices of the Civil Rights Movement, Black American Freedom Songs 1960–1966; Smithsonian Collection of Recordings CD SF 40084*; and Mathew A Jones Jr.: "Freedom Fighter" in Erenrich, ed., *Freedom is a Constant Struggle.* 161.

29. Ibid.

30. Ibid.

31. Juan Williams, *Eyes on the Prize.*

32. Pete Seeger and Bob Reiser, *Everybody Says Freedom: A History of the Civil Rights Movement in Songs and Pictures* (New York: W. W. Norton and Company, 1989). 82.

33. Len Holt, *The Summer that Didn't End: The Story of the Mississippi Civil Rights Project 1964, and its Challenges to America* (London: Heinemann, 1966). 84.

34. Bob Cohen, "Sorrow Songs, Faith Songs, Freedom Songs: the Mississippi Caravan of Music in the Summer of '64 ", in Erenrich, ed., *Freedom is a Constant Struggle.* 183.

35. Bernice Johnson Reagon, "Songs". 156.

36. "Without These Songs . . ." *Newsweek*, August 31, 1964, 74.

37. Ed King, interviewed by Linda Gold.

38. Phil Hood, *Artists of American Folk Music* (New York: William Morrow, 1986). 35.

39. Pete Seeger, interview by H. T. Holmes and Bill Hanna, November 2, 1979. Mississippi Department of Archives and History, Jackson, Mississippi. Acquisition Number: OH 80-02, 5.

40. Ibid.

41. Ibid., 6.

42. Ibid., 2

43. Ibid., 10.

44. Thomas Dent, Richard Schechner, and Gilbert Moses, *Free Southern Theater by the Free Southern Theater* (Indianapolis: Bobbs-Merrill Company, 1969). 3.

45. "A General Prospectus for the Establishment of a Free Southern Theater," Papers of the Free Southern Theater, King Center, Atlanta.

46. Thomas Dent, et. al, *Free Southern Theater*. xii.

47. Ibid., 6.

48. Ibid., 6.

49. Ibid., 8.

50. "Announcing a Summer Stock Repertory Theatre in Mississippi, May 30, 1964-August 22, 1964." Papers of the Free Southern Theater, King Center, Atlanta.

51. Denise Nicholas, "The Free Southern Theater," in Erenrich, ed., *Freedom is a Constant Struggle*. 252

52. Papers of the Free Southern Theater, King Center, Atlanta.

53. Nicholas, "The Free Southern Theater," in Erenrich, ed., *Freedom is a Constant Struggle*. 252.

54. Len Holt, *The Summer that Didn't End: The Story of the Mississippi Civil Rights Project 1964, and its Challenges to America* (London: Heinemann, 1966). 83.

55. *Vicksburg Citizens Appeal* 1, no. 1, (August 22, 1964). 5.

56. Elizabeth Sutherland, ed., *Letters from Mississippi* (New York: McGraw-Hill Book Company, 1965). 99.

Chapter 10   Freedom Summer: Mississippi Freedom Democratic Party

1. Otis Pease , *The Development Of Negro Power In American Politics Since 1900 – a narrative and interpretive survey*, SNCC, The Student

Nonviolent Coordinating Committee Papers, 1959–1972 (Sanford, NC: Microfilming Corporation of America, 1982) Reel 67, File 340, Page 0830. can be viewed at http://www.educationanddemocracy. org/FSCfiles/C_CC3f_DevelopmOfNegroPower.htm

2. Freedom School Curriculum, Unit VII, Part I

3. (http://www.educationanddemocracy.org/FSCfiles/C_CC7_UnitVII. htm)

4. Kay Mills, *This Little Light of Mine* (New York: Penguin, 1993). 135.

5. Charles M. Payne, *I've Got the Light of Freedom* (Berkeley: University of California Press, 1995). 321.

6. Charles Marsh, *God's Long Summer* (Princeton: Princeton University Press, 1997). 149.

7. Ibid., 118.

8. Charles Marsh, *God's Long Summer.* 124.

9. Ed King, interview by Linda Gold, Jackson, Mississippi, 19 August 1998.

10. Christopher Wren, "An Insider Stays to Fight: A Profile of Edwin King," *Look*, September 8 1964, 27–28. 28.

11. Eric Burner, *And Gently.* 97.

12. Ed King, interview.

13. Ibid.

14. John Dittmer, *Local People: The Struggle for Civil Rights in Mississippi* (Chicago: University of Illinois Press, 1994). 280.

15. Ibid., 280.

16. Sally Belfrage, *Freedom Summer* (Charlottesville: University Press of Virginia, 1990). 187.

17. Ibid., 188.

18. Mary King, *Freedom Song: A Personal Story.* 341.

19. United States Commission on Human Rights, 1965 Voting Rights Hearings.

20. Iris Greenberg Collection (New York: Schomberg Library).

21. Kay Mills, *This Little Light.* 107.

22. Ibid., 109.

23. Joanne Grant, *Ella Baker: Freedom Bound* (New York: John Wiley and Sons, 1998).163.

24. Ibid., 164.

25. Mary King, *Freedom Song: A Personal Story.* 341.

26. Henry Hampton and Steve Fayer, *Voices of Freedom: An Oral History of the Civil Rights Movement from the 1950s through the 1980s* (London: Vintage, 1995). 198.

27. Ibid.

28. Hampton Fayer, *Voices of Freedom* (London: Vintage, 1995). 180.

29. Eyes on the Prize, Documentary, "Mississippi. Is this America?"

30. Eric Burner, *And Gently.* 87.

31. Kay Mills, *This Little Light of Mine.* 45.

32. Henry Hampton and Steve Fayer, *Voices.* 198.

33. Juan Williams, *Eyes on the Prize: America's Civil Rights Years, 1954–1965* (New York: Viking, 1987). 134.

34. Kay Mills, *This Little Light of Mine.* 24.

35. Ibid., 37.

36. Mildred Pitts Walter, *Mississippi Challenge* (New York: Alladin Paperbacks, 1992). 110.

37. Kay Mills, *This Little Light of Mine.* 53.

38. Ibid., 85.

39. Bernice Johnson Reagon, "Songs of the Civil Rights Movement, 1955–1965: A Study in Cultural History," (Washington: Schomberg Library, 1975). 155.

40. Kay Mills, *This Little Light of Mine.* 41.

41. Mary King, *Freedom Song.* 340.

42. Iris Greenberg Collection (New York: Schomberg Library).

43. Kay Mills, *This Little Light.* 153

44. Clayborne Carson and et. al, eds., The Eyes on the Prize Civil Rights Reader (New York: Penguin Books, 1991). Brown cover, 141.

45. Kay Mills, *This Little Light.* 122.

46. Ibid., 117.

47. Ibid., 120.

48. Ibid., 118.

49. Ibid., 121.

50. Carson, *Eyes on the Prize.* 145.

51. Kay Mills, *This Little Light.* 117.

52. *CORE-LATOR*, Schomberg materials, September, October 1964, No. 108

53. Kay Mills, *This Little Light.* 153.

54. Ibid., 154.

55. Ibid., 129.

56. Eric Burner, *And Gently*. 182.

57. Ibid., 183.

58. Kay Mills, *This Little Light*.

59. Eric Burner, And Gently. 189; and John Dittmer, *Local People*. 299.

60. Kay Mills, *This Little Light*. 160.

61. Jack Minnis, "The Mississippi Freedom Democratic Party: A New Declaration of Independence," *Freedomways*, Second Quarter, 1965, 271.

62. Eric Burner, *And Gently*. 184.

63. James Forman, *The Making of Black Revolutionaries* (Seattle: University of Washington Press, 1997). 391–392.

64. Nicolas Mills, *Like a Holy Crusade*. 158.

65. Eric Burner, *And Gently*. 186.

66. James Forman, *The Making of Black Revolutionaries*. 392.

67. John Dittmer, *Local People*. 300.

68. Higgs as quoted by Eric Burner, *And Gently*. 187.

69. James Forman, *The Making of Black Revolutionaries*. 395.

70. Henry Hampton and Steve Fayer, *Voices*. 198.

71. Eric Burner, *And Gently*. 189.

72. Eric Burner, *And Gently*. 180.

73. Dittmer, *Local People*. 314.

Chapter 11   Beyond Freedom Summer

1.   Cleveland Sellers as quoted in John Dittmer, *Local People*. 302.

2.   L.C. Dorsey, interviewed in "Freedom on My Mind" (movie)

3.   Cobb, in *Freedom is a Constant Struggle*. 137.

4.   Polly Greenberg, *The Devil Has Slippery Shoes A Biased Biography of the Child Development Group of Mississippi* (London: The Macmillan Company, Collier-Macmillan, 1969). 3.

5.   Ibid., 42.

6.   Ibid. 99–102.

7.   Ibid., 102.

8.   Ibid., 114.

9.   Ibid., 657–8.

10.   Dittmer, *Local People*. 316.

11. Carson, *In Struggle*, pp. 157–162 and pp. 171–174.

12. Polly Greenberg, *The Devil Has Slippery Shoes*, (1969). 681.

13. Quarles, B., *The Negro in the Making of America*. 270.

14. Zinn, *People's History*. 457.

15. *National Roster of Black Elected Officials*, Vol 3 qtd in Grant, *Black Protest*. 532.

16. Meier and Rudwick, *Black Leaders*. 346–7.

17. Zinn, *People's History*. 458

18. Wilson, J.Q. "The Negro in American Politics: The Present." In *The American Negro Reference Book*, Prentice-Hall (1966), p. 456; qtd in Piven and Cloward, *Poor People's Movements*. 257.

19. from a Mississippi Labor Union Mimeograph qtd in Grant, *Black Protest*. 498.

20. Ibid. 499–500.

21. Dittmer, *Local People*. 367–68.

22. From "We have no government", transcript of press conference, Feb 1, 1966, qtd in Grant, *Black Protest*. 505.

23. Dittmer, *Local People*. 368.

24. For information on the Algebra Project visit its website at www.algebra.org/

25. From website: members.aol.com/taylorteri/hamer.html

26. *San Francisco Chronicle*, Aug 26, 2000. A7. Wire service.

27. Hollis Watkins, interviewed by Linda Gold.

28. Ed King, interview by Linda Gold, Jackson, Mississippi, 19 August 1998.

29. From *Humanity*, December, 1964. 239 – 243.

30. Barbara Ransby, *Ella Baker and the Black Freedom Movement* (Chapel Hill: U of NC Press, 2003). 303.

31. Clayborne Carson, *In Struggle*. 169.

32. Ibid., 173.

Appendix   Further Research, Debate and Activities

1. From *Readings on Nonviolence* in Freedom School Curriculum in the Iris Greenberg Collection (New York: Schomburg Library).